HISTORY OF

United States Naval Operations

IN WORLD WAR II

★

VOLUME NINE

Sicily–Salerno–Anzio

January 1943–*June* 1944

HISTORY OF UNITED STATES NAVAL OPERATIONS

IN WORLD WAR II

By Samuel Eliot Morison

I *The Battle of the Atlantic*, September 1939 – May 1943

II *Operations in North African Waters*, October 1942 – June 1943

III *The Rising Sun in the Pacific*, 1931 – April 1942

IV *Coral Sea, Midway and Submarine Actions*, May 1942 – August 1942

V *The Struggle for Guadalcanal*, August 1942 – February 1943

VI *Breaking the Bismarcks Barrier*, 22 July 1942 – 1 May 1944

VII *Aleutians, Gilberts and Marshalls*, June 1942 – April 1944

VIII *New Guinea and the Marianas*, March 1944 – August 1944

IX *Sicily – Salerno – Anzio*, January 1943 – June 1944

X *The Atlantic Battle Won*, May 1943 – May 1945

XI *The Invasion of France and Germany*, 1944 – 1945

XII *Leyte*, June 1944 – January 1945

XIII *The Liberation of the Philippines: Luzon, Mindanao, the Visayas*, 1944 – 1945

XIV *Victory in the Pacific*, 1945

XV *Supplement and General Index*

Also

Strategy and Compromise

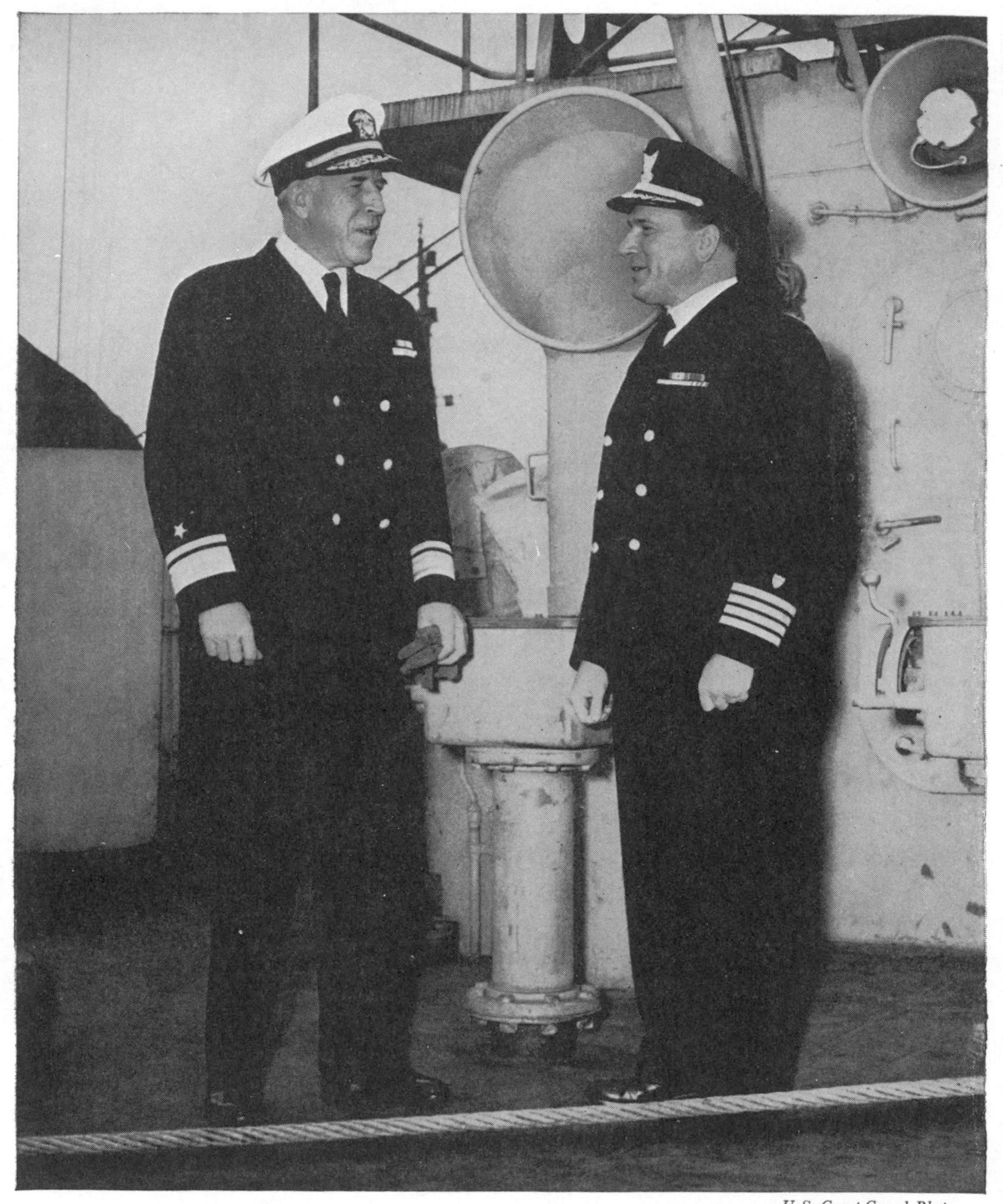

U.S. Coast Guard Photo

Rear Admiral John L. Hall USN *and Captain Roger C. Heimer* USCG

On deck of U.S.S. *Samuel Chase*

HISTORY OF UNITED STATES NAVAL OPERATIONS IN WORLD WAR II

VOLUME IX

Sicily—Salerno—Anzio

January 1943 - *June* 1944

BY SAMUEL ELIOT MORISON

With Illustrations

LITTLE, BROWN AND COMPANY
BOSTON • NEW YORK • TORONTO • LONDON

LIBRARY OF CONGRESS CATALOG CARD NO. 47-1571

20 19 18 17 16 15

KPT

Published simultaneously in Canada
by Little, Brown & Company (Canada) Limited

PRINTED IN THE UNITED STATES OF AMERICA

To

The Memory of

LYAL AMENT DAVIDSON

1886–1950

Vice Admiral, United States Navy

I think, therefore, that we ought to take . . . great numbers also of archers and slingers, to make head against the Sicilian horse. Meanwhile, we must have an overwhelming superiority at sea, to enable us the more easily to import what we want; and we must take our own corn in merchant vessels.

— SPEECH OF NICIAS on eve of Sicilian Expedition, in THUCYDIDES *Peloponnesian War* (Livingstone trans.) vi. 22.

The Navy, in its escorting, supporting, and maintenance functions, performed miracles and always in exact coördination with the needs and supports of the other arms.

— GENERAL EISENHOWER *Crusade in Europe* p. 179.

Preface

THIS volume picks up the story of the United States Navy in the Mediterranean where Volume II left off. It covers three major operations, the first two of which may be likened to giant strides – from North Africa to Sicily (HUSKY) and over to the Italian mainland at Salerno and Naples (AVALANCHE) – and the third, to Anzio (SHINGLE), a big side-step. The first of these amphibious operations began the Sicilian campaign; the second opened the long-drawn-out Italian campaign, to which the third was planned as a diversion – but it developed into something else. All the actions described in this volume extended from 13 May 1943, when the Axis forces in Tunisia surrendered, to 5 June 1944 when the Allied armies entered Rome. And on the following day began the Allied invasion of France, to which the Italian campaign was a logical prelude.

If the reader finds this volume somewhat complicated, I beg his indulgence; because the campaigns that it covers were very complicated. In contrast to those in the Pacific, where the United States Navy called the tunes to which a single enemy had to dance, here in the "Med" we had a very important ally, and two major enemies. The Royal Navy of Great Britain in this theater was stronger than the United States Navy, and both navies realized that they were there mainly to take the United States and British Armies where the Combined Chiefs of Staff wanted them to go, and to support them. Although General Eisenhower was Supreme Allied Commander in the Mediterranean until January 1944, his subordinate Air, Naval and Ground Force Commanders were British; and the British government as represented by Mr. Churchill took a continuous and even intrusive interest in everything that went on in that "Sea of Destiny," the importance of which, in the major strategy of the war, the "P.M." certainly did not underestimate.

Thus, warfare in the Mediterranean is too complicated to be told with any justice or accuracy in terms of what the United States Navy alone accomplished. An American historian can no more neglect the part that the Royal Navy played than he could ignore the French Navy's part in the War of American Independence. In the Mediterranean in 1943–1944, the United States and British Navies, first under Admiral of the Fleet Sir Andrew B. Cunningham RN, and then under Admiral Sir John Cunningham RN, acted in a close and intimate concert that had hitherto been considered impossible. Nor could one neglect events on shore, because the ships, after covering the soldiers' landings, stood by "dishing it out" as long as the enemy was within gunfire range, and at all times handled the armies' logistics supply and protected their communications. Air operations, too, contributed greatly to victory in the Mediterranean, although the aviators' desire to fight the war in their own way made their contribution less than it might have been under a more resolute control, such as both Admiral Nimitz and General MacArthur exercised in the Pacific. Higher strategy, and events such as the Italian surrender, must also be considered, because they helped to build the framework within which American naval forces operated.

Vice Admiral Hewitt's Eighth Fleet United States Navy, which conducted the American share of these naval operations, included neither battleships, aircraft carriers nor heavy cruisers; it had no air arm or other air component except the cruisers' own SOCs; it fought no sea battles of the classic kind. Its main mission was amphibious warfare, the most ancient form of naval fighting, practised in the Mediterranean since the dawn of history, and now waged with the most modern vessels, devices and tactics. There is not much glamor in setting troops ashore on enemy territory where the Army wants to operate; but an amphibious operation can be a débâcle for everyone concerned, if the naval planning, preparation and execution are defective. Here in the Mediterranean all three aspects were phenomenally good in comparison with Operation TORCH of 1942.

Although the constant and recurring theme of this volume is the landing of troops on hostile shores, there is a secondary theme which rises to major importance in the course of the story: naval gunfire support of troops ashore. These Mediterranean operations of 1943–1944 were a turning point in that aspect of naval warfare. Since the invention of gunpowder, land-based artillery had maintained superiority over naval gunfire. Guns emplaced on the firm base of the earth could naturally be directed and fired with greater accuracy than those in a ship whose motion, however slight, deflected the most carefully aimed projectile from its target. But, during the period immediately before World War II and during the opening years of that conflict, a revolution had been brought about through the operation of several factors and devices. (1) Fire control equipment which compensated for every move of the ship and provided for naval guns as stable a base as if on land. (2) The greater accuracy of range-finding, both by radar when conditions were favorable, and by the stereographic optical range-finder. (3) The distribution of a gridded chart of the target area, which enabled officers to assign shore targets to a ship by accurate coordinates. (4) Observing the fall of shot by airplane, preferably one belonging to a battleship or cruiser; and (5) the shore fire-control party (called F.O.O. by the British), which, trained in naval gunfire capabilities, accompanied a battalion ashore, called for naval gunfire by radio and controlled it just as if it had been the Army's own artillery. Hitherto the Army had been indifferent or even hostile to naval gunfire support because their own facilities for determining range had been greatly superior to anything that the Navy possessed. But at Gela in Operation HUSKY the Navy, by showing what it could do under new and unusual conditions, almost completely changed the Army's attitude. Thus the Navy acquired a new function in amphibious warfare; and its development is one of the fascinating and significant things related in this volume.

At the same time, the ancient doctrine that a naval vessel should not expose herself to a coastal battery was disproved again and again. I know of but one case of an enemy coastal battery in the

Mediterranean registered a hit on any Allied naval vessel larger than an LST, or more than a mile from shore. This superiority of floating over fixed fire power developed faster than many senior officers appreciated; otherwise, three German divisions would not have been allowed to escape across the Strait of Messina. But the enemy appreciated what was going on. Frequently, in Italian and German sources, we find that this ferocious and devastating intervention of the Allied Navies was the crucial factor that forced Axis ground forces to retire.

All Mediterranean campaigns are charged with controversy. At the highest level of strategic decision there was an almost complete cleavage of opinion, between the British who wished to nourish the Mediterranean at the expense of the build-up for OVERLORD (the cross-channel operation into France); and the Americans, who stood firm in their belief that a frontal attack was the only way to defeat the German armies, and resisted every proposal to divert forces to the Mediterranean. It is a tribute to the leaders of both countries that they were able to compose these deep differences in conference and to put on the three major operations described in this volume, without compromising the success of OVERLORD. In all three, the British gained a new respect for the fighting qualities of Americans; and we learned anew the truth of Emerson's dictum on "aged England" one hundred years earlier, "that in storm of battle and calamity, she has a secret vigor and a pulse like a cannon." The comradeship in arms displayed by forces of the United States and the British Empire, whether on the sea, in the air or on the ground, was remarkable all through those campaigns. First under General Eisenhower and later under General Maitland Wilson, these forces fought together as a single, integrated team. Other armed forces of the United Nations – French warships and French North African troops, the Italian Navy after the Armistice, the Netherlands Navy, the Polish Navy and Army, the Indian Army, and (somewhat later) the Brazilian Army, contributed a willing share to these operations in so far as their resources permitted. But the Mediterranean campaigns were predominantly fought by the British, the Canadians and the Americans, and it was British and American leadership that planned them and directed them to a successful conclusion.

This volume has been under way intermittently for ten years, while six volumes on the war in the Pacific were being completed. The first research for it was performed by Lieutenant (jg) Henry D. Reck USNR. Coming to me in February 1944 from the staff of Commander Destroyers Atlantic Fleet, he was immediately sent to temporary duty on the staff of Vice Admiral H. Kent Hewitt, Commander U. S. Naval Forces North African Waters, under whom I had been proud to serve in Operation TORCH. Lieutenant Reck divided his time between Algiers, Palermo, Corsica and various North African bases, made several visits to Anzio beachhead in the course of Operation SHINGLE, and subsequently took part in the invasion of Southern France. He was assiduous in gathering information from participants, in collecting important reports and documents of which no other copies can now be found; and his own observations, too, were most valuable. Early in 1945 I visited the Salerno and Anzio beachheads, studied the records and talked to participants at Admiral Hewitt's headquarters in Naples. After Lieutenant Commander Reck retired from the active Naval Reserve in 1948, work on this volume was suspended until January 1953, when I began to concentrate on it myself.

During the summer of 1953, numerous Sicilians dwelling near the coast were puzzled by the movements of a certain United States Navy car driven by a stalwart Seabee Chief, Thomas F. Grady, with Lieutenant Emidio Mancini USN next him in the front seat. In the rear they observed a young, beautiful and auburn-haired American lady – Priscilla B. Morison – and her historian husband, dimly visible behind enormous binoculars. Mrs. Morison and Lieutenant Mancini, who between them could cope with any Sicilian dialect and deal with any situation, frequently inquired the way to obscure beaches in which no tourist had ever been interested. Whenever a crowd gathered, as it did at every stop, they interrogated all and sundry about the events of 1943. There was great excitement when our party debouched on a quay where a smart *motosilurante* of the Italian Navy took us on board and put to sea in order to enable the historian to approach the landing beaches of 1943 from the proper direction. A few natives suspected something sinister in this reconnaissance and tentatively made the Communist gesture of defiance; but by far the greater part were satisfied with the explanation that we were working for *La Stória della Marina da Guerra Americana* – a Navy that seems to have left very pleasant memories in those parts. We shall never forget the kindness and courtesy with which we were everywhere received on Italian soil.

We are indebted to Vice Admiral Jerauld Wright, Commander in Chief U. S. Naval Forces Eastern Atlantic and Mediterranean, and to Admiral Ferreri, Commander in Chief of the Italian Navy, for making possible this historical tour; and for their complete understanding of what we were trying to do. We are grateful to Admiral Girosi at Naples for detailing fleet tug *Tenace* to conduct us to the Salerno landing beaches, and to Admiral Mirti della Valle at Messina for placing *MAS–831* at our disposition in Sicily. Also, to the U. S. Naval attachés in Rome and Paris, who helped us in numerous ways; and to Captain Forrest Close, "Comsubcomnelm" and senior U. S. Naval officer at Naples.

Upon my return to the United States, Rear Admiral Bern Anderson USN, who had helped me with Volume VIII, was recalled to active duty in order to assist me with this one. Mr. Roger Pineau, for many years my "chief of staff," worked almost continuously on research for this volume in 1953, and into the new year. His major contribution was to straighten out the Navy's share in repelling the German tanks on the Gela plain. With such outstanding assistance, I was able to finish the complicated if fascinating task of research and writing in a little more than a year. Mr. Donald R. Martin compiled the task organizations, and Miss Antha E. Card did some valuable text revision as well as accurately typing my repeated and much scratched-up drafts. Roger F. Schofield, Yeoman 1st Class, also helped with the typing.

The maps and charts fall into two classes: (1) the double-page charts of the three Sicilian areas and the Gulf of Salerno. These were drafted by the U. S. Navy Hydrographic Office in Suitland, Maryland, by permission of the Chief Hydrographer, Captain J. B. Cochran USN, with Mr. Fulton B. Perkins overseeing and Mr. Edgar A. Lewis drafting. The basis for these charts was the maps prepared for the operations themselves by the Hydrographic Office of the British Admiralty, which kindly lent me the few surviving copies. (2) The rest of the charts were executed in the drafting room of the U. S. Naval War College, Newport, R. I., under the oversight of Admiral Anderson, the direction of Mr. John Lawton, with Mr. Frederick J. Wagner and Mr. Robert P. Grondin drafting. Basic charts and data for the tri-color situation maps of Sicily were furnished by the Historical Office of the Italian Army.

Neither the official U. S. Army history nor the official British war history has yet touched the Mediterranean theater, and the official U. S. Air Force history has covered it very sketchily. Consequently, I have had to extend my research into (1) Army sources, both American and Canadian – and here the U. S. Army historians Colonel Kent R. Greenfield and staff, and the Canadian Army historians Colonel C. P. Stacey and Lieutenant Colonel G. W. L. Nicholson, have been most helpful; (2) British Admiralty Records, where Rear Admiral Roger Bellairs RN and Commander Titterton RN have extended every possible courtesy and facility – and, I may add, Admiral of the Fleet Lord Cunningham of Hyndhope, the beloved "A. B. C." of 1943, has patiently answered my questions and firmly but courteously parried some of my criticisms of command decisions; (3) German military records, both those that were captured, and the reports written after the war for the Canadians and ourselves by German Army and Navy officers, to which General von Senger und Etterlin has kindly added some personal explanations; (4) Archives of the French Marine de Guerre, where the head of the historical section, Commander Rostand, placed everything needed at my disposal; and (5) Archives of the Italian Army, Navy and Air Force.

It would be difficult to exaggerate my indebtedness to the chiefs of the historical sections of the three Italian armed forces – Rear Admiral Giuseppe Fioravanzo of the Navy, Colonel Giuseppe Giammarino of the Army, and Colonel Vincenzo Lioy of the Air Force. These gentlemen not only allowed me to use their archives, but compiled special reports for this History and patiently answered my numerous queries.

President Eisenhower and the Honorable Walter Bedell Smith, Under Secretary of State, have spared the time, in their exceedingly busy lives, to discuss with me the strategy of the campaigns covered by this volume. Two Chiefs of Naval Operations, Admiral William M. Fechteler and Admiral Robert B. Carney, have continued the Navy's support of this series, as have the Vice Chief, Admiral D. B. Duncan, and two successive Deputy Chiefs, Vice Admiral John E. Gingrich and Rear Admiral Frank T. Watkins.

Rear Admiral John B. Heffernan, Director of Naval Records and History, has continued to afford me encouragement, support and constructive criticism. Admiral H. Kent Hewitt has been consistently helpful and benevolent. Vice Admiral Richard L. Conolly and Rear Admiral Thomas H. Robbins, respectively President and Chief of Staff of the Naval War College, have given generously of their time and placed the resources of the War College at my disposal. At the historical section of the Joint Chiefs of Staff, Lieutenant Ernest R. May USNR continued the checking of my pages on higher strategy that was begun by Lieutenant Grace P. Hayes USNR. At the British Embassy in Washington, Commander R. N. D. Porter RN has answered numerous questions. Many other officers of the United States Army and Navy, and Dr. Albert F. Simpson and Mr. Robert T. Finney of the Air Force historical staff, have responded to requests for information and are individually acknowledged in footnotes.

This volume is dedicated to the memory of Vice Admiral Lyal A. Davidson, whose exploits are written at large in the text. Admiral H. Kent Hewitt has well characterized him as "A splendid, resourceful and determined flag officer, who never thought of anything but the task to be accomplished, and never spared himself."

Samuel E. Morison

Harvard University
March 1954

Notes on Italian Names, RCTs, Time Zone and Distances

Accents on Italian place names indicate the syllable to be stressed; if no accent is printed, the stress is on the penult, the next to the last syllable. By exception, no accent is printed on certain place names, long familiar in English, that are accented on the antepenult – as Anzio, Calabria, Campania, Catania, and Spezia.

In the United States Army a Regimental Combat Team (abbreviated RCT), constantly employed in amphibious warfare, consists of an infantry regiment with a battalion of artillery, a company of engineers, a supply company, a medical detachment and other units attached. It is commanded by the infantry regiment's colonel and bears the same number as that regiment. The RCT, unless it is the only one in an operation (which was never the case in this theater), is broken up shortly after landing, when the artillery and other attached units revert to corps or divisional command. Assuming that each RCT employed in this theater was broken up on D-day, I have alluded to infantry regiments as such, not as RCTs, in the fighting ashore.

The time in all operations in the Mediterranean covered by this volume was that of Zone "Baker," two hours later than Greenwich Civil Time. Thus, when it was 0900 in Sicily, the Greenwich time was 0700, and the Eastern Standard Time in the United States was 0200.

Distances given in this volume are in nautical miles, except on shore when I have endeavored always to give them in statute miles.

Contents

PART III

SALERNO

PART IV

ANZIO

List of Illustrations

(Illustrations appear between pages 192 and 193)

(All photographs not otherwise described are Official United States Navy)

List of Charts

Abbreviations

Officers' ranks and bluejackets' ratings are those contemporaneous with the event. Officers and men named will be presumed to be of the United States Navy unless it is otherwise stated; officers of the Naval Reserve are designated USNR. Other service abbreviations are USA, United States Army; USCG, United States Coast Guard; USMC, United States Marine Corps; RAF, Royal Air Force; RN, Royal Navy; RNR, Royal Navy Reserve; RNVR, Royal Navy Volunteer Reserve.

A.A.F. – United States Army Air Force
AGC – Amphibious Command Ship
AP – Armor-piercing Ammunition
C.A.P. – Combat Air Patrol
C.C.S. – Combined Chiefs of Staff
Cincmed – Commander in Chief Mediterranean
CL – Light Cruiser
C.N.O. – Chief of Naval Operations
C.O. – Commanding Officer
CTF – Commander Task Force; CTG – Commander Task Group
DD – Destroyer; DE – Destroyer Escort
Dukw – 2½-ton amphibian truck
E-boat – German Motor Torpedo Boat
F-lighter, *see* MFP
F.O.O. – Forward Observation Officer
GI – "General Issue," U. S. Infantryman
H.C. – High Capacity Ammunition
H.M.S. – His Majesty's Ship; H.N.M.S. – Her Netherlands Majesty's Ship; H.H.M.S. – His Hellenic Majesty's Ship
J.C.S. – Joint Chiefs of Staff
LC – Landing Craft. U.S.N. types: LCI – Landing Craft, Infantry; LCM – Landing Craft, Mechanized; LCT – Landing Craft, Tank; LCVP – Landing Craft, Vehicle and Personnel. British types: LCA – Landing Craft, Assault; LCF – Landing Craft, Flak; LCG – Landing Craft, Gunboat
LS – Landing Ship. LSI – Landing Ship, Infantry (British); LST – Landing Ship, Tank

MAS – Italian Motor Torpedo Boat
MFP – Marinefährprähme, German Armed Motor Barge
MTB – Motor Torpedo Boat (used mainly for those of the R.N.)
N.O.B. – Naval Operating Base
O.N.I. – Office of Naval Intelligence
O.T.C. – Officer in Tactical Command
PC – Patrol Craft
P.O.W. – Prisoner of War
PT – Motor Torpedo Boat
R.A.F. – Royal Air Force
RCT – Regimental Combat Team
Sacmed – Supreme Allied Commander, Mediterranean
SC – Subchaser
SS – Submarine; S.S. – Steamship
TF – Task Force; TG – Task Group; TU – Task Unit
YMS – Motor Minesweeper

AIRCRAFT DESIGNATIONS

Numeral in parentheses indicates number of engines

United States Army Air Force

A–36 – Invader dive-bomber (1)
B–17 – Flying Fortress heavy bomber (4); B–24 – Liberator heavy bomber (4); B–26 – Marauder medium bomber (2)
C–47 – Skytrain transport (2); C–53 – Skytrooper transport (2)
P–38 – Lightning fighter (2); P–51 – Mustang fighter (1)

United States Navy

SOC – Seagull scout observation float plane (1)

Royal Navy and Air Force

Albacore – Torpedo-bomber (1)
Barracuda – Torpedo-bomber (1)
Beaufighter – Bristol fighter (2)
Martlet – Fighter (1); same as U.S.N. Wildcat
Seafire – Fighter (1); Carrier-based Spitfire
Spitfire – Vickers-Armstrong fighter (1)
Wellington – Vickers-Armstrong medium bomber (2)

Luftwaffe

FW–190 – Focke-Wulf fighter (1)
Ju–88 – Junkers medium bomber (2)
Me–109 – Messerschmitt fighter (1)

PART I

Forward in the Mediterranean

CHAPTER I

The Mediterranean and World Strategy[1]

1. *Strategic Questions at the Turn of the Year*

ON NEW YEAR'S DAY 1943 the Second World War had not progressed much further than the phase well described by Winston Churchill as "the end of the beginning." In the Mediterranean theater, the Western Allies had just scored their first major success in the entire war – Operation TORCH, the Anglo-American landings in North Africa which secured French Morocco and Algeria. The Axis had made a strong stand in Tunisia, but the British Eighth Army under General Montgomery was rapidly exploiting its victory at El Alamein, charging westward with great speed and success. Egypt had been saved and the friendly neutrality of Turkey now secured the Levant; but Greece and the Ægean, Italy and the Adriatic, Sicily, Sardinia, Corsica, and the whole of France, were under Axis control.

In the United Kingdom the build-up (Operation BOLERO) for an eventual cross-channel attack on occupied France continued. Neither of the long-discussed invasions of France – the limited bridgehead concept known as SLEDGEHAMMER or the full-scale ROUNDUP – had been authorized for 1943; and the British Chiefs of Staff were already insisting that neither could be attempted with

[1] Based largely on the Joint Chiefs of Staff Records and the ms. History prepared by the Historical Staff of the J.C.S. There are useful accounts of Casablanca in General Eisenhower's ms. "Dispatch" on the Sicilian Operation; R. E. Sherwood *Roosevelt and Hopkins* (1948) ch. xxvii; Winston Churchill *The Hinge of Fate* (1950) pp. 674–715; E. J. King and W. M. Whitehill *Fleet Admiral King* (1952) pp. 414–34, and *The War Reports of Marshall, Arnold and King* (1947) pp. 121, 155–6.

any prospect of success before 1944. This suggestion dismayed the American Joint Chiefs of Staff, and, when whispers of it leaked out, disgusted those elements in both countries who had been insistently demanding, "Open a second front against Germany!" But one did not have to be a left-winger or Soviet sympathizer to see that something must be done in 1943 to take the pressure off Russia, whose armies were then engaging something like 185 German divisions. Although Allied statesmen and soldiers no longer feared, since the relief of Stalingrad, that Russia would be knocked out of the war, they still had to take that possibility into consideration; for if the entire military machine of the Axis were turned against the Western Allies, they would have to prepare for a ten years' war at least.

At the moment, the Russians were doing well. In December 1942 they had started a strong offensive movement to the southwest. But the problem of supplying them with the tanks and heavy weapons that they required to keep up their momentum was very serious. There were only two supply routes besides the long one across the Pacific to Siberia: the northern to Murmansk and Archangel, and the southern around the Cape of Good Hope to the Persian Gulf. U-boats challenged both. It is true that the Battle of the Atlantic had been somewhat eased up; the Allies had lost 344,000 tons of shipping to submarine attack in December 1942 as against the colossal total of 711,880 tons in November; but they had destroyed only 25 German and Italian submarines in the last sixty days, and the Axis was producing more than that every month.[2]

In the Pacific, the long-drawn-out Guadalcanal and Buna-Gona campaigns were almost over, but Japan still held most of her important conquests — the Philippines, Indonesia, Malaya, Burma, the Gilbert Islands, the Bismarck Archipelago, and most of the Solomons and New Guinea. China was now completely cut off from Western help, except by air. Japan was still in a strong position inside a defensive perimeter that ran from the Western Aleutians through the Marshall, Caroline, and Solomon Islands to New

[2] See Vol. I of this History chapter xiv and pp. 412–15.

Guinea. Allied forces could not hope to break it or exploit their hard-won victories at Midway, Guadalcanal and Papua, unless a greater proportion of Allied resources was allotted to the Pacific theater than the 15 per cent which (in Admiral King's estimate) were actually deployed there at the end of 1942.

In January 1943 a conference was called at Casablanca between the Combined (British and United States) Chiefs of Staff, President Roosevelt, and Prime Minister Churchill, in order to resolve a serious divergence of views both as to the next move and on the grand strategy of the war.

Fortunately, both sides agreed on three fundamental concepts: —

1. The basic strategic principle of March 1941 that the European Axis, as the most dangerous enemy in military might and potentiality, must be defeated first.

2. Anti-submarine warfare was the most pressing and urgent problem.

3. Some sort of "second front" must be opened against Germany in 1943.

The divergences, however, were very wide. The British wished almost complete concentration on the European war and merely to "hold" or "contain" Japan until Germany was defeated. The Americans, especially General Marshall and Admiral King, felt that it was absolutely essential to maintain momentum in the war against Japan, lest she consolidate her conquests and become impregnable. Regarding China as having the same geopolitical relation to Japan as Russia had to Germany, they believed that something must be done in 1943 to relieve Chiang Kai-shek. Admiral Leahy at J.C.S. meetings kept saying to General Marshall: "Remember this: who controls China at the end of the war, controls Asia. Don't overlook China." The British, on the contrary, regarded China as of slight account as an ally, Chiang as undependable, and the obstacles to rendering him aid through the Japanese blockade as insuperable.

The English-speaking allies also disagreed as to their next move after TORCH. The Americans wished to leave only token forces in North Africa, to concentrate on the United Kingdom build-up and the bomber offensive, and prepare to launch a cross-channel invasion during the summer of 1943. The British, on the contrary, believed that no cross-channel operation had any chance of success before 1944. They proposed to exploit the capture of North Africa by using the ships and troops already there to take Sardinia or Sicily around midsummer 1943, in the hope of knocking Italy out of the war, and perhaps bringing Turkey in on the Allied side.

2. *The Casablanca Conference, 14–23 January 1943*

Such, in general, were the opposing strategic views when the war lords of the two Western Allies met at Hotel Anfa in the suburbs of Casablanca. This small modern hotel, within sight and sound of the long Atlantic rollers constantly breaking on the rocky coast of Morocco; the bright, clear air of the African winter; the gardens gay with bougainvillea and hibiscus, made an appropriate setting for a very important strategic conference. The President and Prime Minister were accommodated in nearby villas, and security measures were so strict that few people in Casablanca suspected what was going on until Mr. Roosevelt's insatiable appetite for sightseeing tipped them off. Marshal Stalin, though invited, declined; so meetings of the C.C.S. and the three plenary conferences between them and the two chiefs of state were conducted in English, with plenty of friendly give and take. Almost everyone there, British and American, had met often enough to call one another by his Christian name.

Admiral King and Generals Marshall and Arnold represented the Joint Chiefs of Staff; [3] Admiral of the Fleet Sir Dudley Pound RN, General Sir Alan F. Brooke and Air Chief Marshal Sir Charles F. A. Portal were the British Chiefs of Staff. These six comprised the Combined Chiefs of Staff. Among others who attended and took part in the discussions were Admiral of the Fleet Sir Andrew B. Cunningham RN, commanding Western Allied naval forces

[3] Admiral Leahy fell ill en route and was unable to attend.

Mediterranean; Vice Admiral Mountbatten, commanding British amphibious training; Lieutenant General Sir Hastings Ismay, Churchill's chief of staff; Rear Admiral C. M. Cooke and Brigadier General A. C. Wedemeyer USA of the J.C.S. planning committee; and Lieutenant General Brehon B. Somervell USA, head of the United States Army Services of Supply. Harry Hopkins attended all three plenary sessions with the President, and General Eisenhower attended one, but was too busy with the Tunis campaign to remain longer.

The meetings were conducted with the utmost frankness and cordiality despite a profound divergence. The two teams were like two steeplechasers, the one concentrating on leaping the next obstacle, the other thinking mainly of the last stretch and taking each fence in his stride. As Mr. Churchill wrote to the President before the conference, the British preferred "to take a particular major operation to which one is committed and follow that through vigorously to the end, making all things subordinate to it, rather than to assemble all the data from the whole world scene in a baffling array." But the Americans insisted on considering remote as well as immediate objectives. They were always asking "Where do we go from here?" until the British became rather irritated by the phrase.[4] General Eisenhower did not see how he could intelligently plan an operation unless he were informed what the next one was likely to be. When he appeared before the C.C.S. at Casablanca he asked the embarrassing question "What next?" and was as much as told to mind his own business; to which he replied, "Oh, you just want to go on fighting, do you? Well, we can find plenty of places to do that!"

Early reverses had made the British reluctant to assume great risks. They tended to look on the Americans as impatient amateurs in the art of war, who happened to have the "arsenal of democracy" at their disposal and so must be humored. Sir Hastings Ismay well said, three years later, that in modern war "the fighting services are only the cutting edge of a war machine which embraces

[4] So President Roosevelt told the writer in 1943.

. . . all the national energies."[5] But at Casablanca the British seemed to regard transatlantic energy and resources as inexhaustible; America was expected to shift from one major operation to another at a moment's notice and to produce astronomical quantities of ships, weapons and matériel. General Marshall pointed out that the build-up in Britain had been disrupted and the anti-submarine campaign hampered by TORCH; that American shipyards had given top priority to landing and beaching craft for BOLERO at the expense of carriers and destroyer escorts urgently needed for convoy protection; that every diversion drew strength from the main effort. General Arnold stated flatly that priorities could not be determined unless and until the Allies decided what they would do in 1944 as well as in 1943. Flexibility in war plans is desirable, but too much of it wastes national resources to the point of disaster, as Hitler found when he called off the invasion of England and plunged into Russia.

General Brooke pointed out that, if forces were diverted from North Africa to Britain for a 1943 cross-channel operation, the Western Allies would be putting no pressure whatsoever on Germany during six to eight months; that even if nothing further were done in the Mediterranean, by mid-September 1943 only 21 to 24 British and American divisions could be readied in the United Kingdom. That number would get us nowhere, since Germany already had 44 divisions in France and could pull out more from the Russian front at short notice. Marshall and King then urged that a small cross-channel operation (SLEDGEHAMMER), to seize the Cotentin or the Brest Peninsula as a bridgehead, be firmed up for 1943; but the British argued that no such "token invasion" would help, and stood firm on the principle that no invasion of France begin until Germany had been sensibly weakened.

So the conference adjourned without any commitment for a cross-channel operation in 1943 or, for that matter, in 1944. Undoubtedly the British were right in this. All serious students of the Normandy campaign now agree that a token invasion in 1943

[5] Royal United Service Inst. *Journal* XCI (Feb. 1946) p. 68.

would have been useless, and a full-scale invasion in 1943 fraught with disaster.

Respecting the Pacific, Admiral King and General Marshall overcame the untenable British concept of a passive defense against Japan until the Axis was defeated. They obtained a C.C.S. resolution to the effect that, in the Pacific and Far Eastern areas, there should be allotted forces adequate to "retain the initiative" and "attain positions of readiness" for a full-scale offensive against Japan as soon as the war in Europe was over.[6] The C.C.S. also authorized an amphibious operation to free the Burma Road to China; but, as Marshall predicted, Mediterranean campaigns acted as a suction pump on other areas, and the attack on Burma, postponed again and again, never came off.

Thus, the important strategic compromise at Casablanca was to postpone the cross-channel operation beyond 1943, while the United States retained its initiative in the Pacific.[7] It was implicit in the compromise that *something* must be done in the European theater in 1943, as soon as Tripoli and Tunis were secured. But what?

The British Chiefs proposed occupying Sardinia; the Americans, Sicily. Sardinia as the less strongly held of the two could probably be taken about two months earlier and with fewer forces. It would be a good base for bomber raids on the industrial cities of northern Italy, and for commando raids on the coast. But, although Nelson once called Maddalena Bay "the finest harbor in the world," it was not ample enough to mount a large modern amphibious operation. Admiral King scoffed at the Sardinia proposition as "merely doing something just for the sake of doing something." He predicted that Sicily would have to be taken eventually, and that it could best be taken immediately. Admiral Pound and General Somervell pointed out that the Straits of Sicily were still too risky for troop and tanker convoys, that Allied possession of Sicily would render

[6] *War Reports of General Marshall* p. 179.

[7] See chapter xi below for the misunderstanding created by the vagueness of this formula, and the redefinition of Pacific operations at the TRIDENT Conference; see Vol. VI pp. 6–7 for other data on Pacific decisions at Casablanca.

unnecessary the roundabout Cape route to India, affording a saving in time equivalent to the employment of 225 freighters. On 19 January 1943, the C.C.S. decided on the occupation of Sicily, with four objects in view: (1) securing the Mediterranean line of communications, (2) diverting German forces from the Russian front, (3) increasing the pressure on Italy, and (4) creating "a situation in which Turkey can be enlisted as an active ally."

This boils down to the fact that the Sicilian operation was entered upon as an end in itself, with limited objectives; not as a springboard for Italy or anywhere else.

On 20 January the British produced a rough plan for the invasion of Sicily (now designated Operation HUSKY), by a British force mounted in the Near East and an American force mounted in North Africa. And the C.C.S. on 22 January set D-day for 25 July.

There was some question as to whether Lieutenant General Eisenhower should be relieved by his senior, General Sir Harold R. Alexander, commander in chief of British Forces in the Middle East, and allowed to return to his European theater command at London, of which he had never been formally relieved. But Eisenhower had conducted Operation TORCH so ably that everyone from Roosevelt and Churchill down wanted him to stay at least another six months; and the matter of rank was settled by his promotion to General on 11 February 1943. He was unanimously chosen to be Supreme Commander North African Theater of Operations, and on 23 January the C.C.S. in plenary session issued a directive to him for Operation HUSKY:—

> An attack against Sicily will be launched in 1943 with the target date as the period of the favorable July moon. . . .
>
> You are to be the Supreme Commander, with General Alexander as Deputy Commander in Chief. . . . Admiral of the Fleet Cunningham is to be the naval and Air Chief Marshal Tedder the air commander.
>
> You will submit to the C.C.S. your recommendations for the officers to be appointed Western and Eastern Task Force Commanders.
>
> In consultation with General Alexander you will set up at once a

special operational and administrative staff . . . for planning and preparing the operation.

On that day, 23 January, the Casablanca Conference broke up. It had accomplished a great deal. It had reaffirmed the basic strategy of the war, declared that nothing less than unconditional surrender would be accepted from Germany and Japan, given the United States Navy a somewhat qualified free hand in the Pacific, postponed the cross-channel invasion of France another year, decided on an air-bombing offensive against Germany, and ordered the invasion of Sicily. But no Mediterranean operation beyond Sicily was authorized, because the British and the Americans could not agree whether there would be any, much less what it might be. The J.C.S. hoped that possession of Sicily might put a stopper on Mediterranean campaigns; the British, Mr. Churchill in particular, hoped that the conquest of Sicily would open opportunities for more thrusts at what he mistakenly called the "soft underbelly" of the Axis.[8] So it turned out; but the underbelly proved to be boned with the Apennines, plated with the hard scales of Kesselring's armor, and shadowed by the wings of the Luftwaffe.

[8] Apparently his first use of this phrase, but without the qualifying adjective, was in a dispatch to President Roosevelt, dated 18 Nov. 1942, answering one of the day before in which the President suggested numerous operations to follow TORCH, including "the possibility of obtaining Turkish support for an attack through the Black Sea against Germany's flank."

CHAPTER II

Planning and Training for Sicily[1]

January–June 1943

1. *Evolution of the Plan*

NOT EVEN Mr. Churchill expected Sicily to be soft. As an historian he knew that Greeks, Carthaginians, Romans, Byzantines, Saracens, Normans, Angevins and Spaniards in succession had had their will of this great and fair island, that each conquest had taken many years to complete, and that Sicily had never been so defensible, at least in theory, as now. By March 1943 Sicily contained about a dozen airfields,[2] and its garrison was formidable, at least on paper. The greater part of the island is mountainous, difficult to traverse except by main roads. The Strait of Messina is so narrow that Sicily is far easier to reinforce from Italy than to

[1] Commander Western Naval Task Force (Vice Adm. H. K. Hewitt), *Action Report: The Sicilian Campaign, Operation* HUSKY, *July–August 1943*, Part III "The Plan," p. 16 *et seq.*, and his article "Naval Aspects of the Sicilian Campaign," U.S. Nav. Inst. *Proceedings* LXXIX (July 1953) pp. 705–23. General D. D. Eisenhower USA "Revised C-in-C Dispatch on Sicilian Operations," with the General's final emendations (early 1944); and *Crusade in Europe* (1948) pp. 159–78. Cincmed (Admiral of the Fleet Sir Andrew B. Cunningham RN) "Despatch on Invasion of Sicily" 1 Jan. 1944 (Supplement to *London Gazette* Apr. 25, 1950, pp. 2077–97) and *A Sailor's Odyssey* (1951) chaps. xxxix-xli. Field Marshal the Viscount Alexander of Tunis, "Despatch" 9 Oct. 1945 (2nd Supplement to *London Gazette* 10 Feb. 1948); Field Marshal the Viscount Montgomery *El Alamein to the River Sangro* (1948) Part ii. Col. A. H. Head of the British Army, who observed both Western and Eastern Task Forces, wrote valuable "Notes on Planning, Training and Execution of HUSKY" 26 July 1943.

[2] Gen. Alexander's "Despatch" and other sources state that the number was 19 in May or June and increased to 30 by 10 July. Italian Air Force Historians assure me that this is not correct; that the number of usable fields had decreased rather than increased, owing to the attacks of Allied Air Forces. Even the number 19 can be reached only by counting "satellite" strips at some of the fields, especially Gerbini.

invade from Africa; although Africa is near enough – only 90 miles separates Cape Lilibeo from Cape Bon, Tunisia.

Three capes which Ceres called "the three horns of her land" make the three angles of triangular Sicily – Cape Lilibeo on the west, Cape Peloro on the northeast, and Cape Pássero on the southeast. Measuring about 180 statute miles from Marsala to Messina, the same from Marsala to Portopalo, and 125 miles from Messina to Cape Pássero, Sicily covers the water route from Africa to Rome, and Pachino airfield is only 55 miles distant from Malta.

On 19 January 1943, when the Allies decided to invade Sicily, they assumed that the Tunisian campaign would not be over before 30 April; and until Tunisia was secured no one could predict what troops, ships, or staging areas would be available for invading Sicily. There were other variables, too. General Mark Clark's Fifth Army had to be retained on the border of Spanish Morocco lest Franco give trouble or Hitler strike through Spain at Gibraltar. The political situation in French North Africa was still in ferment. President Roosevelt had persuaded Generals Giraud and DeGaulle to shake hands at Casablanca; but Giraud, though a good soldier, was a poor politician, and General Eisenhower had to spend an inordinate amount of time and energy bringing disparate French elements to coöperate with the Allies. Admiral Darlan, a much easier man to deal with, had been assassinated; but the undeserved bad odor of the "Darlan deal" still worried the British and American governments, as well as their generals in Africa.

Top naval commander for Operation HUSKY (the invasion of Sicily), as for TORCH (North Africa), was Admiral of the Fleet Sir Andrew B. Cunningham RN,[3] the shrewd and capable flag officer of the Royal Navy who had been appointed Commander in Chief Mediterranean in the summer of 1939 and had exercised that com-

[3] Born 1883, entered R.N. 1898, served with distinction in World War I; Naval A.D.C. to the king 1932; Rear Admiral commanding destroyer flotillas Mediterranean Fleet 1933–6, Vice Admiral commanding battle cruiser squadron 1937–8, Deputy chief Naval Staff 1938, Cincmed 1939, Admiral 1941, head of Admiralty delegation to Washington and top Allied Naval commander for TORCH 1942; Admiral of the Fleet, First Sea Lord and Chief of Naval Staff 1943–6, created Viscount Cunningham of Hyndhope 1945.

mand with ever-increasing skill and energy. By this time he knew intimately the leading American military and naval commanders in his theater. "Ike" found "A.B.C." congenial and coöperative; Admiral King regarded him as the nearest modern equivalent to Admiral Jervis, Lord St. Vincent. General Sir Harold R. Alexander, commanding the 15th Army Group, was on the same echelon with Cunningham; Air Chief Marshal Arthur W. Tedder commanded all Allied air forces in the Mediterranean theater. Directly under Cunningham were Vice Admiral H. Kent Hewitt and Vice Admiral Sir Bertram H. Ramsay RN, commanding respectively the Western and Eastern Naval Task Forces for the invasion of Sicily. They were not so designated until 19 May 1943, after they had been planning the operation more or less in the dark for two or three months.

Anyone who knows about the North Africa landings will need no introduction to Admiral Hewitt.[4] In overall command of the Western Naval Task Force in Operation TORCH, he had planned and personally conducted the landings in Morocco. In amphibious experience he was surpassed by none and equaled by few. And he had qualities of mind and heart that especially fitted him for this particular position; the tact necessary to deal with the French, on whose soil the Allied forces were based; with the Royal Navy, accustomed to supremacy in the Mediterranean; and with the Allied armies and air forces which, in this theater of war, called the tunes.

[4] See my Vol. II, with portrait as frontispiece. Henry Kent Hewitt, b. New Jersey 1887, Annapolis '07. Sea duty in *Missouri*, *Connecticut*, *Flusser* and *Florida;* instructor math., Naval Academy; C.O. survey ship *Eagle* in Caribbean, 1916–1917; C.O. *Cummings* in convoy duty, World War I; gunnery officer *Pennsylvania* 1921, and head of gunnery section fleet training div. Office of C.N.O. 1923; Battle Force gunnery officer 1927; Naval War College course and staff 1928; Comdesdiv 12, 1931; as Capt. head of dept. of math. Naval Academy 1933; C.O. *Indianapolis* 1936; chief of staff to Rear Adm. Taussig 1937; Rear Admiral 1939 with command Special Service Squadron and Cruisers Atlantic Fleet. In 1942 commanded Amphibious Force Atlantic Fleet and Western Naval Task Force in TORCH; Vice Admiral 17 Nov. 1942. Commander U.S. Naval Forces Northwest African Waters and Commander Eighth Fleet, March 1943. Commanded all Allied naval forces in AVALANCHE and in ANVIL, 1944. Promoted Admiral 3 April 1945 and Commander U.S. Naval Forces Europe. Representative of C.N.O. on Security Council United Nations 1947; retired 1949.

He had the power to make positive decisions; he was respected by his equals and beloved by the sailors of his Eighth Fleet.

Admiral Hewitt's chief of staff was now Rear Admiral Spencer S. Lewis, and Captain Jerauld Wright, who had been on the combined planning staff for TORCH and had conducted several special missions with skill and discretion,[5] was his assistant chief of staff for plans and operations. Commander Robert A. J. English was still Hewitt's war plans officer, and Commander Leo A. Bachman the head of his Intelligence section. Commander H. R. Brookman USNR planned the logistics, and the alterations of various vessels to enable them to exercise new functions in amphibious warfare.

General Eisenhower, preoccupied with the Tunisian campaign, could give little personal attention to planning HUSKY. At Algiers on 10 February he set up a planning staff for that one purpose, headed by Major General C. H. Gairdner of the British Army.[6] This staff was first known as "Force 141" from the number of the room at the Hotel St. George where it first met. Since that famous hostelry was already full to overflowing, Force 141 and a planning section of Admiral Cunningham's staff were moved to the École Normale at Bouzarea, a suburb of Algiers, where some key members of Admiral Hewitt's staff participated.[7] Admiral Ramsay's planning staff was at Cairo, since the Eastern Naval Task Force was largely mounted in the Middle East. But the planning staffs for the Army and Air Force units participating in the American part of HUSKY were far distant from Algiers – at Arzeu and Constantine respectively.[8]

Admiral Hewitt established headquarters in Algiers on 17 March 1943, in order to be in close contact with Admiral Cunningham. "We worked together like brothers," said Cunningham of Hewitt;

[5] See Vol. II pp. 21, 177, 182, 186, 252.

[6] Relieved by Maj. Gen. Arthur A. Richardson, British Army, in early May.

[7] Cdr. English, Cdr. Brookman and a few others of Admiral Hewitt's staff joined Force 141 to coördinate naval plans with military plans on the highest level. That task completed, they reverted to the lower echelon and prepared Hewitt's plans for the Western Naval Task Force.

[8] Gen. Eisenhower Dispatch on Sicilian Operation p. 8.

"we became the greatest of friends." [9] The planning staff of General Patton, designated to command the Army in the Western Task Force, was at Mostaganem, 165 miles west of Algiers. Despite their physical separation, United States Army and Navy plans for HUSKY were well coördinated; but those of the Northwest African Air Forces remained inchoate to the last minute, and a mystery to their companion arms.

Although Air Chief Marshal Tedder had a planning staff in the École Normale at Bouzarea, it might as well have been in a blimp over the Atlantic, since it would have nothing to do with tactical problems, only with strategic bombing. "So far it has been impossible to pin the air down to anything," wrote Hewitt early in April to Admiral Kirk at Norfolk. "It appears that the air show is to be run entirely independently." And indeed it was. Hewitt sent Captain Wright to General Spaatz's headquarters to ask that either he be given control of a certain amount of air power in the assault, or that the General place on board his flagship an officer who had power to order close air support. These requests were refused, on two grounds: the targets against which the Admiral proposed to employ planes, such as enemy coastal batteries and strong points (so Captain Wright was told), were naval and not air targets; and there would be no need for local control of air power at the beaches, because all proper air targets — enemy planes and airfields — would by that time have been driven away or destroyed!

General Eisenhower defends this attitude on two grounds: that major air operations "never ceased," and that the enemy air force was "a fleeting and frequently a fugitive target, impossible to pinpoint in advance." Consequently, "the air plan was certain to appear imprecise when compared with military and naval plans." [10] True enough; but the real reason that the Allied Air Forces refused to coöperate was the current doctrine of their leaders that they should not coöperate; they did not wish to support ground or naval

[9] *A Sailor's Odyssey* p. 522.
[10] Eisenhower Dispatch pp. 20–21; *cf.* Vice Adm. Hewitt *Action Report* p. 91.

forces at a beachhead. The top air commanders of both countries were trying to prove that air power, alone and uncoördinated, could win the war. They almost managed to prove the opposite.

Want of an explicit directive was another cross to Admiral Hewitt, and to Army planners as well. "I am going ahead," he wrote, "on rough plans based on what I think the plan is going to be." But it was not until 3 May that the top echelons of command could agree on how, where and when Sicily was to be assaulted. Even D-day was not set until 13 April. It had to be fixed in a particular phase of a waxing moon, when it sets around midnight, because the Army planned to spearhead the assault with paratroops, and paratroops prefer to drop by moonlight; whilst the ground forces wished to be set ashore in the dark of the moon to secure a beachhead before daybreak. The tenth day of July suited both: the moon would be shining for the air drop, but would set before the troops landed.

The *when* decided, there remained the important *how.*

The Initial Appreciation [11] for HUSKY produced by General Gairdner's planning group about 17 March, and accepted by General Eisenhower as a basis for planning, may be summarized as follows: —

1. The capture of Messina to isolate Sicily is the ultimate goal, but it will have to be taken from the land side; no amphibious assault within the Strait of Messina is feasible because the Strait is too far from Allied air bases for fighter-plane cover. (We shall return to this point in Chapter X.)

2. At least two good Sicilian harbors, preferably Catania and Palermo, must be captured early, since without good harbor facilities it would be impossible to maintain and supply a sufficient number of troops to conquer the island. (The growing production of beaching craft and their excellent performance removed this limitation.)

3. Since we had learned at Oran in November 1942 not to assault a strongly defended harbor from the sea, initial landings must

[11] Similar to the U.S. "estimate of the situation."

be made over beaches. (As it turned out, some Sicilian harbors had formidable defenses, but none except Messina were stoutly defended.)

4. Beaches must be selected to meet three requirements – favorable topography, ready access to the interior, and accessibility to airfields which are wanted for Allied air forces.

5. Nine divisions (four American, four British and one Canadian) will be available for the assault, and a defense force of at least two German and six Italian divisions will be encountered. Additional German divisions may well be ferried across the Strait of Messina before D-day. (They were.)

6. It is essential to secure command of the air over Sicily before D-day, and promptly to capture enemy airfields in the southeastern part of the island. (Both were done.)

7. Command of the surrounding waters is assumed, but measures must be taken to contain the Italian Fleet in harbor.

The initial plan, worked over by Force 141 in February and March, called for a series of assaults at two widely separated parts of the island. The British Eastern Task Force, with three infantry divisions, would land at four places between Gela and Ávola on D-day, in order to capture the southeastern airfields and the ports of Syracuse and Augusta. Also on D-day, one American division would land at Sciacca and Selinunte in the west, to capture the Castelvetrano airdrome. On D plus 2, two American divisions would land at each side of Palermo, and take that city. Next day (D plus 3), the Eastern Task Force would put ashore two and a half divisions (one airborne) near Catania, to capture that port, the plain, and the Gerbini airfields. Floating reserves would be ready to land at Palermo and Catania when secured. After more discussion, the Sciacca assault was deferred to D plus 2 and the Palermo assaults to D plus 5 or later, so that air cover could be furnished from captured fields in southeastern Sicily.[12] That was the main reason for planning staggered assaults, but it was also hoped that this series

[12] This modified initial plan, dated 6 April, is in Vice Admiral Hewitt's *Action Report* p. 21. Gen. Alexander's Despatch pp. 1011–12 has the most details.

of blows extending over the better part of a week would send the German and Italian defenders rushing wildly about from one end of Sicily to another.

The initial plan was flown back and forth between Algiers, Cairo and London for months. Owing to the deep involvement of Generals Eisenhower, Alexander, Montgomery and Patton in the Tunisian campaign, they were unable to give it much attention. Army planners had to function without guidance from the generals who would be responsible for executing the operation, and Navy planners spent time and effort on landings that were never carried out.[13] When Montgomery found time to examine the plan, on 23 April, he objected to it on many counts. Not enough strength was allotted to assault eastern Sicily, which the enemy could quickly reinforce from Italy; the Eastern Task Force was spread too thin; the plan almost invited the enemy to drive a wedge between British and Americans; the Eighth Army could not possibly be maintained over beaches alone; no provision had been made for capturing the Cómiso and Ponte Olivo airfields. But, if the plan were changed, how could Palermo and Catania be secured promptly?

General Eisenhower "struggled with the dilemma between two risks" – the risk of vital airfields remaining in enemy hands and the risk of trying to maintain an expeditionary force without harbors. "We are arriving at a state of deadlock out here over HUSKY," wrote Admiral Cunningham on 28 April. "Here we are with no fixed agreed plan . . . two months off D-day and the commanders all at sixes and sevens." [14] Finally, after the reluctant admission by American logistics experts that they might be able to supply the Army over beaches alone, if necessary, owing to the growing numbers of dukws and beaching craft, a new outline plan was accepted by Generals Eisenhower and Alexander on 3 May and approved by C.C.S. on the 13th, day of the Axis collapse in Tunisia.

[13] Capt. Bachman points out that these efforts were not wasted; they increased the planners' proficiency and improved the final result, just as a singer's long hours of practice improve a concert, even if different arias are selected. See Vol. VI pp. 9–15 for the importance of sound naval planning.

[14] *A Sailor's Odyssey* pp. 536–37.

Admirals Cunningham and Hewitt and General Patton hated to give up the assault on Palermo, but they had no choice. Patton said they could land him on any beach in Sicily, he'd get to Messina first – which he did.[15]

Although the new plan owed its birth to General Montgomery's dislike of the old one, it did incorporate recent experience and new devices in amphibious warfare. Here, as in the Pacific, the prompt capture and reactivation of enemy airfields rather than enemy harbors had become a major factor in planning. And, to anticipate, the success of the initial assault on Sicily, without using a harbor, had a vital influence on planning for Normandy.

The 13 May plan covered both preparatory measures and initial assaults. The first, designed to gain complete air superiority and to contain the Italian Fleet, included the capture of Pantelleria to provide a new base for fighter planes. Initial assaults, instead of being spread over four days, were now scheduled for 10 July at the same H-hour (0245) and concentrated in southern and eastern Sicily. In the reallotment of objectives, Admiral Hewitt's Western Task Force took over the south coast between Licata and Scoglitti, while the British Eastern Task Force concentrated on the Pachino Peninsula and the Gulf of Noto, short of Syracuse. All elements of the assault would be within supporting distance of each other, strung along more than one hundred miles of coast.

This was a very bold plan. No amphibious operation on so broad a front – practically eight reinforced divisions landing abreast – had ever been tried before; nor was it ever tried again, even in Normandy, where the initial assault force was less than this strength.[16]

[15] Patton, when urged by naval officers to protest against the new plan, said: "No, goddammit, I've been in this Army thirty years and when my superior gives me an order I say 'Yes, Sir!' and then do my goddamndest to carry it out." Very different from the British Army, where "Monty's" objections broke up the initial plan. Admiral Cunningham still believes that the initial plan was the better, and so do many others.

[16] In order to persuade the Axis that landings in western Sicily were coming off after all, Admiral Hewitt had organized a Demonstration Group under Cdr. Hunter R. Robinson USNR in *PT-213*, with 10 air-sea-rescue (often called "crash") boats. The "Beach Jumpers," as they were nicknamed, were to operate off Cape

Admiral Hewitt pleaded to be allowed to deliver a pre-landing naval bombardment. The Army still insisted that naval gun power was not suitable for land bombardment [17] – old doctrine that would shortly be discredited. Nor was the Air Force given the task of neutralizing the beach defenses, because its chosen rôle in this operation was to be "the destruction of enemy air power." But the sailors were not denied their share; scores of enemy targets observed by air reconnaissance were assigned to them, and shore fire-control parties with naval liaison officers were assigned to each regiment, in order to call for naval gunfire after the landings. As it turned out, the beach defenses in Sicily were so weak that a pre-landing bombardment would have helped very little.

Another reason for denying a pre-landing naval or air bombardment on the assault beaches was the desire to obtain tactical surprise. Similarly, a dawn assault, which the Navy always wanted (and in the Pacific obtained),[18] in order to avoid the foul-ups inevitable in night landings, was rejected because it was hoped to get the troops ashore before the enemy knew what was up. Admiral Hewitt, like every sailor, liked tactical surprise, that elusive nymph pursued by all; but he believed that too high a price might be paid for a mere pursuit, in which the gal was not likely to be caught.

The highest air commanders believed that the proper way to help Operation HUSKY was to destroy enemy air power and to render enemy airfields unusable – to "seal off the beachhead" from the enemy was their slogan. For this primary object Lieutenant General Carl Spaatz USA, commanding the Northwest African Air Force, had organized the Northwest African Strategic Air Force under Major General James H. Doolittle USA. But he also had a North-

---

Granítola in the early hours of D-day, emitting false radio messages, firing rockets and other pyrotechnics, playing gramophone records simulating the rattling of anchor cables and the clanking of landing craft, with other intriguing noises supposed to give the impression that a full-scale assault would be delivered there before daylight. It was postponed, owing to heavy weather, until the night of 10–11 July, when it failed to impress the enemy.

17 Vice Adm. Hewitt *Action Report* p. 42.

18 General Eisenhower in his Dispatch (p. 38) adverts to the "demands of the Navy for darkness." He must mean darkness for the approach, because the Navy always wanted dawn landings.

west African Tactical Air Force, under Air Vice Marshal Sir Arthur Coningham RAF, which included the XII Air Support Command, charged with direct air support of Army and Navy during the amphibious operation.[19] Although this command included over 400 planes, it would give no advance assurance to Army or Navy as to the kind and quality of support they could expect on D-day or thereafter. This refusal stemmed from the reluctance of top air commanders to sacrifice flexibility: "Tactical" might be wanted to support "Strategic" in action against enemy air forces.

Thus the United States Army and Navy sailed to Sicily with no knowledge of what bomber or fighter support they could expect. They merely had assurance that after D-day requests for air support "could be submitted with not less than twelve hours' notice to a target committee located in North Africa." [20]

Indignation over the Air Force attitude was not confined to the Navy. General Patton, recalling the performance of escort carriers off Casablanca,[21] begged Hewitt to procure some. "You can get your Navy planes to do anything you want," he remarked; "but we can't get the Air Force to do a goddam thing!" But Hewitt knew he could get no escort carriers; the few then in the Atlantic were desperately needed for anti-submarine work. Nor did he feel that the Army was justified in asking the Navy to provide close air support when it had airfields within a hundred miles of the target; after all the Air Force was supposed to be an integral part of the Army.[22] The results of depending on A.A.F. tactical support were so disappointing that next time, at Salerno, the Royal Navy managed to produce a few escort carriers.

It is pleasant to record that a third Allied air force, the Northwest African Coastal Command, coöperated to the limit of its ca-

[19] Same p. 22. The XII Air Support Command comprised two dive-bomber groups, one fighter squadron, one reconnaissance squadron, and three fighter groups. Two of the fighter groups were based on Gozo and Pantelleria for the invasion.

[20] Vice Adm. Hewitt *Action Report* p. 18.

[21] See Vol. II of this History, index under *Suwannee*.

[22] Admiral Louis E. Denfeld in *Collier's* 25 Mar. 1950 p. 46; information from Admiral Hewitt in 1953.

pacity. "Coastal," predominantly British as "Tactical" was predominantly American, was commanded by Air Vice Marshal Sir Hugh Pugh Lloyd, the gallant defender of Malta. It not only furnished air cover for all convoys passing into and through the Mediterranean, but protected Bizerta and other staging ports, and covered the Western Task Force up to Malta. And when it became evident that no adequate photos of Sicily could be had from the Northwest African Photo Reconnaissance Wing, since the aviators could not be persuaded to give proper attention to beach gradients and approaches, a search through some 100,000 prints in the files of Coastal Command produced a fairly good series for beach characteristics' studies.[23]

The Hydrographic Office of the Admiralty got out excellent maps, a combination of the 1 to 100,000 Italian topographical survey of Sicily with Admiralty charts, giving complete land and hydrographic data, with a grid for artillery and naval gunfire. And, on the basis of air photos, tourists' snapshots, maps and other Intelligence data, Ensign Edouard Sandoz USNR, of Admiral Hewitt's staff, drew a series of perspective views of the coast that were placed in the hands of boat and troop commanders. In the end, the whole Western Task Force was unusually well supplied with information.[24]

The Sicilian beaches and shores were far from ideal for amphibious landings. There were no jagged coral reefs or other hard obstacles as in the Pacific, but the gradients were too easy, and the beaches were fronted by shifting "false beaches." The underwater shelf sloped seaward so uniformly and gradually that transports could anchor several miles from shore, instead of lying-to. The

[23] Information from Capt. Bachman and Capt. English in 1953. Capt. Bachman adds that the failure of the recce. planes was due to the aviators' lack of understanding of Navy requirements, that they improved greatly before Salerno, and by the time of the Southern France landings left nothing to be desired.

[24] The commander Salso Attack Group, Cdr. W. O. Floyd, noted, "The information furnished . . . was most helpful and proved amazingly accurate, particularly respecting beach defenses, surrounding terrain and contours, nature of the beach, beach exits and adjacent roads, and seaward approaches. . . . I found the silhouette of my beach unmistakable; there wasn't the slightest doubt in my mind as to its location and limits."

SICILY
1943
Heights in Feet, Soundings in Fathoms
Nautical Miles
Statute Miles
KEY
Principal roads
Railroads
100-meter contour, marking edge of plain
50-fathom line
TYRRHENIAN
C. Gallo
PALERMO
C. Zafferano
Gulf of Términi
Términi
C.S. Vito
Gulf of Castellammare
Carini
Monreale
TRÁPANI
M. Erice
Castellammare
Segesta
Calatafimi
Camporeale
Corleone
Lercara
Prizzi
Castronovo
Cammarata
I. Lévanzo
ÆGADES IS.
I. Favignana
I. Grande
C. Lilibeo
Marsala
Milo
Chinisia
Salemi
Gibellina
Castelvetrano
Mazara
Campobello
Selinunte
Sciacca
MONTI SICANI
Bivona
S. Stefano Quisquina
Verduro R.
Belice R.
S. Leonardo R.
Platani R.
Ribera
Casteltérmini
S. Cataldo
Serridafalco
Raffadali
Aragona
Canicatti
AGRIGENTO
Porto Empedocle
Favaro
Naro
Naro R.
Campobello
Ravanusa
Palma
Marina di Palma
Torre di Gaffe
M. SOLE
Licata
Caltavuturo
Sommatino
Salso
Gulf
Lascari
13°
38°
37°
F.J.W.

SEA
C.Peloro
C.Milazzo
Milazzo
C.Calavà
C.d'Orlando
Brolo
Patti
Fúrnari
Castroreale
Spadafora
MESSINA
STR. OF MESSINA
Scilla
S.Giovanni
Reggio
Scaletta
Ali
S.Teresa
Taormina
PELORITANI
S.Agata di Militello
Caronia
Cefalù
S.Stefano di Camastra
S.Fratello
Rosmarino R.
Zappulla R.
CARONIE
Randazzo
Cesarò
Alcantara R.
Petralia
Cerami
Troina
Linguaglossa
Fiumefreddo
Bronte
Nicosia
MT. ETNA 10,741
Giarre
Adrano
Regalbuto
Leonforte
Agira
Assoro
Centúripe
Simeto R.
Paternò
Acireale
ENNA
Dittaino R.
CALTANISSETA
Misterbianco
Gerbini
CATANIA
Gulf of Catania
Piazza Armerina
CATANIA PLAIN
Agnone
Lake Lentini
Lentini
C.S.Croce
Riesi
S.Michele
Caltagirone
Grammichele
Augusta
Gela R.
Butera
M.Desusino
Niscemi
Vizzini
Priolo
Gulf of Augusta
P.Olivo
Acate or Dirillo R.
Anapo R.
Palazzolo
Floridia
SYRACUSE
Gela
Gulf of Gela
Biscari
Chiaramonte
C.Murro di Porco
Comiso
Cassibile
C.Ognina
Vittoria
RAGUSA
Avola
Noto
Scoglitti
Marina di Ávola
S.Croce Camerina
Módica
Irminio R.
P. Braccetto
Scicli
Ispica
Pozzallo
Marzameni
Pachino
C.Pássero
P. Religione
Portopalo
I.Correnti
15°
37°
38°

enemy might have planted mines and underwater obstacles but neglected to do so. Tides could be ignored, since the normal range on the south coast of Sicily is only nine and a half inches.

Reinforcement and supply convoys were worked out in great detail, for the era when the Navy could land soldiers and sail away was long past. A modern army, even if it meets little opposition, must be continuously fed provisions, motor fuel, clothing, replacements, and all manner of matériel. Adequate stockpiles had been accumulated in North Africa, and a shuttle service of LSTs and Liberty ships was provided to run the stuff into Sicily quickly. All logistic phases were well taken care of in HUSKY.

General Alexander's Operation Instructions, dated 19 May, divided the operation into five phases: —

1. Preliminary measures by the two Navies and Air Forces to insure mastery of sea and air, and so far as possible to destroy Axis air forces and bases.

2. A pre-dawn amphibious assault, assisted by air drops, securing an initial beachhead to include airfields near the coast, and the ports of Licata and Syracuse.

3. The establishment of a wider base from which to capture Augusta, Catania and the Gerbini airfields.

4. The capture of these places.

5. Reduction of the island.[25]

Thus everything after the seaborne assault and the capture of the Catania plain was left for future decision. But there was a general understanding, which reached down to Army and Naval Task Force command levels, that the British would endeavor to rush through to Messina and dominate the Strait, while the Americans protected their flank and captured important airports. Once Messina was secured the two armies would be maneuvered in order to trap the enemy somewhere north or west of Mount Etna, and prevent his escape to Italy.[26] That is what should have been done, and what

[25] Alexander Despatch pp. 1013–14.

[26] "The major objective was Messina. . . . During the preliminary phase of the advance the rôle of the U.S. Seventh Army on the left was to protect its captured

General Alexander hoped to do; but he was thwarted, as we shall see, by Axis forces on the Catania plain.

The capture of Sicily was both planned and executed as a limited objective. In contrast to the Pacific, where a series of operations was planned in definite stages, Combined Chiefs of Staff had to follow HUSKY with hasty concepts and even hastier plans which proved to be costly and tortuous in execution. Both British and Americans were responsible for this strategic vacuum. The Joint Chiefs of Staff were resolved to protect their Fortress OVERLORD from mines and saps, while the British Chiefs and Mr. Churchill dreamed of a series of brilliant thrusts into the "soft underbelly." Nobody could plan anything ahead, since nothing was authorized.

Nevertheless, the irregular and often stormy planning for HUSKY was a test of moral strength for American and British planners on all echelons. It was the first time that these men had had to work so long and close, and in a theater of combat. The vast assault on *Festung Europa* that started almost a year later would have been impossible but for the intimate knowledge that American and British planners, as well as commanders, had acquired of each other in the Mediterranean.

2. *Forces and Training*

The American Western Naval Task Force for Operation HUSKY, commanded by Vice Admiral Hewitt, and charged with landing General Patton's Seventh Army on beaches between Torre di Gaffe and Punta Braccetto, was divided into three Attack Forces. From west to east these were: —

---

port and airfields . . . and to guard Eighth Army's left flank from enemy reserves which were likely to be drawn in from Western Sicily." Eisenhower Dispatch p. 50. Adm. Hewitt informs me that this was the general understanding at Algiers headquarters. Gen. Leese of XXX Corps, at a conference with Gen. Montgomery on 9 June, informed Gen. Simonds that Eighth Army's objective was "to dominate the Messina Straits as soon as possible." Quoted in Lt. Col. G. W. L. Nicholson *The Canadians in Italy* chap. iv.

TF 86, the Licata or JOSS Force, Rear Admiral Conolly, transporting the 3rd Infantry Division, Major General Lucian K. Truscott USA, and two Ranger battalions. Light cruisers *Brooklyn* and *Birmingham* and nine destroyers for escort and gunfire support.

TF 81, the Gela or DIME Force, Rear Admiral Hall, transporting the 1st Infantry Division, Major General Terry Allen USA, one combat team of the 2nd Armored Division, and a Ranger battalion. Light cruisers *Savannah* and *Boise* and 13 destroyers for escort and gunfire support.

TF 85, the Scoglitti or CENT Force, Rear Admiral Kirk, transporting the 45th Infantry Division, Major General Troy Middleton USA. Light cruiser *Philadelphia* and 16 destroyers for escort and gunfire support.

The Floating Reserve or KOOL Force, commanded by Captain K. S. Reed, transporting two combat teams of the 2nd Armored Division, Major General Hugh J. Gaffey USA, and one of the 1st Division, operated with DIME Force.

As General Reserve, the 9th Infantry Division was readied in North Africa.

On the right flank of TF 85 began the assault area of the British Eastern Naval Task Force, Vice Admiral Sir Bertram Ramsay RN, which landed General Montgomery's Eighth Army of five divisions on the beaches between Pozzallo and Cape Murro di Porco.

Admiral Hewitt had under his command 580 ships and beaching craft that came up on their own bottoms, and 1124 shipborne landing craft;[27] Admiral Ramsay had 795 of the one and 715 of the other for the Eastern landings and follow-up convoys. If covering forces are added, the total number under British tactical command in HUSKY rises to 818.[28] American and British ground forces were substantially equal in numbers. It was the greatest amphibious

[27] See Appendix I. The figure of 580 includes every vessel that took part in HUSKY under Admiral Hewitt's command down to 17 Aug. It includes 37 British ships.

[28] Including 25 U. S. Liberty ships. Mr. Churchill's estimate (*Closing the Ring* p. 26) that 80 per cent of Allied naval forces in HUSKY were British must be based on some method of computation unknown to me. For ground forces committed

operation in recorded history, if measured by the strength of the initial assault.

Neither naval task force was exclusively of one nation. The United States Navy provided many beaching craft and Liberty ships for the Eastern Naval Task Force; the Royal Navy provided beacon submarines, a monitor, and four fast transports [29] for the Western Naval Task Force, as well as battleships, carriers, cruisers and destroyers to cover both. The covering forces were under the direct command of Admiral Cunningham, who established his headquarters at Malta about 5 July. Generals Eisenhower and Alexander joined him there to keep a finger on the assault and also to profit by the island's excellent communications facilities.

By that date all troops, ships and landing craft in Operation HUSKY had been training for weeks and even months – Kirk's CENT Force in Chesapeake Bay; the 1st Canadian Division in Scotland; and the rest in North Africa, all the way from Ouidja on the Moroccan boundary to the Levant. But the most complex of the three American attack forces was Admiral Conolly's JOSS Force, the first to test the new beaching craft on a large scale. New techniques and procedures had to be devised so that these LSTs, LCTs and LCIs could move a reinforced division of some 25,000 men from Africa to Sicily.

Admiral King had long had his eye on a destroyer squadron commander, Captain Richard L. Conolly.[30] In February 1943 he had him promoted to flag rank and gave him the new command of Landing Craft and Bases North African Waters, facetiously abbreviated as Comlandcrabnaw. His training center was at Arzeu, Algeria. The 3rd Infantry Division, which had fought in Operation TORCH, was given the honor of handling the important left flank of the Sicilian assault, but there were no transports to lift

---

in HUSKY to 17 Aug. 1943 the nearest figures I can arrive at are: American Seventh Army, 228,000; British Eighth Army, 250,000, officers and men.

[29] See Appendix I under TG 86.5 and TG 81.2. These LSIs (Landing Ship, Infantry) were 3000-ton, 23-knot Belgian cross-channel steamships, converted to transports and carrying 10 or more landing craft each. They were named after Belgian princes and princesses.

[30] Brief biography in Vol. VII of this History, p. 232.

it from Africa. Could it make-do with LSTs and the like? Conolly was sure it could, and he showed such energy and skill in converting these beaching craft to troop-carrying purposes that at his urgent request Admiral Hewitt chose him to be JOSS Force commander — CTF 86.

Major General Lucian K. Truscott USA, commanding general of the 3rd Division, also was an ideal choice. He had served at Combined Operations Headquarters in London, had supervised the training of the first Ranger Battalions, had taken part in the raid on Dieppe, and, in November 1942, commanded the 30th Regiment in its difficult assault on Mehedia and Port Lyautey. The British, through their frequent commando raids on enemy-held coasts, had learned more than the Americans about tricky shore-to-shore amphibious technique; and General Truscott brought this knowledge with him to Africa.

According to Thucydides, the Greeks who invaded Syracuse in 413 B.C. had most to fear from the Sicilian cavalry, against which, for want of a "landing ship, horse," their only defense was archery. Enemy tanks, the modern cavalry, are now the bane of amphibious landings. In order to prevent their working havoc on the GIs, as the Sicilian horse had done on the Athenian hoplites, it was necessary to land our own tanks and antitank guns immediately after the assault troops. That was the main function of the LST (landing ship, tank), a 328-foot, square-built shoal-draft ark with an enormous bow ramp, and also of the 112-foot[31] LCT (landing craft, tank), which resembled a floating flatcar. These craft were supposed to be able to ground on a beach and lower their ramps, over which tanks, guns and vehicles could roll ashore.[32]

But the beaches of southern Sicily were not amenable to this procedure. Most of them were fronted by "false beaches" — sand bars with enough water over them to float landing craft or LCTs,

[31] Length of the LCT-5s used in Sicily; the later LCT-6s were 120 feet long.

[32] See Vol. II pp. 266–74 for the adventures of these craft, and the LCIs, in crossing the Atlantic. The amphtrac (LVT), essential in Pacific landings, was not wanted here, owing to the absence of hard reefs; and the Landing Ship Dock (LSD), which might have been useful, was not yet ready.

but not LSTs; and between the false and the real beaches would be a "runnel," a miniature lagoon deep enough to drown a tank or vehicle. Some ready means of bridging the runnels had to be provided, or LSTs would be unable to land their cargoes directly on the beaches.[33]

The answer was the pontoon causeway. A number of standard 5 x 5 x 7-foot steel pontoon units were clamped together in suitable lengths to make a portable causeway. These units were brought from the United States in freighters, with their "jewelry" (as the bluejackets called the massive pelican hooks and other hardware that clamped them together), and Conolly set up assembly plants for them at Arzeu and Bizerta. The pontoon causeways could be slung along the sides of LSTs, or towed to Sicily.

Since there were not enough of them to discharge all LSTs expeditiously, an alternate unloading method had to be devised. A certain number of LCTs had large hinged sections cut out of their topsides and were provided with special "jewelry" so that each could be "married" to an LST with its bow ramp lowered, at right angles to the LST's axis. The tanks could then be driven right across the "married" LCT into a second LCT, which closed the first bow-on, lowered its ramp and took the tanks on board and ashore. Both methods worked, and the pontoon causeway became standard equipment for LST flotillas everywhere.

Although Admiral Hall's DIME Force and Admiral Kirk's CENT Force used plenty of LSTs and LCTs for vehicles and equipment, they had big attack transports (APAs) and attack cargo ships (AKAs) to lift the bulk of their troops. To land the troops, the transports carried on their davits the new 36-foot plywood LCVP (landing craft, vehicle and personnel) with bow ramp and gas or diesel engine, which had replaced the rampless Higgins boats used in Operation TORCH. They also carried a few of the big LCM

[33] False beaches are a product of surf breaking on a beach in an almost tideless sea. The sand-charged undertow meets static water about 100 yards off shore, and drops its sand. Gaps can always be found in the false beaches, and these were possible to detect by aërial photography and other methods; but the technique at this time had not been perfected.

(landing craft, mechanized). Admiral Conolly had no big transports for JOSS Force. He was allotted 40 LCIs (landing craft, infantry) — the 158-foot craft designed to carry 200 men directly to the assault beaches, on which they landed over two gangplanks rigged fore-and-aft. But 40 LCIs were not nearly enough to lift the 3rd Division. So Conolly converted 36 LSTs to transport infantry, fitting four additional sets of Welin davits; each LST could now carry six LCVPs and about 500 men, most of whom slept in the vehicles or topside.

Another new amphibious craft was the dukw, a two-and-a-half-ton truck, designed both to swim in the water and roll on the land. The dukw was not big enough to carry a tank, but it could take one 105-mm gun. Launched from an LST at sea, it could drive ashore with its own propeller and roll inland on its wheels. Dukws were used in large numbers for the first time in every part of HUSKY and won golden opinions from all hands.

"Comlandcrabnaw" was not only working for his own JOSS Force, but for DIME and CENT as well. He trained all the beaching craft attached to Hall's and Kirk's task forces, and they too profited by his experiments. But Arzeu, Admiral Conolly felt, was too far from the scene of the future operation. Force 141, the original combined planning staff, had long wanted Bizerta, which fell to Major General Omar N. Bradley's II Corps on 7 May. Commodore William A. Sullivan, the Navy's No. 1 salvage expert, had by 6 June cleared the narrow channel into the great salt lake which makes the harbor. Leaving a staff at Arzeu to train the beaching craft that were still coming over from America, Admiral Conolly and General Truscott moved into the French seaplane base at Bizerta about the first of the month. Here were big cranes and a ramp where 18 LSTs could be loaded simultaneously. Tanks were ferried to Bizerta in the same vessels that would take them to Sicily; troops came over the road; intensive joint training was carried on in the waters of Lake Bizerta and nearby beaches and terrain. Here too the entire JOSS Force had its dress rehearsal.

The Luftwaffe, observing the great concentration at Bizerta, subjected that base to many night air raids, none very destructive. Their lack of success is credited by Admiral Conolly to the British air defense organization at Bizerta, which he persuaded Coastal Command to retain there when the rest of the British forces moved on to Tunis. This air command had some efficient Beaufighters, at a time when the American Army Air Force had not a single night fighter in Africa; and the British antiaircraft batteries, also excellent, fitted neatly into our own air defense. "Best integrated air defense of a harbor that I saw anywhere in the war," said Admiral Conolly. Planes and gunners, between them, shot down three to five German bombers out of every night raid, so that enemy air strength gradually diminished. But on the night of 6–7 July, just after JOSS Force sortied from the harbor, a specially big raid was put on, holing tug *Resolute* so that she could not take part in the operation.

Material readiness was very good, but JOSS Force had already been deprived of three beaching craft. *LST-333* and *LST-387*, each carrying troops especially trained to fight fires, were torpedoed by submarine *U-593* on 22 June en route to Bizerta. Together they lost 45 killed or missing and 75 injured. *LST-333* had to be beached and abandoned, but *LST-387* was towed into Dellys for repair. *LCT-208* buckled en route to Bizerta, probably because of overloading, and was lost.

All units celebrated the Fourth of July in proper style. At Allied Force Headquarters, Algiers, General Eisenhower and Admirals Cunningham and Hewitt reviewed honor guards from United States and British armed services and from the French Army. A French band rendered the three national anthems, H.M.S. *Maidstone* in the harbor fired a salute of 48 guns, one for each state (breaking the King's regulations), as no United States ship was in position to fire the usual 21 guns. At Bizerta there was a full-scale review, after which General Truscott addressed the entire 3rd Division by loud-speaker system. He ended with a crisp command which gave the final fillip to an aggressive spirit: "You are going to meet the Boche. Carve your name in his face!"

CHAPTER III

The Axis on the Defensive[1]

January–July 1943

1. *The Royal Italian Navy*

THE FASCIST government of Italy, seeking to revive the might and glory of the Roman Empire, made every effort to build a powerful navy. It was a costly endeavor for so poor a country, and it never had the success of similar efforts by Japan.

Mussolini and his admirals sought to fashion a fleet containing all types of naval vessels except aircraft carriers, which they deemed unnecessary for operations in narrow seas. The result was impressive, on paper. When the Duce declared war on France and Great Britain on 10 June 1940, he had almost completed two 35,000-ton

[1] The best Italian accounts in print of the Sicilian campaign are Adm. Romeo Bernotti *La Guerra sui Mari 1943–45* (Livorno 1950), Marc' Antonio Bragadin *Che ha Fatto la Marina?* (2nd ed. 1950), and Gen. Emilio Faldella (chief of staff to Gen. Guzzoni) "Questa è la Verità sulla Battaglia di Sicilia" in newspaper *Roma* 10–21 July 1953.

Manuscript sources: Rear Adm. Pietro Barone (commander at Messina) "Estratto della Relazione sull' Occupazione della Sicilia" (1944); Col. Barrille "1943 – Operazioni in Sicilia" (1951); a special report prepared for this History in 1953 by the Historical Office of the General Staff of the Italian Army "Operazioni Juglio 1943 in Sicilia"; extracts from Supermarina War Diary, and other records furnished by the Historical Office of the General Staff of the Italian Navy; and, "L'Opera dell' Aeronautica Italiana durante l'Invasione della Sicilia," prepared for this History by the Historical Office of the General Staff of the Italian Air Force. The statements quoted from Italian documents are indicated by footnotes and, as translated by myself, enclosed in quotation marks.

Principal German sources are *The Fuehrer Conferences on Matters Dealing with the German Navy* (vol. for 1943), and *Fuehrer Directives 1942–1945*, lithographed publications by C.N.O. 1948; the Conferences are also printed in *Brassey's Naval Annual* for 1948. These are summarized in Anthony Martienssen *Hitler and His Admirals* (1949). Felix Gilbert *Hitler Directs His War* (1950). The three best books covering this campaign are Marshal Albert Kesselring *Soldat bis zum Letzen Tag* (1953); the English ed. is called *Memoirs of Marshal Kesselring;* the

battleships (*Littorio*[2] and *Vittorio Veneto*) with nine 15-inch guns each; a third (*Roma*) was building; he also had four remodeled battleships with 12.6-inch guns and of 27-knot speed; 7 heavy and 12 light cruisers; 59 destroyers and 69 more of average 1000-ton displacement, called torpedo boats; 117 submarines, and many fast, light torpedo craft (the MAS), smaller than British and American motor torpedo boats. It was a new fleet of handsome ships, powerful for their class and unusually speedy. But the Italian Navy was doomed to defeat by three factors: lack of radar, a continual shortage of fuel oil, and want of a fleet air arm. *Regia Aeronautica*, the Royal Italian Air Force, was supposed to give air cover to the ships at sea, but seldom could and almost never did.

Command of the Italian Navy centered in Rome. Under Mussolini, General Ambrosio filled the post of *Comando Supremo*, Chief of all Armed Forces, with the task of coördinating all martial activities of the Fascist state. Under him was *Supermarina*, the General Staff of the Navy, whose chief throughout the war was Admiral Arturo Riccardi. He corresponded to the American Chief of Naval Operations, and under him Vice Admiral Luigi Sansonnetti was comparable to the Vice Chief of Naval Operations.

The Duce intended his fleet to be aggressive, and so ordered

American ed. is *A Soldier's Record* (1954); Gen. Siegfried Westphal *German Army in the West* (1951), and Enno von Rintelen *Mussolini als Bundesgenosse* (1951).

Important reports were compiled after the war for, and at the request of, United States Armed Forces: Vice Adm. Eberhard Weichold "Survey from the Naval Point of View of the Organization of the German Air Force for Operations over the Sea, 1939–45" and the same officer's "Axis in the Mediterranean, Phase Four" (O.N.I. *Review* Aug. 1946). Vice Adm. Friedrich von Ruge "Report on the Evacuation of Sicily" (1946); Gen. von Senger und Etterlin "The Battle for Sicily" (1951); Gen. Walter Fries "Operations of 29th Panzer Grenadier Division in Sicily," and "The Fight for Sicily" (1947); O. B. South (Marshal Kesselring) "Official Report on the Fighting in Sicily" (1943). The War Diary of the German Naval Staff, a day-by-day entry of events, is also useful. The Canadian Military Mission, Berlin, obtained from Col. Bogislaw von Bonin, chief of Marshal Kesselring's special staff for Sicily, a report entitled "Considerations on the Italian Campaign 1943–44" (1947); and the Historical Section Canadian Army compiled a report, "Sicilian Campaign, Information from German Sources," copies of which were kindly lent to me by Col. C. P. Stacey, Director Historical Section Canadian Army.

For British sources, see Chapter VIII.

[2] Name changed to *Italia* after the fall of Mussolini.

when Italy entered the war; but the British Navy promptly challenged his *mare nostrum* concept, and circumstances forced him to employ his light craft largely in escort of convoy, while the capital ships stayed safely in port. Italian naval officers accepted the rôle of a "fleet in being" with distaste, hoping that someday there would occur a favorable break when they might sally forth and win another Actium. For had not Polybius written that the Carthaginians excelled in naval science, but the Romans always won naval battles through the superior courage of their sailors? To Grand Admiral Doenitz, head of the German Navy, the passive policy of his Italian ally was exasperating. "It would be better for the Italian ships to get into a fight even at the risk of heavy losses," he reported to Hitler after a fruitless attempt to stir up Mussolini, "rather than fall into the hands of the enemy in the harbors, perhaps even without a fight." Better indeed for Germany but not, in the end, for Italy.

Italian naval officers who craved action found plenty of it in the submarine service, which fully sustained the Roman reputation for superior courage. Fleet submarines operated in the Atlantic, the Caribbean and the Mediterranean. Midget submarines, one-man explosive motorboats and "human torpedoes," effectively attacked Allied ships in the harbors of Alexandria, Gibraltar, Suda and Algiers. But, despite its greater numerical strength, the Italian surface navy for the most part stayed in port; and, although it performed some brave escort-of-convoy missions from Italy to Africa, its few clashes with the British Navy, especially the one with Rear Admiral Vian's light cruisers, were unfortunate. Even Italian harbors afforded no sanctuary, since the British aircraft often struck them with deadly effect. Service in the Italian Navy was very hazardous. Up to 1 July 1943 losses had been 1233 officers killed or missing and over 12,000 officers and men taken prisoner – some 10 per cent of the entire naval establishment.[3]

The Italian Navy grew no stronger in 1943. On 10 April the

[3] Information prepared by Operations Statistics Office of Italian Ministry of Marine.

photographic wing of the Northwest African Air Force discovered several large warships snugly anchored behind nets in Maddalena Bay, Sardinia. Shortly after, 24 B-17s sank cruiser *Trieste*, bombing her from 19,000 feet altitude, and 36 others concentrated on cruiser *Gorizia*, so damaging her that she was forced to proceed to Spezia, where she was soon under attack by the R.A.F. On 6 June a 100-plane high-level attack on Spezia destroyed many shore installations at that famous naval arsenal, and damaged three battleships with near-misses. This was followed 24 June by another attack which made two hits on battleship *Roma*, and she was still under repair when Sicily was invaded. The repeated bombings of Sicilian ports rendered Palermo and Messina untenable for naval vessels larger than motor torpedo boats. As the Italian admiral at Messina wrote, "There no longer existed a harbor or naval base in Sicily where ships great or small could remain in safety." The Sicilian navy yards ceased to function; shore installations were destroyed. Moreover, in the first half of 1943, almost 400 Italian merchant ships totaling over half a million tons were sunk by British submarines or Allied bombers.[4]

Still, the Allies had to reckon with the Italian Navy. There was always the possibility that it might choose "to be a lion for a day," in the words of the Duce's favorite maxim; and if it had so chosen it would have been a lion with teeth. If the Allied intentions as to Sicily had been known or correctly guessed, a resolute sortie of the Italian ships from Spezia and Taranto could have offered battle to the covering forces of the Royal Navy on at least equal terms; or, if they had eluded those forces they could have played the devil with the amphibious convoys. Fortunately nobody in Rome or Berlin knew when or where the Allies were about to strike until the evening before D-day.

Admiral Doenitz argued, at his conference with the Italian naval

[4] Craven and Cate II 194–95; Bernotti p. 42; Barone p. 3; *La Marina Italiana nella Seconda Guerra Mondiale: Navi Perdute*, II (1952). According to this list, 29 merchant steamers were sunk by air bombs in harbors from Leghorn to Catania between 14 May and 28 July 1943, and the number of sailing vessels and auxiliaries lost was much greater.

chiefs at Rome in early May, that the entire Axis naval effort must now be directed toward the supply of Sicily, Sardinia and other islands still in their possession. "The battle on land alone is decisive," he is quoted as having told the Italians; "therefore, the most important part of the Navy's mission is to make battle on land possible. That means safeguarding the supply lines across the sea. . . . It must not happen again, as it did in North Africa, that we are defeated because our supply system failed." [5] He agreed to send more U–boats into the Mediterranean to be used as supply vessels, and proposed that the Italians use everything from cruisers down for the same purpose – as the Japanese were doing for their threatened Pacific islands. But the Italians did not like the idea. Comando Supremo felt that "submarines and cruisers should fight"; and the Duce declared that his ground forces, with a little German help, would be able to defend Sicily.

The German Admiral, nonplussed, told Hitler upon his return that only an attack on Gibraltar through Spain could draw off the Allied forces and save Sicily, Sardinia, or whatever their target might be. Hitler replied he could not spare the troops, and that he did not care to risk starting a guerrilla war in Spain.[6]

When Supermarina took cognizance of the situation on the morning of 10 July, it had to consider that a challenge to Allied sea supremacy at that point would be hazardous, if not suicidal. What was available? At Taranto, old battleships *Doria* and *Duilio*, light cruiser *Cadorna*, and two old destroyers. It would take them about ten hours to reach Sicilian waters, and without air cover; besides, two more powerful British battleships, covered by carrier planes, were out looking for them. So the Taranto squadron had better be reserved for defense against a possible landing on the heel

[5] *Fuehrer Conferences, 1943* pp. 54–55.

[6] Same pp. 66–67. As an example of the interconnection of different phases of the war, another extract from the same conference minutes is relevant. Doenitz observed that, by clearing the Mediterranean, the Anglo-Saxon powers had gained 2,000,000 tons in shipping space. "Which" (interrupted Hitler) "our trusty submarines will now have to sink." Doenitz continued: "Yet we are at present facing the greatest crisis in submarine warfare . . . heavy losses – 15 to 17 submarines per month." "These losses are too high," interjected Hitler; "something must be done about it."

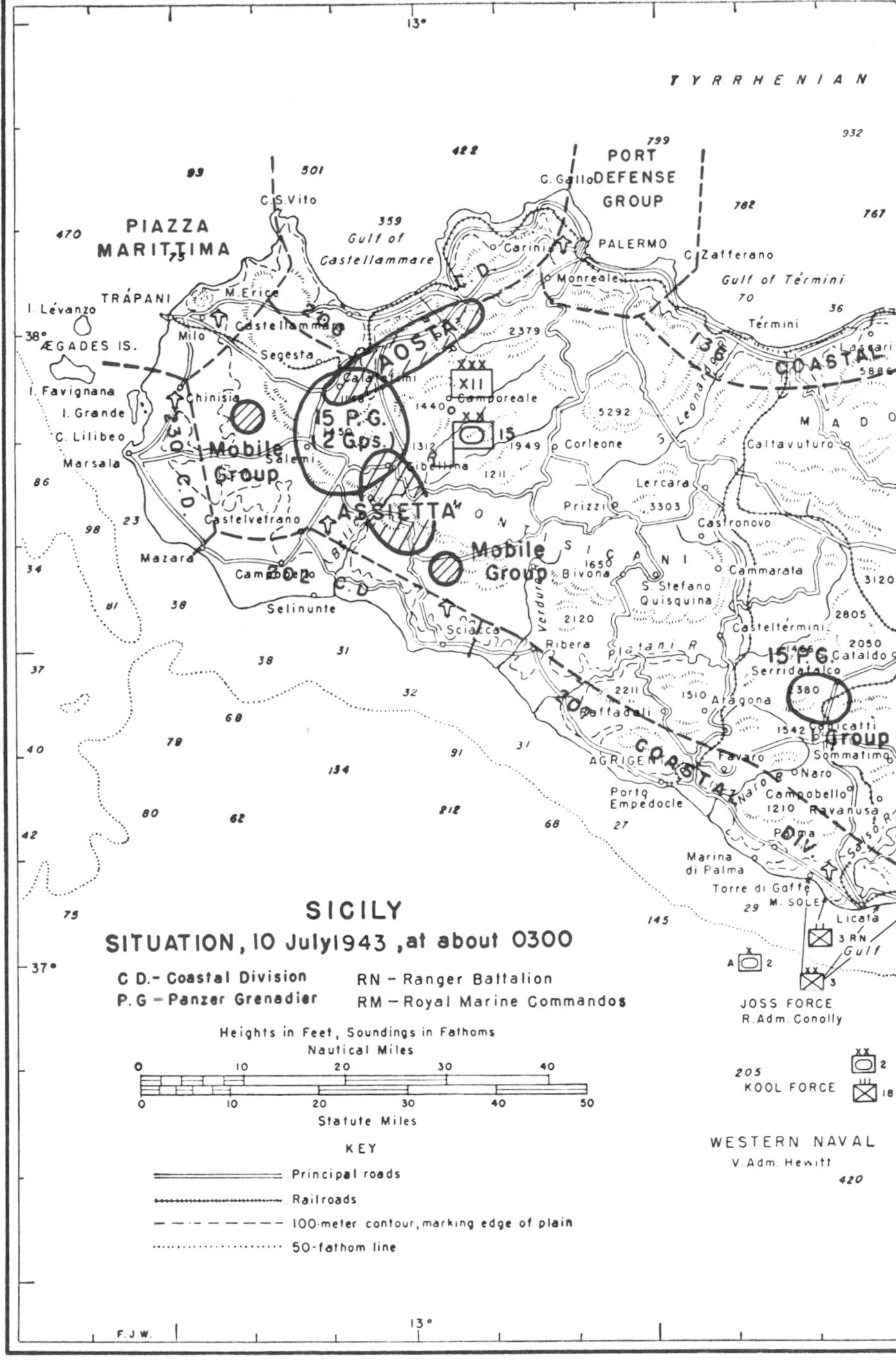
TYRRHENIAN
PIAZZA MARITTIMA
PORT DEFENSE GROUP
PALERMO
TRÁPANI
ÆGADES IS.
Gulf of Castellammare
Gulf of Términi
AOSTA
15 P.G. (2 Gps.)
Mobile Group
ASSIETTA
COASTAL
COASTAL DIV.
15 P.G.
Group
XII
JOSS FORCE
R. Adm. Conolly
KOOL FORCE
WESTERN NAVAL
V. Adm. Hewitt
SICILY
SITUATION, 10 July 1943, at about 0300
C D.- Coastal Division
P. G - Panzer Grenadier
RN - Ranger Battalion
RM - Royal Marine Commandos
Heights in Feet, Soundings in Fathoms
Nautical Miles
Statute Miles
KEY
Principal roads
Railroads
100-meter contour, marking edge of plain
50-fathom line
F.J.W.

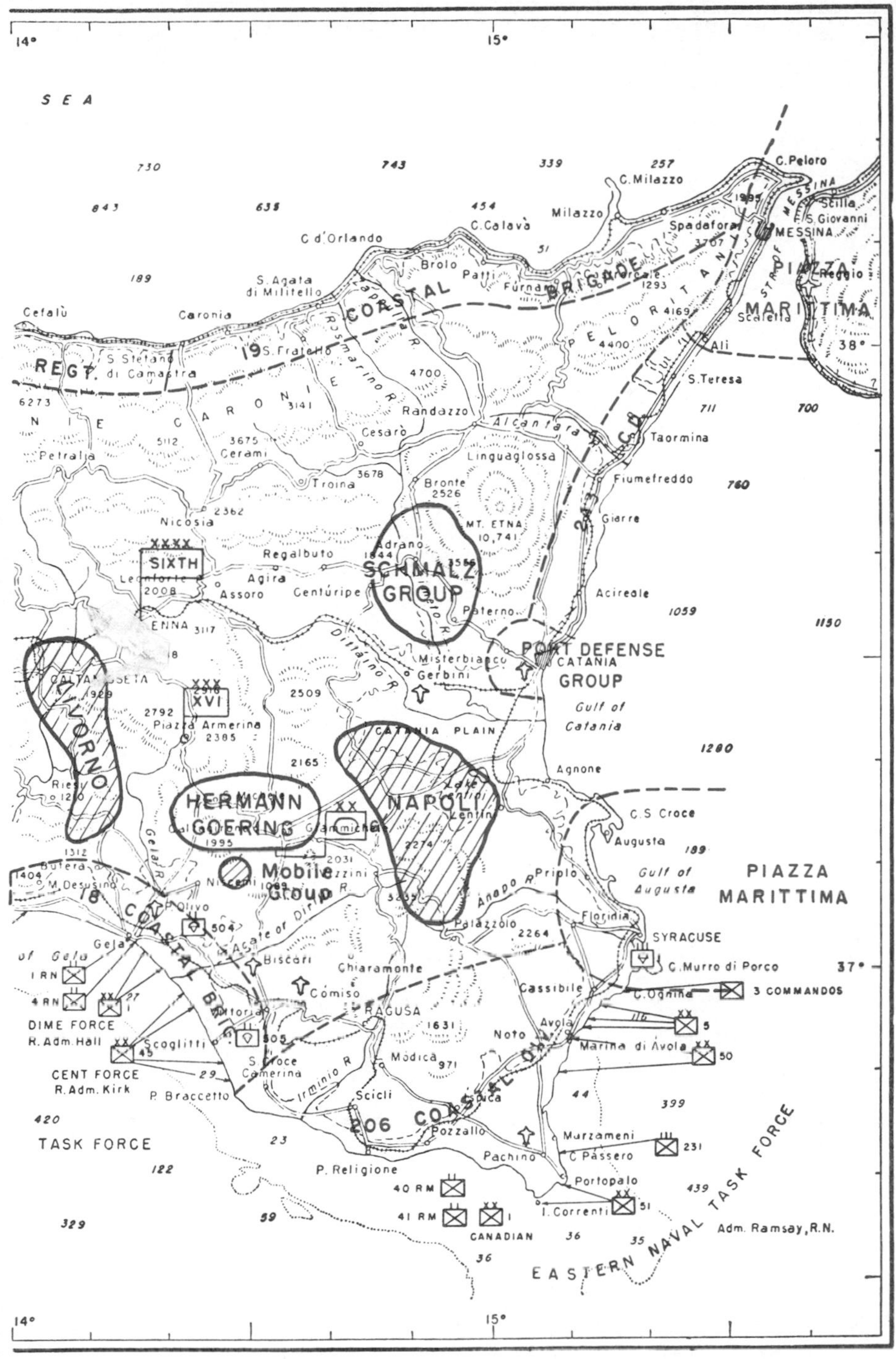

SEA
SCHMALZ GROUP
PORT DEFENSE CATANIA GROUP
HERMANN GOERING
NAPOLI
LIVORNO
Mobile Group
SIXTH
XVI
PIAZZA MARITTIMA
3 COMMANDOS
TASK FORCE
EASTERN NAVAL TASK FORCE
Adm. Ramsay, R.N.
DIME FORCE
R. Adm. Hall
CENT FORCE
R. Adm. Kirk
CANADIAN
Gulf of Catania
Gulf of Augusta
MESSINA
SYRACUSE
Taormina
Catania Plain
MT. ETNA 10,741

of the Italian boot. At Spezia two modern battleships, five light cruisers and eight destroyers were ready for sea. Comando Supremo wished to commit them at once. But the General Staff of the Navy, considering that they would require at least 25 hours, mostly without air cover, to reach Augusta, decided against it. There was no possibility of surprise, without which any surface counterattack would be "a sterile sacrifice"; the Spezia fleet had better be saved for the defense of Sardinia or the Italian peninsula. Comando Supremo then proposed to move the ships to Naples, where they would be in a position to exploit a favorable tactical opening. But he was answered that any such deployment would merely expose the ships to frequent and devastating air attacks.[7]

According to Western principles of strategy, especially that of "calculated risk," Supermarina was right. And the best explanation of the Italian Navy's inactivity came from Vice Admiral Weichold, the former German naval commander in Italy. In an essay written after the war, he stated a doctrine that the United States Navy would certainly not dispute: —

> The Axis war in the Mediterranean was lost principally because of the dual control of naval operations by the Navy and Luftwaffe. *If there had been an efficient naval air arm of either Axis partner, the Italian naval forces would have had positive operational possibilities. . . . The single air force was not suited to the conduct of a naval war.*

Add to this the lack of radar. Would any modern navy, except the Japanese, have sought battle under like conditions?

The only German naval vessels in Sicilian harbors in June 1943 were an indeterminate number of E-boats, the German motor torpedo boats.[8] Most of these were dispatched to the Peloponnesus as a result of the "Major William Martin" discovery, to be mentioned shortly. One squadron, left at Porto Empédocle on the south coast, was transferred to Trápani (where it was useless) just before the

[7] Bernotti pp. 61–67. Light cruiser *Muzio Attendolo* had been sunk there by air attack 4 Dec. 1942.

[8] The Germans called them S-boats; but they are so consistently called E-boats in Allied accounts of the war that I have followed suit to avoid confusion.

invasion. At the same time, or shortly after, the E-boats at Salerno and Palermo were shifted to Messina, as were the Italian MAS boats formerly stationed at Trápani.

Finally, there were the submarines, of which ten Italian and six German were immediately available in the central Mediterranean.[9] Doenitz had earlier persuaded Hitler not to send more U-boats into the Mediterranean, for two excellent reasons: he had found out (as the United States Navy had learned in the Philippines in 1941–1942) that an amphibious operation cannot be stopped by submarines; and there were none to spare after the recent Allied offensive in the Atlantic Ocean – 41 U-boats lost in May alone. At a conference in Rome on 8 July, Supermarina proposed to deploy all available submarines in the Strait of Sicily "to resist an enemy landing," but Admiral Sansonnetti and Captain Kreisch (Captain U-boats Italy) declined to do this for the curious reason that they were still ignorant of the positions of their own mine fields. So it was decided to employ all submarines to the south of Sicily *after* the invasion, in the hope of breaking up supply convoys. This was accordingly done, with melancholy results for the Axis underwater fleet.

We may first tell their few successes. On 22 June *U-953* sank two American LSTs. The same boat, and *U-375*, sank three vessels from a slow British convoy off Algiers on 4–5 July. *U-453* sank *S. S. Shahjehan* on the sixth, when steaming with a Middle East convoy off Derna. *U-371* cut Liberty ship *Matthew Maury* and tanker *Gulf Prince* out of an American convoy off Bougie on 10 July.

Allied counterattacks almost wiped out these Axis submarines. Shortly after sunrise 12 July (D-day plus 2) British destroyer *Inconstant*, escorting a convoy of transports returning from Sicily to the United Kingdom, made sound contact on *U-409* off Dellys, Algeria. Before the boat could get into a firing position, it was

[9] War Diary Captain U-boats Italy 8–10 July 1943. Italy had 5 more and Germany 11 more in the eastern and western ends of the Mediterranean that could be diverted to Sicilian waters.

depth-charged to the surface and then sunk by gunfire; 35 survivors were recovered.

On the night of 12 July, three British motor torpedo boats based on Syracuse were patrolling the Strait of Messina, right up to the city, when they flushed two U-boats proceeding south. *MTB–81* sank *U–561* with a single torpedo fired at a range of 100 yards; the other escaped by a prompt dive.

From D-day until the end of the Sicilian campaign, the Germans kept from three to four U-boats operating around Sicily.[10] Captain Kreisch called for a situation report from two of them on 18 July, expressing his astonishment that they had been so unsuccessful in seas swarming with fat targets. The reason, of course, was the excellent anti-submarine protection given by United States and British escorts, and by planes of Coastal Command Northwest African Air Force. One boat, *U–81*, presumably stung by this reproof, was responsible for sinking Liberty ship *Empire Moon* off Cape Pássero on the 22nd.

U.S.S. *PC–624* obtained partial revenge for the losses when, escorting a small convoy from Sicily to Africa, she encountered *U–375* a few miles southeast of Pantelleria at 0230 July 30. The boat surfaced, made a torpedo attack which closely missed the patrol craft, then dived. *PC–624* promptly peeled off from the convoy and made a depth-charge attack. Lieutenant Commander R. D. Lowther USNR, the skipper, modestly claimed only "possible damage" to the submarine, but it is now certain that he did so much damage that it was never heard from again.

The Italian submarines fared even worse than the German.[11] *Flutto*, after passing through the Strait of Messina, had a running fight with three British motor torpedo boats off Catania at 2130 July 11. She was sunk after killing or wounding 17 British sailors. *Bronzo*, ignorant that the British had already taken Syracuse, sur-

[10] Commander U-boats Mediterranean War Diary pp. 542, 640.

[11] Full details, from the Italian point of view, are in the official *La Marina Italiana nella Seconda Guerra Mondiale. Navi Perdute*, I (1951). Most of the Italian boats were dispatched from the submarine base at Pozzuoli in the Bay of Naples.

faced outside that city at noon 12 July, to find herself inside a formation of a dozen British ships. Three minesweepers, H.M.S. *Seaham*, *Boston* and *Poole*, turned on a brisk fusillade which scored many hits and killed her captain and eight others. *Seaham* closed, sent over a boarding party, captured *Bronzo*, and towed her into Syracuse. Eventually she was given to the French Navy.

On 13 July light cruiser Force "Q" of the Royal Navy encountered *Nereide* 40 miles east of Augusta. A series of depth-charge attacks by destroyers *Ilex* and *Echo* forced the boat to the surface where it was sunk by gunfire; 22 survivors were rescued. On the same day *Acciaio*, approaching the Strait of Messina from the north, encountered H.M. submarine *Unruly* off the Gulf of Gioia and was sunk. *Ascianghi* had the satisfaction of making one torpedo hit on H.M.S. *Newfoundland* off Catania on 23 July before being sunk by destroyers *Laforey* and *Eclipse*. The captain and 27 Italian sailors were rescued.

All the above-mentioned boats were rated between 600 and 750 tons, and these were the only submarines especially deployed to harass the invasion. But others suffered as well. A class of cargo submarines, rating from 1370 to 2220 tons, had recently been built in Italy to run the Allied blockade and obtain rubber from Malaya. Three which were at Taranto on D-day were then ordered to Naples. All three were sunk before reaching the Strait of Messina – *Remo* by H.M. submarine *United* on 15 July, *Micca* by H.M. submarine *Trooper* on the twenty-ninth, and *Romolo* by planes of the R.A.F. off Augusta on 19 July.

Hitherto, Italian submarines had avoided waters where the United States Navy operated. *Argento*, a 630-tonner based on La Maddalena, was making a reconnaissance of the south coast of Sicily on the evening of 2 August when she encountered, within sight of Pantelleria, a convoy of six vessels en route Licata to Oran, escorted by United States destroyers *Buck* and *Nicholson*. Lieutenant Commander Millard J. Klein, *Buck's* skipper, challenged the boat. No reply. The target disappeared. *Buck* picked up sound contact, and dropped 16 depth charges at 2311. While the convoy passed on, Klein pursued his contact for over two hours, dropped another full pattern of depth charges at 0026 August 3, and had the satisfaction of seeing a submarine surface 1200 yards dead astern. *Buck* opened fire with all guns that would bear. *Argento* retaliated with a torpedo which missed. *Buck* turned to bring her forward 5-inch mounts to bear, and the C.O. with gratification observed a "hail of lead and steel hitting on, around and near the submarine," which fired a second torpedo and again missed. *Buck* closed to within 50 feet of the boat, already dead in the water. Shouts of Italian sailors who had abandoned ship were heard. After making certain that the submarine was abandoned and sinking, *Buck* lowered her motor whaleboat and spent an hour searching for survivors in the dark: she rescued 46 out of the crew of 49, including the Italian C.O., who informed Klein that *Buck's* "cannon fire" had blown a large hole in the base of the conning tower through which most of the crew had escaped.[12]

This was a good break for a devoted crew who had endured almost two years of grueling North Atlantic convoy duty. But the gallant *Buck* had not long to live.

All in all, the Axis submarines put in a miserable performance, comparable to that of the Japanese submarine screen that tried to stop Admiral Spruance's fleet in 1944.[13] Three U-boats and nine Italian submarines were sunk within three weeks; and they had nothing to show for their sacrifice except five merchant ships, a tanker, and two LSTs.[14] Casualties on both sides were remarkably few.

[12] Cinclant "Report of Destruction of Italian Submarine *Argento*" 13 Sept. 1943.

[13] See Vol. VIII pp. 222–31.

[14] Kesselring, in his official report, claimed the sinking of a U.S. light cruiser by a U-boat. Actually no U.S. warship larger than an LST was conscious of having been the target of a submarine attack. He also credits Italian MAS boats with sinking one cruiser and one destroyer.

2. *Where Will the Allies Strike?*

On 13 May, General Sir Harold Alexander signaled his Prime Minister: "Sir, it is my duty to report that the Tunisian campaign is over. All enemy resistance has ceased. We are masters of the North African shores."

If the Allied divisions then in Africa could have embarked promptly for Italy, they would have had that peninsula at their mercy; it was almost denuded of trained troops, Italian or German. But one cannot stage a big amphibious operation overnight.

On the day that Tunisia fell, Admiral Doenitz, Commander in Chief of the German Navy, was in Rome for a conference with Italian admirals and the Duce. In the course of these conversations it was revealed that nobody could guess where the Allies would strike next. The concentration of shipping, landing craft, aircraft and troops in North Africa from Oran to Port Said told the knowing ones that the next great operation would be carried out in the Mediterranean; but the Mediterranean is a big sea. What island or coast would be the exact target? The wildest rumors flew about Rome and Berlin. A "high British personality" at Lisbon was overheard telling a Portuguese friend that what the Allies needed was a "fixed airplane carrier" from which to start the invasion of Europe, and that Sardinia filled the need better than Sicily. The Spanish ambassador to Portugal told the Italian minister at Lisbon that he was sure the Allies would try three separate and simultaneous landings: in Southern France to seal off Spain; in the Balkans to capture the Rumanian oil fields; and in Sardinia or Sicily. "An official neutral foreign intelligence report from the U.S.A." confirmed this, as did the Italian consul general at Tangier, from "a printed British plan captured by German agents at Algeciras"; all this was to happen on 17 June. A "high personality" on the general staff of the Spanish Air Force told an Italian agent at Madrid on 19 June that the Allies positively would land on Sardinia "that very night or tomorrow." But the Turkish military attaché at Budapest, believed trustworthy because he had a German mother-in-law, was certain that the main Allied thrust would be in Apulia. On 18 June a "reliable agent" in Portugal reported that 85,000 men were to land at Trápani, Marsala, Agrigento, Licata, Gela and Pozzallo.[15] This agent really had something; he must have had word of the earlier, discarded Allied plan.

And on 24 June Supermarina informed Comando Supremo that he expected the enemy to land shortly in one or more of these three areas: Trápani to Gela, Gela to Syracuse, and the Gulf of Cagliari in Sardinia; he inferred from the ports where landing craft had gathered that the "center of gravity" of the attack would be in the west.

At the Rome conference on 13 May between Admirals Doenitz and Riccardi and other high naval officers, Vice Admiral Sansonnetti pinned his hopes on mines. He predicted that it would take the American and British Navies from one to four weeks to sweep up the mine fields between Sicily and North Africa; therefore the Allies would attack Sardinia first, sweep next, then attack Sicily. But Sansonnetti was only talking – the mines were not yet laid, and the next episode explains why they never were laid, except off harbors where they were of little use.[16]

When Admiral Doenitz returned to Germany on 14 May and presented Hitler with this welter of uncertainty and speculation, he found the Fuehrer hoodwinked by the discovery of an alleged "Anglo-Saxon order that the Allied attacks will be directed mainly against Sardinia and the Peloponnesus." This was the result of a "plant" by the Royal Navy, so elaborate and important as to be dignified by the name Operation MINCEMEAT.[17] With the permission of his heirs, the body of a man who had died of pneumonia was placed in cold storage, renamed "Major William Martin of the

[15] Captured Italian documents at Adjutant General's Office, It. 106.

[16] In the course of the U. S. Navy's minesweeping all the way from Scoglitti around to Palermo, only 162 mines were swept – almost all off Porto Empédocle, Marsala and Trápani. Capt. E. D. McEathron "Minecraft in the Van," an unpublished ms. in Office of Naval History.

[17] Ewen Montagu *The Man Who Never Was* (1953).

Royal Marines," provided with forged identification papers and important documents, and propitiously set afloat off the coast of Spain from a submarine in such manner that anyone who recovered it would assume that the "Major" had been killed in a plane accident. The body floated ashore near Cadiz, whence an Axis agent, as had been planned, forwarded everything found on the "Major" to Berlin. The key documents were (1) a "letter" from the Vice Chief of the Imperial General Staff to General Alexander, informing him that Sicily was to be a mere cover or diversion in Operation HUSKY, the real target being the Peloponnesus; and (2) a "letter" from Admiral Mountbatten to Admiral Cunningham introducing Major Martin as a landing craft expert and adding, "Let me have him back, please, as soon as the assault is over. He might bring some sardines with him!" Teutonic Intelligence experts inferred from this labored pun, as they were meant to do, that Sardinia also was a target in HUSKY. Hitler himself was completely deceived. As a result, in June, several large consignments of good troops and matériel were sent from Adriatic ports and France to the Peloponnesus, a Panzer division was sent to Sardinia, coastal batteries were installed on the Greek coast, and German motor minesweepers already laying mines off the south coast of Sicily were diverted to Greece, together with most of the motor torpedo boats then in Sicilian waters.[18] On 21 May the High Command of the German Army instructed Marshal Kesselring that "measures to be taken in Sardinia and the Peloponnesus have priority over any others," and as late as 9 July the German Admiralty signaled to Admiral von Ruge in Italy, "Sardinia and Corsica are the first targets. . . . An assault on Greece is most probable."

All this, especially the interruption to the mining of Sicilian waters, was much to the Allies' advantage. The hesitating dispatch of troops to Sicily and the refusal to send air reinforcements, reflecting Hitler's anxieties, even worried the Japanese war lords,

[18] Ruge p. 5. Small Italian minesweepers took up the minelaying work, but they were so slow that they dared not operate by day, and when the invasion started there were hundreds of mines at Porto Empédocle waiting to be sown off Gela.

who demanded a "second front" to draw off American power from the Pacific.[19]

Yet, in contrast to the gullibility of Hitler and his entourage, responsible Italian admirals and German generals acted with good sense and resolution. Italian Intelligence .discounted "Major Martin" from the first, and the Supermarina "appreciation" of 26 June ruled Greece out; deployment of Allied beaching craft, it said, proved that the certain target was Sicily.[20] Nor did Marshal Kesselring fall for the mythical Major. On 20 June, he began sending the Hermann Goering Panzer Division across the Strait of Messina to reinforce the Sicilian garrison; and his "appreciation" dated 28 June anticipated landings in Sicily, possibly in Sardinia as well; not a word as to Greece.

3. *The Defenses of Sicily*

This Hermann Goering was the second German division to reach Sicily before the Allies struck; Hitler in early May had offered to send three more, but Mussolini refused to accept them; thus proving, remarked Kesselring, "that the Italians want to remain masters in their own house." [21]

The Italian government by July 1943 had placed Sicily in a fair military posture, at least on paper. Naval defenses, as we have seen, were almost nil; and air defenses would be drastically reduced; but the ground forces were sufficient to repel an invasion or to confine it for a long time to narrow beachheads (as later at Anzio), provided they had the will to fight.

After the fall of Tunis the Italian Army comprised 64 combat divisions, of which only 7 were in the Peninsula, 4 in Sardinia, and 4 in Sicily.[22] These four, the "Assietta," "Aosta," "Livorno" and

[19] "The Sicilian Campaign, Information from German Sources" pp. 4, 7.

[20] "Apprezzamenti sulla Situazione," extracts from archives of the Italian Navy.

[21] Martienssen *Hitler and his Admirals* pp. 168–9.

[22] Gen. Faldella "La Battaglia di Sicilia," *Roma* 14 July 1953. Of the rest, 38 were in the Balkans and France, 9 had been largely destroyed in Russia.

"Napoli" Infantry Divisions, together with two German divisions, were the core of the Sixth Army for the defense of Sicily.

A melancholy tale of the state of Sicilian defense was unwound by Admiral Riccardi at the Rome conference of 13 May. Allied air bombardments had cut off coastal traffic by which Sicily was mainly supplied; only 40 small vessels were still available. Bread and other provisions were short, for the wheat grown in Sicily is suitable only for *pasta*, and the island produces plenty of wine but not much meat. During the next two months, as air bombardment accelerated, conditions grew worse. All railway locomotives in Sicily were coal-burning, and only a few days' supply of coal was on hand by 1 July. Most of the matériel, originally earmarked for Sicily, especially concrete for coast defenses, had been diverted to Africa and there lost.[23] Civilians evacuated from the cities were living under deplorably unsanitary conditions. The great majority of Sicilians had lost all hope of winning the war. Von Neurath of the German diplomatic corps at Rome, who visited the island in early May, told Hitler that the Germans were unpopular there; that the peasants were hoping the Allies would strike soon and get the war over; that General Roatta, the island commander, was a defeatist.[24] On 30 May General Roatta, possibly at Hitler's insistence, was relieved by General Alfredo Guzzoni, who had commanded the Italian expeditionary force against Albania in 1939. The new Sixth Army Commander, sixty-six years old, was a sound strategist and in every way an able soldier; and because he saw clearly the real situation, he was far from optimistic. On 14 June General Guzzoni visited Rome and "exposed the reality to Mussolini without reticence." The Duce, nevertheless, sounded off with one of his eloquent orations in which he predicted that the Italian Army would defeat the enemy "at the water's edge."

* * *

[23] "Operazioni Juglio 1943" p. 3 states that the Army wanted 160,000 tons of cement a month in 1943 to construct fixed defenses; but only 7000 tons a month were sent, and much of that went to the Navy and Air Force. In consequence, few antitank traps had been constructed.

[24] Gilbert *Hitler Directs His War* pp. 29–30.

Here is the actual deployment on 9–10 July 1943: –

Sixth Army, headquarters at Enna, was divided into two corps, the XII in the west, and the XVI in the east. It comprised three categories of defense forces: – [25]

1. Most numerous in man power, but least important in strength, were six coastal divisions, two coastal brigades and one coastal regiment. These were charged with beach defense of the entire perimeter of Sicily except for three gaps filled by the *piazze marittime*, and two port defense groups. Each coastal division comprised two to four infantry regiments normally of 1600 men each, with independent machine-gun units, fieldpieces and mortars; it was they who manned the coast defense batteries. The men were mostly Sicilian reservists, since Mussolini thought that such soldiers would be the best defenders of their homeland. He could not have been more wrong. The Sicilians, though by reputation the best of Italian fighters, had never been good Fascists; they disliked the war and hated Germans, and felt they were being sacrificed to an alien power. Moreover these troops were spread out much too thin to stop a modern amphibious assault. The entire attack area of the Seventh Army – Licata, Gela and Scoglitti – had only 22 batteries of 75-mm to 100-mm guns, and two of 149-mm guns. So it is not surprising that coastal troops at the points of contact, although ordered to fight *à l'outrance*, in order to give time for the mobile divisions to counterattack, surrendered or fled for the most part.[26]

2. The *piazze marittime*, literally "maritime strong points," which took over coastal defense at three places thought to be especially menaced – Trápani, Messina-Reggio and Syracuse-Augusta. In each piazza, under an admiral's command, were large-caliber coast defense batteries, antiaircraft and mobile batteries, motor torpedo boats, special troops and everything conducive to a vigorous defense against air or sea assault. Similar in purpose but

[25] See our Situation Map based on that in Barrile "Operazione" p. 73. I have not included in this enumeration the German "fortress battalions" or numerous independent Italian groups such as the Bersaglieri.

[26] Gen. Guzzoni's General Order of 20 June; "Nota sulla Divisione Costiere" prepared for this History by the Historical Office of the Italian Army, 1953.

much weaker in strength were two port defense groups charged with protecting Catania and Palermo.

3. Six mobile divisions of the Italian and German armies, which were counted on to deploy promptly while the coastal troops held, and "hurl the enemy back into the sea." These, as well as the coastal divisions, were divided between two army corps: —

(*a*) The XII Army Corps (General Mario Arisio) with headquarters at Corleone on the Agrigento-Palermo road, charged with the defense of western Sicily, west of the Cefalù–Licata line. It included six groups of artillery, two Italian infantry divisions (Assietta and Aosta), each of about 11,000 men and 84 artillery pieces (mostly horse-drawn), and two combat groups of the German 15th Panzer Grenadier Division,[27] motorized and provided with tanks. These were deployed along the road from Sciacca to Palermo, and a detached Bersaglieri regiment was in the hills above Agrigento.

(*b*) The XVI Army Corps (General Carlo Rossi), with headquarters at Piazza Armerina south of Enna, was entrusted with the defense of eastern Sicily. It comprised (1) the Livorno Division, two-thirds motorized, which, together with one combat group of the 15th Panzer Grenadiers and the Niscemi mobile group of about 50 Italian light tanks, was deployed in a rough arc running from Canicattì through Caltanissetta and almost to Gela; (2) the Hermann Goering Panzer Division, comprising four infantry battalions, 100 medium or heavy tanks, and 60 guns, totaling 8739 officers and men, deployed around Caltagirone northeast of Gela; (3) the Napoli Division, divided into five or six tactical groups that were deployed south of the Catania plain, and as far south as Palazzolo; (4) a German combat group of brigade strength, consisting of infantry, tanks and antitank guns, called "Battle Group Schmalz" from the name of its colonel,[28]

[27] So designated 29 June; earlier called the Sizilien. A Panzer Grenadier division consisted of 3 motorized regiments (2 infantry, 1 artillery) and 6 battalions of supporting troops, one being tanks; a Panzer division differed mainly by including a tank regiment in place of an infantry battalion.

[28] The Schmalz belonged to the 15th Panzer Grenadiers but was under XVI Corps command.

deployed on and near the Catania plain. Six mobile batteries of 90-mm guns were directly under Sixth Army command.

This deployment, which may best be grasped by consulting our Situation Map for 10 July, was decided upon at a conference between Marshal Kesselring and General Guzzoni at Enna on 26 June. Guzzoni, who guessed nearly correctly where the Allies would land, wished to keep both German armored divisions together in the eastern half of the island, readied to deliver a strong counterattack. He believed that this would be the only chance to defeat the invasion, and he was none too confident at that. Kesselring, however, was an incurable optimist. Heedless of the lessons of Operation TORCH, he kept repeating that the invasion of Sicily would be in a class with the Dieppe raid of 1942. He proposed to make an all-out attempt to defeat it on the beaches, and to abandon a defense in depth, which is the best way to defeat a modern amphibious operation. And he wished to deploy one German division in western Sicily, where he expected the Americans to land. The actual deployment was a compromise: the headquarters and two combat groups of the 15th Panzer Grenadier Division were sent west, while the third group, and the weaker Hermann Goering Division commanded by a general whom Senger describes as a "former police officer," were deployed around Caltagirone, north of Gela.[29]

Both Germans and Italians expected a landing near Gela, and had already held anti-invasion exercises there.[30]

Although everyone except the Duce and Marshal Kesselring regarded a victory "at the water's edge" as impossible, the Axis military situation in Sicily was far from hopeless. The Northwest African Air Force, in all its bombings, had not blocked the Strait of Messina, the funnel of supply and reinforcement; nor would it ever do so. Two of the four big train-ferries, with a total capacity of

[29] Senger (who was present at the conference) "The Battle for Sicily" sec. 3 (pp. 13–20 of trans.). This is confirmed by a German General Staff Situation Report of 5 July sent to me by the Canadian Army Historical Section.

[30] Seventh Army *Report of Operations* p. C–31, information from a P.O.W.

5600 men or 800 tons of supplies, were still able to make regular trips.[31] Troops were pouring down the roads and the railroad from central Italy to Reggio and the Germans had provided armed barges to get them and their supplies across. There were in Sicily on 10 July between 300,000 and 365,000 men under arms, at least one third of them in mobile divisions.[32] One can easily imagine what would have happened to the Seventh and Eighth Armies on an island the size of Sicily defended by that many Japanese.

But these were not fanatic Japanese; the greater part belonged to a perceptive and Christian people who realized that the game was up, now that the democracies were armed and aroused. Every Italian knew it but nobody could do anything about it while Mussolini was in power. General Faldella, Guzzoni's chief of staff, remarked in June 1943 to General von Senger, the German liaison officer with him: "Clausewitz has written that when it becomes evident a war can no longer be won, you ought, with the aid of the politicians, to try and obtain an honorable ending to the affair."

"I entirely agree," replied Senger, "but Hitler has positively never read Clausewitz!"[33]

[31] "Dati riguardanti le Navi Traghetto," compiled for this History by the Historical Office of the Naval General Staff.

[32] Westphal *German Army in the West* p. 142 says about 300,000; my computation of the figures, furnished me by the Historical Office of the General Staff of the Italian Army, gives 350,000; Gen. Alexander's Despatch (Supplement to *London Gazette* 10 Feb. 1948 p. 1016) estimates 365,000, of which 50,000 were German; Senger confirms this number of Germans. But Ruge's figures show that over 60,000 Germans were committed in Sicily.

[33] Gen. Faldella in *Roma* 10 July 1953; confirmed by Senger in letter to me.

PART II

The Sicilian Campaign[1]

(*Operation* HUSKY)

13 May–18 August 1943

West Longitude Dates
Zone "Baker" Time (add 2 hours to Greenwich Time)

[1] General sources, especially for the American part, are Eisenhower's "C-in-C Dispatch" to the C.C.S.; Vice Admiral Hewitt *Action Report Western Naval Task Force. The Sicilian Campaign, July-Aug. 1943* (126 pp., undated but completed in July 1944); an excellent O.N.I. Combat Narrative *The Sicilian Campaign* (1945) prepared by Lts. Winston B. Lewis USNR and John LaMont USNR; Lt. J. J. Altieri USA *Darby's Rangers* (1945); *Report of Operations of the U.S. Seventh Army in the Sicilian Campaign* (1944, mimeographed with abundant maps and illustrations); "Seventh Army Statistical Data 10 July–18 Aug. 1943", pub. Sept. 1943 by the Seventh Army. Ernie Pyle covers the invasion in *Brave Men* (Henry Holt, 1943); nobody equals him in conveying the feeling of an amphibious operation. Admiral Sir Andrew B. Cunningham RN (Viscount Cunningham of Hyndhope) *A Sailor's Odyssey* (1951); General George S. Patton USA *War As I Knew It* (1947); General Omar N. Bradley USA *A Soldier's Story* (1951); General H. H. Arnold USA *Global Mission* (1949). For Axis sources, see Chap. III footnote 1.

CHAPTER IV

Preliminary Movements

13 May–9 July 1943

1. *The Air Offensive*[1]

ALTHOUGH the landings in Sicily started on 10 July, Operation HUSKY properly begins on 13 May, when the Tunisian campaign ended; that was the day when the Combined Chiefs of Staff accepted General Eisenhower's final plan.

As soon as Axis forces in Tunisia surrendered, Northwest African Air Force was able to turn its entire attention to softening up Sicily, to bombing continental and Sardinian airfields whence enemy airplanes could operate, and to the capture of Pantelleria to provide an advance airdrome. The Air Forces certainly performed valuable and vital services before Operation HUSKY even started. They won air supremacy over the Axis, which otherwise might have decimated the amphibious forces; they destroyed naval and air bases in Sicily before the landings, and they notably helped to beat down enemy morale.

It was to obtain more space for fighter planes nearer the target that General Eisenhower authorized the capture of Pantelleria, which lies 60 miles SSW of the western coast of Sicily. After several days of intensive air bombing and naval bombardment, Pantelleria surrendered 11 June.[2] Three days earlier, Aviation En-

[1] Preliminary account in *Participation of the IX and XII Air Forces in the Sicilian Campaign*, Army Air Forces Hist. Studies No. 37 (1945); definitive in Craven and Cate *Army Air Forces in World War II* II (1949) pp. 419–49. For the enemy side, "L'Opera dell' Aeronautica Italiana" prepared for this History by the Historical Office of the General Staff of the Italian Air Force, 1953; and Admiral Pietro Barone "Relazione sull' Occupazione della Sicilia," prepared for the Italian Navy after the war.

[2] See Vol. II (revised ed.) chap. xii for the Pantelleria operation.

gineers of the A.A.F. started to build a new base on Gozo, the small island next to Malta. In record time – and to the astonishment of the British who predicted it would take months – an airfield with two runways, taxiways and hard standings was completed 25 June, when the field was turned over to R.A.F. Spitfires for tactical defense of landing forces in Sicily.[3]

For a month or more before the landings, bombing missions were flown almost daily against airfields and harbors in Sicily, Sardinia, Greece, and Italy as far north as Leghorn, with special attention to the Sicilian airdromes, and to continental ones from which enemy planes might operate against HUSKY task forces. The weather was perfect for flying – unlimited ceiling and visibility.

There was not much that Regia Aeronautica or Luftwaffe could do about this. The effect of the North African campaign on the former has been well described as a hemorrhage; from 1 November 1942 to 30 June 1943 Italy lost, from all causes, 2190 military planes, together with 1790 damaged. Its power of recuperation, by new construction and pilot training, was inadequate – 300 planes and 75 pilots per month. By 1 July Regia Aeronautica had fewer than 900 military planes, of which not even 300 were ready to fly, and by D-day its strength had been very little increased, as the following partial table of its deployment[4] indicates: –

	1 July		*10 July*	
	Total	*Operational*	*Total*	*Operational*
Sicily	232	98	220	79
Sardinia and Corsica	195	112	179	114
Calabria	98	58	142	94
Central and Northern Italy	76	22	85	37
Total	601	290	626	324

Similar statistics for the Luftwaffe are not available; but on 1 July the total number deployed in Sicily, Sardinia, Corsica, Italy

[3] Extracts from A.A.F. study "Airfields in the Med. Theater of Operations," communicated by Dr. Albert F. Simpson, Air Force Historian; Eisenhower *Crusade in Europe* p. 171.

[4] Tables of deployment furnished by Historical Office of the General Staff of the Italian Air Force. Reggio is included with Sicily.

and Provence, which could be immediately employed in defending Sicily, amounted to 780 military planes of all kinds.[5] Thus the total Axis air strength that could be deployed in this new theater of action numbered about 1400 to 1500 planes, as against 3680 in the Northwest African Air Force. Hitler declared, shortly after the campaign started, that he would send no more planes to help his army in Sicily — he needed every one in Russia — but he soon relented.

In view of this disparity of air forces, and of the continuous attacks on their Sicilian airfields, General Fougier, the head of Superaereo, and Marshal von Richtofen, commanding Second Air Fleet of the Luftwaffe in Italy, agreed on 22 June to retire most of their bombers to continental fields. Thenceforth Italian torpedo-bombers and four-engined aircraft were based at Pisa and Perugia, leaving only fighter planes on the Sicilian and southern Sardinian fields, together with a few bombers in Sardinia. These were readied to strike Allied ships.[6]

On 1 July Sicily had 11 or 12 airfields and seaplane bases with permanent installations and antiaircraft defense. The actual fields in operation 1 and 10 July, with the total numbers and kinds of planes based on them, were as follows (VF=fighters; VT=torpedo-bombers; VO=Scout-observation; and the numbers in parentheses are those operational): —

EASTERN SICILY	*1 July*	*10 July*
Catania	18 VF (10)	None
Gerbini and satellites	9 VO (6), 13 VF (6)	11 VO (6)[7]
(Finocchiara, San Salvatore, etc.)	38 VF (23)	4 VT (0), 48 VF (13)
	plus an unknown number of German VF	
Cómiso	21 VF (7)	21 VF (0)
Caltagirone	German VF, number unknown	
Augusta seaplane base	27 VO (5)	27 VO (16)

[5] "Opera dell'Aeronautica" pp. 2–4; 500 of these were Ju-88s; and 200 were Messerschmitt-109 fighters, of which 70 were in Sardinia. The Luftwaffe then had no torpedo-bombers. Kesselring's Appreciation of the Situation, 28 June, states that in all Italy he then had about 850 fighters (including some "modern Italian fighters") and 600 German and Italian bombers.

[6] Information from Col. Vincenzo Lioy of the Historical Division Italian Air Force. Superaereo for the air force corresponded to Supermarina for the Navy.

[7] Divided between Gerbini and Reggio.

	1 July	*10 July*
Western Sicily		
Sciacca	34 VF (10)	25 VF (16)
Castelvetrano, Trápani (Milo)	German planes, number unknown	
Chinisia (Borizzo)	18 VF (10)	21 VF (0)
	(Also some German planes)	
Stagnone seaplane base	13 VO (4)	8 VO (5)[8]
Palermo	13 VO (5)	13 VO (5), 7 VT (3)
Strait of Messina		
Reggio	37 VF (18)	37 VF (17)

The other Sicilian fields which figured largely in Allied planning – Ponte Olivo, Biscari, Licata, Pachino – were called *campi di fortuna*, landing strips lately cut out of the wheatfields, where no air squadrons were based. But the first two were stoutly defended, and when captured were found to contain an appreciable number of damaged and destroyed Axis planes.

On the night of 2–3 July the Northwest African Air Force began (as the Italians described it) "an implacable hammering of all the insular airports, especially the Sicilian, with the object of paralyzing all activity." As usual in Allied bombing operations, the American B–17s and B–24s struck by day and the British Wellingtons by night. Some 1520 tons of bombs were dropped on the Gerbini-Catania fields alone. The Foggia airdrome on the Adriatic coast of Italy, and the southern Sardinia fields, also received unwelcome attention. Regia Aeronautica and Luftwaffe made every effort to intercept these raids; it is claimed that 690 Italian and 500 German fighter-plane sorties were made during the first nine days of July, and the losses that they inflicted on the Northwest African Air Force were not inconsiderable;[9] but they were unable to protect their Sicilian bases. By the morning of D-day, 10 July, the only fields still functioning were some of the Gerbini satellite strips. A Superaereo report of 12 July states that in eastern Sicily only one Gerbini strip was usable; and, in western Sicily, only emergency landings could be made on the Palermo field and on Chinisia.[10]

[8] Divided between Stagnone and Milazzo, near Messina.

[9] Craven and Cate II 485 say "around 375" Allied planes were lost and "approximately 740" Axis planes destroyed in combat in the whole of HUSKY, but there has been no breakdown as to dates, types or missions.

[10] 'L'Opera dell' Aeronautica" pp. 6–8.

All planes that could rise had already taken off for Sardinian or Italian bases, whence air attacks on the Allied forces in and around Sicily were mounted after 12 July. The exact number of enemy planes destroyed in those attacks cannot be stated accurately, but it can hardly have been much over one hundred, as the total number of Axis planes destroyed from 3 July to 17 August did not exceed two hundred.[11]

Nor were these furious attacks the only contribution of the Allied Air Forces during this initial phase. The Northwest African Photo Reconnaissance Wing covered important Axis-held ports from Spain to Corfu, photographing Spezia and Taranto twice daily to discover if the Italian Navy had sortied. Coastal Command of the Northwest African Air Force covered all convoys that passed Gibraltar. On 26 June an eastbound convoy was attacked by over a hundred German planes off Cape Bon, but Coastal's fighters kept them so busy that not one ship was seriously damaged. Coastal also undertook the protection of North African harbors where troops were being trained and assault forces mounted.

The penultimate contribution of the Air Forces was delivered on 9 July and the night before the landings. During daylight, 21 bombing and strafing missions[12] struck airfields and other selected targets all the way from Sciacca to Taormina, sparing the beaches with the idea of concealing where the landings would take place.[13] Luftwaffe headquarters in Taormina, as well as the nearby Church

[11] Information from Col. Lioy of Historical Division Italian Air Force. It was reported in the British *Weekly Intelligence Report* 20 Aug. 1943 that 800 damaged, destroyed, or abandoned aircraft had been counted on Sicilian fields. Gen. Alexander fleeted the number to "over one thousand" (Churchill *Closing the Ring* p. 40) and Craven and Cate II 485 make it eleven hundred – more than all the Sicilian fields together could hold. Col. Lioy states that several Sicilian airports had an "air cemetery" of planes that had been damaged, destroyed or discarded for years back, and that there might well have been 500 such relics on hand before HUSKY started.

[12] Comprising 411 bombers escorted by 168 fighters, plus 78 fighters to strafe radar stations, etc. Data in this paragraph from Dr. A. F. Simpson.

[13] This seems to have had the contrary effect: "In the course of the last few days the attacks on Sicilian airfields have skipped certain areas which are in the neighborhood of harbors or landing areas. Enemy landing activities can be foreseen in these areas." War Diary German Naval Command Italy, 7 July 1943.

of San Domenico, were destroyed.[14] Between sunset and midnight, 63 British and 44 United States bombers, in eight separate missions, bombed Syracuse, Catania, Caltagirone, Palazzolo and various airfields. Then followed the air drops, so close to the actual landings that we shall consider the two together.

The Army Air Forces, as usual at this period of the war, were not always discriminating in target selection. The cities of Palermo and Catania were bombed without affording the Allies any military advantage. Churches were damaged or destroyed, many noble buildings gutted and civilians buried under the ruins of their dwellings. On the other hand, beach defenses "had neither been bombed, nor shelled, nor in any way attacked before Zero hour," [15] nor had the mobile divisions in the interior been strafed.

There is little charm to the towns in the part of Sicily where the Americans landed. They have names that sing of romance and history — Vittoria, Ragusa, Campobello, Raffadali, Aragona — but all are closely built huddles of gray stone houses with gray tiled roofs, and no open space but the piazza facing the church; narrow cobblestone streets along which heavy-laden donkeys patiently carry enormous loads; and a few fountains where the women fill their earthern water jars and wash their clothes. But each town, by reason of its thick stone walls, is a natural fortress.

Sicily was still Sicily, anxiously awaiting another assault as she had met those of the Greeks and Carthaginians, the Romans and Saracens, the Angevins and Aragonese. She would not exactly open her arms to the invaders, as she had to Garibaldi and his Thousand in 1860; but she was ready to be delivered from the hardships of a war that she detested. The Sicilians, fatalistic as orientals under bombing, continued to ply their usual simple tasks. Spring, when the almond trees are in blossom and the rivers are full, and the wheatfields are a tender green, was long past. The island, as viewed from the air or the sea, was parched to a dusty brown. Most of the water courses had dried up. The wheat and barley had been har-

[14] Information from Admiral Mirti della Valle, Messina, 1953. There is a tablet to the memory of the civilians killed, about 45 in number, in a nearby piazza.

[15] Col. A. H. Head USA "Notes on HUSKY" 25 July 1943 sec. 61.

vested by hand with sickles; and the sheaves were strewn on antique threshing floors in the open, for the grain to be trodden out by the hoofs of horses and donkeys. Withered beanstalks, from which the beans had been threshed by primitive flails, were stacked in neat bundles to be used for winter fuel. The only relief to the prevailing brown stubble was an occasional vineyard where bunches of grapes were forming, a gray-green olive grove, or a deep-green almond orchard.

2. *Approach of the Western Naval Task Force*

The Western Naval Task Force was mounted at, or staged through, six harbors along the North African littoral between Oran and Sfax. Rear Admiral Alan Kirk, commanding CENT Force, wrote to Cinclant, Admiral Royal E. Ingersoll, on the eve of departure from Oran: "We are off tomorrow. . . . wish we had our own air under our own control . . . planning to get transports out of Gela Gulf . . . in four days. Patton said eight days and I have bet him a quart of Scotch I beat that figure. Everybody is in fine shape, all ships waiting, and the gunners itching to do some shooting." [16]

The troop transports which lifted the 1st Division in Rear Admiral Hall's DIME Force for Gela loaded at Algiers. "Four agencies had a finger in the pie," wrote Admiral Hall — "the 1st Infantry Division, the Mediterranean Base Section, the British Naval and Military Port Authorities, and the 384th Port Battalion." Army officers circulated amongst the ships like "shipping brokers to obtain or to sell ship space independently for their particular interest." And the Admiral had to fly his flag in an ordinary transport, *Samuel Chase.*

Admiral Hewitt's flagship *Monrovia,* which accompanied DIME Force, was the most crowded of all. She embarked the Admiral's staff, a fighter control group of the Army Air Force, and General Patton, commanding the Seventh Army, with his staff. Three sep-

[16] Office of Naval History "Admin. Hist. of U. S. Atlantic Fleet" I, iii 525.

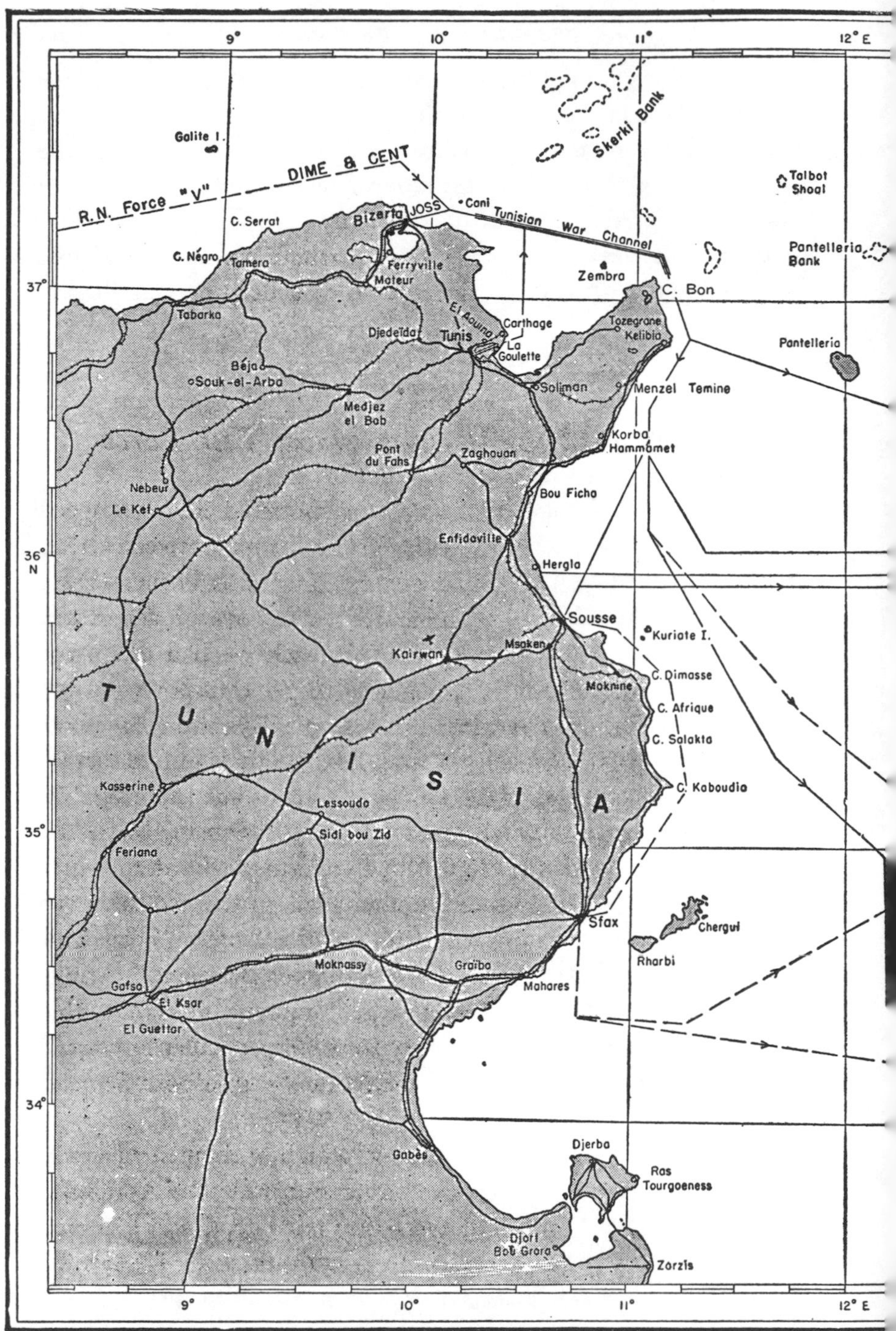

9°
10°
11°
12° E
Galite I.
R.N. Force "V"
DIME & CENT
Skerki Bank
Talbot Shoal
Bizerta
JOSS
Coni
Tunisian War Channel
C. Serrat
C. Négro
Tamera
Ferryville
Mateur
Zembra
C. Bon
Pantelleria Bank
37°
Tabarka
El Aouina
Carthage
Djedeïda
Tunis
La Goulette
Tozegrane
Kelibia
Pantelleria
Béja
Souk-el-Arba
Soliman
Menzel Temine
Medjez el Bab
Korba
Hammamet
Pont du Fahs
Zaghouan
Nebeur
Bou Ficho
Le Kef
Enfidaville
36° N
Hergla
Sousse
Kuriate I.
Kairwan
Msaken
C. Dimasse
Moknine
T U N I S I A
C. Afrique
C. Salakta
Kasserine
C. Kaboudia
Lessouda
Sidi bou Zid
35°
Feriana
Sfax
Chergui
Rharbi
Moknassy
Graïba
Gafsa
Mahares
El Ksar
El Guettar
34°
Djerba
Ras Tourgoeness
Gabès
Djorf
Bou Grara
Zarzis
9°
10°
11°
12° E

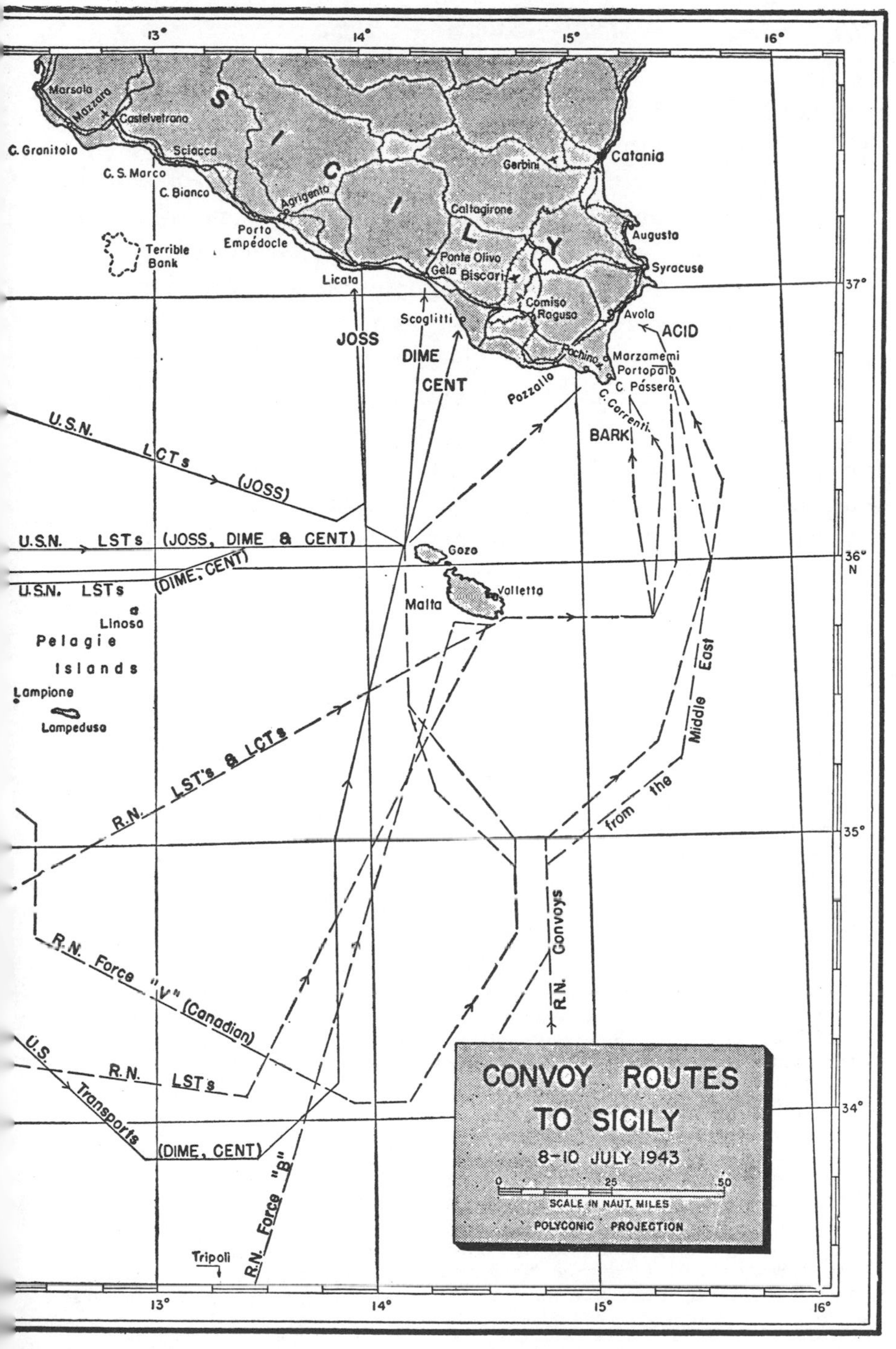
CONVOY ROUTES
TO SICILY
8-10 JULY 1943
0
25
50
SCALE IN NAUT. MILES
POLYCONIC PROJECTION
13°
14°
15°
16°
37°
36° N
35°
34°
SICILY
Marsala
Mazzara
Castelvetrano
C. Granitola
Sciacca
C. S. Marco
C. Bianco
Agrigento
Porto Empédocle
Terrible Bank
Licata
Caltagirone
Gerbini
Catania
Augusta
Syracuse
Ponte Olivo
Gela
Biscari
Comiso
Ragusa
Scoglitti
Avola
Pachino
Marzamemi
Portopalo
C. Pàssero
C. Correnti
Pozzallo
JOSS
DIME
CENT
ACID
BARK
U.S.N. LCTs (JOSS)
U.S.N. LSTs (JOSS, DIME & CENT)
U.S.N. LSTs (DIME, CENT)
Gozo
Malta
Valletta
Linosa
Pelagie Islands
Lampione
Lampedusa
R.N. LST's & LCTs
from the Middle East
R.N. Convoys
R.N. Force "V" (Canadian)
R.N. LST s
U.S. Transports (DIME, CENT)
R.N. Force "B"
Tripoli

arate code rooms had to be provided. *Monrovia* managed to accommodate 126 officers and 670 men over and above her own complement of 48 officers and 566 men.[17] There was a brief ceremony on board shortly after sailing, when Admiral Hewitt presented General Patton with the first Seventh Army flag. One who was present remembered the "fire of pride" in the General's eyes. "It was to him not a ship's deck he stood upon, but a peak of glory." [18] And that flag stayed with him as long as he lived.

It was feared that security had been violated by distribution of a "Soldier's Guide to Italy" while transports were still alongside the dock; and "scuttlebutt" had it that the French pilot, upon taking leave of *Monrovia* off Algiers, had cheerfully wished the commanding officer "a pleasant trip to Sicily!" But there was no leak. Such knowledge as the enemy had of our destination was based on inference and plane reconnaissance.[19]

Admiral Kirk's CENT Force, floating the 45th Infantry Division United States Army (Major General Troy H. Middleton USA), crossed the ocean in 28 combat-loaded attack transports and cargo ships, in two convoys, one escorted by cruiser *Philadelphia* and nine destroyers, the other by cruiser *Brooklyn* and nine destroyers. Kirk's flagship *Ancon* was the only really complete AGC in the Western Naval Task Force; so well equipped, in fact, that Admiral Hewitt was tempted to requisition her for his own use. He did not long resist the temptation, and "Hotel *Ancon*," as she was nicknamed, became his flagship for Salerno.[20]

CENT Force staged through Oran, where it tarried less than a

[17] *Monrovia* "Report of Operations – HUSKY" 17 July 1943, and conversations with her C.O., Cdr. T. B. Brittain. *Monrovia* was a new ship, built in 1942 for Delta Lines and converted by the Navy into an attack transport.

[18] Hal Boyle in *Rome Daily American* 10 July 1953. Photo in U. S. Naval Inst. *Proceedings* LXXIX, 814 (July 1953).

[19] It is a curious reflection of fighting men's psychology that almost inevitably some apocryphal warning of violated security circulates on board during the approach phase of an amphibious operation. In the Pacific, it was usually to the effect that "Tokyo Rose" had announced the code name of the target.

[20] Formerly a passenger-cargo ship on the New York-Cristobal run, *Ancon* was converted in early 1942 and made two voyages to Australia as an Army transport before being taken over by the Navy. She was converted to an AGC early in 1943 and was first of this class to be finished. She owed her nickname to the old

week; hardly long enough to let the GIs make the acquaintance of the "A-rabs." There *Ancon* took on board Lieutenant General Omar N. Bradley USA [21] and his II Corps staff. Off Bizerta the force picked up its LSTs, LCTs and minesweepers, which had been trained by Admiral Conolly; his JOSS Force, too, started from Bizerta.

Approach routes to Sicily for these various task forces, groups and support forces, including the British, had to be worked out in great detail and at the top level of Admiral Cunningham's command, with the help of Admiral Hewitt's planners, so that they would not interfere with each other. The one British and three American task forces approaching from the west steamed at well-spaced intervals through the mine-protected, ten-mile-wide Tunisian War Channel between Capes Serrat and Bon. They then split, a few going north but most of them south of the Pelagies; and, after being joined by elements from Sousse and Sfax, converged at a point off Gozo, whose waters acted as a sort of maritime marshaling yard. This routing, it was hoped, would convince snooping Axis planes that the Allied target lay somewhere east of Sicily.

The procession was headed by the Western Task Force LCIs. A convoy carrying the Canadian 1st Division of the Eastern Task Force came next, entering the Tunisian War Channel at about 0100 July 8. Admiral Hall's DIME Force, destination Gela, followed; Admiral Kirk's CENT Force, destination Scoglitti, had fallen in behind, off Algiers. Joss Force waited at Bizerta to take the tail end. By 1600 July 7, Admiral Conolly had every one of the 276 vessels of his force except flagship *Biscayne* anchored in Bizerta roadstead. Then the flagship slipped out of the harbor. Ernie Pyle, a passenger, describes how, as *Biscayne* passed through the narrow harbor entrance, the order came over the loudspeaker: "Port side, Attention!" On the flat roof of the bomb-shattered customs house at the end of the mole stood in parade formation

Hotel Ancon, C.Z., an old-Navy idea of luxury and splendor. She was Admiral Hall's flagship in the Normandy invasion, Admiral's Wright's flagship at Okinawa, and Admiral Barbey's at the time of the surrender of Japan.

[21] II Corps included troops in DIME and CENT, but not those in JOSS.

two guards of honor composed of British and American sailors, each flying their country's flag. The ship's bugler played, the officers saluted, bluejackets stood rigidly at attention. "When the notes died down there was not a sound. No one spoke. We slid past, off on our mission into the unknown. . . ." [22]

At daybreak 8 July JOSS Force formed up in Bizerta roads, in two separate convoys, the slow and the medium. When fully deployed, JOSS slow convoy steamed in seven columns. Joss medium convoy comprised all 38 LSTs in seven columns, a dozen PCs and SCs, half a dozen small minesweepers and screening destroyers.

On 9 July, as all convoys were heading toward Gozo, there was relayed to every ship an inspiring message from the supreme naval commander, Admiral of the Fleet Sir Andrew B. Cunningham RN: —

> We are about to embark on the most momentous enterprise of the war — striking for the first time at the enemy in his own land.
>
> Success means the opening of the "Second Front" with all that it implies, and the first move toward the rapid and decisive defeat of our enemies.
>
> Our object is clear and our primary duty is to place this vast expedition ashore in the minimum time and subsequently to maintain our military and air forces as they drive relentlessly forward into enemy territory.
>
> In the light of this duty, great risks must be and are to be accepted. The safety of our own ships and all distracting considerations are to be relegated to second place, or disregarded as the accomplishment of our primary duty may require.
>
> On every commanding officer, officer and rating rests the individual and personal duty of ensuring that no flinching in determination or failure of effort on his own part will hamper this great enterprise.
>
> I rest confident in the resolution, skill and endurance of you all to whom this momentous enterprise is entrusted.[23]

For days the weather had been fair and the sea calm, with only a slight chop. But "if the western horizon is red at sunset or misty

[22] *Brave Men* p. 8.

[23] Dated 2 July. From the signed copy given to Maj. Gen. W. Bedell Smith, and by him to the Naval Historical Foundation.

at dawn, strong westerly winds are indicated," says the sailors' guide, *Sailing Directions for the Mediterranean.* Sunset 8 July was blood-red. The wind died down during the night, but after a murky dawn there suddenly blew up a stiff norther, one of those mistrals that have bedeviled sailormen in the Mediterranean since the dawn of history. It was just such a one that Poseidon raised on the "wine-dark sea" to pester Menelaus, or that wrecked St. Paul on the coast of Malta. During the afternoon watch the wind increased from force 3 to 6, some say to 7; and a nasty, steep sea made up athwart the convoys' courses. Five miles west of Gozo was the "marshaling yard," through which all United States convoys and the Canadian convoy passed, where the LST and LCI groups split up to join their respective forces, and where approach dispositions for JOSS, DIME and CENT were formed. In a strong wind and high sea these difficult and even dangerous maneuvers were executed in a thoroughly seamanlike manner. The LCTs, their passengers drenched to the skin, at times slowed down to 2½ knots; the LCIs, endeavoring to keep schedule, were taking seas over solid; and their soldier passengers, battened down in unventilated compartments, were hot, seasick and miserable. What if the plunging and wallowing beaching craft were so dispersed as to miss their rendezvous? Would the big transports, over whose decks water was now breaking, be able to lower landing craft? As Ernie Pyle described the scene:

> The little subchasers and infantry-carrying assault craft would disappear completely into the wave-troughs as we watched them. The next moment they would be carried so high they seemed to leap clear out of the water. . . . An Army officer had been washed overboard from one craft but had been picked up by another about four ships behind. During the worst of the blow we hoped and prayed that the weather would moderate by dusk. It didn't. The officers tried to make jokes about it at chow time. . . . Never in my life had I been so depressed.[24]

Most of the troops, and many of the sailors, too, wondered whether the expedition would not have to be called off and start

[24] *Brave Men* p. 14.

afresh. Old Boreas seemed to be just as powerful in A.D. 1943 as he had been in 249 B.C. when he had scattered a great Roman fleet in those very waters. During the first watch, Admiral Hewitt seriously considered signaling Admiral Cunningham to recommend that the assault be delayed. After a searching consultation with his force aërographer,[25] who predicted that the mistral would die down by eight bells, he decided to go ahead. At Malta, General Eisenhower and Admiral Cunningham were very anxious. But they did not interfere, and the expedition went on – a firm resolution that was repeated by General Eisenhower eleven months later before Normandy.

The open LCTs were drenched with spray and making so much leeway that Admiral Conolly expected them to be blown miles to leeward of their proper beaches. Although his orders from Cincmed were "under no circumstances" to alter convoy courses, he wisely decided to disobey; thrice on 9 July he sent orders by destroyer *Swanson* to Commander Durgin, leading the slow convoy in *Buck*, to alter course a point to the north.[26] After dark, conditions became even worse. *LCI–10*, flotilla leader for JOSS Force, rolled and pitched so horribly that her gyro compass threw its mercury; and as the magnetic compass was unreliable, owing to a last-minute radio installation, Captain Sabin had to signal minesweeper *Seer* to keep good dead reckoning, so that the other craft could follow her. And *Seer*, though badly tossed herself, did a perfect piece of navigation.[27]

By 2100 all but a few stragglers had passed through the Gozo "yards," and by 2230 the vans of the three United States forces were within radar hail of Sicily. At that hour, providentially, the wind began to moderate.

There is nothing in warfare, or perhaps even in life, to be compared with the hushed mystery of the final approach in a night

[25] Lt. Cdr. R. C. Steere, the same who made the accurate forecast en route to Morocco. See Vol. II of this History, pp. 49–50.

[26] D. G. Taggart *Hist. of 3rd Inf. Div.* p. 53; confirmed by Rear Adm. Conolly.

[27] Capt. Sabin and Cdr. Floyd Action Reports.

landing. Everything ahead is uncertain. There is no sound but the rush of waters, the throbbing of your ship's engines and of your own heart. You cannot see your friends on either flank, nor anything but the ship ahead and the ship astern. The shore, if dimly visible, is shrouded in darkness. Suppose the beacon submarine has been driven off? Can we locate the right beaches in complete darkness, with a heavy sea running? Have we surprised the enemy, or is he merely watching and waiting to unleash fierce dogs of death and destruction? A few mistakes on our part, or clever thrusts on his, may utterly wreck this vast and long-planned effort. There can be no drawn battle, no half-success, in an amphibious landing; it is win all splendidly or lose all miserably.

The enemy was not taken by surprise; yet he was far from ready. Nobody but Hitler and Keitel seems to have been fooled by the "Major William Martin" hoax. Early on 8 July Admiral Sansonnetti, Vice Chief of the Italian Naval Staff, told the German Commander of U-boats, Italy, that he expected landings in Sicily at any moment. During that day the folbots (folding canvas boats) which took scouts ashore from beacon submarines were observed from the Gela beaches. At 0320 July 9 a convoy was sighted south of Pantelleria. Supermarina estimated that this convoy was to be added to others at Malta, and that all would land after the storm abated. At 1630 July 9, five convoys steering northerly from Malta were spotted by an Italian plane. At 1840 all German troops in Sicily were alerted.[28] At 1935 a German plane sighted a convoy 33 miles NW of Gozo, and reported it promptly. Before 2000 Superaereo had ordered a torpedo-plane attack on the ships, to be launched from Sardinian fields. More contact reports came in every 20 or 30 minutes, indicating assaults all the way from Porto Empédocle to Syracuse. At 0100 July 10, before any landing craft had left the American transports, General Guzzoni, commanding all Axis forces in Sicily, declared a state of emergency and ordered the harbor obstructions at Licata and Porto Empédocle to

28 "The Sicilian Campaign, Information from German Sources" p. 6.

be blown.[29] And before D-day was many hours old he had correctly estimated that there would be no landings west of Licata, and ordered his mobile units in western Sicily to make best speed east.

Surprise, like speed, is relative; the defenders of Sicily were well enough surprised for Allied purposes. Supermarina analyses in Rome did not reach the first line of defense; many officers of coastal divisions, in view of the foul weather, turned in to sleep; [30] German crews of search radar stations would not believe the enormous "blips" they saw on their screens, and waited until daylight to report.[31]

Better than surprise was the "imposing and terrifying spectacle" [32] that the first light of dawn afforded to the defense. There had been nothing like it in Sicilian history since the Athenian expedition against Syracuse, "not less famous for its wonderful audacity, and for the splendor of its appearance, than for its overwhelming strength." [33] As Sicilians described the scene of 10 July to me, "There were thousands of vessels in the roadstead; one couldn't see the horizon for the ships. Thousands of troops were landing every minute." A pardonable exaggeration; but in truth the Allies had ringed a good third of Sicily with a wall of ships. No power on earth could prevent them from establishing their beachheads.

[29] Supermarina appreciations, extracts furnished by Historical Office of the Italian Navy; "Opera dell' Aeronautica Italiana" p. 6; War Diary of Captain U-boats Italy.

[30] The alert reached General d'Havet, commanding 206th Coastal Division, at 2220 July 9; but his naval adviser told him the weather was too rough for landing.

[31] Ruge "The Evacuation of Sicily" p. 9.

[32] Gen. Faldella in *Roma* 17 July 1953.

[33] Thucydides *Peloponnesian War* vi. 31.

CHAPTER V

The Licata Landings (JOSS Force)[1]

10–12 July

1. *Terrain, Arrival and Plan*

LET US take a look at the entire Western Naval Task Force target area, the Gulf of Gela. The shore extends 37 miles from the Torre di Gaffe to Punta Braccetto, and on its rim are two small cities, Licata and Gela, and a fishing village, Scoglitti, convenient foci for the three American attack groups – JOSS, DIME, and CENT. Over half the shore line is sand beach; the rest, rocky points and low cliffs. Behind the coast, at distances varying between fifty yards and five miles, runs a railway and the Southwest Sicily Coastal Highway (No. 115). Three rivers, the Salso, the Gela and the Acate, empty into the gulf, flowing through flat and fertile coastal plains – the small Piana di Ginisi behind Licata; the wide Piana di Gela in the center; and the Piana di Camerina behind Scoglitti. Around these plains is a scalloped mountain wall, from which close-built hill-towns look down on the valleys and the beaches. From each plain a main road pushes into the interior of Sicily. The area was well chosen for an amphibious force to land, consolidate and deploy; but it was also an ideal theater for counterattack.

[1] CTF 86 (Rear Adm. Conolly) Action Reports and Comments on HUSKY 5 Aug. 1943, and those of his group commanders: Cdr. R. E. Nelson, Lt. Cdr. S. H. Pattie, Cdr. W. O. Floyd and Cdr. Robert M. Morris (*cf.* Appendix I). Comcrudiv 13 (Rear Adm. DuBose) and Comdesron 13 (Capt. Durgin) Action Reports, and those of individual ships, especially *Birmingham, Brooklyn,* and *Bristol;* D. G. Taggart *History of the 3rd Infantry Division in World War II* (1947). Useful for a detached view is "Notes on Planning and Assault Phases of Sicilian Campaign" by a British liaison officer with JOSS Force, issued by Combined Ops. Hq., London, Oct. 1943.

Ex Africa semper aliquid novi – "Something new is always coming out of Africa" – is an ancient motto. This time it was JOSS Force, first amphibious expedition against Sicily since the days of the Saracens to be mainly shore-to-shore; that is, in which the troops are landed from the very craft in which they embark. And it was also the first to use large numbers of the new beaching craft.

On the beaches just east of the Salso River mouth, probably those that we designated Yellow and Blue, M. Atilius Regulus in 256 B.C. embarked a Roman army in 350 ships, which a few days later defeated the Carthaginians in the Battle of Ecnomus, laying Carthage open to attack. And in the next Punic War, 211 B.C., Marcellus beat the Carthaginians near Licata and captured eight elephants – the tanks of antiquity.

"Line Yellow," the first objective line of Seventh Army, was so drawn along the semicircle of hills that the enemy, when pushed beyond it, would be unable to reach Licata, Gela or the airfields with long-range artillery. With this line secured, a beachhead roughly 40 miles long (counting the American sector only) and 15 to 25 miles deep would serve as a great sally port from which columns of American troops could knife through to the north coast or, if necessary, help the British to take Messina. It was assumed that at least five days would be required for the Seventh Army to reach Line Yellow; but on 12 July JOSS Force had even pressed beyond the western segment, which ran between Palma, Campobello and Canicattì.

Beacon submarine H.M.S. *Safari* was the first Allied ship to arrive off Licata, on 5 July. Her commanding officer, and Captain G. B. H. Fawkes RN of the 8th Submarine Flotilla, had conferred with Admiral Conolly and even exercised with his ships off Bizerta. *Safari* buoyed her beacon position, sent scouts ashore in folbots to reconnoiter the beaches, lay on the bottom during the day, and at nightfall took station five miles south of the Castel Sant'Angelo that overlooks Licata.

At 1615 July 9 destroyer *Bristol* forged ahead of the JOSS convoys to locate *Safari*. After dark a lucky rift in the clouds enabled her navigator to obtain star sights and to shape her course correctly. Commander Glick, her skipper, seeing a dark shape in the water only a few hundred yards away, bore down on it and, for-

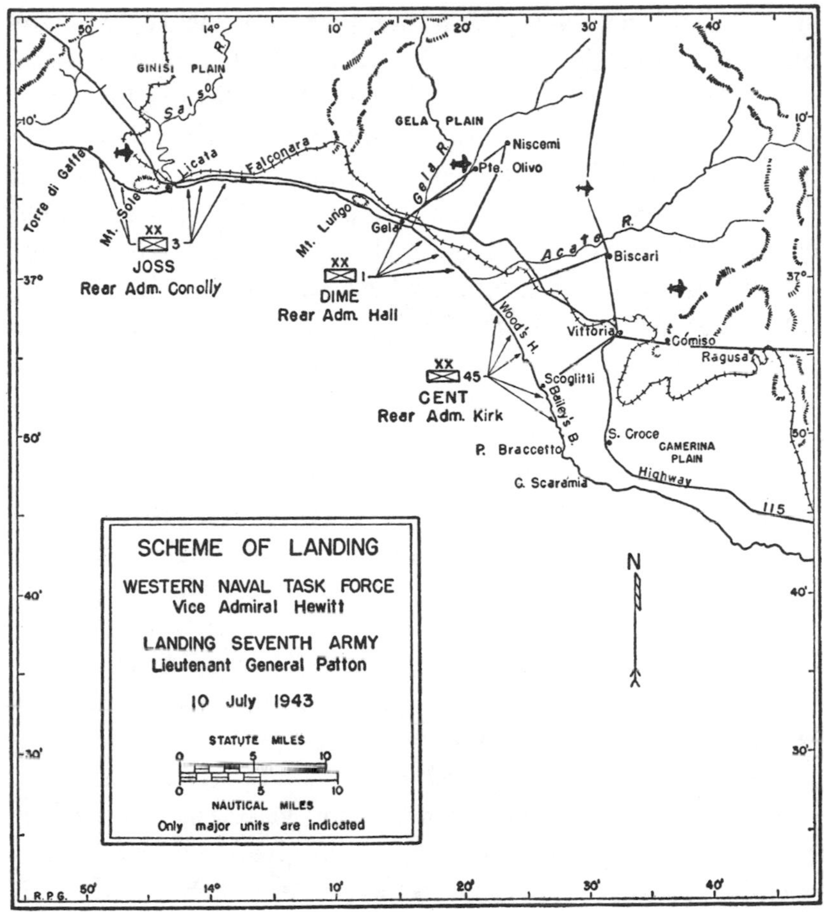

bidden to use radio or blinker, hailed "Hello!" A pleasant English voice replied, "Hel-lo!" That was around 2230. *Bristol* then took her planned station exactly five miles to seaward of the submarine and directed a searchlight beam due south as a beacon. *PC–546* located *Bristol*, took station five miles outside her (at the 15-mile point) and began blinking seaward. The other patrol craft, one for each beach, were thus enabled to find *Bristol,* fan out, and take their stations 6000 yards off shore. This plan worked almost without a hitch. It was the key to the success of the JOSS landings.[2]

During the first watch cruisers *Brooklyn* and *Birmingham,* flagship *Biscayne* and the two fast transports approached, with five columns of beaching craft trailing them, all struggling with the heavy wind and sea. Fires and flashes ashore, lighted by the air bombers, were sighted from the flagship at 2200. *Brooklyn* pushed ahead to locate *Bristol,* did so at 2310, then covered the approach of the two westernmost attack groups, which Admiral Conolly released one minute before midnight. *Birmingham* did the same for the two easternmost groups, which *Biscayne* led in.

Although the wind had abated, the sea was still very rough. LSTs for Beach Blue, first of their class to arrive, began anchoring and lowering boats at 0115. Within half an hour *Biscayne* had anchored two and a half miles SE of Licata breakwater. The anchor chain, remarked one of her sailors, "made a noise you could have heard clear to Rome"; and it did seem that someone ashore had heard it, since presently three and then five searchlights converged on the flagship. They lighted her for fully twenty minutes, during which one could read a book on deck. The Admiral ordered gunfire withheld, and eventually the searchlights shifted. The failure of the enemy to fire until fired upon long remained a wonder to the Americans, but the reason was simple enough. Behind these beaches the only artillery consisted of ancient Italian fieldpieces with a maximum effective range of 9000 yards, and most of the transports were anchored too far out to give them any hope of accomplishing anything, except to reveal their position. So the commanding generals ordered their artillery to reserve fire for landing craft and troops ashore.[3]

[2] As part of the plan, *PC–543* closed *Safari* at 2245 to screen her against possible attack, which she did successfully when Axis dive-bombers went for the submarine shortly after 0500. "*Safari* was an interested spectator and was happy to congratulate this vessel on her excellent shooting." *PC–543* Action Report, Lt. (jg) M. W. Silverstein.

[3] Information from Historical Office of the General Staff of the Italian Army, 1953.

At 0300 destroyer *Buck*, escorting the JOSS slow convoy, was maneuvering near *Bristol*, checking off the LCTs as they passed and directing them by bull-horn into their proper areas.

Joss Force landing plan was so complicated that we have left it to the moment of execution to describe.

Licata, an active little city with a small artificial harbor, a center for sulphur manufacture and export, was too well protected and fortified for a frontal assault. The town lies between the mouth of the Salso River and Monte Sole, which rises to a height of 560 feet and extends for about five miles along the coast. The coastal highway and railroad from Gela cross the Salso near its mouth, cut through the edge of the town and run behind Monte Sole to Palma di Montechiaro, which stands on the western foothills of the mountain range that forms a semicircle around Licata. Another important highway runs north across the Ginisi plain to Campobello, Canicattì and Caltanissetta.

With reference to our chart, here is the detailed plan. Joss Force was divided into four attack groups, as follows, from west to east: –

1. *Gaffi Attack Group*, Captain Lorenzo S. Sabin in *LCI–10.* To land the 7th Regimental Combat Team of the 3rd Division (Colonel Harry B. Sherman USA) on Beach Red about five miles west of Licata, from 7 LSTs, 17 LCIs and 21 LCTs. Their mission was to occupy the western section of the initial beachhead line.

2. *Molla Attack Group*, Commander Robert M. Morris in *LST–6.* To land 3rd Ranger Battalion (Lieutenant Colonel H. W. Dummer USA) and 2nd Battalion 15th RCT on the two Beaches Green at the western end of Monte Sole, and march on Licata.

3. *Salso Attack Group*, Commander William O. Floyd in *LCI–95.* To land the 1st and 3rd Battalions of the 15th RCT (Colonel Charles E. Johnson USA) on Beach Yellow, a mile and a half east of the mouth of the Salso River. Half these troops were to join the Rangers in a pincer movement on Licata; the other half to take a strong point on the 980-foot Monte Gallodoro.

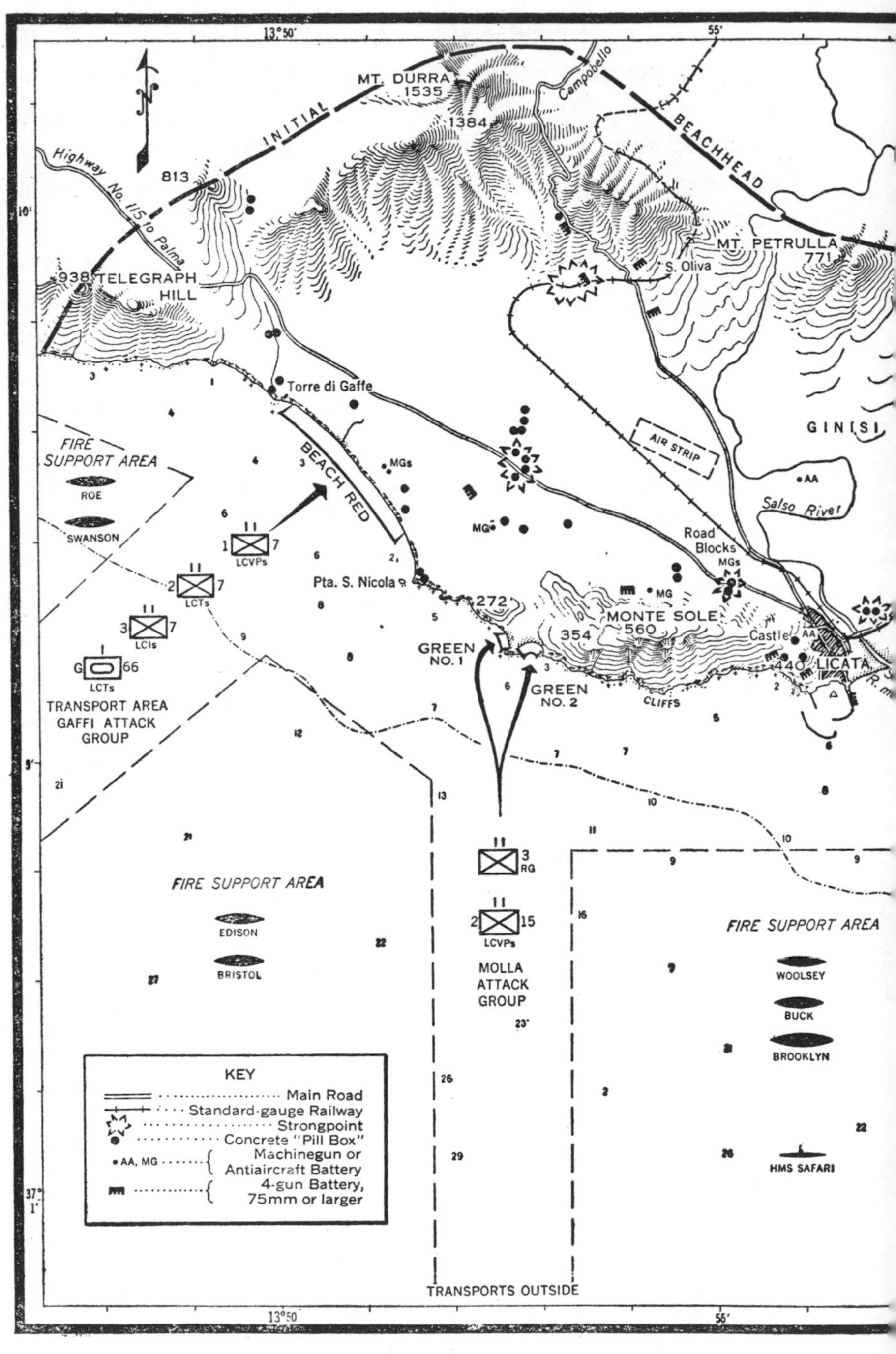

13°50'
55'
MT. DURRA
1535
1384
Campobello
INITIAL
BEACHHEAD
Highway No. 115 to Palma
813
938 TELEGRAPH HILL
MT. PETRULLA
771
S. Oliva
Torre di Gaffe
AIR STRIP
GINISI
FIRE SUPPORT AREA
ROE
SWANSON
BEACH RED
MGs
AA
Salso River
LCVPs
Road Blocks
MGs
Pta. S. Nicola
272
MG
MONTE SOLE
560
354
LCTs
LCIs
Castle
AA
440 LICATA
GREEN NO. 1
GREEN NO. 2
CLIFFS
LCTs
TRANSPORT AREA
GAFFI ATTACK GROUP
RG
FIRE SUPPORT AREA
EDISON
BRISTOL
LCVPs
MOLLA ATTACK GROUP
FIRE SUPPORT AREA
WOOLSEY
BUCK
BROOKLYN
HMS SAFARI
KEY
Main Road
Standard-gauge Railway
Strongpoint
Concrete "Pill Box"
AA, MG
Machinegun or Antiaircraft Battery
4-gun Battery, 75mm or larger
TRANSPORTS OUTSIDE
13°50'
55'

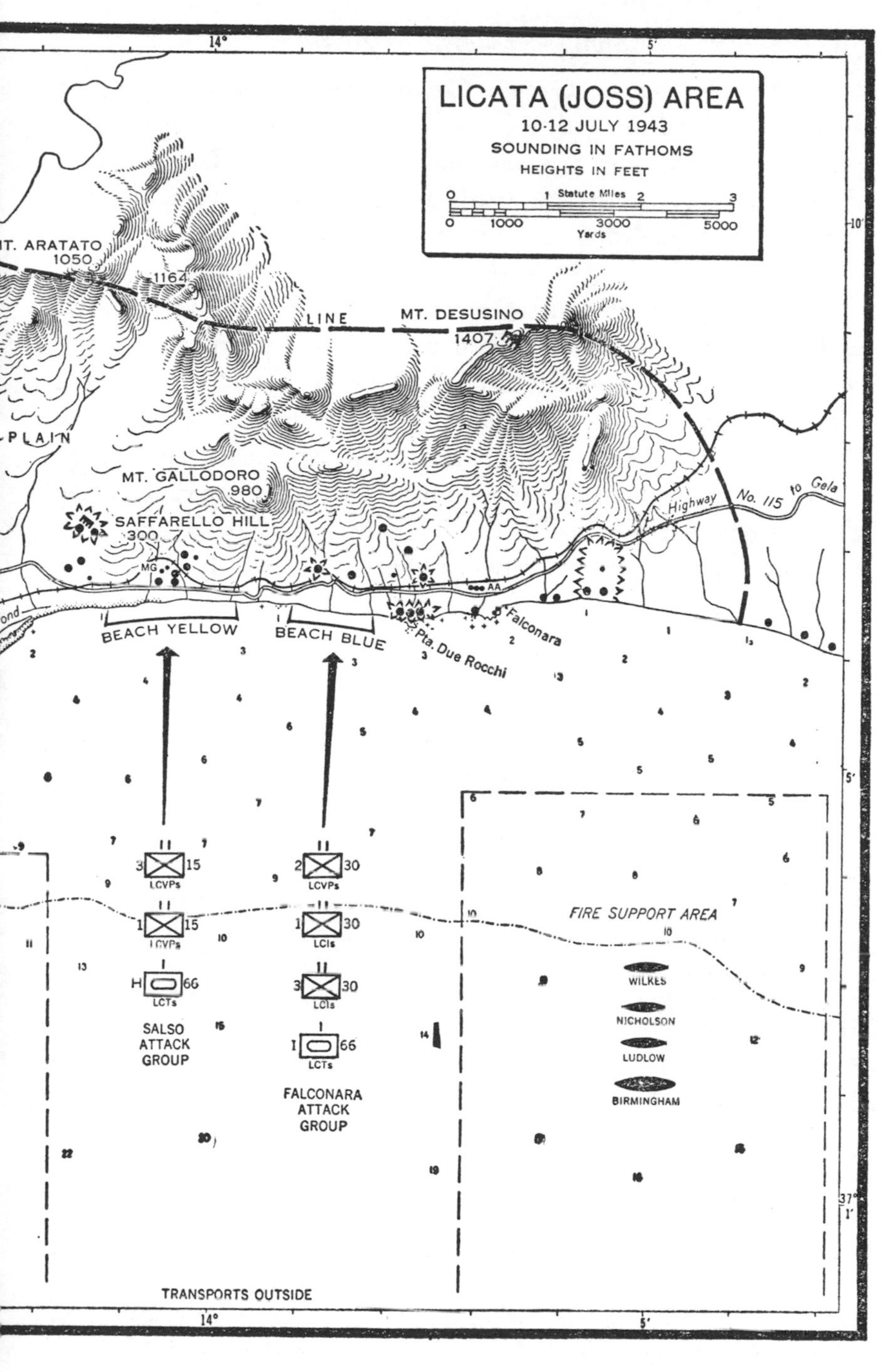
LICATA (JOSS) AREA
10-12 JULY 1943
SOUNDING IN FATHOMS
HEIGHTS IN FEET
Statute Miles
Yards
MT. ARATATO
1050
1164
LINE
MT. DESUSINO
1407
PLAIN
MT. GALLODORO
980
SAFFARELLO HILL
300
MG
AA
Highway No. 115 to Gela
BEACH YELLOW
BEACH BLUE
Pta. Due Rocchi
Falconara
LCVPs
LCIs
LCTs
SALSO
ATTACK
GROUP
FALCONARA
ATTACK
GROUP
FIRE SUPPORT AREA
WILKES
NICHOLSON
LUDLOW
BIRMINGHAM
TRANSPORTS OUTSIDE

4. *Falconara Attack Group,* Commander Roger E. Nelson in *LCI–86.* To land the 30th RCT (Colonel Arthur H. Rogers USA) on Beach Blue. Their mission was to take Monte Desusino and the strong points on the east flank, and to make contact with CENT Force to the east.

The first-quarter moon set at 0023, but the stars were bright, and as long as they are out it is never completely dark in a Mediterranean summer. The first light of D-day began to steal over the sea shortly before 0500; the coast was then visible from seaward. Sun rose at 0550. For an hour longer the morning haze reduced visibility to 1500 yards, but it soon dissolved, and at no time during this fair day was even half the sky obscured by clouds. Owing to the mistral it was a comparatively cool day for Sicily, with temperature not above 77° F.

NOTE ON THE LEFT FLANK SCREENING GROUP

Parallel to the JOSS Force approach and on its west flank steamed a special screening group composed of 17 motor torpedo boats of Squadron 15 commanded by Lieutenant Commander Stanley M. Barnes and led by Lieutenant Commander Robert Brodie in destroyer *Ordronaux.* Their object was to neutralize a nest of German and Italian motor torpedo boats reported to be based on Porto Empédocle, 24 miles west of Licata. Empédocle, with a bigger harbor than Licata, had not been included in the initial assault for two reasons: — a mine field correctly reported by Intelligence, and the respect that we had for the Italian MAS boats. This screening group arrived at its destination off Empédocle about 2300 July 9. *Ordronaux* started an offensive sweep outside the mine field while Barnes's PTs patrolled the eastern edge of it. The Brodie-Barnes screening group had been left under Hewitt's direct command instead of being placed under Conolly's. It had no orders from Commander JOSS Force, or even communication with him. Lieutenant Commander E. L. Robertson, commanding the westernmost fire support unit of JOSS Force, destroyers *Swanson* and *Roe,* had no knowledge of friendly PTs being in the area, and no information of *Ordronaux's* whereabouts. But he had been told to look out for E-boats

— as we called the German PTs. Observing small pips on his radar screen, he suspected that enemy small craft had broken loose; he moved over with *Roe* to investigate, and ran down his radar contacts to within 1500 yards. Lieutenant Barnes flashed a recognition signal but it did not register; and at 0255, as Robertson was about to order both destroyers to open fire, *Roe*, swerving to avoid the Porto Empédocle mine field and at the same time fall in astern of *Swanson*, hit her at right angles on the port side abreast her forward stack when she was making 25 and *Swanson* 20 knots. *Roe's* bow crumpled, and the two destroyers came almost parallel as they went dead in the water. Miraculously, nobody was even injured on either ship, but both vessels were so badly damaged that they had to be sent to Malta and Bizerta for repairs.[4]

Not a single motor torpedo boat was sighted — but some were there. Supermarina at 1930 July 9 ordered all Italian boats at Empédocle to move to Augusta; they started off, took fright at the immense concourse of shipping off Licata, turned back and made for Trápani, alleging "violent enemy reaction."

2. *The Gaffi and Molla Landings*[5]

The Torre di Gaffe,[6] a stone tower on a rocky cliff about 75 feet above the sea, marks the western end of Beach Red. There were pillboxes on the cliff; the two beach exits, dry channels of streams, were well wired; and the beach could be swept by guns located at the Torre and on the Punta San Nicola that makes out from the coast beyond the southern end of the beach.

General Truscott had intensively trained his division in the

[4] *Roe* Report of Collision 23 July; information from Capts. Robertson and Barnes in 1953. *Swanson* had to fire all torpedoes on account of steam coming up around them. The bulkhead between forward fire and engine rooms was buckled; the fire-room crew, after securing, repeatedly dove down into their flooded fire room in complete darkness to stop the leaks with blankets, etc. As steam from the after boiler room was available for pumping, the forward engine room was in operation by 0500. Shortly after, when there was just enough light to see, a Ju-88 flew in; *Roe* and *Swanson* shot it down with 7 and 6 rounds respectively of proximity influence-fuzed 5-inch .38. This was one of the first times that this new fuze had been used in antiaircraft fighting, and the exploit of shooting down a plane with so few rounds was so sensational that Robertson, when he reached Malta, was summoned by Admiral Cunningham to tell the story.

[5] Com LCI(L) Flot 2 (Capt. L. S. Sabin) Action Report 27 July 1943.

[6] The tower is so spelled; but we called the landing group the "Gaffi."

right sort of tactics to meet the situation. The first battalion to land was to "work like a pack of hounds, hunting out beach defenses and keeping them occupied whilst the remaining infantry battalions, by-passing resistance, penetrate inland to seize and consolidate key areas." [7] Combat engineers accompanied the initial assault to help dispose of beach defenses, but they had also been trained and equipped to fight as infantry. All troops, in fact, had been taught to fight with their own weapons and not count on constant artillery support, but that did not make General Truscott any less keen to get his tanks and artillery ashore at the earliest possible moment. Troops of this and all the other United States forces in Sicily were landed in light order, carrying only their own weapons, two canteens of water per man, gas mask, and combat pack for toilet kit, K-rations and extra ammunition. They were uniformed in olive drab woolen trousers and shirts, and netted steel helmets painted the same color; the trousers were tucked inside short canvas leggings. Blouse, blankets, herringbone twill fatigue clothing, mess kit and other gear were in barracks bags on board ship, to be landed later.

All craft of the Gaffi Attack Group sailed in the slow JOSS convoy, and all arrived late. The van, seven LSTs commanded by Lieutenant Commander Samuel H. Pattie, lifting the assault battalion of the 7th RCT, anchored between 0200 and 0215 in very straggling fashion, the nearest two and one half miles and the farthest six miles off shore.[8] Sweeper *Seer* and her train of LCIs got there first, which almost upset the landing plan.

The Gaffi landings were very rough, as Beach Red was completely exposed to the westerly surf. Yet the landing craft of the initial waves, launched from the LSTs in darkness, came through well. Machine-gun and artillery fire began to fall on the beach and its approaches at 0410, when LCVPs carrying the spearhead of Lieutenant Colonel Roy E. Moore's assault battalion were on their

[7] Col. Head "Notes on HUSKY" p. 14. Note the similarity to the tactics employed by the Marines in amphibious assaults in the Pacific.

[8] Lt. Cdr. Pattie Action Report 31 July 1943. Sabin gives the 6-mile figure.

way in. As the boat carrying the beach scouts [9] was late, the landing craft had no guide except the PC stationed three miles off shore; but the young officers designated as flotilla leaders skillfully led their boat waves, at proper intervals. All the first wave had beached by 0435. Ten minutes later, enemy dive-bombing attacks began on the Gaffi Group. Antiaircraft fire from all calibers between 20-mm and 3-inch 50 was opened in the direction of the sound of motors, since it was still too dark to see a plane. Captain Sabin's LCI was lifted partly out of the water by a big bomb that exploded 300 yards away, but she suffered no damage, and no vessel was hit.

Second wave for Beach Red consisted of six Landing Craft Infantry under Lieutenant Commander Edward W. Wilson USNR, which landed the rest of the 2nd Battalion. They started in at 0415 and were close to Beach Red within 30 minutes.

By this time most of the local defenders of pillboxes had fled, appalled at the magnitude of the assault,[10] but some machine-gunners held their ground, and there were two coast defense batteries sited about 5500 yards inland, in a good position to cover Beach Red. Wilson's LCIs became the first targets. *LCI–1* had her controls and communications shot away and her helmsman and engine-room telegraph man killed as she was about to hit the beach, which she did at full speed with no steering control. She broached and swung around, but landed her troops over the stern. Her crew, inspired by Lieutenant Carl F. Robison, fired off all their ammunition in a duel with machine-gun nests upon the cliff. Although subjected to a wicked crossfire and riddled with holes, *LCI–1* lost only three men. *LCI–2*, Lieutenant John D. Ogilby, also put up a stout fight when beached. Three more

[9] A Scout and Raider Group of the Navy was supposed to be carried by a specially equipped motorcraft, brought to the area by a larger vessel, to each landing beach, where the scouts were to land in rubber boats and flash appropriately colored blinkers to help the landing craft find the right spot. If a scout boat happened to be carried by an LST or transport that arrived late, its mission was thwarted.

[10] Information from the owner of the Torre di Gaffe. He added that those who fired on our troops "must have been Germans; they had no more sense than to fight"; but no Germans were there.

beached successfully; the sixth grounded on the false beach and later transferred her troops to an LCI of the next wave.[11] By 0500 the entire assault battalion was ashore, most of the LCIs had retracted, and the third wave, consisting of nine LCIs under Lieutenant Commander Robert G. Newbegin USNR, was coming in. Day was breaking, there was just enough light to see the shore from the sea, but sunrise was still three quarters of an hour away.

Newbegin's LCIs, too, came under heavy fire; and so close that one of them, as she beached, sighted an Italian soldier on the cliff twenty-five yards away, preparing to toss hand grenades into her; he was quickly disposed of. Another, before she was fairly ashore, took five prisoners — troops who rushed out from a pillbox on which she had fired, and surrendered. At 0515 *LCI–5*, bearing Colonel Harry Sherman of the 7th Infantry, and staff, beached in a ring of gunfire that came from near the Torre di Gaffe and also from the east end of the beach. Her port ramp was carried away by the heavy surf after only a dozen soldiers had landed, and her starboard ramp was fouled by another LCI. The troops started to flounder ashore as best they could, but a number were drowned, and a 90-mm projectile from an Italian mobile battery entered a troop compartment and killed several men. As a last resort the C.O., Lieutenant Richard W. Caldwell USNR, deliberately broached his craft, and the rest of the troops landed over her port side.

The gallantry and intelligence with which these LCIs of the Gaffi Group were handled in heavy surf under severe gunfire, and mostly in complete darkness, is a notable feature of the western landings. And it must be remembered that the Gaffi people had very little fire support because of the mishap to *Roe* and *Swanson;* except for a few British LCTs converted to gunboats they had none until *Brooklyn* and *Buck* moved in after daylight.

[11] Combat Narrative *The Sicilian Campaign* pp. 80–82. Capt. Sabin Action Report p. 10. Nos. 1 and 2 were later pulled off and salvaged, owing to good work by Cdr. Imlay USCGR. The LCI ramps, one on each bow, which the British call "brows," proved not robust enough for heavy-surf landings, and most of Wilson's were wrenched off. After the operation was over, he returned to Beach Red and recovered 18 out of 23 craft that had been given up as lost, and these were refitted in time to take part in the Salerno landings.

Twenty-one LCTs, carrying most of the vehicles, tanks and equipment of the 7th Regiment, were yet to be heard from. Commander Durgin had done his best to herd them along, but heavy seas impeded. Captain Sabin in *LCI–10* closed *Biscayne* at 0512 to report that as yet only three LCTs of the Gaffi Group were in sight, and that the LCIs were catching it hot and heavy on Beach Red. Half an hour later, daylight had so increased that the beachmaster signaled the Captain, "Enemy field artillery getting close. Hold the wave. Give us support." Beachmaster then signaled that this Italian mobile battery was located 1500 yards behind the right flank of the beach. The information was conveyed to Lieutenant Commander Millard J. Klein of destroyer *Buck*, which "went in at high speed with guns blazing and did a beautiful job of silencing these batteries." [12]

Captain Sabin knew of General Truscott's eagerness to get his fieldpieces and tanks ashore promptly; and the LCT crews did so well that, by 0630, three American field artillery battalions had gone into position 500 to 1500 yards inland and were supporting the infantry.[13] But things were so hot on the beach that at 0645 the beachmaster again requested that all landing be held up. Now cruiser *Brooklyn*, which had been firing on the batteries on Monte Sole, moved over to Beach Red, and delivered a few 6-inch salvos. By 0715 enemy fire on Beach Red had ceased. As the General was becoming impatient, Admiral Conolly at 0722 directed all remaining Red-bound LCTs to "charge the beach" and land regardless of cost. He sent destroyers *Edison* and *Bristol* to join *Buck* and cover their approach with a smoke screen. Under that cover, as well as gunfire from *Brooklyn*, all remaining LCTs landed safely by 0800.

A very difficult, complex and contested landing of troops and artillery had been accomplished by the Navy with a minimum of casualties. And the troops were going to their allotted task without the slightest hesitation. Nothing is more astonishing to sailors

[12] Sabin Report p. 4. *Buck* closed the beach so near that the wash from her passing at 20 knots freed *LCI–218* which had grounded on a false beach.

[13] Taggart p. 55.

in an amphibious operation than the quick recovery of GIs, once ashore. At one moment they are seasick, weak, miserable boys, helpless in the landing craft; once they hit the beach they become fighting men. And the 7th Infantry Regiment, the "Cotton Balers,"[14] were just that. Its 1st Battalion overcame all local defenses. While engineers removed barbed wire from beach exits and blew up pillboxes, the infantry assembled on the plain a mile north of the beach. By the end of D-day the 3rd Battalion was well on its way to Campobello; and the other two had passed the initial beachhead line and were "Truscott-trotting"[15] halfway to Palma di Montechiaro.

Endeavors to unload vehicles from the LSTs into "married" LCTs for landing were unsuccessful until next day, owing to the heavy ground swell; and it was too rough to launch dukws. At 1000 Captain Sabin ordered six LSTs to beach. They, too, were unsuccessful. The only pontoon causeway available to the Gaffi Group broached and became unmanageable, the LSTs grounded on the offshore bar, and the runnel was too deep for vehicles to negotiate. After attempts extending all day, these craft retired off shore and anchored for the night — all except *LST–348*, which hit a lucky gap, and landed her 105-mm guns under their own power.[16]

Commander Robert M. Morris's Molla Attack Group, so called after an upstanding rock which separates the two beaches, encountered much less opposition than the Gaffi Group. Beaches Green were two little pockets in the western end of Monte Sole, with narrow rocky entrances through which the surf was roaring on

[14] So called from their use of cotton bales as barricades in the Battle of New Orleans, 1815. The second oldest regiment in the U. S. Army, the 7th has always lived up to its motto, *Volens et Potens.*

[15] By this method of march, in which General Truscott had trained the 3rd Division, 30 statute miles could be covered on foot in less than 8 hours by troops carrying their weapons and full packs. They hit a pace of 5½ m.p.h. for the first hour, 4 for the next two, and 3½ for the rest. Taggart p. 42.

[16] *LST–348* Report enclosed in Lt. Cdr. Pattie's. Most of the JOSS Force LSTs were eventually unloaded early 12 July, at the mole in Licata Harbor, leading one observer to remark, "On a rough coast, the most insignificant harbor is better than the best beach." Beach Red was abandoned that day.

D-day. Although difficult for boats to locate in the darkness, they made excellent sally ports.

The Molla Group, headed by destroyer *Edison*, included minesweeper *Sentinel*, *LCI–32* carrying the naval and military commanders, and the two "Princesses" carrying most of the Rangers. Commander Morris, having reached the transport area three miles off shore, at 0120 gave the order to deploy, close up, anchor and lower boats. The British landing craft were smartly handled, taking Rangers into these two small and dangerously rocky coves with the aid of a Scout and Raider company which landed on the entrance rocks and flashed signals seaward. Admiral Conolly attributed this success to the excellent mock-up of rocks and landscape that Morris had used in the African rehearsals.[17] The Rangers began to hit the beach at 0300. Only 40 minutes after them came LCVPs from the six LSTs of this group, carrying the 2nd Battalion 15th Regimental Combat Team of the 3rd Division.

The Rangers did not wait for their vehicles, which were not landed from LCTs until 0605. They pressed ahead through barbed wire, accepted the surrender of sundry Italian troops and moved along the northern edge of Monte Sole. A strong point that dominated the road was overcome, and by dawn the Rangers were entering the suburbs of Licata.[18] In the meantime the 15th Regiment was swarming over the crest of the mountain. Sailors off shore were watching the flagstaff on Castel Sant'Angelo. At 0735 they observed the Italian flag coming down and the Stars and Stripes being run up immediately thereafter.

Minesweeper *Sentinel*, Lieutenant Commander George L. Phillips, was the only important casualty of the Molla Group. At 0510 when she was on anti-submarine patrol near the patrol craft at the 15-mile mark, and before it was light enough to see aircraft from the deck, an enemy dive-bomber holed her at the after engine room. Within the next hour she received four more air attacks, resisting each one strenuously but suffering another hit that flooded

[17] Cdr. Morris Action Report 2 Aug. 1943 and endorsements.
[18] Lt. J. J. Altieri USA *Darby's Rangers* p. 53.

the forward engine room. At 0615, when it became apparent that this ship was doomed, Phillips summoned assistance from the Molla Group. *SC–530,* superbly handled in the heavy sea, took on 31 wounded men; *PC–550* rescued the remainder. *Sentinel* capsized at 1030. She lost 10 killed or missing and had 51 wounded, from a ship's company of 101.

3. *The Salso and Falconara Landings* [19]

About 3000 yards east of the Salso River, separated from it by a marshy tract and a pond, begins Beach Yellow; Beach Blue is separated from it by a rocky gorge with high banks. These proved to be the best beaches for a night landing in the entire Gulf of Gela. Landmarks were conspicuous, even in the darkness: on the left flank the city of Licata and unmistakable Monte Sole, then Saffarello Hill and Monte Gallodoro directly behind Beach Yellow. The 1400-foot Monte Desusino makes a perfect landmark for Beach Blue, which ends at the Punta Due Rocchi, whose pair of rocks could hardly be missed; if they were, Falconara Point half a mile farther east, with a modern imitation castle sitting conspicuously on it, served as a good warning. The Southwest Sicily Highway (No. 115) runs very close to these beaches — less than a hundred yards distant in some places; the railway, for the most part, parallels the road. On 10 July the rising ground between shore and road was wheatfield in stubble, with a few tomato gardens; across the road harvested wheatfields rose to almost every high point that the troops had to take.

Beach Yellow was taken by Commander Floyd's Salso Attack Group, consisting of two battalions of the 15th RCT; Blue by Commander Nelson's Falconara Attack Group, the 30th RCT. Over 60 beaching craft lifted the two groups; sundry patrol craft and subchasers acted as guides; three destroyers and nine of the

[19] Action Reports of Adm. Conolly, Com Falconara Attack Group (Cdr. Nelson) and Com Salso Attack Group (Cdr. Floyd).

converted British LCTs stood by for fire support. Commander Floyd sighted the two PCs detailed to act as approach markers, at 0045 and 0123; but the one close to Beach Yellow was out of position, and Floyd had a hard time rounding up his flock. All LSTs were anchored by 0141, and put their landing craft into the water promptly. Beach Yellow had been well marked by Scouts and Raiders commanded by Ensign P. H. Bucklew USNR, and the first wave touched down at 0340. All but one of the craft that landed there retracted successfully.

Surprise here seems to have been complete; the beach command post was abandoned before the Americans had time to fight for it. One of the first to enter was Michael Chinigo, a news correspondent, who, thanks to his good knowledge of Italian, enjoyed a unique experience. A telephone rang. Chinigo picked up the receiver and said "*Che è?*" ("Who's there?") An Italian general answered querulously. He had been aroused from his slumbers by a disturbing report that Americans were landing in his sector. He hoped it wasn't true; didn't see how it could be on such a night. Chinigo in firm, authoritative tones assured the General that all was quiet on the Licata beaches; and both parties, well satisfied, hung up.[20]

The 3rd Battalion 15th Infantry, after landing under light machine-gun fire, cleared the defenses and seized a good position across the road. In the meantime the 1st Battalion, which had landed at 0445, marched straight to its objective, a coast defense battery spotted by air reconnaissance northwest of Saffarello Hill, and took it at 0800. An hour and a half later it received orders to ford the river and march into Licata, detaching a platoon to prevent the Italians from blowing up the bridge over the Salso. *Bristol*, no longer needed as a beacon after sunrise, steamed to a point off Licata and pummeled a railroad battery located on the harbor mole.

Nine LCTs destined for Beach Yellow lost sight of their guide during the night and ran blind. At an early morning hour they were hailed by an SC which signaled, "Follow me!" and led the entire formation over to Gela. But the mistake was remedied after day-

[20] Taggart p. 51.

light and these LCTs reached Beach Yellow at 0800. The new system of unloading tanks from LSTs over a "married" LCT worked well here in spite of the swell. All Salso Group LCTs had tanks ashore by 0914.

Although the scout boat for Beach Blue did not arrive in time to mark it, the mountain silhouettes were so unmistakable against the starry sky that the first wave of Commander Nelson's Falconara Attack Group, carrying the 2nd Battalion 30th RCT, touched down at 0315, beating Floyd by twenty-five minutes. LCIs of this group began to beach at 0422 and discharged their troops, in water knee- to waist-deep, within ten minutes. Enemy gunfire from a fieldpiece and a few mortars and machine guns now began to fall on Beach Blue, but it was feeble and ineffective. All but four LCVPs, which hit the Punta Due Rocchi instead of the beach, retracted successfully, as did all but one of the LCIs.

About 6000 yards inland from Beach Blue in a northeasterly direction is the summit of Monte Desusino, commanding not only the JOSS beaches but the Gela plain. On its slopes were enemy batteries which were not given a chance to shoot. *Brooklyn* began bombarding them at 0445, as soon as there was light enough for her spotting planes to see.[21] The mountain targets were silenced after 713 rounds of 6-inch HC had been expended. One of *Birmingham's* planes was badly shot up by a Messerschmitt and "a friendly ship's antiaircraft batteries," but returned safely; a crewman was shot out of the other plane by similiar "friendly" fire and drowned. Destroyer *Buck* helped the advance of Colonel Rogers's 30th Infantry by firing on various other targets, such as Monte Gallodoro, at ranges from 10,000 to 13,000 yards.

By 0530 nine dukws were churning ashore from *LST–318*, and about that time a hitherto unlocated Italian battery began shooting at the ships, but did slight damage. The first LCTs, late at Beach Blue as elsewhere, began beaching only at 0627. Yet they were not too late. The historian of the 3rd Division states that "with minor exceptions" all divisional artillery landed and got in position as

21 Hewitt and DuBose Action Reports.

soon as needed,[22] and Colonel Rogers, moreover, had the support of Company I of the 66th Armored Regiment to help his advance to objectives north and east. All were taken by about 0930. The assault battalion, the 2nd, after destroying all beach defenses, marched west along the coastal road and crossed the bridge into Licata at about 1130. At the same time the 1st Battalion 15th Infantry, which had forded the Salso, entered the town from the north, and the troops which had landed on Beach Green entered from the north and east.

For almost seven hours the fire support ships had been firing intermittently on assigned targets to open the way for this triumphal entry, and during the first four hours of this shoot they were not in touch with shore fire-control parties.[23] That did not greatly matter, as most of the targets were conspicuous and had been designated beforehand. The cruisers' spot planes worked steadily and valiantly despite lack of fighter protection and a morning mist which made it difficult to sight targets. There were several air attacks on the ships by Axis planes, some delivered even before it was light; but no damage was done except (as we have seen) to *Sentinel*, and shots from coast defense batteries were rare; one missed *Bristol* by a thousand yards; and another near-missed flagship *Biscayne* by a scant fifty yards. Admiral Conolly had her anchor weighed in a jiffy, and indulged in a short tour of duty as fire support ship. *Biscayne* steamed up and down the coast belching gunfire, greatly to the delight of her crew and of passenger Ernie Pyle.

The Italian defenders of Licata were completely upset by the night assault and never recovered balance. At no point did they put up stout resistance; there was no street fighting, and at every opportunity they surrendered. *Birmingham* still had a job to do on a battery located on Monte Desusino back of Beach Blue. After she had disposed of that, there were no more targets, and at 0918 Ad-

[22] Taggart p. 56.

[23] Admiral Conolly thought that this was the result of communications equipment having arrived late and drenched in LCTs, and *Wilkes* complained that she could get nothing but Italian music on her shore fire-control frequency!

miral Conolly signaled, "Hold all gunfire. Objectives taken." [24] Presently the LSTs with pontoon causeways were rigging them on Beaches Yellow and Blue for the expeditious landing of supplies; tanks were already rolling ashore over two of them at 1000. The unloading proceeded quietly and efficiently.

Licata was completely in American hands by 1130. The harbor had already been partially cleared by salvage parties landed from two patrol craft. Shortly before noon General Truscott and staff went ashore from *Biscayne* and set up command post in the Palazzo La Lumia. The port was open for LSTs and small shipping before dark.[25] Follow-up beaching craft convoys were handled over the Licata mole and quays, but the port is so small that Liberty ships were unloaded by LCTs on Beaches Yellow and Blue.

Before dark, the 3rd Division had more than attained its initial beachhead line. The 7th Regiment had good defensive positions in the hills overlooking Licata; Rangers and the 15th Regiment had taken city and airfield; the 30th Regiment had occupied Monte Desusino and other hills that threatened the right flank of JOSS Force. The Italian XII Corps was already moving forces from western Sicily to halt the advance of the 7th toward Palma, but so far the Americans had sustained few casualties, while capturing some 3000 Italian prisoners. These were "the happiest crowd you ever saw," said one officer who conducted a boatload of them to the transport which would convey them to Algiers. "Those who could speak English even joked with their GI guards, saying, 'We're going to Brooklyn – you poor guys have to stay in Sicily!' "

Although JOSS landings in Sicily can hardly compete with those on Tinian a year later for the title of the "perfect amphibious operation," as night landings they were very smooth and successful. The individual initiative in meeting unexpected situations and straightening out foul-ups was remarkable. Coöperation between

[24] *Brooklyn* Action Report; but Adm. Conolly's Report gives time as 0948.
[25] Col. A. H. Head "Notes on HUSKY."

Army and Navy could not have been better. Night landings by small craft on rough beaches were accomplished with slight delay and few casualties; the enemy was kept continually off balance; the troops captured all objectives ahead of schedule. Thus, the left flank of the entire Allied assault was secured by a bold offensive, and an ample beachhead with a feeder port was obtained for the conquest of western Sicily; and all this with minimum air support.[26]

[26] Statistics of discharge of troops, vehicles and supplies at Licata and on beaches of JOSS Area, from Seventh Army *Report of Operations* pp. E–15, 16:

	No. Troops	*No. Vehicles*	*Supplies (long tons)*
10–12 July	20,470	3,752	6,614
13–31 July	29,294	7,967	31,152
August	6,325	2,430	51,003

CHAPTER VI

The Gela Landings (DIME Force)[1]

10–13 July

1. *The Rangers' Assault on Gela*

THE GELA landings in the center of the Western Task Force sector turned out to be the most bitterly contested. Fortunately the command had been entrusted to one of the most competent, level-headed, and highly respected flag officers in the Navy, Rear Admiral John L. Hall.[2] "Jimmy" Hall (his nickname since Naval Academy days) has rugged features that remind one of the less flattering portraits of his fellow Virginian, George Washington; and he has a twinkle in his eye that Washington lacked. His immediate preparation for Operation HUSKY was of the best. Coming to Africa as chief of staff to Admiral Hewitt, he became, one

[1] CTF 81 (Rear Adm. Hall) Action Report 14 Aug. 1943, and those of his group and unit commanders and of individual ships; *Danger Forward, the History of the 1st Division*, Seventh Army *Report of Operations* and the Italian and German sources mentioned in Chapter iii footnote 1.

[2] John Lesslie Hall jr., b. Williamsburg, Va., 1891; son of a professor at the College of William and Mary, where he was graduated before entering the Naval Academy; prominent athlete in the Class of 1913. Served in battleships in World War I; Engineer Officer of destroyer *Philip* and in battleship *Pennsylvania;* "exec." and C.O. of *Schenck;* instructor at Naval Academy, 1920–22; staff duty with destroyer squadrons 1923–25; C.O. *Childs* 1928–30; three years' duty at Naval Academy; 1st Lt. of *Augusta* in Asiatic Fleet 1934–35; C.O. *Asheville* and Comdesdiv 15, 1935–37; senior course and staff duty at the War College; C.O. *Arkansas* 1940–41; staff of Com Battleships Atlantic Fleet and chief of staff to Comcrudiv 7, 1941–42. He took command of XI Amphibious Force in England in Nov. 1943 and commanded the force that landed on OMAHA Beach in the Normandy operation. Comphibgrp 12 Pacific Fleet Oct. 1944 and of the Southern Attack Force at Okinawa, 1945. After the war, Comphibforcespacfleet, Com 14th Naval District, Com Armed Forces Staff College and Com Western Sea Frontier. Retired 1953.

week after the North African landings, commander of the naval operating base and sea frontier forces at Casablanca. Since February 1943 he had become Commander Amphibious Forces Northwest African Waters, including Admiral Conolly's training command. He knew very well the capabilities of the ships and craft allotted to him as the DIME Force. These included eight big transports which carried the bulk of the 1st Infantry Division.

The 1st Infantry Division, called the "Fighting First," or "Pershing's Own," from its distinguished record in World War I, had been trained for amphibious warfare with the 1st Marine Division in 1941 and later in England under Major General Terry de la M. Allen USA, who commanded them now; Brigadier General Theodore Roosevelt jr. was the assistant division commander. They had also fought in the Tunisia campaign.

Off Gozo Admiral Hall formed DIME Force in three long columns: cruisers and transports, including Admiral Hewitt's flagship *Monrovia*, in the center; LCIs and LSTs on either flank; *Savannah* in the lead. The Admiral was so eager to make it on time that he passed the minesweepers who were supposed to sweep ahead of his disposition; fortunately the waters off Gela were not mined. The approach here was less complicated than off Licata — a British submarine five miles south of Gela, and an American destroyer five miles to seaward of her, were enough to direct the transports. These were only 20 to 30 minutes behind schedule, but two or three hours were required for the LCIs and LSTs to straggle in. Three of the latter lost their way, ending up with Admiral Kirk's force off Scoglitti.

DIME Force took station in conspiratorial silence. All hands topside, from *Monrovia's* crowded bridge to that of the lowliest subchaser, watched the fires and flares ashore, wondering what they meant. This display had been triggered off by our own bombers and paratroops. Here, and behind the British assault beaches as well, was staged the first large-scale air drop for the Allies. That type of warfare had been practised successfully by the Germans on

Crete in May 1941, but this was the first time that any army had dropped at night.

No fewer than 227 transport planes (C-47s) of Northwest Africa Troop Carrier Command flew in 3405 men of Major General Matthew B. Ridgway's 82nd Airborne Division U. S. Army, commanded by Colonel James M. Gavin USA, to be dropped inland, east of Gela. Their mission was to capture roads and high ground commanding the plain. In order to provide check points, the planes were routed east from Tunis to Malta, north to Sicily, and west along the coast until they found Lake Biviere, then north along the right bank of the Acate River to drop men at four different places short of Niscemi.

The dusk take-off from Kairouan in Tunisia went well, but high winds and want of experience caused some of the pilots to miss Malta; 25 of them mistakenly joined the British airborne force flying to the east coast, and dropped near Noto. Others were confused by the fires lighted on Sicily by the bombers who preceded them. Consequently, the Gela-bound parachutists were dispersed along 50 to 60 miles of coast. Only a part of one battalion dropped where it intended, the junction between Highway No. 115 and the Niscemi road. They blocked this road, very tenaciously; twice on D-day holding up a German tank column. One group of about a hundred troopers organized a strong point around a building described as a "château" on the south side of Niscemi, which commanded the road thence to Gela. These were a thorn in the side of the Hermann Goering Division, a whole battalion of which they ambushed on its retreat, 11 July; and, though frequently attacked, they held out until relieved on the 13th. A battalion which dropped near Cape Scarámia frightened nearby Italian troops into retreat, captured the village of Marina di Ragusa, and on D-day joined the 45th Division in taking Santa Croce Camerina.[8]

Although Sicily was the scene of the first successful air landing in history, or mythology – that of Dædalus from Crete – she

[8] Maj. Gen. James M. Gavin USA *Airborne Warfare* (1947) chap. i, with maps; Craven and Cate II 449.

had never experienced anything like troops dropping from the heavens. In the light of a setting moon, the air seemed full of parachutists; Italian prisoners estimated their numbers at between twenty and thirty thousand. Despite faulty navigation and wide dispersal, the paratroops helped greatly to demoralize the defense of Sicily.

The plan for DIME Force was relatively simple. Since the cliffy part of the coast between Manfria and Cape Soprano was topped by a number of 100-mm coast defense batteries, no landing place could be found short of Gela itself. There the Rangers planned to make the initial assault. A stretch of shore beginning a mile east of the Gela River mouth, and about 5000 yards long, was chosen for the principal landing by the 1st Division. Here the plain is very broad; one cannot see the mountains from half a mile off shore. So it was hoped that the 1st Division could organize and deploy quickly, to capture the Ponte Olivo airfield six miles inland. Unfortunately enemy dispositions had been made expressly to prevent this. The Hermann Goering Panzer Division, the Livorno Division and the Niscemi Combat Group, which included most of the Italian tanks in Sicily, were poised above the edge of the plain, ready to strike.

Gela, on a plateau 150 feet above the Mediterranean, with olive groves, vineyards and wheatfields on three sides, is one of the oldest Greek sites in Sicily. In 1943, as seen from the sea, it was a fairly imposing little chalk-gray city. Since there was no harbor, the Italian government had built a long steel pier out into the roadstead, and a winding road up the cliff to connect pier with town. The seasoned Rangers were given the tough assignment of landing on two beaches (Red and Green) on either side of the pier and right under the cliff. They were brought up in transport *Joseph T. Dickman*, manned by coastguardsmen, and in the two Belgian "Princesses." The scout boat, launched at 0044, located these beaches so quickly that *Dickman's* skipper actually found time on his hands — a unique experience in amphibious warfare. With H-hour two hours away, he proposed to delay lowering boats, in order to spare the men seasickness. Enemy searchlights playing over the waters caused him to change his mind; for where searchlights are, shore

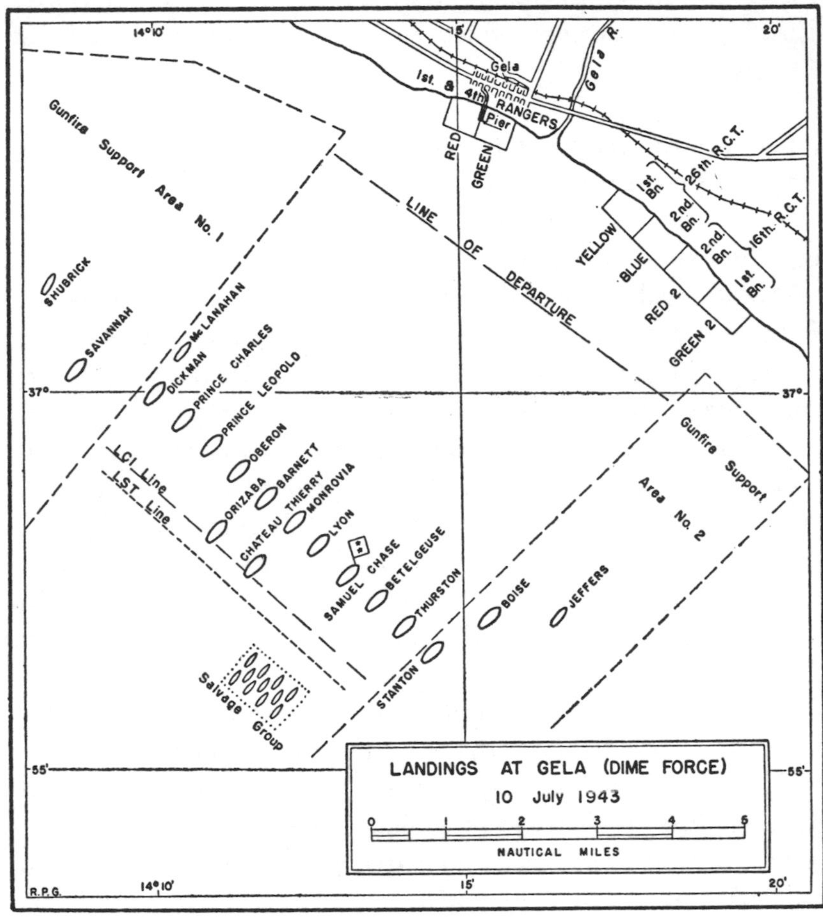

batteries should be expected. So by 0125 he had lowered 30 loaded landing craft, to which the "Princesses" shortly added 14 British LCAs.[4] The boats had to wait half an hour for their subchaser control craft to show up and lead them in. Fire support ships, as General Allen requested, kept silent as long as there seemed any

[4] Landing Craft Assault. These were 41½ feet long, ramped, took 35 troops besides crew of 4, and resembled the LCVPs of the U. S. Navy.

possibility of surprise, but at 0310 destroyer *Shubrick*, to everyone's relief, extinguished two of the more persistent searchlights.

On their way in, men in the first boat wave heard a loud explosion ashore; the central portion of Gela pier had been blown. A three-foot surf and a strong lateral set on both beaches caused some boats to broach, but the greater part landed, retracted and returned to their transports. The nimble Rangers, touching down at 0315, quickly made up for lost time. And a tough time they had, too, since Beach Red, thought to be safe because air photographs showed it to be covered with fishing boats, was heavily mined. (The boats turned out to be old hulks, which had been lying there for months.) One company lost almost an entire platoon, partly because they landed under crossfire from two pillboxes. The remainder of the company, led by a wounded first sergeant, pressed forward and captured the pillboxes. In the meantime, three companies fought their way into the center of Gela, seized the town square and set up battalion headquarters. By 0800 the whole of Gela had been cleared of organized resistance.[5]

Three LCIs carrying infantry and a motorized chemical battalion (equipped with 4.2-inch mortars) followed the Rangers' landing craft, and all but two of them grounded on the false beach. *LCI–188* managed to float off and make Beach Green, where there were very few mines – for the good reason that the civilians ordered to plant them, a few days earlier, had lost two of their number in the process and the rest had quit.[6] One LCI experienced such difficulty debarking 24 heavy carts bearing the mortars that she stayed there almost four hours, suffering many casualties from machine-gun and shell fire.[7]

Fire support ships promptly disposed of coastal batteries on the Gela water front and on the Lungo plateau, where only one piece remained intact by the afternoon. On Monte San Nicola, over

[5] Altieri *Darby's Rangers* (1945) pp. 49–50.

[6] Information from Hon. John T. Koehler, who as Lt. Cdr. Koehler USNR was "exec." of the Advanced Base Group. The widow of one of the civilian victims called on him after the landings to demand compensation for the death of her husband!

[7] Enclosures in CTG 81.4 (Capt. Leppert) Action Report 26 July.

8000 yards from the coast, a 149-mm battery held out until the afternoon of 12 July, when it was captured by troops of the 1st Division.

2. *Attack, Counterattack and Naval Gunfire, 10 July*

The Gela River mouth is marshy, but about a mile southeasterly begins a long sandy beach. A 5000-yard stretch of this — designated Beaches Yellow, Blue, Red 2 and Green 2 — was chosen for the main landings of DIME Force. Not that it was ideal for that purpose! The false beaches here are numerous, the sandy shore and the exits through sand dunes are too soft for vehicles unless covered with steel matting, landmarks are few, and the beaches had been mined. But the choice turned out to be fortunate, because the dunes protected the beaches from enemy fire and because the troops, once they had deployed along the highway, were in position to meet counterattack from the north. Also, on the cheerful side, the dunes were planted with melons, ripe and ready to refresh many a parched GI during the next few days; a delicious relief from the halazone-disinfected water from Africa supplied by the Army.

The combat-loaded transports of DIME Force began easing into their unloading area, seven miles off the beaches, precisely at midnight. Hove-to, they promptly hoisted out landing craft. A heavy swell was running parallel to the shore, but the wind had dropped, and, as the landing craft crews had been well trained, few boats were damaged. Those of *Barnett* and *Lyon*, aided by boats from the other transports, set Colonel John W. Bowen's 26th Regimental Combat Team ashore on Beaches Yellow and Blue, while the 3000 men of Colonel George A. Taylor's 16th Regimental Combat Team were put ashore on Beaches Red 2 and Green 2 from *Thurston* and *Stanton.*

Jack Belden describes the motion of the LCVP that took him ashore as "totally unlike anything we had experienced on the ship.

It pitched, rolled, swayed, bucked, jerked from side to side, spanked up and down, undulated, careened, and insanely danced on the throbbing, pulsing, hissing sea. The sea itself flew at us, threw the bow in the air, then, as it came down, swashed over us in great roaring bucketfuls of water." The first troops landed precisely at H-hour, 0245, and the men were glad to be ashore. "As they poured from the boats onto the firm, solid ground, the soldiers shed their nausea and fear as easily and as quickly as they dropped their life belts on the beach. They stamped their feet on the steady ground, and so strong was their sense of relief and release that each one of them felt a new surge of life, hope and satisfaction at a danger already past." [8]

No machine-gun or other enemy fire was received until the men had been ashore for 20 minutes. LCIs, carrying more troops, came in after the fourth assault wave, the first beaching at 0330. About half the LCIs discharged troops directly on the beach; the other half grounded on a false beach and needed the aid of LCVPs or of rubber boats. First phase of the assault ended with the successful landing of the six remaining LCIs on Green 2 at 0430, just as the first glimmer of morning twilight began. All retracted except *LCI–220*, which, after sticking on a false beach exposed to enemy shellfire, managed to make the real beach at 0500; but, having sprung a plate from a near miss, lost her stern anchor and the use of her port propeller, and broached. Captain John H. Leppert, LCI group commander, had given orders, "If any ship becomes high and dry, it is still a fighting unit as long as it has guns and is above the surface of the water." [9] Accordingly, *LCI–220* kept her guns firing until next afternoon, when bulldozers and tugs managed to pull her off.

A battalion of dukws, launched from LSTs, mostly made their objectives. Then their troubles began. The beaches were heavily mined against vehicles, and a number of dukws, trucks and bulldozers were blown up.

[8] Belden *Still Time to Die* (Harper and Bros., 1943) pp. 251, 256.
[9] Capt. J. H. Leppert Report of Operation HUSKY 26 July 1943.

Except for these contretemps, the landing of two regimental combat teams on the eastern beaches went off without a hitch. As an example of the many instances of courage and resourcefulness of the landing craft crews, one may take Thomas B. McMonagle, Seaman 2nd class, coxswain of one of *Barnett's* LCVPs. He grounded his boat at Beach Yellow in the face of machine-gun fire which so frightened the troops that they refused to land. Although badly wounded, McMonagle retracted, silenced the machine gun with his boat gun and beached his LCVP at another spot where the passengers consented to leave. On the way back to his transport he was overcome by loss of blood, but eventually recovered.[10]

Everything in this eastern sector of DIME went well until daylight, when the LSTs, endeavoring to unload tanks and heavy vehicles, got into trouble, and the enemy began to show his hand.

Although *Shubrick* had shot out a searchlight as early as 0310, Admiral Hall did not pass the word "to commence schedule of prearranged fires" until 0400. *Boise* and *Jeffers* then fell to with a will, knocking out a pillbox near the beach from which flashes were observed, and attempting to silence the batteries that were firing from inland positions.

Ships' antiaircraft batteries swung into action when the first enemy air attack, aimed principally at the ships off Scoglitti, spilled over to Gela roadstead. The planes concentrated on destroyer *Maddox*, patrolling alone about 16 miles off shore to protect the transports against submarines. At 0458, just as daylight began to spread over the sea, she was attacked by a Stuka. A bomb exploded under her starboard propeller guard, completely demolishing the stern and probably exploding the after magazine. An officer in a distant ship observed: "A great blob of light bleached and reddened the sky, tearing the night into shreds. It was followed by a blast more sullen and deafening than any we have so far heard." [11] Within two minutes *Maddox* rolled over and sank, taking down most of her

[10] *Monrovia* Action Report.
[11] John Mason Brown *To All Hands* p. 131.

crew. Beacon submarine *Safari*, on her way out, was straddled by two sticks of bombs in the same attack; unhurt, she hastened to the spot where *Maddox* had disappeared, and, in conjunction with a stray landing craft, searched for survivors, but found none. Eventually tug *Intent* recovered 9 officers and 65 enlisted men, who apparently had drifted to leeward. The destroyer's skipper, Lieutenant Commander Eugene S. Sarsfield, 7 other officers and 203 men perished.[12]

All that morning, the Axis air marshals at Rome were sending planes from Italian fields to Sardinia, there to fuel and take off to attack the invading ships. There were two bombing attacks on the Gela transport area during the afternoon of D-day, with only minor damage to destroyer *Murphy* from near-misses; and one dive-bomber attack on the beaches, which inflicted a few casualties. At nightfall a single Me–109 attacked, and, although the transports escaped, *LST–313* was destroyed, as we shall see presently. There was also a high-level bomber attack, which did no damage, at 2200.

Fortunately the aim of most of the Axis bombers was very inaccurate. The Western Task Force had virtually no air protection until 12 July. The Northwest African Tactical Air Command had provided close air support to the invasion from Pantelleria and Malta when and if needed; their own headquarters in Tunisia to decide whether or not the call should be answered. Since all estimates depended on reports sent by dispatch from Admiral Hewitt to Admiral Cunningham at Malta, and from him to Marshal Tedder at Tunis, after which tactical air headquarters had to figure out what planes could be spared and issue the orders, the need was generally obsolete by the time air cover arrived. Combat air patrol over DIME area never amounted to more than two to eight planes at any time during the first two crucial days, and for the most part none were present. These few and far-between friendlies were of slight assistance; because, in the first place, no Air Force officer embarked with Admiral Hewitt had any au-

12 *Maddox* Report 15 July 1943; Admiralty Records.

thority over them,[13] and, second, because the Army fighter-director team in *Samuel Chase* did not know its business. The fighter-director unit in *Monrovia* did a little better, but was apt to announce "Red" alerts without stating the direction from which the attackers, or their interceptors, were approaching.[14] A formation of 32 German planes once flew over the transports without any interference from Allied fighters that were supposed to be protecting them. All this time, the Air Force was giving much indirect and remote support by striking enemy airfields, which the sailors did not then appreciate.[15]

Admiral Hall, as we have seen, charged into the DIME area ahead of the minesweepers, which at 0600 started combing the waters off Gela. No mines were found, so the transports and cargo ships moved closer inshore, anchoring in 7 to 9 fathoms between 0830 and 1000. LSTs nosed hopefully in toward the broad beaches on the right flank; landing craft and subchasers plied to and fro; four SOCs, catapulted from *Boise* and *Savannah* in the early light, hovered over the Gela plain without fighter protection. Within a few minutes several fast-climbing Messerschmitts flew over from the Gerbini airdrome and beat them back. Lieutenant C. A. Anderson, *Savannah's* senior aviator, was killed in flight; his radioman, Edward J. True, skilfully landed the riddled plane on the sea, only to have it sink immediately. He was rescued. *Savannah's* second plane also splashed and sank. Captain R. W. Cary, the ship's commanding officer, sent his two remaining planes into the air at 0827. One was shot down by German fighters and the other was driven off.[16] Lieutenant C. G. Lewis USNR, in one of *Boise's* planes, radioed, "Two Messerschmitts on my tail, stand by to pick me up." And, a

13 He had an Air Force colonel, with authority only to transmit requests for air support, on board *Monrovia*.

14 *Monrovia* Action Report p. 6.

15 Adm. Hall Action Report, Annex D, p. 5. Craven and Cate II 451–2 admit the above reasons for poor air support, plus "heavy commitments to fighter escort for bombing missions."

16 *Savannah* Action Report 19 July 1943, Enclosure E.

few moments later, "Belay that, they've gone back for reinforcements!"

This same Lieutenant Lewis, at 0830, reported tanks and vehicles lumbering south down the Niscemi–Priolo–Gela road. General Guzzoni had set this counterattack in motion before dawn, in the hope of wiping out the Gela beachhead. He ordered the Goering Panzer Division to take part. The western column of it moved very slowly, checked by the paratroops and delayed by breakdowns. It left the entire onus of the counterattack in this sector on the Italian Niscemi Mobile Group, which had about 32 ten-ton Renault tanks, 16 tiny three-tonners, and a few still smaller Fiats of World War I vintage.[17] These approached Gela by two different roads. At 0900, Lieutenant Lewis observed some of them about three miles from the coastal highway. Before being chased away by two Me–109s, Lewis passed coördinates of the tanks' position to *Boise* with a request for one-turret salvos. The first salvo hit, at 0910; and for two minutes *Boise* fired as rapidly as possible with one turret. "Had we only known what we were shooting at," said Captain Thébaud, "we would have cut loose with the whole 15-gun battery." [18] That stopped this column. At the same time, or a little earlier, a naval liaison officer with a shore fire-control party called for gunfire from destroyer *Jeffers*, which delivered 19 salvos on the same road from Niscemi.

Destroyer *Shubrick* had been shooting furiously since 0830 at another procession of 25 light Italian tanks moving down the road from Ponte Olivo. Her fire was directed by an efficient shore fire-control party, which credited her with knocking out three tanks and slowing down the rest. Nine or ten of the 25 actually reached Gela, entered the town about 1030, and acted in a timid and uncertain manner – obviously not trained for street fighting. The Rangers fought them from rooftops and alleyways with bazookas, dynamite charges and one 37-mm antitank gun.

[17] Special Report by Historical Office of General Staff Italian Army.

[18] Capt. Thébaud and his gunnery officer inspected the place about 14 July and saw the destroyed tanks lying about. The range was about 10,000 yards from the ship

Two were knocked out by rockets, one surrendered, and the rest withdrew after having spent only 20 minutes in the town.[19]

On the right flank the 16th Regiment moved easily along the coastal highway, and at about 0700 reached the junction with the dirt road to Niscemi. It then searched for the American paratroops who were supposed to have been dropped there around midnight, and at 0842 it found a group of them near Priolo, valiantly engaging ten Italian tanks. This reinforcement was opportune, because the Italian mobile group had begun to commit the rest of its tanks; but the 16th was forced back to the road junction, around which there was bitter fighting during the rest of D-day.

Returning to the fire support ships, we find that *Boise* and *Jeffers* had been shooting not only at tanks but at shore batteries whose fire was so heavy as to interdict use of the landing beaches for short periods. Admiral Hall ordered *Boise* to close the beach and knock out a battery that was enfilading the troops there. She closed to 3000 yards, located the guns behind a sand dune and silenced them. Brigadier General Clift Andrus of the divisional artillery, who was about 500 yards from the target, reports that the effect was terrific. In the meantime Admiral Hewitt had ordered H.M.S. *Abercrombie* to move over from CENT Force to assist DIME. She was asked first to fire on Niscemi, eight statute miles inland, which was known to be an Axis observation post and strong point. Captain Faulkner, her C.O., was so eager to help that he actually shifted ballast to obtain higher elevation for his 15-inch guns. Next day, when Niscemi was captured, it was found that the monitor had hit enemy headquarters.

Boise's two planes gamely returned to scour the land for tanks, and detected some that were moving down the Niscemi road. Both planes were damaged and forced out to sea by vigilant German fighters, as was *Savannah's* sole surviving SOC. Captain Thébaud, skipper of *Boise*, decried the use of cruiser spotting

[19] Altieri *Darby's Rangers* p. 50, checked by conversations with Lt. Col. Roy A. Murray and Capt. H. Avedon of the Rangers in 1953, and by 1st and 4th Ranger Reports.

planes without fighter protection. His planes managed to get back only, he said, because they were "flown by pilots of great skill, determination and courage." [20]

All day the big transports were busy discharging cargo by landing craft and dukws. Admiral Hewitt left in minesweeper *Steady* at 1015 to inspect the other two areas under his command, and returned to *Monrovia* at 1925.

Tank and air attacks were not the only things that slowed up the troops' advance. Beach congestion and unloading the LSTs were perhaps the most serious problems in Admiral Hall's force.[21]

3. *Troubles of the LSTs,*[22] *10–11 July*

Owing to the early morning counterattacks, General Terry Allen urgently needed more tanks, vehicles and heavy guns to support his troops. These, with few exceptions, were in the LSTs – and there was hardly a spot in the DIME area where an LST could land vehicles directly onto the beach. Since it had been assumed that Gela pier would be available, only three pontoon causeways had been provided, and these were not enough. No LSTs were supposed to beach until scouts had located the gaps in the false

[20] *Boise* Report on Shore Bombardment, Gela Area, 6 Aug. 1943 p. 1. Compared with the brilliant performance of cruiser-based aircraft in the invasion of Morocco, the Sicilian experience was a distinct shock to the Navy; but French opposition there was not comparable to that of the Axis. The vulnerability of SOCs was so clearly demonstrated in the Sicilian invasion that Admiral Hewitt wished to abandon the type; but Rear Adm. Davidson stood up for it and the debate went on in planning circles until the invasion of Southern France.

[21] Altogether 23,161 troops were landed at Gela and on the beaches 10–12 July, and 12,214 more during the rest of the month. Of supplies, 3351 long tons were landed 10–12 July, and 31,959 more during the rest of the month, mostly at the town pier after it had been repaired. Vehicles numbering 1464 were landed 10–12 July, and 4383 during the rest of the month. The port was closed 7 August except for tankers, as the Army Engineers had in the meantime laid pipelines from the pier to the Cómiso and Biscari airfields. Seventh Army *Report of Operations* pp. E-15, 16.

[22] Adm. Hall's Action Report; CTG 81.3 (Cdr. W. D. Wright) Action Report 3 Aug. 1943; CTU 81.2.3 (Capt. R. A. Dierdorff) "Report of Landing Combat Team 16 near Gela, July 9–12, 1943," July 18; Action Reports of the LSTs, especially *LST-344* (Lt. R. B. Hensley).

beaches and the best spots for rigging causeways; but demands for tanks and vehicles were so insistent that as early as 0633 Admiral Hall ordered *LST-337* and *LST-338*, each carrying a pontoon causeway, to go right in. He did not know that the first-named had missed her destination in the darkness and at that time was about nine miles away, off Scoglitti. Thus the whole LST unloading problem devolved upon *LST-338*. In she went to Beach Red 2, and at 0803 began the dangerous task of rigging her causeway amid falling shells and against a strong current. Three Me-109s tried skip-bombing the LSTs at 1000, but all their bombs missed. *LST-338* had unloaded her 63 vehicles and 300 troops by 1030, when *LST-344* took her place at the causeway and began to discharge. Two or more 88-mm guns were firing on her all this time, but made not one direct hit.

Here, as on most of the Sicilian beaches, the sand was too soft for wheeled vehicles to negotiate. That had been anticipated in the planning. Bulldozers were landed from LCTs towing "sleds" loaded with sections of prefabricated beach mat. Six sleds could carry 400 yards of this metal track, which made a fairly good roadway on the beaches and over the exits between sand dunes.[23]

Most of the unloading of Army artillery was done by 140 Army-driven dukws, launched from the ramps of the LSTs. This was the first time dukws had been used to bring artillery ashore ready for immediate action. Everyone was pleased with their performance; too well pleased, in fact, since once they had reached a supply dump they were apt to be diverted by Army officers to land trucking. Dukws were capable of carrying a load of three tons only; they would have been swamped by any tank. Sherman tanks, if they could not roll ashore directly from LSTs, had to be lightered in by LCTs or LCMs.

The late afternoon scene on Beach Red 2 is vividly described by Jack Belden: —

> From one end to the other the beach provided an astounding spectacle. Tiny infantry landing craft were coming in all up and down the

[23] Col. A. H. Head "Notes on HUSKY."

sea front, and other larger boats were edging toward the shore to swell the monstrous and ever-growing heap of beached matériel. There was an endless, confused mass of men, of tiny jeeps, huge, highsided dukws and more jeeps and heavily loaded trucks, stuck and straining in the thick sand or moving clumsily on the wire netting that the engineers had already laid down in some places as a road. . . . From every conceivable direction there was the roar of motors, the sound of spinning wheels, the puttering of incoming craft, the buzzing of planes overhead, shouts of drivers, the curses of soldiers, mechanics, gun crewmen and officers. In the surf at the edge of the beach I saw abandoned trucks, overturned jeeps and smashed boats, and on the sands there were blown-up cars, a tank with its tread off, heaps of bedding rolls and baggage with soldiers sitting on them waiting for transportation, mechanics struggling over broken-down vehicles, and supply troops gathering up broken-open boxes of rations. Where the wire-screen road had not been laid down, the crush of men, vehicles and guns became greater, and there sounded a ceaseless roar of shouts, curses and anguished straining machinery. Trucks, floundering to their hubcaps in the sand, futilely raced their engines as jeeps, jerking this way and that, tried to pull them out and soldiers put their backs against the trucks and heaved. . . .[24]

"An inadequate labor force for unloading was the chief bottleneck."[25] There was nobody here with the voice and energy of the famous Commander "Squeaky" Anderson, who had resolved many a "snafu" in similar situations on Pacific beaches. Officers of the naval beach party and the Army Engineers shore party rode up and down in jeeps bellowing orders which made slight impression amid the uproar; but traffic did slowly move inland, because the first object of every soldier was to get off the beach and out from under enemy fire.

At 1835, just as the sun was setting, an Me-109 bomber, approaching low from the direction of the sun, picked on *LST-313*, which was helping *LST-311* to rig a pontoon causeway on Beach

[24] Belden *Still Time to Die* p. 267.

[25] Gen. Eisenhower Dispatch p. 47. The Army's insistence on making naval beach parties part of the army shore parties resulted in the beach parties, generally commanded by a naval lieutenant, being "pushed around" by senior army officers so that they were unable to perform effectively their proper function of routing and directing the landing craft.

Green 2. No. *313* carried well-gassed trucks, jeeps, half-tracks and ambulances, together with 37-mm guns, ammunition and land mines. One bomb, exploding below the tank deck, turned this craft into a raging inferno and deathtrap; burning fragments of trucks rained all around. Several brave soldiers and sailors swam out to the ship's bow – fortunately her ramp was down – and passed wounded men ashore. Another courageous rescue was made by *LST–311*. Her skipper, Lieutenant Robert L. Coleman USNR, abandoned the pontoon causeway (blown apart by the bombing), swung his ship around and placed her bow, with a section of the pontoon attached, against the stern of burning *LST–313*. By this fine feat of shiphandling the young reservist saved about eighty men trapped on the fantail of the perishing vessel. A score of soldiers and one sailor were killed, and many guns and vehicles destroyed.[26]

The situation on the eastern beaches was bad when darkness fell. Only three LSTs had been fully unloaded. Pontoon units strewn along the beach were impossible to get at, owing to ammunition exploding in the abandoned *LST–313*. Fully loaded *LST–312*, which had broached on the beach, was showered by shell fragments from her sister ship.

During the greater part of D-day KOOL Force, the floating reserve consisting of the 18th RCT of the 1st Division and two combat teams of the 2nd Armored, in transports *Orizaba* and *Chateau Thierry* and eleven beaching craft, lay in the roadstead near flagship *Monrovia.* General Patton decided in the early afternoon to commit this reserve. Owing to beach congestion and to the sending of the order by roundabout Army channels instead of through the Admiral, the movement did not begin until 1800. Surf and the false beach made it impossible to get any tanks ashore on D-day; and, although many vehicles and supplies were landed, the movement stalled around 0200 July 11 because men of the shore

[26] *LST Reports of Damage to 7 Dec. 1943;* War Damage Report No. 46, Sept. 1, 1944, p. 67; *Danger Forward: Story of the 1st Division in World War II* (1947) pp. 103–4; conversations with Capt. Thomas E. Bennett USA, assistant division operations officer, one of those who rescued people from *LST–313*.

party and the beach party alike, completely fagged out after working round the clock, began dropping off to sleep. After sunrise the landing of KOOL Force was resumed and 62 tanks were put ashore on 11 July. Only five of them, however, came up from the beach in time to meet the enemy tanks, and they were too short of ammunition to engage.[27]

That night, 10–11 July, was an anxious one for all responsible officers. The Gela beaches were so congested that many landing craft had to return to their ships fully loaded; others that did beach swamped through open ramps, because nobody would help their own exhausted crews to unload. Many officers were wondering whether they could hold on to the beachhead. The enemy had almost full control of the air; only good luck and inaccurate bombing saved other ships from the fate of *Maddox* and *LST–313*. The cruisers' float planes could not spot for more than a few minutes without fighter-plane protection, which they could not obtain from the A.A.F. A renewal of tank counterattacks at daylight was certain, but how could they be met? There was slight prospect of getting tanks ashore with the pier destroyed, only one pontoon causeway operating, and false beaches holding up LSTs. Unless more tanks and heavy guns got ashore promptly, or the naval vessels produced a miracle in gunfire support, Axis armor might well force the 1st Division off the beaches. As at Tarawa, "the issue was in doubt" until well on into D-day plus 1.

4. *Navy Stops Tanks, 11 July*

That day opened fair for the weather men,[28] but dismally for the invaders. At 0635 twelve Italian bombers from Sardinia made for the transports, which hastily weighed anchor and scattered. *Bar-*

[27] "Historical Record Operations 2nd Armored Division 22 Apr.–25 July 1943" (5 Aug.) p. 5; conversation with Lt. Col. Charles P. Stone USA.

[28] Light airs from the NW, rising to force 3 at 0700; the wind veered again to the north in the afternoon, and from then on the invasion forces enjoyed fair weather. The temperature ranged from 68° to 75° F. on the 11th, and clouds never covered more than one third of the sky.

nett took a near-miss so close on her port bow as to kill seven soldiers and start a fire in the hold. And there were now plenty more targets for the enemy, because at 0815 the first follow-up convoy of seven Liberty ships and three minelayers, escorted by four destroyers, arrived. Minecraft *Keokuk*, *Salem* and *Weehawken*, starting about noon, planted an anti-submarine minefield about Gela roadstead.[29]

Air cover was again absent; early morning mists over Pantelleria were the excuse for A.A.F. fighter planes not taking off at dawn. General Eisenhower ordered the British Spitfires based at Malta to provide air cover for the Western Naval Task Force;[30] but the effect of this order was not felt until 13 July, when enemy aircraft laid off the Americans and began to concentrate on the nearer British forces.

Savannah and *Boise* remained watchfully on the scene; destroyers *Butler* and *Glennon* came in at 0530 to relieve *Shubrick* and *Jeffers*, which had almost exhausted their 5-inch ammunition. Owing to the activities of enemy fighter planes on D-day, the United States cruisers had no SOCs to spot for them; and so they did not learn promptly that tanks of the Hermann Goering Panzer Division were rolling down two roads to Gela, south from Niscemi and west from Biscari.[31] This was a resumption of the counterattack ordered by General Guzzoni on D-day, in which the Germans had not participated. The western group, which the Germans called Combat Group Right, came in contact with American troops on the plain, about two miles south of Ponte Olivo airfield, at 0700. But naval gunfire was not called in for over an hour and a half. What were the shore fire-control parties doing? Nobody seemed to know.[32]

Combat Group Right fanned out into units of two to three tanks with infantry support, some coming down the open plain between

[29] *Brooklyn* and *Woolsey* blundered into this field on 14 July but were not badly damaged.

[30] Butcher *My Three Years with Eisenhower* p. 360.

[31] See insert on the double-page chart of this area.

[32] The suggestion has been made that smoke from burning wheatfields obscured the targets.

the Niscemi and Ponte Olivo roads, some down the Niscemi road itself. At 0640 they began shooting at an advance patrol of the 26th Regiment which was approaching the Ponte Olivo airfield.

Brigadier General Theodore Roosevelt, at the battalion command post east of Gela, phoned General Allen at the divisional command post behind Beach Green 2, "Terry – look! The situation is not very comfortable out here. . . . 3rd Battalion has been penetrated. . . . No antitank protection. If we could get that company of medium tanks it sure would help." [33]

The situation as to tanks and antitank weapons was serious indeed. All antitank guns of the 26th RCT had been lost in the burning of *LST–313*. During the previous night and early morning, Army artillery had been coming ashore in dukws, but tanks had to be landed directly from LSTs, or lightered ashore from them by the "married" LCT method. Although pontoon units were badly damaged and scattered, Commander Wright managed to get two causeways operating by 0800 July 11, in order to enable LSTs to resume the unloading of 2nd Armored Division tanks. These tanks did not start to roll ashore until 1130; and as neither Navy beachmaster nor Army shore party was promptly informed of the desperate need for their service, an hour or more was wasted in de-waterproofing. By exception, *LCT–197* took five tanks off an LST of the KOOL Force at 1025 and rushed them in to Beach Blue; they went straight into action without waiting to de-waterproof, but soon ran out of ammunition. The rest, too late to get into the fight, were posted on the shore side of the dunes "to engage the enemy in case of further penetration." [34]

Thus the main burden of defeating the German tanks fell on the Navy, and on divisional artillery. Shortly before 0830 came the first call for naval gunfire. *Savannah*, first to respond, put 24 rounds around several tanks reported to be on the Ponte Olivo road only two miles from Gela, and at 0902 shifted to another group

[33] *Danger Forward* p. 105; Hq 26th RCT Reports After Action Against Enemy, 10 Aug. 1943, S–1 Journal; Patton *War As I Knew It* p. 54.

[34] Cdr. W. D. Wright Report pp. 4–5; "Hist. Record Operations 2nd Armored Division" p. 5.

rolling down to support them, less than a mile farther up the road. Then she shifted to the Butera road, down which infantry was pouring, and took care of that until 1700. Destroyer *Glennon* got the word that her gunfire was wanted at 0847: "Enemy counter-attack, need all support available." She obliged with 193 rounds of 5-inch shell on the Niscemi road. By 0930 some of the German tanks were on the plain within four miles of Gela, all headed toward the beaches. General Patton, who had just come ashore from *Monrovia*, intended to visit 1st Division headquarters on Highway 115, but decided to pay a call on Colonel Darby first. He found the Ranger commander triggering a captured Italian fieldpiece in the direction of Italian tanks which were advancing on Gela down the Ponte Olivo road. The General decided to occupy the Rangers' observation post in one of the taller buildings of Gela, which had an unobstructed view of the plain. Seeing the Italian tanks even nearer, he broke out into a more than ordinary torrent of expletives. A young naval ensign in the building, who had a walkie-talkie radio, said "Can I help you, Sir?" "Sure, if you can connect with your —— —— Navy, tell them for —— sake to drop some shellfire on that road." Miraculously the ensign was able to get cruiser *Boise*, which began shooting at 1040. The result of her 38 rounds of 6-inch was devastating to the tanks, and General Patton's conversion to the value of naval gunfire support dates from that moment.[35]

We do not claim that the Navy did it all! Two field artillery battalions, carried by dukws right off the ships, moved to the crest of the dunes, fought the tanks at ranges down to 500 yards, and expended their last shells. The command post of the 18th Regiment was forced back from a position north of the highway to the railroad. Tank shells fell on the beaches, killing men and smashing equipment;[36] the Germans afterward claimed they could have

[35] Told to me by Vice Adm. Jerauld Wright, 1953. Bob Landry's *Life* photo shows the scene as Gen. Patton saw it.

[36] *LST–2* Action Report 20 July 1943 p. 9, and conversation with Capt. William Friedman, transport QM of 26th Regiment; "History of 531st Engineer Shore Regiment, year 1943."

KEY TO NAVAL GUNFIRE SUPPORT ON GELA CHART, JULY 1943

No. in Chart	*Ship*	*Time*	*Rounds*	*Target*
		10 July		
1	SAVANNAH	0806–0915	126	Italian tanks
	SHUBRICK	0830–0920	100	
2	JEFFERS	0842–1512	184	Italian tanks
	BOISE	0910–1255	162	
		11 July		
3	GLENNON	0847–0957	193	German tanks
		2025–2057	165	
	BOISE	1102–1611	48	
4	SAVANNAH	0829–0843	24	German tanks
		0902–0909	15	
5	BOISE	1040–1130	38	German tanks
6	BUTLER	1316–1324	48	
7	BEATTY	0738–1047	799	German tanks close support of troops
	LAUB	1100–1225	408	
		1547–1711	343	
	COWIE	1112–1521	200	
	TILLMAN	1813–1855	46	
8	SAVANNAH	0917–1231	474	Italian infantry
		1621–1928	393	
		12 July		
9	BOISE	0719–0732	5	Retreating tanks and troops
		1635–2048	96	
10	SAVANNAH	0740–1246	519	Enemy infantry
		1445–1456	21	Butera
		1659–1721	60	Enemy infantry
11	BOISE	0913–0957	107	Retreating tanks and troops

done far more damage if the beaches had not been hidden from sight by sand dunes.

At 1100 came the crisis. All the small groups of tanks which had fanned across the plain were approaching Highway 115, apparently intending to cross it and wipe up the landing beaches. The Gela plain became an arena of free-for-all battle. *Savannah*, *Boise*, *Glennon* and *Butler* anxiously awaited calls for gunfire, but none came; friend and foe were too closely intermingled. General Pat-

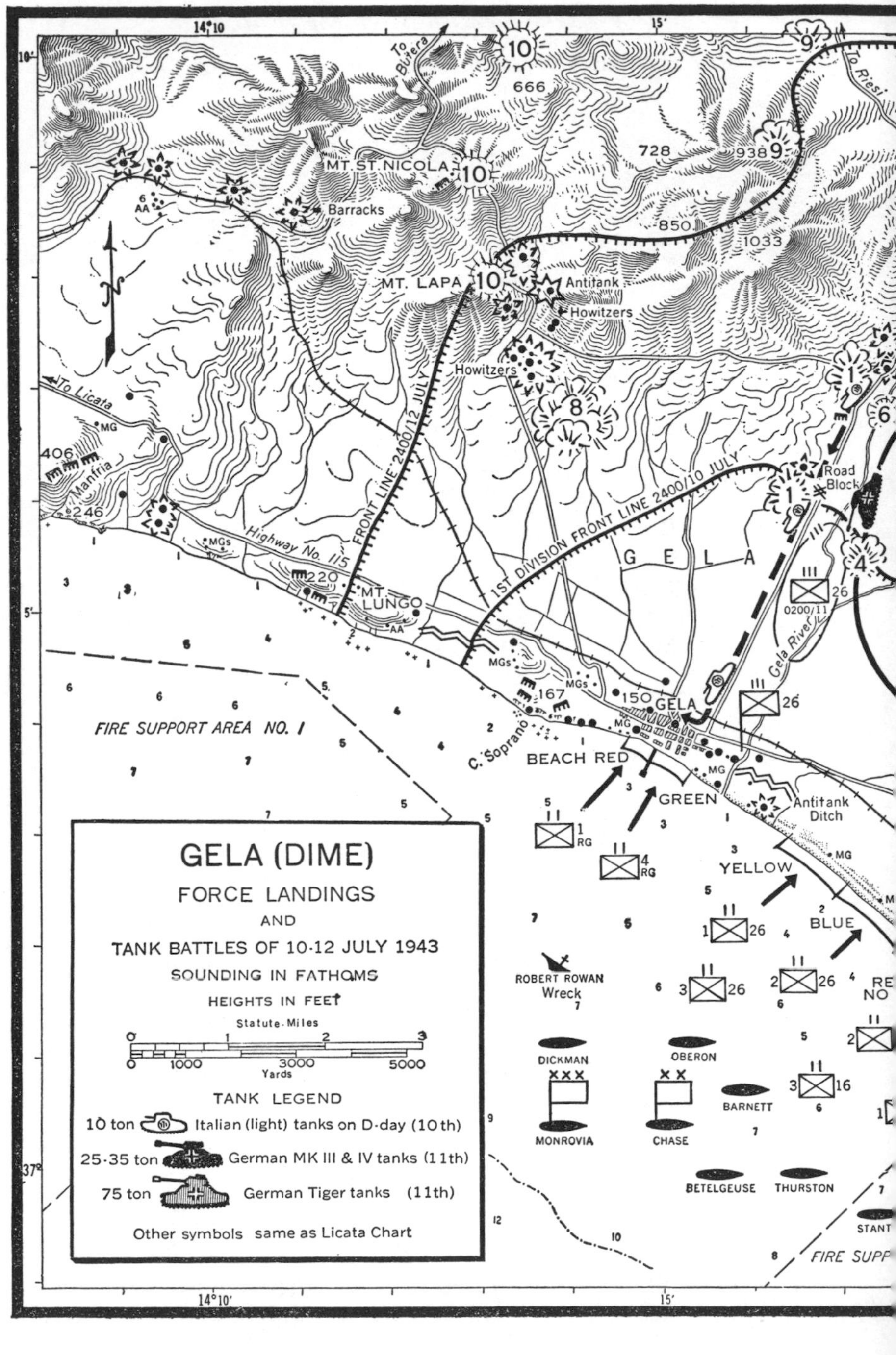
GELA (DIME)
FORCE LANDINGS
AND
TANK BATTLES OF 10-12 JULY 1943
SOUNDING IN FATHOMS
HEIGHTS IN FEET
Statute Miles
Yards
TANK LEGEND
10 ton Italian (light) tanks on D-day (10th)
25-35 ton German MK III & IV tanks (11th)
75 ton German Tiger tanks (11th)
Other symbols same as Licata Chart
MT. ST. NICOLA
Barracks
MT. LAPA
Antitank
Howitzers
Howitzers
To Butera
To Riesi
To Licata
Manfria
Highway No. 115
FRONT LINE 2400/12 JULY
1ST DIVISION FRONT LINE 2400/10 JULY
MT. LUNGO
GELA
Road Block
Gela River
C. Soprano
BEACH RED
GREEN
YELLOW
BLUE
Antitank Ditch
FIRE SUPPORT AREA NO. I
ROBERT ROWAN Wreck
DICKMAN
OBERON
MONROVIA
CHASE
BARNETT
BETELGEUSE
THURSTON
14°10′
15′
37°

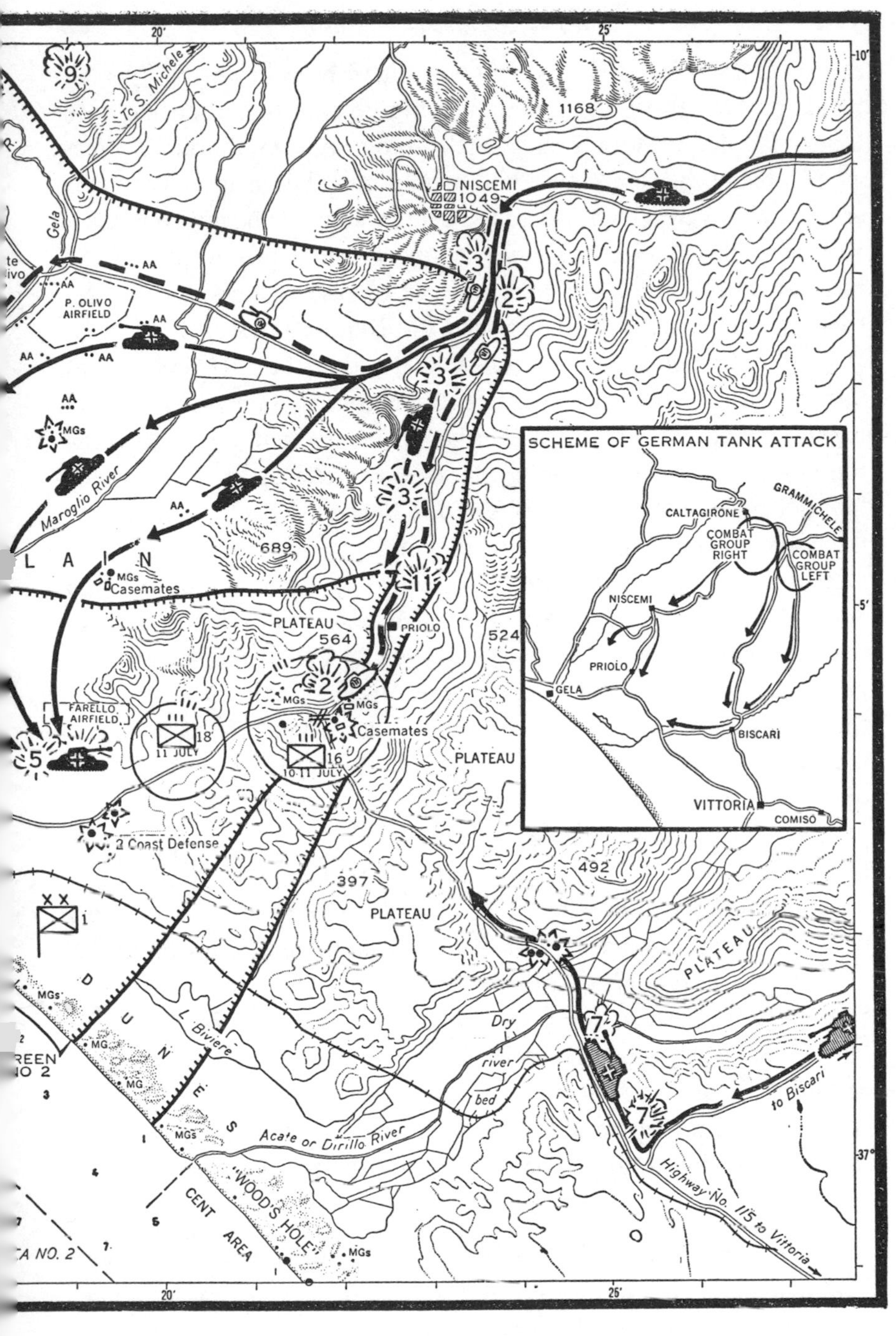

SCHEME OF GERMAN TANK ATTACK
CALTAGIRONE
GRAMMICHELE
COMBAT GROUP RIGHT
COMBAT GROUP LEFT
NISCEMI
PRIOLO
GELA
BISCARI
VITTORIA
COMISO
NISCEMI 1049
1168
Tc S. Michele
Gela
P. OLIVO AIRFIELD
AA
MGs
Maroglio River
689
PLATEAU
564
524
PRIOLO
Casemates
FARELLO AIRFIELD
11 JULY
18
10-11 JULY
16
PLATEAU
2 Coast Defense
492
397
PLATEAU
PLATEAU
L Biviere
Dry river bed
Acate or Dirillo River
to Biscari
Highway No. 115 to Vittoria
"WOOD'S HOLE"
CENT AREA
MG
20'
25'
10'
5'
37°

ton in Gela ordered the Navy's advanced base group to "get all hands up here to fight." Up they came, to find that they were no longer wanted.[87] With a tank battle going on a few hundred yards away, this naval base group had a wild day; but neither they nor anyone else were given orders to reëmbark, as the enemy reported. In this battle, 14 German tanks in one group were destroyed. As the rest retired, the Navy was allowed to resume firing on the retreating enemy, and this continued until late afternoon.[88]

While the battle raged east of Gela, the 16th Regiment was fighting on the Niscemi road with a column of German Mark III (20-ton) and IV (30-ton) Panther tanks, which penetrated infantry units unable to stop them. At 1105 the order was passed: "Under no circumstances will anyone be pulled back. Take cover from tanks, but don't let anything else get through." The men were cut off, fighting in isolated groups. Only two out of nine antitank guns remained. Naval gunfire helped here too, starting with a shoot by *Glennon* at 0847. *Boise* at 1119 fired on another group that had just started south from Niscemi. Shortly after noon the long-sought-for cannon company, with a few Sherman tanks, moved directly into action from the beach, helped to destroy ten to fifteen enemy tanks and drove off the rest.[39] *Boise* sped the departing tanks with 18 rounds of 6-inch laid down on the upper part of the road.

She also hastened the departure of a distinguished witness to this battle, General von Senger und Etterlin, German liaison officer at Sixth Army headquarters and commander of all German troops in Sicily. He had driven down from Enna to a bare hill five miles behind Beach Blue; and as he looked out over the sea on the spectacle of hundreds of ships all around the horizon, and the multitude of landing craft plying to and fro, he concluded that nothing could stop the invasion; only a delaying action was practicable.[40]

[87] Conversation with Lt. Cdr. John T. Koehler USNR, "exec." of this group.

[88] Conversations with Lt. Col. J. K. Rippert, Operations Officer 26th Regiment, and Capt. Crawford.

[39] 16th Regiment S-1 Journal, sheets 6 and 7, and Reports After Action p. 5.

[40] "Battle of Sicily" p. 64 of translation.

All in all, this was a memorable battle. "The manipulation of the fire from six ships, four organic field artillery battalions and three infantry cannon companies, was a sight never to be forgotten," wrote a participant. "There was close coördination between the fire-direction center on board flagship *Samuel Chase* and division artillery headquarters. The fact that none of our troops were hit by this volume of fire coming from the south, east, west and northeast attests the excellence of the fire control system and the accuracy of the observers and gun crews." [41]

During the afternoon and evening, gunfire support ships supplied abundant call fire, chiefly on the rolling country west of the Gela River. *Butler* at 1316 fired 48 rounds on a tank concentration, which was a regrouping after the morning repulse. *Boise*, moving in close to the beach with leadsmen in the chains taking soundings, shot up targets around Ponte Olivo and ended her day's work with salvos on Niscemi, eight miles inland. *Savannah* at 1700 helped the Rangers to repel an Italian infantry attack, which came down the road from Butera. *Glennon* closed the day with 165 rounds in support of the 16th Regiment on the right flank. At 2057 her shore fire-control party signaled "Cease fire, good shooting!" since darkness had closed over the Gela plain.

Shooting like this wrung a bitter threat from a retreating colonel of the Hermann Goering Division: "Naval gunfire forced us to withdraw, but if the Allies pursue too far inland they will be engaged by superior German forces and destroyed!" [42] The Oberst planted this naïve message with some Sicilian farmers in the hope that it would intimidate the 1st Infantry Division when they came along! Closer to the truth was a captured order from Major General Conrath, commanding the Goering Division, to rally his men; he admitted that these choice members of the Master Race were spreading false rumors, throwing away supplies and equipment, and "running to the rear hysterically crying." The division had lost

[41] Maj. Gen. Clift Andrus USA (who then commanded 1st Div. Artillery). Letter to Mr. Pineau 13 Dec. 1953.

[42] Lt. Col. R. W. Porter USA, (1st Div. Intelligence Officer) "Messages to Accompany S-1 Journal, 16th Regiment, July 10 to 16."

30 officers, 600 men, and between 40 and 50 tanks, but still had 45 tanks intact.[43]

Naval gunfire here, as on the other Sicilian beachheads, was of such high quality as to wean high-placed Army officers from their ancient prejudice against this form of support: "So devastating in its effectiveness," wrote the Supreme Commander, "as to dispose finally of any doubts that naval guns are suitable for shore bombardment. Modern guns in cruisers and destroyers," he observed, "are of high angle, capable of ranging on reverse slopes and on targets inland. The fire power of vessels assigned to gunfire support exceeded that of the artillery landed in the assaults, and the mobility of the ships permitted a greater concentration of fire than artillery could achieve in the initial stages." [44]

Naval gunfire was resumed on 12 July. At 0740 *Savannah* fired 519 rounds of 6-inch, range 23,000 yards, in support of Rangers advancing toward Butera. *Boise* dropped 255 rounds in front of our troops headed north of Ponte Olivo, toward Piazza Armerina, over eight miles inland.

With the exception of a few shoots at Guadalcanal, this was the first time that the Navy had given prompt and effective gunfire support to troops engaged in a purely land battle.[45] It had often covered landings, but heretofore enemy troops and tanks had not been accepted as suitable targets for naval bombardment. And, it is important to remember, this close coördination of fire, the Army using naval guns afloat just as if they had been corps artillery, was not an improvisation. It had been carefully planned in North Africa between 1st Division Artillery and the staff of Admiral Hall, who

[43] *Danger Forward* pp. 108–10; "The Sicilian Campaign. Information from German Sources" p. 12, and count from unit reports.

[44] Eisenhower Dispatch pp. 45–6. And Gen. Patton in his "Notes on Sicilian Campaign" says, "In daytime, Navy gunfire support is of immeasurable value, and the means now developed by the Navy for putting it on are extremely efficient."

[45] Royal Navy had given 1st Division some support near Oran, and United States Navy had given 3rd Division some support at Mehedia, in Operation TORCH, Nov. 1942 (see Vol. II pp. 117–18), but, owing to lack of shore fire-control parties and apprehension of misdirected fire, this support was sparingly, even fearfully, called for, and was of comparatively slight effect. The Navy had worked out this system with the Marine Corps, and it had been in the Navy manuals since 1938; but the Army would have none of it until 1943.

told his officers that "their job was to get the Army where it wants to go, and when it wants to get there, and then to support it as far as we can shoot." Navy shore fire-control parties practised with artillery ashore, and artillery officers lived on board ship, so each arm understood the other's language; and the divisional gunnery officer shared an office with the task force gunnery officer on board flagship *Samuel Chase*. But in every case the Army ashore called the tune – no more wild firing on "targets of opportunity." It all worked out exactly as planned. Thus, this tank battle on the Gela plain is a milestone in the development of naval gunfire support, and a shining example of Army–Navy coöperation.

It may be said that the tank counterattack was defeated in the nick of time. General Guzzoni, in the early hours of D-day, had ordered two combat teams of the 15th Panzer Grenadier Division to make all haste from western Sicily to the Gela plain. They arrived at the 1st Division front on the 12th, but by that time the battered Livorno and Goering Divisions were moving east, where Guzzoni planned to use them to defend the Catania plain against the British Eighth Army.[46]

5. *Beachhead Secured, 11–13 July*

Beach conditions improved during 11 July; Army shore parties turned to, Navy beachmasters managed to control the situation, and by using LCTs and one rebuilt pontoon causeway, all LSTs finished unloading by 1600 when the crisis had passed.[47]

Ships' war diaries are crowded with notes of air raids on the 11th, some of great ferocity and well coördinated with the attacking tanks. Between two and three dozen Ju–88s bombed the transport area at 1540 and hit Liberty ship *Robert Rowan* of the first follow-up convoy. Fire-fighting efforts failed, her cargo of

[46] Gen. Faldella in *Roma* 17 July 1953.

[47] Comtransdiv 3 (Capt. Edgar) Action Report 23 July p. 5; Cdr. W. D. Wright Report p. 4. All LSTs left for Tunis at 1100 July 12, for reloads.

ammunition started to explode, and the ship was abandoned without loss of a single life. She exploded in a single shattering detonation at 1702 and burned for hours, resting on the bottom in shallow water.

The saddest event of this day was an attempted parachute drop. In late afternoon, Admiral Hewitt was informed by Tactical Air Force headquarters in Tunisia that the 52nd Troop Carrier Wing would fly 144 transport planes into the combat zone that evening, to drop paratroops on an emergency airstrip near Gela, the Farello.[48]

There was a mad scramble to alert all ships and antiaircraft batteries ashore, but it was too late to pass the word to everyone. It seemed incredible that the Air Force would lay on so hazardous a flight at low level — over an assault area heavily committed in combat, where enemy raids had been frequent for two days — and for no sound purpose.[49] The course that the planes were ordered to take "followed the actual battle front for about 35 miles; and the antiaircraft gunners on ship and shore had been conditioned by two days of air attack to shoot at sight." [50] And what if an enemy air raid were taking place when the transport planes arrived? Nobody seems to have thought of that.

That night, 11–12 July, was hellish in appearance and in fact. A heavy pall of smoke from burning *Robert Rowan* hung over the water, a perfect shield for enemy bombers against antiaircraft fire; and the light from her fires silhouetted the ships in the roadstead. As if to avenge their stinging repulse on the ground that day, the

[48] Message logged on board *Ancon*, which Adm. Hewitt was visiting at the time, at 1747.

[49] "The decision to mount this operation was not reached until the day it was to be carried out, and insufficient time was allowed for warning the naval vessels along the route." *Participation of the IX and XII Air Forces in the Sicilian Campaign*, Army Air Forces Historical Studies No. 37, Nov. 1945. NAAF Troop Carrier Command Report p. 84 states that the purpose of this drop was to "attack and hold strategical positions in the vicinity of Gela." But the spot selected, Farello, was already held by our own troops. Gen. Arnold, in a letter to Gen. Spaatz a few days later, said it was obvious to him that the real reason for the drop was desire to commit paratroops waiting in Africa. These could better have been sent in by ships of the follow-up convoys.

[50] Eisenhower Dispatch p. 41.

Germans staged their heaviest air raid between 2150 and 2300. All ships got under way as the bombs began to drop; tracer bullets laced the sky; parachute flares lit up the scene. And, on top of this, came the American transport planes. In order to escape anti-aircraft fire of the Army ashore, which was very severe, the pilots tried to save themselves and their passengers by flying out over the roadstead at low altitude, right in the midst of the German bombing attack. Recognition signals were of no avail in the smoke- and tracer-filled night sky. Stricken planes plummeted into the sea and onto the land. Destroyer *Jeffers* picked up two rubber boats containing seven survivors from a transport plane; one of them was a paratrooper, who was promptly placed under arrest by a fellow survivor for having refused to jump! [51]

All next day paratroop survivors were trickling into Gela. Twenty-three of the 144 planes failed to return and almost half of those which did return were badly damaged; 60 pilots and crewmen were lost, in addition to about 40 troop passengers drowned or shot down. General Eisenhower ordered a searching inquiry into these aborted airborne operations. The special board that he convened to study this and an equally unfortunate drop over the British sector concluded that airborne troops should be employed only on missions suitable for them, and then only when the task could not be accomplished by other means; that all friendly ground and naval forces should be notified of an impending air drop at least twelve hours in advance; that in the case of a sea approach a "safety corridor" ten miles wide should be evacuated by naval vessels; and that every troop-carrying plane must identify itself to ships.

In justice to the Air Force, we must remember that its main effort against enemy airfields and lines of communication was so successful that air attacks on our amphibious forces were kept to a minimum, and that no air attacks were delivered in the JOSS, DIME

[51] *Jeffers* Action Report. This ship congratulated herself on not firing on friendly planes, for the good reason that Ens. D. W. McClurg USNR, a graduate of the Plane Recognition School at Columbus, O., had insisted on carrying on intensive daily training in plane recognition by all hands.

and CENT areas after 13 July. But as soon as our naval forces came "round the mountain" to Palermo, the Luftwaffe found them again.

By daybreak 12 July the enemy was retiring from the Gela plain. Ponte Olivo airstrip, prime objective of the DIME landings, was captured at 0845 by the 26th Regiment. Lieutenant Colonel Rippert set up his regimental command post in the Italian officers' mess hall, which had been so hastily vacated that undrunk glasses of wine still stood on the tables. A fighter wing of the R.A.F. occupied the field next day. The 18th Regiment pushed north and seized 1300-foot Monte Ursitto; the 26th took an even higher mountain which dominates the road to Riesi. The Navy, too, was in on this. In answer to calls from shore fire-control, *Savannah* and *Boise* fired for extended periods on batteries high in the hills, and on troop concentrations far inland. *Savannah*, for instance, shot up Butera, on a 1300-foot pinnacle some 11,000 yards from the beach, while *Boise* took on Niscemi, a good 17,000 yards inland — as did H.M.S. *Abercrombie*, whose 15-inch shells had an extreme range of 32,200 yards. This performance so impressed Brigadier General Clift Andrus USA, commanding 1st Division artillery, that he reported to General Terry Allen:

> We have handled the fire support of the ships in exactly the same manner that we handled reinforcing artillery of our own. At no time has the Navy hesitated to do anything requested, and their answers to calls for fire have invariably been in the form of remarkably accurate fire delivered in surprisingly short time.
>
> First Division Artillery recognizes superior gunnery when it sees it, and we are unanimously stating that the support rendered by Admiral Hall's command has been more than we could have expected even from the United States Navy.[52]

By 1800 July 12 the 1st Division had so much of its own artillery and armor ashore, and was fighting so far inland, that it released all naval gunfire support parties, which returned on board ship.

[52] HQ 1st Div. Artillery, Unit Journal, 5–16 July 1943.

Afloat, too, the situation of DIME Force vastly improved. On 12 July Tactical Air Command began to provide adequate combat air patrol. Even before dawn, *Savannah* cheerfully observed "friendly planes continually overhead," and later in the day, "many Spitfires . . . flying around." [53] A bombing attack at 0936 was actually broken up by Allied fighters and antiaircraft gunners. This was the last day of enemy air attacks on the American beaches and amphibious forces off the south coast of Sicily.

It was also a day of official visits. General Eisenhower steamed over from Malta in British destroyer *Petard*, took a quick look at the beaches, and at 0630 boarded *Monrovia*. He found General Patton, who had returned on board, in excellent spirits; and, as few progress reports of the Seventh Army had reached Malta, their conference was most fruitful.[54] At 0715 the Supreme Commander resumed his cruise in *Petard*, steaming about two miles off shore on "a lovely sunny Mediterranean morning . . . There was hardly a shell or a bomb to be heard, and the outstanding impression was one of complete serenity. Landing craft were proceeding on their lawful occasions from ship to shore; it looked more like a huge regatta than an operation of war. Convinced that the invasion had been successfully launched, I returned to Malta and thence to Tunis to await General Alexander for a conference on subsequent operations." [55]

By noon Admiral Hall, too, decided that the assault phase of the Gela landing was complete and made plans to return to North Africa. The LSTs were already on their way back to Bizerta for a second load. Transports and cargo ships were almost completely unloaded. Fire support ships remained on call, with about half their ammunition on board.

As the assault phase drew to a close, more and more Italian prisoners were herded into Gela en route to North African stockades.

[53] Rear Adm. Hall Action Report p. 8; *Savannah* Action Report pp. 12–13.

[54] It was also friendly; Capt. Butcher's report of an altercation between the two, I am informed on good authority, is without foundation. The General did not then learn of the shooting down of transport planes the night before, because word of it did not reach *Monrovia* until half an hour after he had shoved off.

[55] Eisenhower Dispatch p. 49.

The Naval Advanced Base group organized as the fighting proceeded inland. Intelligence officers interrogated fishermen in the hope of detecting subversive characters; soundings were taken around Gela pier; radios, blinkers and even an American post office were set up. The townspeople were not yet convinced that the Americans came as "liberators," but they gave little trouble.[56]

On the afternoon of the 12th the Western Naval Task Force command was rearranged. Admiral Conolly reported in *Biscayne* to take tactical command of all naval phases. Admiral Hewitt transferred his flag to destroyer *McLanahan* in order to report in person to Admiral Cunningham at Malta, and General Patton went ashore from *Monrovia* for the last time to take over complete responsibility for land operations. Just as he shoved off from *Monrovia* in an LCT at 1700, a lone fighter plane, an Italian Macchi–202, dove down to strafe, so suddenly that nobody had time to fire before it got away. Fortunately for us, all bullets struck the water between the LCT and the flagship; unfortunately for the bold aviator, he returned for a second try and was promptly shot down.[57]

An hour later the flagship, five transports, two cargo ships, *Samuel Chase* with Admiral Hall on board, seven destroyers and various other vessels departed for Algiers. Presently this convoy was augmented by ten transports from Admiral Kirk's CENT Force, with his flagship *Ancon*, U.S.S. *Andromeda* and nine destroyer escorts, bound for Oran. The return passage was uneventful, except in the sick bays where doctors and pharmacist's mates worked night and day tending wounded soldiers and sailors.

Around Gela all was quiet again. Niscemi fell to the 16th Infantry on 13 July. That day there was but one call for naval gunfire, on the high hill-town of Butera, which *Savannah* answered with several salvos. Her shore fire-control party with the 1st Division sent her this warm message before pressing on into the interior of Sicily: —

[56] Naval Advanced Base Gela, War Diary July 1943; and Intelligence situation reported to Admiral Hewitt by Lt. A. J. Marzullo USNR and Ens. J. F. Murray USNR.

[57] Information from Lt. Col. Francis M. Rogers USMCR, who observed this from *Monrovia*. The Italian Air Force is unable to identify the pilot.

We are saying goodbye. We cannot sufficiently thank you for rapid and accurate fire support you have given us. Among other things you have been responsible for crushing three infantry attacks and silencing four artillery batteries. Italian prisoners have been demoralized by the effect of your fire. We are saying goodbye until we meet again.[58]

Meet again they did, at Omaha Beach, in June next, when the 1st Division was again landed and supported by a task group commanded by Admiral "Jimmy" Hall.

Seabees, using pontoon causeways, constructed a temporary pier at Gela, where LSTs of follow-up convoys could unload easily; and for a week or more the town was an important port of entry.

Gela has forgiven what she suffered in the invasion, and has not forgotten that the Americans brought liberation and peace. On the tenth anniversary of the landing, the townspeople packed the Chiesa Matrice to attend a requiem high mass celebrated for the souls of the war dead. While church bells tolled, the people moved in solemn procession down the zigzag road to the shore, and to the end of the reconstructed pier. There, Monsignor Giochino blessed the fallen warriors; and three wreaths, one given by Italian veterans, a second by American veterans, and a third by the town of Gela, were lowered into a fishing vessel to be carried far out and deposited off soundings in their – and our – Sea of Destiny.[59]

[58] *Savannah* Action Report 13 July, Enclosure C. She and *Boise* retired to Algiers on 14 July and returned on the 20th to relieve *Philadelphia* and *Birmingham* off Porto Empédocle.

[59] Rome *Daily American* 12 July 1953.

CHAPTER VII

The Scoglitti Landings (CENT Force)[1]

10–14 July

1. *The Beaches and the Assault, to 0630 July 10*

THE CENT landing area, on each side of the small fishermen's town of Scoglitti, lay between Admiral Hall's DIME area on the west and the Anglo-Canadian BARK area on the east. Admiral Hewitt and General Patton considered CENT to be the most important of the three American landings, because it lay nearest the Cómiso and Biscari airfields. Almost 26,000 troops (about 6600 more than in DIME) were allotted and placed under the senior force commander, Rear Admiral Alan G. Kirk.[2] This reliable, ex-

[1] CTF 85 (Rear Adm. Kirk) Report on Operation HUSKY 21 July 1943; Comtransdiv 7 (Capt. D. W. Loomis) War Diary; CTU 85.1.2 (Capt. W. B. Phillips) Report of Operation HUSKY; Action Reports and War Diaries of other vessels involved; Gen. Omar N. Bradley *A Soldier's Story* (1951); "After Action Report of 45th Inf. Div. in Sicilian Campaign," compiled from the G–3 Journal; "Report of Operations of 180th Infantry in Sicilian Campaign," 10 Oct. 1943; "179th Infantry RCT History"; Maj. Gen. T. H. Middleton USA "Comments and Recommendations, 45th Division" 31 July 1943; Lt. Col. L. V. Bishop *et al.*, *History of the 45th Division* (1946); Lt. Col. Ernest H. Daniel jr. "Observations of the Sicilian Campaign" Sept. 1943.

[2] Alan G. Kirk, b. Phila., 1888; Annapolis '09; in Asiatic Fleet until World War I, when he became an ordnance expert, and, after sea duty as gunnery officer and "exec." of presidential yacht *Mayflower*, was detailed to Buord. Gunnery officer *Maryland* 1924 and on staff of Commander Scouting Fleet; Naval War College course and staff; C.O. *Schenck;* "exec." *West Virginia* 1932; Office of C.N.O. 1933; C.O. *Milwaukee* 1936; operations officer to Admiral C. C. Bloch 1937; naval attaché London 1939, Director of Naval Intelligence Mar.–Oct. 1941; a desron commander in escort of convoy duty to May 1942, when he became chief of staff to Admiral Stark; Commander U.S. Naval Forces Europe; Commander Amphibious Force Atlantic Fleet Feb. 1943; Commander U.S. Naval Forces for Invasion of Normandy Oct. 1943. Subsequent to OVERLORD he commanded all U.S.

perienced and versatile flag officer had relieved Hewitt as Commander Amphibious Force Atlantic Fleet, and as such had had the responsibility of training the major part of CENT Force in the waters of Chesapeake Bay. His appointment to command in action the force that he had trained in practice was logical and appropriate.

Before entering the Tunisian War Channel, Kirk found the convoy carrying the 1st Canadian Division of the Eastern Task Force, which had come directly from England, on his starboard hand. At the turning point off Gozo he had some difficulty keeping clear of this and of DIME Force too. The necessary delay before he could form approach disposition meant that H-hour off Scoglitti could not be met.

Assault landings in the CENT area were divided between two groups of beaches about seven miles apart, the one selected to be nearest Biscari airfield, the other because it was nearer Cómiso. The northern group (Beaches Red, Green and Yellow), bordering on the mouth of the Acate River, was called by the planners "Wood's Hole"; the southern, compressed between Branco and Braccetto Points, "Bailey's Beach." Both names, well known in New England nomenclature, had also local significance, since *Leonard Wood* was flagship of the transports in the Wood's Hole section, and Captain W. O. Bailey commanded those of the other group. About halfway between the two groups of beaches lies the small fishing village of Scoglitti, built around a tiny beach; two miles north of it is the rocky Punta Zafaglione, and two miles south, Punta Camerina. Behind this coast stretches the Camerina plain, once the seat of a flourishing Greek city.

Both sections of beach, as it turned out, were ill chosen. Wood's Hole, backed by a thousand-yard wide strip of sand dunes and waste land, lies 6500 to 8000 yards from the main coastal highway; landmarks there are none and exits are few and soft. Bailey's Beach, 2500 yards at its nearest point from a secondary road, is backed by bare sand dunes. The 3000-yard stretch of beach north of Branco

Naval Forces in France; Ambassador to Belgium 1946 after retiring as four-star admiral; Ambassador to Russia 1949–50.

Point, behind which the land is dry and level and planted with tomatoes, would have been better for the southern landings,[3] and the several small beaches between Scoglitti and Zafaglione Point could have handled the northern ones. Moreover, since all CENT Force beaches faced the westerly wind, the surf was very severe. On 10 July it was breaking on the false beaches, and a southeasterly set of current carried several boat waves south of their objectives.

The 45th Division (Major General Troy H. Middleton USA) was a National Guard outfit, recruited largely from Oklahoma, Colorado and New Mexico. Two of the regiments, the 179th and 180th, contained a large number of Choctaw, Cherokee, Seminole, Sioux and Apache Indians who, during the training period, acquired wide publicity by staging a war dance on Boston Common for a war bond drive. The "Thunderbirds," as the 45th was nicknamed since it used that familiar Indian symbol as a shoulder patch, had received amphibious training at Little Creek, Virginia, and Solomons Island, Maryland, with the boat crews; but, one hour before sailing for Africa, at least half the well-trained landing craft ensigns and coxswains had been replaced by men fresh from boot camp. This was a severe blow, as there was no further opportunity to train the replacements.

At 2145 July 9 the vessels destined for Bailey's Beach, with LSTs astern, peeled off from the Wood's Holers. Gunfire flashes and fires under the northern sky indicated that the Air Force was not neglecting the Camerina plain. Transport planes bearing paratroops for the inland drop passed to starboard. Beacon submarine H.M.S. *Seraph* appeared on the radar screen of destroyer *Tillman* at 2233, and blinker signals were exchanged. Lieutenant Jewell RN, the submarine's commanding officer, peered at the approaching fleet through his night glasses and reflected that "the English language needs a new descriptive noun to replace the hackneyed word *armada*. After all, the original Invincible Spanish Armada that

[3] Probably the reason these beaches were not chosen was the existence of a strong point on Punta Camerina which could enfilade them, and the planners did not know how weak Sicilian "strong points" really were.

tackled us in 1588 could boast of only 129 sizable ships and a scattering of small fry."[4]

The assault plan in the Wood's Hole area was to put the 1st Battalion 180th Regimental Combat Team ashore on Beach Red, adjoining the mouth of the dry Acate River, to move northeast and capture Biscari, eight miles inland, establish road blocks around that town, and await orders to advance and take the airfield. The 1st Battalion 179th Regimental Combat Team would land on Beach Yellow, and move laterally to take Scoglitti; 3rd Battalion to advance inland and capture Vittoria, nearest town to the Cómiso airdrome. In the meantime the 157th RCT, landing at Bailey's Beach, would take Santa Croce Camerina and provide a second pincer on Cómiso airfield. It was a bold plan; for instead of taking time to consolidate a beachhead all units were to press vigorously inland to capture key points.

Off Wood's Hole the ships anchored in two rows, parallel to the shore and five to six miles out. Owing to the earlier delays in the convoy, boats could not be lowered or troops debarked fast enough to meet the 0245 H-hour. At 0215 Captain Phillips, senior transport commander, requested a postponement of one hour. Admiral Kirk so ordered at 0246, which confused the scout boats and landing craft already in the water.

Six rocket-mounted scout boats were to have supported *Leonard Wood's* initial waves with a barrage on Beach Yellow before the landing. Two were so damaged in lowering that they sank; the other four hurled 84 rockets into the beach, followed by smoke bombs, to blanket the area against snipers and flare illumination.[5] *Leonard Wood*, smartest transport in boat handling, got 28 LCVPs of the first four waves into the water and loaded at 0105, an hour and a half ahead of the others; and her first wave, after a long

[4] Lt. N.L.A. Jewell *Secret Mission Submarine* (1944) pp. 114–15. This was the same submarine that had set General Mark Clark ashore in North Africa, spirited General Giraud out of Southern France in 1942 and set "Major William Martin" afloat.

[5] These few and feeble rocket craft were used in all three landings. They were 36.8-ft. Higgins boats carrying not more than 2 rocket projectors each.

wait, grounded 20 yards off Beach Yellow at 0345, right on time.[6] The anticipated false beach proved to be no obstacle. In a moment, soldiers were wading ashore, waist-deep, greatly encouraged by naval gunfire support. For at 0330, when enemy parachute flares illuminated the scene, Admiral Kirk decided it was time to do some shooting. Destroyers *Tillman* and *Knight* commenced firing on assigned machine-gun emplacements and pillboxes.

The first wave to Beach Green, from *Florence Nightingale*, was only nine minutes behind the winner. This transport managed to get 29 boats into the water by 0043, but it took two and three-quarters hours to load them in the heavy swell, and *Nightingale* was a heavy roller. Her first four boat waves put 748 men on the beach.

The 180th RCT, the larger part of which, spearheaded by its 1st Battalion, was supposed to land on Beach Red, had perhaps the worst time of all. Owing to the lack of landmarks, even the Scouts and Raiders were unable to identify Beach Red in time to help the boat waves in, and the transports that carried the assault battalion had more than their share of completely inexperienced coxswains. Colonel Forrest E. Cookson and staff were set ashore miles to the north, on one of the Gela beaches; part of his regiment was landed at Bailey's Beach, and the rest was scattered along the entire front of Wood's Hole and on unscheduled beaches south of it. Transport *Neville*, a bad roller and pitcher, required two hours to get her landing craft lowered and in the water; but they won the race to Beach Red, touching down at 0434. There was slight opposition and all boats retracted. *Calvert's* landing craft were off to Beach Red at 0250, before her commanding officer got the word that H-hour had been postponed. They were then recalled and made a fresh start at 0320. More delays followed; but the troops began to go ashore around 0445 – mostly wet to the neck. The 1st Battalion commander and staff were landed at a point south of the Wood's Hole area.

All these boat waves had plenty of excitement on the way in,

[6] Rear Adm. Kirk Report, Enclosure H.

since an air attack, heralded by brilliant, slow-descending yellow flares, was delivered at about 0430. This had been ordered by Superaereo at Rome after receiving word of the previous evening's contact on the convoys. It consisted of one squadron of torpedo-bombers from Sardinia and 13 high-level bombers which had come all the way from Perugia. Six bombs landed about 300 yards from destroyer *Tillman*, extinguishing her lights and knocking out her SG radar for a few minutes. Cruiser *Philadelphia*, missed by 35 yards, bent on knots and maneuvered radically. *Jefferson* also was near-missed. Friendly fighter planes – British Spitfires which General Bradley observed "whistling serenely by on their fat wings"[7] – dropped down from higher altitudes in pursuit, but do not appear to have caught any of the enemy bombers; they were probably deterred by "friendly" antiaircraft fire. During three quarters of an hour bombs were falling throughout the transport area, but not one hit was made. All the ships and even small craft opened up with everything they had, but the bombers either stayed hidden in the night sky, or came in undetected from over the land.[8] At 0529 Admiral Kirk ordered all ships to cease fire, thinking that friendly planes were getting hit.

During this uproar an informal but important scouting mission ashore was being performed by Francis Carpenter, seaman 1st class, of *Calvert*. Before the landing he had remarked to one of the ship's officers that he had once attended a house party not far from Wood's Hole and had even ridden a horse on these very beaches. Brought before Lieutenant Colonel William H. Schaefer USA, commanding the 1st Battalion 180th RCT, he was asked to scout ahead of the troops and ascertain whether a line that appeared on the aërial photographs was a road or a fence, and whether a certain field behind the dunes was a vineyard or an olive grove. Carpenter, who was to be bow hook in an LCVP of the first wave, was given permission to leave his boat as soon as she hit the beach, which she did at 0440. He ascertained that the line was a road. Returning

[7] *A Soldier's Story* p. 128.

[8] *Tillman* Action Report 17 July 1943 p. 5.

shoreward to give the prearranged signal with a Very pistol, he pointed out to an Indian GI a place recently dug up as probably concealing a land mine; but the Indian ignored his warning and was blown to bits. Carpenter himself was hurled "quite a distance." He picked himself up and hurried inland again to check on the vineyard or olive grove. It proved to be the latter. After making the proper light signal from a sand dune, he slid down it into the edge of a cornfield, where he found in hiding a very frightened peasant family, complete with babies and donkey. "I gave the men cigarettes," said Carpenter, "told them the Americans were their friends. Sang 'La donna è mobile' from *Rigoletto*, and all in all put them quite at their ease." Carpenter offered to safe-conduct the natives to their cottage, which was south of Beach Yellow, and en route two Italian soldiers surrendered themselves and their rifles to him. While Carpenter was sitting outside the peasants' home "drinking wine and having a beautiful time," who should arrive but Colonel Schaefer, whose aspect (which had earned him the nickname "King Kong" at West Point) so terrified the Italians that they fell on their knees and begged for mercy. Carpenter reassured them, and the Colonel and staff passed on.[9] His appearance with pistol upraised, over the brow of another dune, persuaded 20 more Italian infantrymen to surrender. By 0600, most of the 1st Battalion 180th Infantry, some 3000 strong, was ashore; and all except one platoon, which had been landed on the Gela beaches, was ready to strike out for Biscari.

At 0530, when day was breaking, *Philadelphia* began catapulting four observation planes, two to spot for her and two for the monitor, H.M.S. *Abercrombie*. Later in the morning a *Philadelphia* SOC, in the intervals of spotting fall of fire, flushed Italian soldiers out of the bushes behind Punta Camerina for delivery to Americans on the beach. The pilot "flew low and motioned for them to go in the general direction of our troops; their movement was hurried and guided by the very accurate fire" of his radioman. "They gathered force as they went forward, resulting in what appeared

[9] Carpenter's typed report, 14 July 1943; confirmed by Col. Schaefer in 1953.

to be more than a hundred by the time they reached the beach." [10] A second *Philadelphia* plane was shot down by two Messerschmitts and her crew killed; the Germans might have strafed the cruiser, too, if she had not promptly aimed antiaircraft fire in their direction and chased them away.

Captain Bailey's Transdiv 5, lifting the 157th Regimental Combat Team (Colonel C. M. Ankcorn) of the 45th Division, had a rough time on and around the beaches named after their division commander. Beach Green 2 was known to have wire strung along its entire length of 1000 yards, and Yellow 2, less than half as long, had a stretch of wire perpendicular to the waterline. Aërial reconnaissance showed a flock of pillboxes covering the two beaches; and if the howitzer battery on Cape Camerina had been active (fortunately the guns had been captured from the French and the Italians had no ammunition to fit) it could have raised hob with the landing. There were no distinctive landmarks to serve as signposts for incoming craft, except the rocks of Punta Braccetto, between which and Beach Yellow is a rocky outcrop easily mistaken for the Point.

Transports found their stations with difficulty, owing to the want of radar landmarks, but anchored between 2348 and 0128 in a fairly straight line. The sea was even rougher here than off Wood's Hole. *Biddle's* scout boat, carrying the beach markers, started to sink and put back for repairs. Those of *Carroll* and *Anthony* groped around Punta Braccetto, but were so tardy that the destroyers began to shoot before they had even located Beach Yellow 2. *Jefferson,* last to arrive, rolled so badly that Captain Welch and Lieutenant Colonel I. O. Schaefer USA, commanding 2nd Battalion 157th RCT, decided not to rail-load the troops, but to lower all boats and let the men scramble down debarkation nets in the old-fashioned manner. Her scout boat wandered about blindly, fighting wind and waves, and never locating Beach Green 2. Landing craft had great difficulty staying alongside. Four-inch

[10] *Philadelphia* Action Report including that of the pilot, Lt. (jg) Paul E. Coughlin USNR; his gunner was Richard Shafer ARM2c.

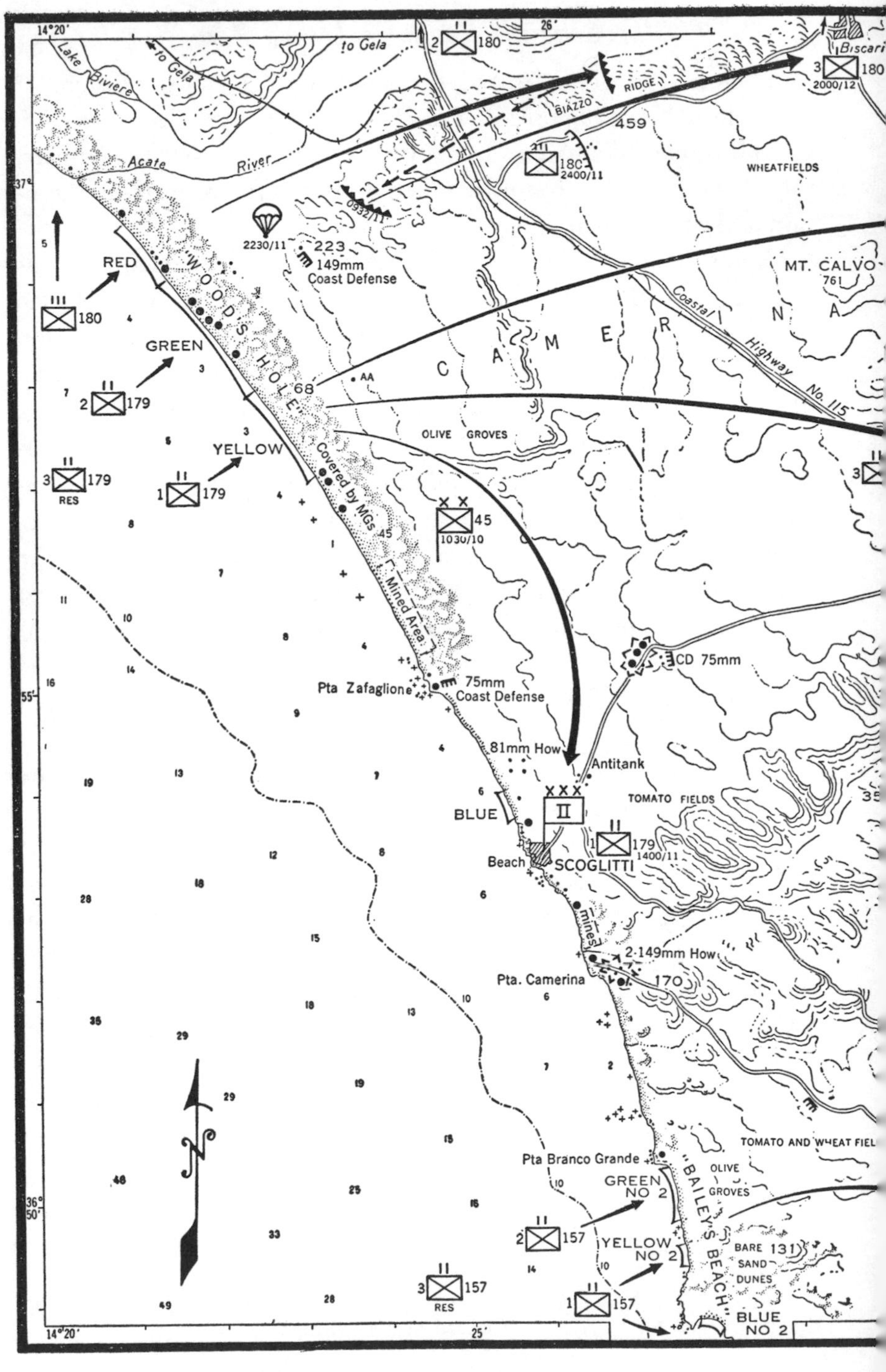

to Gela
Lake Biviere
Acate River
BIAZZO RIDGE
Biscari
WHEATFIELDS
MT. CALVO 761
C A M E R I N A
Coastal Highway No. 115
149mm Coast Defense
"WOOD'S HOLE"
RED
GREEN
YELLOW
Covered by MGs
Mined Area
OLIVE GROVES
75mm Coast Defense
Pta Zafaglione
CD 75mm
81mm How
Antitank
TOMATO FIELDS
BLUE
Beach
SCOGLITTI
mines
2-149mm How
Pta. Camerina
TOMATO AND WHEAT FIEL
Pta Branco Grande
GREEN NO 2
YELLOW NO 2
BLUE NO 2
"BAILEY'S BEACH"
OLIVE GROVES
BARE SAND DUNES
RES

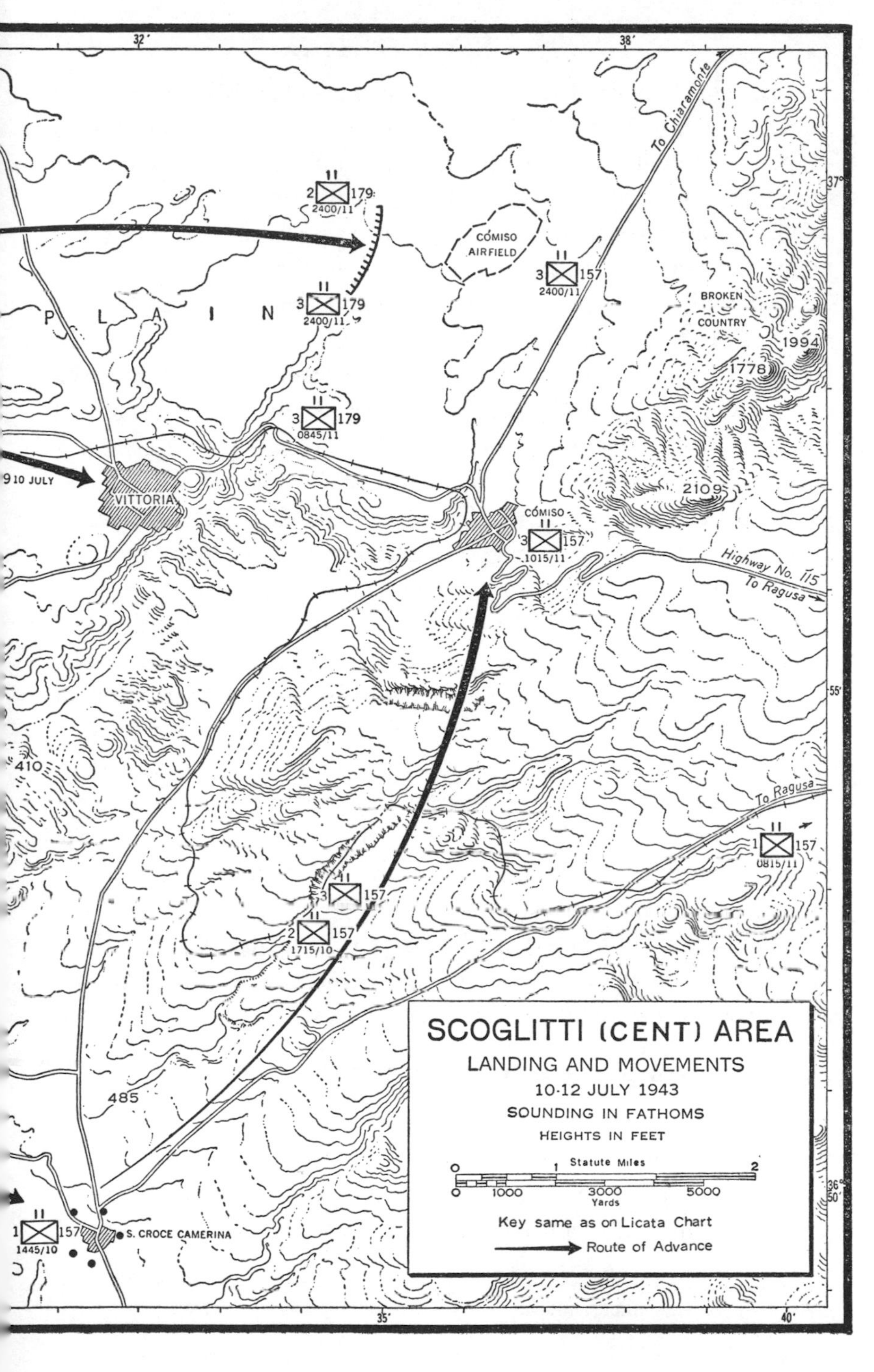

SCOGLITTI (CENT) AREA
LANDING AND MOVEMENTS
10-12 JULY 1943
SOUNDING IN FATHOMS
HEIGHTS IN FEET
Statute Miles
Yards
Key same as on Licata Chart
Route of Advance
COMISO AIRFIELD
VITTORIA
COMISO
S. CROCE CAMERINA
BROKEN COUNTRY
To Chiaramonte
Highway No. 115
To Ragusa
To Ragusa
P L A I N
9 10 JULY
2400/11
0845/11
1015/11
0815/11
1715/10
1445/10

manila painters parted time and again. Seasick soldiers had great difficulty going down the nets, which were almost impossible to drape into a boat. A young assault-wave officer tried to screw up the soldiers' courage by telling them that the foul weather favored them, because the enemy would never expect a landing on such a night. The troops were silenced but far from convinced.

Even with the postponement of H-hour to 0345, net loading was so slow that only three out of four assault waves were ready on time to start for the beaches. In they went with *PC–591*, the control vessel, at 0303. Destroyers *Mervine* and *Doran* protected their left flank, training guns on targets around Beach Green 2 and north of Scoglitti. But the course of *PC–591* was badly deflected by wind and sea to a point off Beach Yellow 2. Real trouble now began. *Philadelphia* opened bombardment at 0334, a few minutes before H-hour. *Mervine* and *Doran* also fired vigorously on prearranged targets, while the landing craft of the first assault wave swarmed into the wrong beach, Yellow 2. Shellfire, suspected to be shots from *Philadelphia*, but more probably shots from the Italian coast defense battery on the Santa Croce road, grazed the landing craft and forced them farther and farther to the right. The support boats launched rockets in correct timing with the troops' landing, but since "the waves did not land on the correct beach . . . the desired geographical objective, Punta Branco Grande, was not hit by our fire."

"We landed right up on the beach in bare inches of water," reported the ensign commanding the first assault wave, "and the Army walked out of the boats, quite surprised at the convenience of a bus ride. They seemed to stand rooted for a minute, not being able to realize the apparent lack of opposition." [11] Time was 0355. *Jefferson* had won the race to Bailey's Beach.

On rocky Punta Braccetto one of *Jefferson's* boats, commanded by Ensign G. P. Limberis USNR, came to grief. The troops, understandably, flinched from debarking in heavy surf on a rockbound

[11] *Jefferson* Action Report 31 July, including reports of Ens. M. S. Hunting USNR, support boat officer, and of Ens. J. L. Bruckner USNR of 1st wave.

coast, but "after much persuasion," reported the Ensign, "every man in my boat was on the beach, and the crew and myself salvaged the two .30-caliber machine guns and a few rounds of ammunition." Four Italians who manned a nearby machine gun were so astonished at this exploit that they surrendered without firing a shot. Presently Limberis and his men heard shouts and screams in the water. Two boats in the second wave, following the same erroneous course, had collided and swamped when their coxswains had sighted the rocks and tried to sheer off.[12] The first-comers scrambled down the steep and slippery rocks and managed to pull four GIs out of the water, but some 38 were drowned. Signalman D. E. True, in one of the unfortunate craft, had the presence of mind to flash an emergency signal to the boat directly astern of him a moment before his own crashed, saving it from a similar fate. The third wave, at 0415, barely escaped crashing and put its troops ashore safely on the rocky point, but lost five boats out of seven. Later assault waves, arriving by daylight, had no trouble finding the proper beaches.

Charles Carroll's story also is full of mishaps. At the time of anchoring, a support boat on deck broke loose, tore away rigging, injured men, and smashed gear, so that the troops' boat stations had to be changed. The patrol craft designated as control boat took such an erratic course to the beach that only the presence of mind of individual boat coxswains saved them from the rocks. Even so, only the first wave landed on the right beach.[13]

The combination of heavy surf, want of definite landmarks, and inexperienced boat crews made landing craft casualties in CENT area almost as great as in the Moroccan landings of Operation TORCH.

[12] Same, reports of Ensigns Limberis and Ross E. Schumann USNR.

[13] "*Charles Carroll* in Operation HUSKY," written for this work by Rear Adm. Harold Biesemeier (her former C.O.) in 1947, and comments by the commander of embarked troops, Col. C. M. Ankcorn USA.

2. *Unloading Problems and Complications, 10–12 July*

When the D-day sun rose over the Sicilian mountains, neither General Middleton nor Admiral Kirk had a clear picture of what was going on at Wood's Hole or Bailey's Beach, and the Army command in *Ancon* was becoming very impatient. At the General's request, Admiral Kirk at 0625 began moving in transports to about 5000 yards from shore. These waters had not yet been swept, but fortunately Intelligence was correct: there were no mines off Scoglitti.

CENT Force found itself in a tight situation not of its own choosing, though to some extent of its own making. Some assault transports were still sending troops ashore with landing craft borrowed from other ships, which were "hollering" to get them back for unloading their own passengers and supplies. But so many LCVPs had broached that serviceable ones were at a premium. The inshore movement of the transports tempted some of the Italian short-range coastal batteries, which had hitherto kept silent, to open up. Bursts bracketed the transports and forced them to retire seaward until *Philadelphia* and other fire support ships could silence the guns.[14] The soft sand of Bailey's Beach immobilized heavy equipment, and Beach Yellow 2 had no fewer than three false beaches on the approach, which caught any boat that tried to cross, unless she rode the crest of a wave. The long stretch of sand dunes and brush behind these beaches made it almost impossible to move vehicles inland.[15]

Shortly after noon, Admiral Kirk decided to abandon the use of Bailey's for landing supplies. A beach on the south side of Braccetto Point, Blue 2, was opened up at 1050 and vigorously used by LSTs, while landing craft were ordered to the fishermen's cove in front of Scoglitti, and to other small beaches north of the town.

Conditions at Wood's Hole were no better. The access road to

[14] According to information from the Italian Army, all guns in CENT sector were knocked out within an hour.

[15] *Anthony* Action Report 27 July 1943 p. 8; Biesemeier Account, p. 15.

Beach Yellow had to carry the traffic from all three beaches. By mid-morning the chaos there was such that Admiral Kirk sent ashore one of his transport division commanders, Captain Loomis, to accelerate the removal of beached boats. He found between 150 and 200 stranded or swamped craft on offshore bars and landing beaches. Salvage parties were overwhelmed with work. Boat handling had been as bad as at the Fedhala landings, and for the same reasons – surf and inexperience. There were not enough beach exits, which made bottlenecks inevitable.[16] Here, for instance, are the experiences of a young boat officer of *Anne Arundel*, attempting to land a 40-mm gun in broad daylight, after he had hit the wrong beach: –

> The boat was broached by the on-rushing surf, simply because we could not get any means of removing the gun. . . . The Army lieutenant in the boat left to get help and never returned, leaving his men behind. We stayed with the boat six hours trying to get assistance to get the gun out of the boat, but no one, including an Army colonel, could get us motorized help. We then salvaged the two .30-caliber guns, ammunition, and other equipment to carry with us. We hiked to Red beach after hitting the sand dunes several times to escape gunfire from enemy planes. At Red beach we reported our problem to the beachmaster. He directed us to take a *Neville* boat which returned us to our ship about 2130.[17]

Captain Loomis, arriving on the beach, immediately directed his ships to send in at least one LCM each, equipped with salvage gear, to drag stranded boats back into the water. This unfortunately deprived each ship of one of her most valuable cargo carriers. LCTs were pressed into service too, and ships' companies sent in working parties to speed up unloading.

General Middleton took the same dim view as did naval officers of the Army Engineers designated as shore party: he referred to them as a "rabble." These men, including rejects from combat units,

[16] Rear Adm. Kirk Report p. A–4; Comtransdiv 7 (Capt. Loomis) Action Report p. 5.

[17] Ens. S. S. Campbell USNR in *Anne Arundel* Action Report p. 47.

were untrained and insubordinate; some even devoted their energies to rifling soldiers' barracks bags and the personal baggage of officers.[18]

Leaving pontoon causeways at Bailey's Beach, Admiral Kirk on the morning of 11 July ordered all unloading by landing craft, from whatever transport, to be shifted to the three little beaches between Scoglitti and Punta Zafaglione. Here the exits were better, but the beaches themselves were just as bad as Bailey's. More boats stranded; shore and beach parties tried to move laterally, but had difficulty in locating the intended landing places. Loaded boats lay off shore or returned to their ships, because nobody could be found to handle their cargoes at the shoreline. A survey of the number of LCVPs and LCMs available to the seven transports of Captain Phillips's division, made at noon 11 July, revealed an alarming loss of boats: only 66 of an original 175 were still usable; the rest were damaged, stranded, sunk, or missing. And that is only half the story. The 18 transports of CENT Force left almost 200 LCVPs on the beach.[19]

General Bradley "thumbed a ride in a passing dukw" and was landed with a few members of II Corps staff at Scoglitti, on the morning of the 11th. His command post was established in the moldy headquarters of local Carabinieri, as the ample palazzo some distance inland, originally selected for that purpose, was still in enemy hands. The corps commander found the invasion beaches "a dismal sight. . . . More than 200 assault craft wallowed in the surf after having burned out their engines in crossing the runnels while coming ashore. Bulldozers churned through the soft sand, dragging pallets of supply from the water's edge to be piled in dumps behind the grassy dunes. A fleet of more than 700 dukws

[18] Gen. Middleton "Comments and Recommendations, 45th Division, Task Force" 31 July 1943; conversations in 1953 with Lt. Gen. Raymond S. McLain USA who commanded the divisional artillery in 1943, and with Col. W. H. Schaefer USA. The lieutenant colonel commanding the shore party was court-martialed.

[19] Cdr. Transports (Capt. W. B. Phillips) Action Report p. 10 and Enc. D; Rear Adm. Kirk gives total losses of boats 10–13 July as 199 LCVPs, 13 LCMs and 10 Scout boats. But many of these were subsequently salvaged.

moved from ship to shore, ferrying the bulk tonnage that would be needed for support." [20]

Admiral Kirk, overly optimistic, reported to Admiral Hewitt at 1700 July 11 that he expected to have seven transports ready to sail by midnight. Hewitt responded by ordering 20 LCMs from CENT Force to help DIME. But at midnight Kirk had to admit "No convoy will sail tonight due to congestion on beaches, causing boats to be held up."

During the morning CENT Force came in for a share of the second big enemy air attack, the one that sank *Robert Rowan* off Gela. The following night, 11–12 July, was cloudless, typical of the Mediterranean summer, with a bright first-quarter moon. The Fleet lay almost motionless off shore on a gently heaving sea. At 2215 destroyer *Murphy* reported "dive-bomber just missed me by 100 yards." Within a few minutes the German air attack swirled like a cyclone into the CENT area. Four flares dropped near Admiral Kirk's flagship. Pandemonium broke loose. Everybody let go; several men in *Ancon* were injured by other ships' flak, and *Anthony* shot down a bomber flying low across her bow, heading for *Philadelphia*. Right on the heels of this enemy attack, came the American transport planes. At 2315 Admiral Kirk ordered his ships not to shoot "toward the beach unless you have a definite target, as friendly paratroopers are landing from friendly planes." But it was too late to prevent mistakes; one could only search for survivors. *Beatty* learned from paratroops she fished out of the water that some of the Army planes had been so badly shot up by "friendly" fire inland that they had decided to make a dash to the sea, splash, and take their chances on being picked up. *Cowie* rescued two sergeants, sole survivors of one plane, who said that their section of three planes passed over assigned objectives, but the Army antiaircraft fire was so dense that parachuting of troops would have been suicidal. The pilot then flew back to the coast and followed it southward until the plane was shot down.

[20] *A Soldier's Story* pp. 129–30.

It is clear where the responsibility for this unfortunate accident lay. Attend the measured words of Admiral Kirk: —

> No control over fighter patrol was delegated to the CENT Attack Force. No bombers were on call. No fighter protection to spotting planes was provided. . . . At no time was the Force informed concerning the degree of air control exercised by our forces and as to what . . . enemy attack might be expected. . . . The air battle was separate and foreign, apparently unconcerned about the situation in the CENT Area.[21]

At 0800 next morning, 12 July, the Admiral went ashore to size up the situation and to call on General Bradley, with whom there had been a brisk exchange of dispatches about lack of progress at the shoreline. He found unloading "completely blocked" by failure to clear the beaches. Fortunately, enemy troops and tanks had now retired beyond reach of naval gunfire, and at 0927 the Admiral requested General Middleton to detach the naval liaison officers from his shore fire-control parties and return them on board ship. Ten unloaded transports, together with *Ancon, Andromeda* and nine escorting destroyers, sailed at 2008 for Oran. Among their passengers were 17 German and 1239 Italian prisoners taken by the 45th Division.

Admiral Kirk now shifted his flag to destroyer *Earle* and supervised unloading of the seven remaining transports, which weighed anchor on the 13th and sailed to Oran, escorted by seven destroyers. The Admiral jubilantly collected the quart of whisky owed to him by General Patton, who had bet it would take the Navy eight days to unload. Early next day he departed for Malta, bequeathing to Admiral Conolly all his tugs, patrol craft, beaching craft and minecraft to perform the necessary tasks of unloading the follow-up convoys of merchant ships.

Scoglitti and its flanking beaches were distinctly not wanted by Army or Navy for further supply. They were closed 17 July, after serving the 45th Division as well as could be expected.[22]

[21] Rear Adm. Kirk Action Report p. 3.

[22] Troops landed in CENT area, 10–12 July, 22,654; 300 on 13th, and none after. Supplies: — 7,801 long tons 10–12 July, and 5,952 13–17 July. Vehicles, 10–12 July 2,179, and 636 after. Seventh Army *Report of Operations* pp. E-15, 16.

3. *The 45th Division Ashore, 10–14 July* [23]

Here, as elsewhere in HUSKY, Army and Navy acted as "one big family," to which they would gladly have admitted the Air Force if that junior service had not preferred to fight its own war. General Middleton, who had sailed to Sicily in flagship *Ancon*, admired the perseverance of Kirk's sailors in setting his division ashore with its mountains of equipment; although it was not done entirely "according to plan," the General knew why. Admiral Kirk wrote, "The Commanding General's plan of assault was excellent, well understood, and executed with celerity and precision. . . . The 45th Division was coöperative, patient and helpful. It was admirably led, of fine fighting spirit, seized all its objectives, and was full of dash and power." Admiral of the Fleet Cunningham, who visited the CENT area on D-day, reported to General Eisenhower that Admiral Kirk's landings "constituted one of the finest exhibitions of seamanship it had been his pleasure to witness in 45 years of sailoring." [24]

Typical of the "snafus" inevitable in amphibious operations was the experience of Lieutenant Colonel R. C. Routh USA, the divisional paymaster. For reasons he never understood, he was ordered ashore from *James O'Hara* before noon on D-day. His six field safes containing about $2,000,000 in United States currency were sent ashore in another LCVP. The Colonel landed on one beach, but the money disappeared. After a frenzied search it was found next day submerged in shoal water off another beach where a coxswain had dumped the safes when his boat couldn't make the shoreline. It took days for the money to dry out, and for "Pay" to recover from the experience.

All in all, the 45th Division had wriggled out of its initial difficulties very well, and lost remarkably little time in going after its

[23] "45th Infantry Division in Sicilian Campaign, as compiled from G–3 Journal for Period 10 July–22 August 1943." This and other U.S. Army documents quoted are from Departmental Records Branch, Historical Records Section, Department of the Army.

[24] Eisenhower *Crusade in Europe* p. 173.

main objectives: the Biscari and Cómiso airfields; extending the beachhead to Line Yellow between Ragusa and Caltagirone; establishing contact with the Canadian division on the east flank.

First objective of Colonel C. M. Ankcorn's 157th RCT, which landed at Bailey's Beach, was the small town of Santa Croce Camerina, about four miles inland. He advanced on it immediately, his route preceded significantly by accurate naval gunfire. "An emplaced battery southeast of the village was silenced early in the day and the gunfire placed on the town was accurate and effective. Hits on buildings near the village public square were very effective and had a marked effect on the garrison commander's attitude." When the 157th approached the town shortly before noon, white flags began to appear, and the Italian troops manning the defenses disappeared or surrendered.[25] Santa Croce Camerina, together with 500 Italian prisoners, was in American hands by 1500 D-day. The Italian divisional commander reported that enemy forces were "overwhelming"; that "hundreds of anchored ships were unloading matériel undisturbed," and that he had no air support.[26]

The 1st Battalion 179th Regiment, at 1400, captured Scoglitti where the fishermen's cove afforded a good landing place for one LCT at a time. A hard road leads from Scoglitti, seven miles, to Vittoria. That small and dirty town was in our hands by the end of D-day.

On the afternoon of the second day, 11 July, the 3rd Battalion 157th assisted the 179th in taking Cómiso airdrome, about ten statute miles north from the coast. There were 25 enemy planes on the ground and the wreckage of a hundred more in the aircraft cemetery. General Bradley rushed an Army antiaircraft battalion in to defend the field. The first "attack" was from a German Ju–88 bomber whose pilot did not know the field had been captured. The

[25] Conversation with Col. Ankcorn.

[26] John Mason Brown *To All Hands* p. 144. This message was taken off a carrier pigeon that roosted on the deck of *YMS–43,* and was delivered to Admiral Kirk who turned it over to Brown to broadcast.

gunners fired at him and missed; he made a good landing, jumped out of the cockpit and cursed the gunners, whom he supposed to be Italian, in good German! Two fighter planes were captured in the same manner.[27]

In the meantime the 1st Battalion 157th pushed along the highway that laces the escarpment on the edge of the Camerina plain, and at 0815 entered the large and imposing town of Ragusa, simultaneously with troops of the 1st Canadian Division, who had landed on the Pachino Peninsula. Italian troops were already packed up and ready to surrender when the GIs arrived; but the Germans retired.

The 180th Regiment had no such easy going. "King Kong" Schaefer, the 1st Battalion commander – whom we left at dawn on D-day accepting the surrender of terrified Italians at Wood's Hole – soon ran into trouble. Although injured in the leg and walking painfully with the aid of a cane, the Colonel insisted on leading his battalion. Gathering what men he could from elements scattered along the whole range of beaches, he passed Biscari railway station on Highway No. 115 and pushed up the road to the town of Biscari. When about three miles short of it, he encountered Combat Group Left of the Hermann Goering Division, the eastern prong of that armored division's drive to push the invading forces into the sea. This group, consisting of a company of "Tiger" (Mark VI, 75-ton) tanks and two battalions of infantry, well equipped with artillery, mortars and automatic weapons, got into action a day earlier than the western half of the pincer, whose battle with the 1st Division we have already described. Schaefer's battalion, with no artillery support, was forced to retire to the high ground south of the main highway, and its intrepid commander, heading the column, was surrounded and captured.

Such part of the 2nd Battalion as could be assembled, after its strung-out landing, had in the meantime seized the important bridges over the Acate River and taken the high ground dominating that valley from the west. This position had to be abandoned

[27] General Bradley *A Soldier's Story* p. 135.

on 11 July when several Tiger tanks stormed across the highway bridge. Supported by infantry, the Germans drove the 180th off the Biazzo ridge, penetrated the regimental command post, and reached a position only a little over two miles from the Wood's Hole beaches. The combined efforts of infantry, paratroops, a battery of 155-mm field artillery, a company of Sherman tanks, and the Navy, managed to "quiet down" the Germans by 1600.[28] The Navy, in fact, had been assisting all day. That section of the main highway between the Acate River bridge and the Biscari road junction was plastered by four destroyers in succession between 0738 and 1855, following the calls of shore fire-control parties. *Beatty* started the shoot; *Laub* took it up at 1047, firing 408 rounds in the next hour and a half, and was credited by her shore fire-control party with the destruction of four Tiger tanks. *Cowie* fired for two hours around noon, and again for half an hour in the afternoon. Shortly after 1800, three minutes' gunfire by *Tillman* on "tanks under trees" elicited a "Very nice, very nice!" from her shore fire-control party; and ten minutes' gunfire on "tanks moving over the hill" was followed by the signal, "Cease fire, tanks destroyed."

On 12 July, owing to their decisive defeat on the Gela plain, all German forces began to retire from CENT area as well. The 180th Regiment caught up to them near Biscari and entered the town at 2000 after a brisk battle. After a day of comparative inactivity, the 180th advanced at first light 14 July on Biscari airfield, and captured it at 0630. Italian infantry and artillery put up a tough fight for this airfield, so that it was not secured until the evening.

On 14 July, just as the southern columns of the 45th Division pressed near the Vizzini-Caltagirone road, which would open up their advance to Enna in the center of the island, General Bradley, to his disgust, received an order from General Alexander to hold his horses. This important road was wanted by General Montgomery for a flanking movement by the Canadian division, in an effort to get around Catania and Mount Etna, where the Germans

[28] Maj. Gen. James M. Gavin USA *Airborne Warfare* p. 11.

were stoutly resisting. Bradley had no other choice but to march the 45th Division almost back to the Scoglitti beaches and place them in a new position on the left of Terry Allen's 1st Division.[29]

The untried troops of the 45th had now tasted blood, and, as part of General Patton's Seventh Army, pushed inland with renewed confidence and dash. We shall meet them again on the north coast of Sicily.

[29] Bradley *A Soldier's Story* pp. 135–6. "I was certain," he remarks, "that Alexander could not have known how awkward was this movement into which his directive had forced our corps. For want of a day and a night on the Vizzini road, we were forced to disassemble our front and patch it together again."

CHAPTER VIII

The British Sector[1]

10–22 July

1. *Commands, Areas and Plans*

VICE ADMIRAL Sir Bertram Ramsay RN, a naval officer second to none in experience, commanded the Eastern Naval Task Force in Operation HUSKY.[2] He had a larger naval force at his disposal than did his opposite number, Vice Admiral Hewitt, and the military force that he landed, General Montgomery's Eighth Army, was somewhat more numerous than General Patton's Seventh Army. Eastern Task Force landings were effected on the same day (10 July) and H-hour (0245) as those of the Western, with which they were beautifully coördinated. Just as the Western Naval Task Force was not wholly American, so the Eastern was not wholly British; it included some 30 American Liberty and other merchant ships, and a few destroyers and gunboats of the Royal Hellenic, Royal Netherlands, and Polish Navies.

[1] Owing to the predominantly R.N. composition and completely British command of the Eastern Naval Task Force I have only attempted a summary of its activities in this chapter. The main printed sources will be found in Chapter II, note 1, above; in addition, the Admiralty has kindly furnished me with numerous documents, and there are some valuable "Notes and Observations" by Capt. J. H. Foskett, the U.S. Naval Liaison officer, dated 19 May 1943.

[2] Bertram H. Ramsay, b. 1883; entered R.N. 1898; commanded *Monitor 25* and *Broke* in Dover Patrol, World War I; various commands and staff service in war colleges to 1933 when he became C.O. of *Royal Sovereign;* Rear Adm. and chief of staff Home Fleet 1935; retired 1938; recalled to active duty 1939, he organized the Dunkirk evacuation, for which he was knighted. Head of British planners for Operation TORCH. As top Allied Naval Commander under General Eisenhower he planned and executed the Normandy landings of 1944. Promoted Admiral, he was killed in an airplane accident on 2 Jan. 1945, shortly after his crowning achievement, opening the port of Antwerp.

British planning for HUSKY passed through much the same vicissitudes as the American, and encountered similar difficulties. Rear Admiral Troubridge remarked that if planning for TORCH was horrible that for HUSKY was hellish. Admiral Ramsay was in Cairo; Generals Eisenhower and Alexander were in Algiers directing the Tunisian campaign, in which General Montgomery was heavily embroiled. "Monty," as commander of the Eighth Army, naturally had to be consulted. He visited Cairo for a couple of days, during which he changed the entire plan. On a lower level, the S.N.O.L.s [3] were in Cairo, while the Brigadiers with whom they were supposed to plan were in Syria. The transports were mostly at Suez, while the Beach Bricks [4] were in the Syrian desert. As a result, decisions which should have been reached in hours took weeks, and last-minute changes in Army plans were so numerous that naval officers, when they opened their sealed orders, "were faced with a pile of volumes which would daunt an ardent bookworm, and every volume had numerous amendment sheets." [5]

Admiral Ramsay, like Admiral Hewitt, was hampered by the lack of adequate Air Force representation in Cairo, and sailed for Sicily completely in the dark as to what the Northwest African Air Force could or would do to protect his ships' unloading. But in one respect he was better off than his opposite number in the west; an air vice marshal of the R.A.F. sailed in his flagship as local air commander, with authority to act.

Admiral Sir John D. N. Cunningham RN, Commander in Chief Levant, in whose bailiwick most of the Eastern Task Force was mounted, was responsible for embarking about 66,000 men, 10,000 vehicles, and 60,000 tons of stores at Alexandria and a number of minor ports between Haifa and Bengasi. And (as we are apt to forget) it was not until after the Axis surrender in Tunisia that merchant convoys could be routed through the Mediterranean. The first one from the United Kingdom via Gibraltar did not reach

[3] "Senior Naval Officer Landing," corresponding to the U.S. control officer in an amphibious operation, but with more authority.

[4] British equivalent to Army Shore Parties.

[5] Cunningham Despatch.

Alexandria until 22 May: before that, all supplies and matériel for this area had to come around the Cape of Good Hope.

The preliminary air landing in the British sector was performed by 1600 British airborne troops in gliders, towed by 134 planes, of which 106 were C–47s of the United States Army Air Force. These troops were even more widely scattered than in the American air drop, and 47 gliders came down in the sea; but the dozen or so which were released within a reasonable distance of their targets accomplished a very essential task.[6]

Starting on the right flank of the American sector (Admiral Kirk's CENT area), the Eastern Task Force landed Montgomery's Eighth Army on four groups of beaches that swept around the Pachino Peninsula, the southeastern promontory of Sicily, to Cape Murro di Porco south of Syracuse. The four areas, with the naval and military commanders responsible for seizing them, follow: –

1. BARK WEST, the west side of Pachino Peninsula. Force "V" (Rear Admiral Sir Philip Vian RN in H.M.S. *Hilary*) here landed the 40th and 41st Royal Marine Commandos and the 1st Canadian Division (Major General Guy G. Simonds), mounted in the United Kingdom.

2. BARK SOUTH, the blunted end of Pachino Peninsula. Force "B" (Rear Admiral Roderick McGrigor RN in H.M.S. *Largs*) here landed the 154th Brigade 51st (Highland) Division (Major General D. N. Wimberley), mounted in North Africa. (This brigade, together with the BARK WEST and EAST Forces, composed the XXX Corps, Lieutenant General Sir Oliver Leese.)

3. BARK EAST, from near Cape Pássero to Vendicari Island. The small Force "N," Captain Lord Ashbourne RN, in H.M.S. *Keren*, here landed the 231st (Malta) Infantry Brigade (Brigadier R. E. Urquhart), mounted in the Middle East.

[6] The C–47s belonged to 51st Wing N.A.A.F. Troop Carrier Command (Brig. Gen. Ray A. Dunn USA). All except 8 of the gliders were American Wacos, but all glider pilots were British. There is a disposition in British circles to blame the aborted glide on the C–47s' releasing prematurely to avoid AA fire. The main reason, according to Craven and Cate II 446–9, was the inexperience of glider pilots, some of whom cut loose before they got the word from tow pilots, while

4. ACID AREAS, the Gulf of Noto, and up to the Maddalena Peninsula. Force "A" (Rear Admiral Thomas H. Troubridge RN in H.M.S. *Bulolo*) here landed the 50th and 5th Divisions (constituting the XIII Corps, Lieutenant General M. C. Dempsey), together with a Commando battalion; mounted in the Middle East.

A glance at our chart of the Eastern Task Force area will make the objectives clear. The Royal Marine Commandos and 1st Canadians were to protect the left flank. The rest of XXX Corps was to take Pachino airdrome and seal off Pachino Peninsula, after which part of it would advance across Sicily parallel to the United States Seventh Army. The XIII Corps was to take Noto and Ávola, press north to capture Syracuse and Augusta, and overrun the Plain of Catania with its important airfields. Messina was the eventual objective. (Page 153.)

The Royal Navy provided gunfire support and escort ships for its own task force, and the covering forces and submarines for both. Owing, however, to British shortage in troop-lift, the United States contributed 30 vessels, including 24 Liberty ships, manned by American merchant mariners and Naval Armed Guards, to the British convoys that loaded in the Middle East. These ships were used mostly for stores and matériel, but each carried a few hundred troops. Those that took part in the D-day assault carried 65 civilian stevedores each, for speedy discharge; and those in the follow-up convoys carried 17 stevedores each.[7] The Royal Navy also used a large number of LSTs, LCTs, and LCIs built in the United States but manned by British seamen. The LSTs loaded at Suez and Alexandria and the LCIs at Sousse; the LCTs, owing to their slow speed, were sent on ahead to Bengasi, whither their loads were dispatched by rail or motor transport.

---

others turned in the reverse direction from the proper course. Not one towing plane was lost.

[7] U. S. Naval Liaison Officer Suez "Report on Operation HUSKY 29 July 1943" (issued by Intelligence Div. Office of C.N.O.) gives complete list with men embarked and tonnage loaded in all merchant vessels, British or American, used in the Middle East convoys, and their complicated routing.

2. *Pachino Peninsula Landings, 10–11 July*

The transports of Admiral Vian's Force "V," which landed the Canadians in BARK WEST, sailed from the Clyde between 19 June and 10 July in four strongly escorted convoys — two "assault" and two "follow-up." The slow assault convoy lost three freighters to U-boat attack, but most of the passengers and crews were saved. Both assault convoys threaded the Tunisian War Channel, rounded Cape Bon, and, so routed as to clear the United States convoys, passed through the Gozo rendezvous. Beaching craft components, which loaded at Sousse and Sfax, made rendezvous at midnight off the beaches. The Royal Canadian Navy manned four flotillas of landing craft, carried in the transports of this and other British forces.

Instead of the American method of marking beaches by Scouts and Raiders, the British used folbots — frail, collapsible canvas boats like kayaks — from the beacon submarines, in which "gallant young men of the Combined Operations Reconnaissance and Pilotage Parties"[8] went ashore to flash signals seaward and set up beach marks. Commandos landed first, before 0200, on the very beach where, traditionally, Ulysses first made Sicily. There was a delay getting the Canadian division ashore, because almost at the last minute Admiral Vian — alarmed like Admiral Kirk at reconnaissance reports of false beaches — decided to do the job in high-powered LCTs rather than the transports' own landing craft; and the LCTs here, as in the American sector, were held up by the weather. But all assault troops were ashore by sunrise; the cheery British signal "Success!" was made from every beach by 0530.

Beach troubles were similar to those in the American sector. Many landing craft, especially the big LCMs, broached and were washed too high on the beach to retract. The fast "Killer" class British LSTs, which drew more water than ours, were completely baffled by the false beaches; and no pontoon causeways had reached

[8] Cunningham *A Sailor's Odyssey* p. 557.

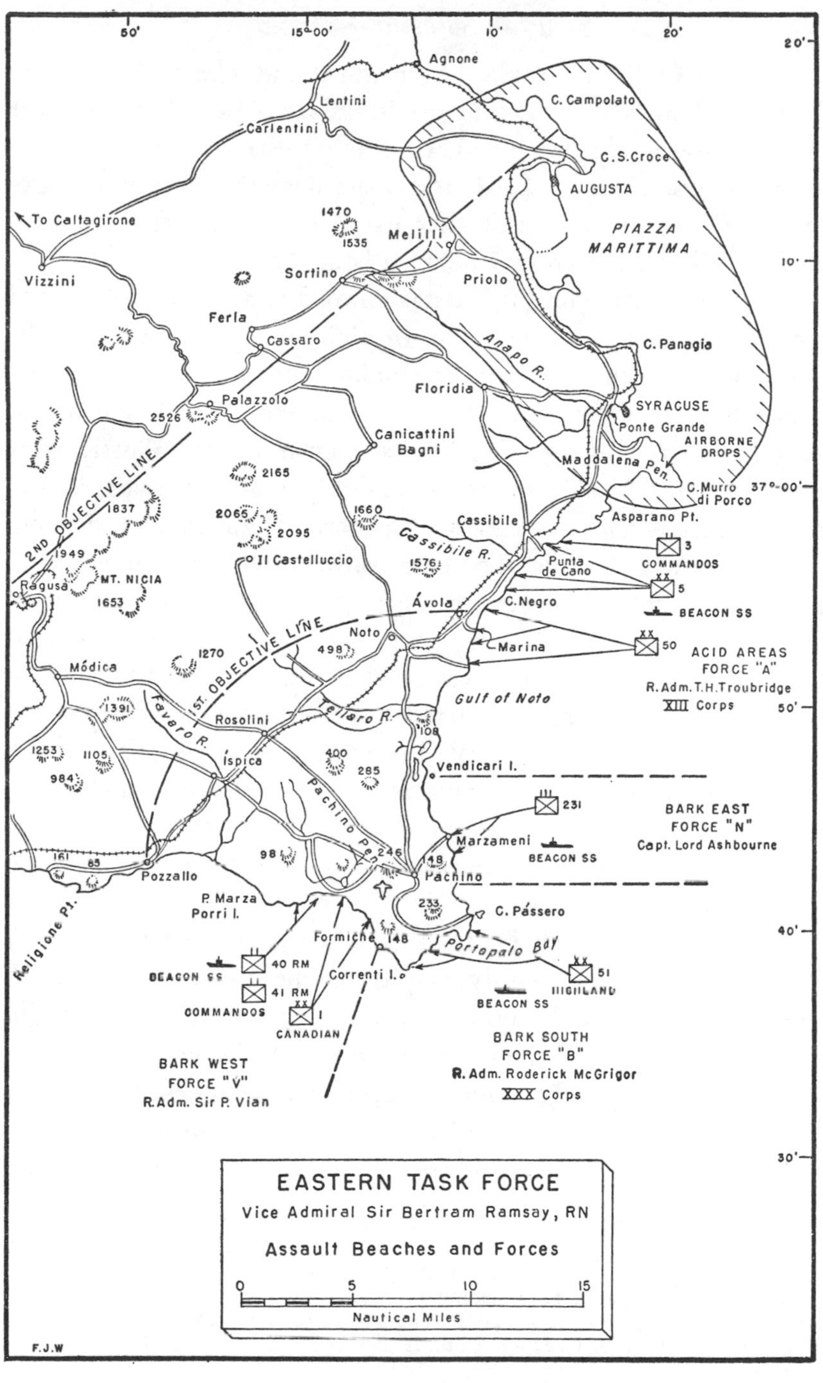
50'
15°00'
10'
20'
20'
10'
37°-00'
50'
40'
30'
Agnone
Lentini
Carlentini
C. Campolato
C. S. Croce
AUGUSTA
PIAZZA
MARITTIMA
To Caltagirone
1470
1535
Melilli
Vizzini
Sortino
Priolo
Ferla
Cassaro
Anapo R.
C. Panagia
Palazzolo
Floridia
SYRACUSE
2526
Ponte Grande
Canicattini
Bagni
AIRBORNE
DROPS
Maddalena Pen.
2165
C. Murro
di Porco
2ND OBJECTIVE LINE
1837
2065
2095
1660
Cassibile
Asparano Pt.
1949
Cassibile R.
Punta
de Cano
3
COMMANDOS
Il Castelluccio
1576
Ragusa
MT. NICIA
1653
5
Avola
C. Negro
BEACON SS
1ST. OBJECTIVE LINE
Noto
498
Marina
50
1270
ACID AREAS
FORCE "A"
R. Adm. T. H. Troubridge
XIII Corps
Módica
Gulf of Noto
1391
Favaro R.
Rosolini
Tellaro R.
108
1253
1105
Ispica
400
285
984
Vendicari I.
Pachino Pen.
231
BARK EAST
FORCE "N"
Capt. Lord Ashbourne
Marzameni
BEACON SS
161
85
98
246
148
Pozzallo
Pachino
P. Marza
Porri I.
233
C. Pàssero
Religione Pt.
Formiche
148
Portopalo Bay
40 RM
Correnti I.
51
BEACON SS
41 RM
HIGHLAND
COMMANDOS
1
BEACON SS
CANADIAN
BARK SOUTH
FORCE "B"
R. Adm. Roderick McGrigor
XXX Corps
BARK WEST
FORCE "V"
R. Adm. Sir P. Vian
EASTERN TASK FORCE
Vice Admiral Sir Bertram Ramsay, RN
Assault Beaches and Forces
0
5
10
15
Nautical Miles
F.J.W

BARK WEST. One small, rocky beach was found where two or three American-built LSTs at a time could unload almost dry-ramp; the "Killers" were unloaded by LCTs. Highest marks, however, went to the dukws. These, said Admiral Vian, were the outstanding success of the operation. Craft that grounded on the false beaches could hardly have been unloaded without them.

Pozzallo, a village on the coastal railroad and an important road junction, lay several miles west of the landing beaches. As the Canadians detailed to capture it encountered opposition, they requested naval gunfire; "V" Force destroyers obliged, starting at 2045 on D-day and resuming fire at noon next day. Shortly after 1330 July 11, white flags were observed ashore. Destroyers *Blankney* and *Brissenden* made up a landing party of sailors who accepted the surrender of Pozzallo. The keys of the town hall, together with a bouquet of flowers, were presented by the postmaster to the naval officer in charge of the landing party, and the population "evinced great friendliness." Pozzallo was all the warmer toward the British sailors because they had delivered the village from an unpopular German garrison which retreated with most of the available food. But the local priest and the postmaster helped the Canadians to break open a granary, averting a threatened famine.[9]

Módica surrendered to the Canadians, as did the commanding general of the 206th Coastal Division, on 11 July; next day the Canadians and the 45th Division entered the important town of Ragusa almost simultaneously. Rapid marches had so tired the Canadians that General Montgomery gave them two days' rest. On the 14th they resumed the advance, and, with the aid of the Highlanders on their right flank, took Vizzini on the important east–west road from Syracuse to Enna. Near Vizzini the commanding general and staff of the Napoli Division were captured.[10] Thus, by the end

[9] Capt. T. Dorling RN "The Navy in the Sicilian Campaign" (British press release of 1943) p. 4.

[10] Col. C. P. Stacey *The Canadian Army 1939–45* (Ottawa 1948) pp. 100–1; J. B. Conacher "Canadian Participation in the Sicilian Campaign" (Harvard doctoral dissertation 1949) pp. 118–34; Lt. Col. G. W. L. Nicholson preliminary draft of *The Canadians in Italy 1943–45* (Vol. II of the *Official History of the Canadian Army*.)

of the fifth day, the Canadians had passed the eastern end of Line Yellow, and had bagged two major generals.

BARK WEST beaches were so rough, compared with those around the cape, that after 22 July, when all ships had finished unloading, they were left to the local fishermen and the shade of Ulysses.

Rear Admiral McGrigor's Force "B," charged with putting the 51st (Highland) Division ashore on each side of Portopalo Bay, the BARK SOUTH area, was the counterpart of Rear Admiral Conolly's JOSS Force – composed of beaching craft and passenger steamers converted to LSIs.

The 51st Division, which included elements of the Seaforth, Cameron, and Gordon Highlanders and of the Black Watch, had been trained at the British combined operations center at Djidjelli, Algeria. The story of its storm-tossed approach is very similar to that of JOSS Force. McGrigor, like Conolly, was forced to break Cincmed's orders and alter course to the north to counteract leeway. During the final stages of the approach, the field was strung out as in a fox hunt with the Bicester.

All assault waves landed successfully on three small beaches between Correnti Island and the west end of Portopalo Bay between H-hour and 0430; even the LCTs had all tanks and antitank guns ashore before sunrise. On the rocky eastern point of Portopalo Bay, where the fishing village of that name is situated, a stone ramp for hauling out fishing boats was of great assistance in landing the Camerons and the Seaforths. The "Jocks" promptly disposed of the Italian defenders, so that the sheltered sand beaches of the bay were ready to take landing craft and LSTs by mid-afternoon. False beaches and runnels there were; but a pontoon causeway was soon rigged, and the dukws took false beaches in their stride. By dark the whole 51st Division, minus kilts but complete with bagpipes and most of its vehicles, was ashore.

Pachino Peninsula is arid, flat, and almost treeless; good terrain for troop deployment. The Highlanders, as early as 0700 D-day, took the poor little town of Pachino and within two hours met the

Canadians at Pachino airfield. That strip had been badly cratered by the 15-inch guns of monitor *Roberts*, and its principal defense, a battery of 6-inch howitzers, had also been silenced by naval gunfire. A British airfield construction group had the strip ready for emergency landings shortly after noon on D-day, and fighter squadrons began to base there on the 14th. And the "sappers" (as the British call their army engineers) soon had the coastal railway running from Pachino to Noto.

BARK EAST area, separated from BARK SOUTH by about five miles of rocky coast, was assaulted by Force "N," the 231st (Malta) Infantry Brigade lifted in three LSIs and three LCIs commanded by Captain Lord Ashbourne RN in H.M.S. *Keren*. The 231st had been trained in Egypt; most of its landing craft were manned by the Royal Canadian Navy. On 6 July, one of the freighters in the first follow-up convoy, S.S. *Shahjehan*, was torpedoed and sunk off Derna by *U-453*. The loss of vehicles and stores that she carried, together with four companies of stevedores, was severely felt.

The beaches in this area, just south of the fishing village of Marzamemi, are well protected by two small islands; but there was no protection for the transports. A heavy sea, running from the north, made the lowering and loading of landing craft a slow and difficult process, and the boats made a ragged run to the beach; but they touched down in time, with over two hours of darkness ahead. Here, tactical surprise was so complete that the assault troops found the entire crew of an Italian 75-mm fieldpiece, concealed in a shed 50 yards behind the beach, fast asleep. A battery of five coast defense guns, which awoke in time to lay a defensive barrage 200 yards off the beach, did not succeed in hitting anything and was quickly silenced by two gunboats, H.N.M.S. *Flores* and *Soemba*. Tanks brought up by LSTs, arriving at 0648, were able to roll directly out of them onto the beaches; and as the LCTs were six hours late Admiral McGrigor sent some from BARK SOUTH to help discharge the Liberty ships that followed the assault shipping.

3. *Ávola-Cassibile Landings, 10–13 July*

The ACID areas, covering the Gulf of Noto and running up toward Syracuse, received the most powerful British assaults. Force "A," commanded by Rear Admiral Troubridge in H.M.S. *Bulolo,* lifted the XIII Corps (5th and 50th Divisions) from Alexandria and Port Said in several separate convoys. Admiral Ramsay sailed from Malta in H.M.S. *Antwerp* at 0630 July 9 to witness a successful rendezvous of these widely spaced convoys near that island in heavy weather. *Bulolo,* pressing ahead, sighted Mount Etna before sunset.

Guided by only one beacon submarine, Force "A" had some difficulty in locating the ten ACID beaches, strung out as they were for eight or ten miles along the Gulf of Noto. This force, too, had trouble lowering landing craft in a short, steep sea and high wind; but the beaches themselves were fairly well sheltered from the mistral, and no searchlights played on the ships. The first wave of assault troops landed around 0410, and within an hour the transports were ordered to close the shore. At first light, Italian coast defense guns around Ávola began shelling the southernmost beaches, until H.M.S. *Eskimo* opened gunfire at 0545 and temporarily relieved the situation. The men ashore, near the Marina di Ávola, a little tuna-fishing port, were also bothered by strafing Me–109s. At 0619, the 50th Division commander signaled: "All troops landed, capture and mopping-up of beach defense completed. Most beaches being shelled."

The coastal highway at this point runs under the foot of the Montagna d'Ávola, a high, arid plateau on the edge of which Noto is poised; the town of Ávola lies just below, between road and bay. It would have been easy to site artillery on the plateau that could have interdicted the landing; fortunately, the Italians did not do this. Their batteries, all close to shore, were silenced by 0800, and two hours later the 50th Division took Ávola. High-poised Noto required more time; but the troops entered early next morning, to be joyfully greeted by the populace of that golden baroque city, fairest town in all Sicily.

In the ACID NORTH area, an excellent landing place was chosen for the 3rd Commandos, who were to advance on Syracuse, and for most of the 5th Division. This was Beach George, a crescent-shaped sand beach from which a narrow but solid road leads between almond groves and across the railway to Cassibile. That village on the main highway was in British hands by 0800; it was here that Italy formally surrendered, just eight weeks later. In this region the country is highly cultivated, with many olive groves and small fields separated by stone walls and cactus hedges, but roads are numerous and the British found good exits from almost all their landing beaches. By the evening of D-day the 5th Division was firmly established on the Montagna d'Ávola, and one combat team was well on its way to Syracuse.

Large transports retired from ACID by 1530, avoiding the biggest air raid of the day, at sundown; but the enemy planes took a nasty revenge by attacking hospital ships *Dorsetshire* and *Talamba*, which were fully illuminated and lay three miles outside the main anchorage. Both were hit, and *Talamba* sank after all patients had been taken off. Thereafter hospital ships in the Eastern Naval Task Force were blacked out.

The story of the master of United States Liberty ship *Colin P. Kelly Jr.*, which landed her men and equipment at Beach George, is a good sample of the performance of the American merchant vessels that were used as AKAs in the ACID area. In June she loaded water, ammunition and 80 trucks at Haifa, and took on three LCMs at Port Said. Thence she sailed to Alexandria for more supplies, embarked 163 British troops, and departed in a convoy on 4 July. At 1000 D-day she arrived at her destination off Beach George. From that time until noon 13 July the ship discharged almost continuously during daylight with the aid of her own LCMs and dukws and landing craft from other vessels; and accomplished this with almost no confusion and few mistakes. "Everyone on the ship pitched in splendidly, Army, Navy and ship's crew alike, all working willingly with absolutely no complaints or confusion. The guns' crews stayed at their posts continually throughout the entire four days, some of them actually sleeping in the harness of Oerlikon guns. The ship's crew brought food to them and assisted in passing ammunition and loading." [11] No fewer than 29 air raids in which bombs were dropped came in. British Spitfires from Malta kept the bombers off by day, but there were not enough Beaufighters to thwart them at night.

Admiral Cunningham went out of his way to praise "the fine spirit, discipline and calm determination of the many officers and men of the Allied Merchant Navies." "They were our real comrades in arms, undaunted by any difficulty or danger." [12] And Admiral Troubridge, an officer hard to please, was delighted with the unloading in ACID Area. The dukws, he said, were "magnificent."

British ground forces, meeting only feeble and sporadic opposition, made as good time in BARK and ACID as the United States forces were doing in JOSS and CENT. Italian coastal troops "stampeded to the safety of our prisoner-of-war cages on the beach in such terrific disorder that our troops faced greater danger from being trampled upon than from bullets." [13] Many of these prisoners even volunteered to do stevedoring work for their captors, rather than be shipped to P.O.W. camps in Africa.

4. *Fall of Syracuse and Augusta, 10–14 July* [14]

The most surprising event in the British sector was the prompt and complete collapse of *Piazza marittima Augusta-Siracusa,* upon

[11] War Dept. Military Intelligence Service Collection Unit, Information from Mariners No. 85, 23 Aug. 1943, signed by Col. R. S. Bratton USA.

[12] *A Sailor's Odyssey* p. 557.

[13] L. S. B. Shapiro *They Left the Back Door Open* (1944) p. 48.

[14] General Alexander Despatch p. 1018; Lt. Gen. Wilhelm Schmalz "The Fight for Sicily in the Section of Brigade Schmalz" (1947); Bernotti *La Guerra Sui Mare* pp. 67–75 with map; Bragadin pp. 255–65; Gen. Faldella in *Il Tempo del Lunedi* 6 July 1953 and comments on same, prepared for this History by the Historical Staff of the Italian Army. I have largely followed the latter account in this controversial subject.

which the Axis had counted to repel any invasion in that quarter. This "maritime strong point," including the two ancient cities and about 30 kilometers of coast, contained at least 23 coast defense batteries (four of them of 6-inch caliber), five anti-paratroop batteries, miles of barbed wire and scores of machine guns. Like other Sicilian *piazze*, it had been set up in the hope of preventing the Allies from capturing important seaports, and so of wrecking their invasion, since nobody imagined that armies could be supported without harbors. From the sea the Augusta-Syracuse strong point looked impregnable, but the British approached it by land, which the Italian planners had not taken into account, and Rear Admiral Leonardi, the commander, had not been given a force commensurate with his responsibilities.

In attacking this strong point, the night-before air landing was decisive. About 160 British airborne infantry glided to earth at a place where there was no anti-paratroop unit to oppose them, the Maddalena Peninsula. Some of them captured nearby coastal batteries and the Cape Murro di Porco radio station; others advanced to the Ponte Grande, a high-arching bridge of the main coastal highway over a canal and the Anapo River, just south of Syracuse. The airborne troops' mission was to prevent Ponte Grande's being blown, and to hold it until the infantry landing farther south came up. The bridge is near the head of Syracuse harbor, which at that point is covered with salt pans and so impassable by troops; and Ovid's "gently flowing Anapo" is too wide and deep to ford.

General Rossi, commanding the XVI Italian Army Corps, got word of the invasion promptly and ordered four combat groups into motion for the defense of the Piazza. Any one of these was more than enough to recapture the bridge and block the road into Syracuse; but none arrived in time, owing to ruptured communications and various contretemps; and Admiral Leonardi was unable to get in touch with any of these units or with the higher command until 1600. The defenders of Ponte Grande, numbering only eight officers and 65 men, had plenty of time to remove demolition charges and set up defenses. At about 1700 they were invested by a superior force of Italian infantry, with artillery and a few tanks, that had moved in on them from the Piazza. Against these heavy odds the airborne troops gamely held their own until after dark, when a vanguard of the 5th Infantry Division relieved them. Only 19 men then survived. Enemy forces now melted away and the 5th Division marched right on into Syracuse by the main highway, arriving at 2100 July 10. That *via dolorosa* for the ancient Athenians had become a *via triumphalis* for the British.

As the Italians report, "The key to the English success was, definitely, the failure to blow the bridge over the Anapo." It started a chain reaction. The German antiaircraft gunners at Syracuse and Augusta retreated north, and this had a demoralizing effect on Italian units. A blackshirt militia officer in charge of other batteries at Augusta followed suit; and Admiral Leonardi, thoroughly discouraged, ordered all remaining defenses of Syracuse destroyed, and concentrated on saving Augusta. During the same evening, units of the 5th Division, supported by naval gunfire, engaged the Schmalz armored group at Priolo and forced it to retire to Melilli.

Syracuse harbor entrance was swept by British minecraft on the morning of 11 July. Shortly after noon, when the channel was reported clear, Rear Admiral Troubridge, flying his flag in a small sweeper, entered the port and went ashore. This famous city, which had baffled the greatest amphibious operation of antiquity, became a British port of entry within 36 hours of the initial landings. Alcibiades had remarked in 415 B.C.: "If Syracuse falls, all Sicily falls also, and Italy immediately afterwards." [15] It did not happen quite so quickly in A.D. 1943, but the omen was good, and Syracuse was the first major European port to be captured by the Allies. The harbor, within which Athenian and Sicilian triremes had fought each other to a standstill, was rather small for modern shipping; but as early as 13 July it accommodated a convoy of 12 troop-laden vessels which discharged in eight and a quarter hours.

Augusta, 15 miles farther up the coast and provided with a large artificial harbor, was the next objective. A vanguard of the 5th

[15] Thucydides *Peloponnesian War* (Crawley trans.) IV. xx.

Division entered the city shortly before midnight 11 July. That night Admiral Troubridge started for the same destination in destroyer *Eskimo.* Off Syracuse she was hit by an air bomb which started a fire in the after fuel tanks and killed 19 men. The Admiral transferred his flag to destroyer *Exmoor.* In the meantime the minesweepers had entered Augusta harbor and reported the channel clear; so at 1035 *Exmoor* proudly steamed in, with Greek destroyer *Kanaris* in her wake. Their appearance did not have the expected effect; and, as Troubridge wryly remarked, "If I was the first admiral to enter Augusta, I was also the first out again, my departure being hastened by a considerable volume of fire from various unfriendly gents ashore!" [16] He might have felt better about it had he known that some shots which near-missed *Exmoor* were fired by Admiral Leonardi and two members of his staff with their own hands, the Italian Admiral here playing the rôle of Casabianca.[17]

After two more unsuccessful attempts to enter and stay, Admiral Troubridge, concluding that he must be a Jonah as far as Augusta was concerned, returned to his own ship; and at 1930 July 12 H.M.S. *Ulster Monarch,* escorted by a destroyer and two motor gunboats, entered and landed troops who succeeded in silencing the enemy. Early next morning a port development party moved in.

But the Eastern Task Force was not allowed to walk away with Augusta. An Italian naval battery northwest of the city, which British gunfire failed to locate, fired into Augusta so frequently that the port development party had to retire until a Commando unit could attend to the Italian gunners. The Commandos embarked at Syracuse in *Prince Albert* on the evening of 13 July, escorted by H.M.S. *Tetcott,* which en route drove off a motor-torpedo-boat attack. They landed on Cape Campolato north of Augusta, com-

[16] Keith Edwards *Britain at War: The Royal Navy, 1943–44* p. 19.

[17] Bragadin p. 464. There was much recrimination within the Axis about the fall of the Piazza. Italians claim that the German AA gunners at Syracuse started it by destroying their batteries and retreating. Senger admits that they retreated but states that they took their 88-mm guns with them and later used them for the defense of the Strait. Mussolini announced, and some Germans still maintain, that Admiral Leonardi "fled treacherously to Messina," which is false.

pleted their mission before sunrise 14 July, reëmbarked, and were back at Syracuse within twenty-four hours. In the meantime, Colonel Schmalz of the German armored combat group, after a conference with Marshal Kesselring on 12 July, had decided to fall back with his supporting infantry to the line Lentini–Francoforte, and to hold that line until the Hermann Goering Division could come to his assistance and occupy prepared positions under Mount Etna. A battalion of the Napoli Division, more brave than wise, managed to break through the British lines on the 13th and to reoccupy the seaplane base at Augusta; but the British moved against their line of communications, and on the morning of 14 July forced them to retire. That afternoon the Royal Navy returned to Augusta in force, this time to stay, and had the harbor in full operation as an Allied port of entry by the 16th.

Docking facilities at Augusta were so limited that only 1600 tons of cargo could be discharged daily, but the Italian seaplane and submarine bases were captured intact, and the harbor promptly became an important base for British motor torpedo boats. Syracuse, though the smaller port of the two, proved the more useful because its installations had not been so heavily damaged by air bombing. Within the harbor where Nicias and Demosthenes met their fate, 18 LSTs and LCTs could unload simultaneously, and over 5000 tons of cargo could be handled daily. Both places were of inestimable benefit in supporting and supplying the Eighth Army.

Both, too, became objects of intense interest to enemy aircraft and to Italian motor torpedo boats based at Messina. In the small hours of 20 July, U.S.S. *Niblack* and *PC–556*, escorting two merchant vessels and two LSTs from Gela to Syracuse, sighted three torpedo wakes when about to enter the swept channel. They heard two explosions – evidently "prematures" – and opened fire on two torpedo boats, which fled northward, making smoke. That brief encounter is but a sample of what went on almost nightly for ten days or two weeks off the former Piazza Marittima.

5. *Air Raids and Unloading, 11–14 July*

The annals of Eastern Task Force beaches for the most part are the same tale of follow-up convoys arriving and departing, of beach congestion and of LSTs making heroic efforts to get discharged, that we have read of in the story of the American sector. But the Eastern area was more enlivened by air attacks, which continued long after 13 July, when Axis bombers decided to lay off the Americans.

The unwisdom of catering to the Air Forces by launching an amphibious assault at the end of a first-quarter moon in July was soon demonstrated. Every night the moon waxed brighter and set later. Every night was crystal-clear. Although the Sicilian airfields were by this time either in Allied hands or abandoned, the Axis-held airfields in southern Italy were so much nearer to the British ships than to the Americans that Luftwaffe and Regia Aeronautica concentrated on the vessels unloading in ACID and BARK EAST. Smoke was extensively used, but not every ship escaped. Besides *Eskimo* and *Talamba* already mentioned, four Liberty ships and a Dutch auxiliary were hit, and two were lost. H.N.M.S. *Baarn*, an ammunition carrier, was set on fire by splinters from a near-miss during a noon air attack on 11 July, and had to be abandoned and scuttled. *Joseph G. Cannon*, after completing her unloading, was hit off Ávola that evening by a dud bomb which went through her bottom. She was able to return to port under her own power; but her sister Liberty ship *Timothy Pickering* was not so lucky. As she was unloading explosives off Ávola at noon 13 July, a direct hit and near-miss by two 500-pound air bombs split her in two. About 100 of the 130 British troops on board were killed, as were 30 Americans of the ship's crew and naval armed guard, and she became a total loss.[18] In an air raid at 0215 July 17, Liberty ship *William T. Coleman* was damaged and H.M.S. *Queen Emma* lost 18

[18] Data from Maritime Commission records. A salvage vessel was working on the wreck when I visited the spot in July 1953.

killed and 70 wounded. *Samuel Parker* lost two men in an air attack on the 22nd.

Despite these losses, Admiral Ramsay was as pleased with his air support as Admiral Hewitt was displeased with what he obtained. Good tactical air cover was furnished from Malta and Gozo; and, although the Eastern lost more ships to air attack than the Western Task Force did, "it appeared almost magical" to Admiral Cunningham "that great fleets of ships could remain anchored on the enemy's coast within 40 miles of his main airdromes, with only such slight losses from air attack as were incurred." For Cunningham well remembered the evil days of the Battle of Crete in May 1941 when the Royal Navy, temporarily without fighter protection, had been at the mercy of Axis bombers.

The second mission of Allied airborne troops, on the night of 13–14 July, met the same devastating reception over ACID as did the American drop over DIME and CENT. Here, as there, the flight was ordered at such short notice that ships did not get the word; here, too, the passenger planes were confused with enemy aircraft which happened to be delivering a bombing attack at that very moment; here, too, several were shot down. Nevertheless, one unit of the airborne troops landed exactly where they were supposed to land, at the Primosole Bridge.

The Royal Navy, in delivering gunfire support to troops on shore, at that time did not use air spot. Apart from top spot (the visual observation of shots from shipboard), it relied on a system similar to the United States Navy's shore fire-control. A team of specially trained Royal Artillery officers was placed on board each ship, and naval communication parties, each headed by Forward Observation Officer (F.O.O.), were attached to troop and artillery units ashore. As soon as radio communication was established between a ship and her special F.O.O., she was "on call" to deliver supporting fire as desired.[19] In HUSKY, 23 F.O.O. parties were attached to army units, and in addition six smaller groups flew in

[19] Cdr. J. G. Hamilton RN "Naval Bombardment" in *Journal of Royal United Services Inst.* XC (1945) p. 346.

with the airborne units. These last proved to be especially valuable in supplying information on the location of friendly troops and for directing fire on targets not otherwise observed.

Although initial enemy resistance in the British sector was light compared with what the Seventh Army encountered, British monitors, cruisers and destroyers made nearly 200 shoots, some at targets designated by F.O.O.s and others on strong points known to be in enemy possession, or guns betraying themselves by flashes. Here, too, enthusiastic converts to naval gunfire support were made among the soldiers. As an instance of accuracy, when H.M.S. *Puckeridge* was called upon to silence a troublesome battery near Portopalo early on D-day, the first salvo fell on the gun parapet and 20 more rounds disposed of the only effective opposition offered to the landing.

At 1400 July 13, Rear Admiral McGrigor, still flying his flag in H.M.S. *Largs*, was appointed Flag Officer, Sicily, by Admiral of the Fleet Cunningham. He thus became the opposite number to Admiral Conolly, with full charge of naval operations in the Eastern sector. Three days later he shifted his anchorage to Augusta.

H.M. destroyer *Brocklesby* arrived off Pozzallo at 1015 July 12 with General Montgomery on board. "Monty" was well pleased with the progress of his Eighth Army. The entire southeastern part of Sicily, up to but not quite including Augusta, was firmly in its possession. The XXX Corps had occupied a large chunk of the interior, up to the line Ragusa-Palazzolo. "The operations were very exhausting for the troops," he wrote, since their advance had been made entirely on foot. But he ordered the advance to continue: XXX Corps toward Enna, XIII Corps toward Catania. And on that day, or early on the next, he decided that the latter should "make a great effort to break through into the Plain of Catania . . . and ordered a major attack for the night 13–14 July." That is where trouble began for the Eighth Army.

6. *Operations of the Covering Forces*

Each Navy provided gunfire support for the troops of its own nation, but the Royal Navy furnished the covering forces for the whole of HUSKY. They were organized as follows: –

Force "H," Vice Admiral Sir Algernon U. Willis RN: battleships *Nelson, Rodney, Warspite, Valiant;* aircraft carriers *Indomitable* and *Formidable;* 18 destroyers.[20] This force included Force "Q," Commodore W. G. Agnew RN: light cruisers *Aurora, Penelope, Cleopatra, Euryalus, Sirius, Dido.*

Force "Z," Captain C. H. L. Woodhouse RN: battleships *Howe, King George V;* six destroyers.

Force "H" – half of which sailed from Mers el Kebir and the other half from Alexandria, in order to cover both groups of convoys – rendezvoused south of Malta and then split three ways. Admiral Willis shaped a course toward Greece with his battleships and carriers, in order to prove that "Major William Martin" was right after all. He reversed course after dark 9 July and made for a point southeast of Sicily, where he cruised about in the vain hope of drawing off enemy air attacks from the amphibious forces. Two light cruisers and two destroyers bombarded railway and power stations at Catania and Taormina in the early hours of D-day, while the rest of Force "Q" began a routine patrol of the northern flank of ACID area. Admiral Willis never raised another enemy target, and failed to accomplish his purpose of tempting the Italian Fleet to leave port.

The absence of enemy torpedo-bombers, a type which had raised havoc with the United States Pacific Fleet in 1942, was gratefully noted until 14 July, when six of them, Italians, attacked H.M.S. *Euryalus, Cleopatra* and two destroyers off Cape Spartivento. All torpedoes were successfully dodged. Two days later, when the moon lacked one day of full, a torpedo-bomber scored on

[20] Of which 3 were Dutch, 1 Greek, 1 Polish, the rest British.

carrier *Indomitable* about 50 miles off Cape Pássero, and got away without even being fired upon. Although the explosion knocked out the port boiler room and adjacent compartments, *Indomitable*, true to her name, turned up 14 knots and made Gibraltar for repairs. There were many red faces in Force "H" after this incident, which Admiral Cunningham ascribed to "a sense of false security."

The same day, 16 July, Italian submarine *Dandalo* got a torpedo into H.M.S. *Cleopatra*, patrolling with Force "Q" north of Syracuse. Again, only a boiler room was knocked out and propulsion was not lost; but 21 men were killed and 23 wounded. Other encounters with submarines *Nereide* and *Ascianghi*, we have already described in Chapter III.

Force "Z" moved from Gibraltar to Algiers before D-day, and on the nights of 12 and 13 July bombarded two of the Ægades Islands off the western cape of Sicily, and the nearby city of Trápani as well. The main object of these shoots was to create the impression that Allied troops were about to land in that part of Sicily. Battleship *Warspite* bombarded Catania at 1845 July 17 in support of the Eighth Army; coastal batteries replied without effect. To reach her bombarding position from Malta, this veteran of the Battle of Jutland made good 23½ knots for five hours, an exploit which led Admiral Cunningham to remark, "There is no question, when the old lady lifts her skirts, she can run!" But Admiral Willis considered the moral effect of the bombardment to have been greater than the material. That is true of all these shoots by the covering forces, including a bombardment of Crotone by Force "Q" on the 21st. The United States naval observer remarked that "neither radar nor airplane spot was used by H.M. ships in bombarding shore objectives during this operation." They were "far behind the U. S. Navy in gunnery fire control, radar equipment and application." [21] Under such limitations a night bombardment could be little more than *brutum fulmen*.

There were several noisy but inconclusive brawls in the early days of the operation, between British motor torpedo boats and

[21] Capt. Foskett "Notes" p. 5.

their Axis counterparts based on Messina. The Germans, who had suffered heavy losses to PTs during the Tunisian campaign, on 17 July set up a special Messina command and a night patrol south of the Strait. They had only seven R-boats (100-ton minesweepers) and a captured French gunboat to do it with, but that appears to have been sufficient. One R-boat was sunk by Allied planes on 25 July, but she was then north of the Strait, trying to locate survivors from a group of transport planes shot down by Allied fighters.

An unpleasant surprise to all hands in Operation HUSKY was the almost total absence of Italian surface warships in the heart of Mussolini's *Mare Nostrum*. On the night of 16–17 July one brief encounter took place, when light cruiser *Scipio Africano* was proceeding from Spezia to Taranto. Four British motor torpedo boats, patrolling two miles south of Messina, ran afoul of her under the full moon at 0215 July 17. *Scipio* hit and sank one boat; the other three fired torpedoes which missed, but they had the consolation of seeing Italian batteries on both sides of the Strait open fire on their own cruiser and straddle her twice.

The Royal Navy's part in Operation HUSKY was conducted with the same verve and efficiency as that of the United States Navy. The British had the easier meteorological conditions for landing, but the worse enemy air attacks. The American troops met stouter initial opposition, but after 15 July it was the other way round. On each side there was that complete coöperation between Army and Navy which we now take for granted, but which pleasantly surprised old hands of both services in 1943. Each task force learned valuable lessons for the future, especially the value of naval gunfire support to troops ashore. And, although the British and the Americans landed on different sections of the coast, the closest coördination was maintained at all upper levels of command, and the two Navies got along so well that a more intimate intermingling could be attempted at Salerno.

But, before the next operation could start, Sicily had to be conquered.

CHAPTER IX

Sicily Overrun[1]

11 July–7 August

1. *Allied and Axis Objectives*

ALTHOUGH General Alexander's Operation Instructions of 19 May were vague as to his intentions subsequent to the landings, there is no doubt that the essence of his plan was a swift advance by the British Eighth Army on Messina via Catania, while the American Seventh Army protected its left flank. Thereafter, presumably, Seventh Army would isolate Axis forces in western Sicily and help the Eighth to push enemy forces in eastern Sicily north of Mount Etna. By this "pincer" type of operation the Strait of Messina, the only evacuation route possible for the Axis, would have been closed, their forces virtually surrounded and forced to surrender. That is how the Allies intended to conquer Sicily and how it should have been done; but of course the enemy had different views. His stiff resistance on the Catania plain forced a complete change of plan.

Now that the beachheads were secure and enemy dispositions had been felt out, General Alexander's staff, on the night of 12–13 July, drew up a plan, and the directives were issued next day. Montgomery was to thrust XIII Corps due north to Catania, while XXX Corps took the road to Enna and continued to the north coast at

[1] General Eisenhower's Dispatch; General Alexander's Despatch (*London Gazette* 10 Feb. 1948); Seventh Army *Report of Operations* (1943); Lt. General L. K. Truscott jr, *Command Missions* (1954); Lt. Colonel G. W. L. Nicholson *The Canadians in Italy* (Vol. II of the Official History of the Canadian Army, seen in ms.); The U.S. divisional histories; Axis sources listed in footnote 1 to chapter iii.

San Stéfano di Camastra "to split the island in half." This left Seventh Army free to pivot on its left and overrun the central and western parts of the island in whatever manner General Patton chose; except that he was ordered, for the time being, not to get involved in a fight for Agrigento.

As it turned out, the Americans had the easier task for the first ten days. Seventh Army, whose total strength stood at 203,204 officers and men on 15 July,[2] overran the western half of the island in record time and entered Palermo 22 July. After that, it had to lend a hand to the British in eastern Sicily.

Marshal Kesselring flew to General Guzzoni's headquarters at Enna on 12 July to find out what was going on. And what he saw and heard deflated his easy optimism. The Allied landings everywhere had been successful. The Hermann Goering counterattack had failed ignominiously. Syracuse and Augusta had fallen. Several airfields were already in Allied possession. Kesselring realized that there was nothing left but to fight a delaying action. But he did ascertain that Guzzoni had shown decision and initiative. As early as noon on D-day he had ordered the two combat teams of the 15th Panzer Grenadiers then in western Sicily, and a mobile group of the Assietta Division, to move into the hills behind Licata and Gela. At 0910 July 12, only five minutes before Kesselring descended from his plane at Enna, Commander Sixth Army had ordered the Hermann Goering Division to move to the Caltagirone-Vizzini road, with the Napoli covering its easterly and the Livorno its westerly flank; the Schmalz Group to try to save Augusta; and the 15th Panzer Grenadiers to block any northern thrusts of the 1st and 3rd United States Divisions. Kesselring confirmed these dispositions.[3]

The Marshal flew back to Rome the same day and informed Mussolini that, owing to the failure of the Italian troops, it would be impossible to defend Sicily. The Duce beat his breast and bellowed, "The occupation . . . it must not come!"[4]

[2] Seventh Army *Report of Operations* p. b–8.
[3] Senger "Battle for Sicily" sec. 4 (pp. 21–37 of trans.).
[4] Westphal *German Army in the West* p. 138.

Hitler, on receiving radio reports from Kesselring at his "wolf's lair" headquarters in East Prussia, on 13 July issued a directive that governed the action of German forces in the Sicilian campaign for the next month. "After the bulk of the Italian forces are eliminated" – apparently a foregone conclusion – "the Germans alone will be insufficient to push the enemy into the sea. It will therefore be the objective of the Germans to delay the enemy advance, and bring it to a halt west of Mount Etna." The initial defense line chosen by Marshal Kesselring started on the north coast road three miles west of San Stéfano di Camastra, passed around Agira and Regalbuto southeast to Catenanuova on the Enna–Catania railway, and along that railway to the sea. And, on 14 July, Hitler confirmed the Marshal's decision to reinforce Sicily with the 1st Paratroop Division, the 29th Panzer Grenadier Division and the rest of the XIV Panzer Corps, whose commander, General Hans Hube, had proved his mettle on the Russian front.[5]

A well-directed attack by the Northwest African Air Force at midnight 12–13 July completely destroyed Sixth Army headquarters at Enna. General Guzzoni, mortified by the poor performance of the Italian divisions, talked wildly of "sharing the fate of his troops," but soon pulled himself together. Unimpressed by diversionary monkeyshines of American "beach jumpers" between Mazara and Sciacca,[6] the General on 13 July decided further to denude his defenses in western Sicily to help his center and east. Leaving certain elements (to be mentioned presently) to protect Agrigento, he ordered the rest of the Assietta Division to traverse the island across the American front, and the Hermann Goering Panzer Division to continue moving east in order to join the defense of the Catania plain. Other tactical regroupings were made in order to protect this movement. "It was no longer possible to think of expelling the enemy," wrote his chief of staff. "Henceforth we must develop tactics of attrition and delay."[7]

[5] *Fuehrer Directives of the German Armed Forces 1942–45* p. 83; Bonin p. 7.
[6] Vice Adm. Hewitt *Action Report* p. 79.
[7] Gen. Faldella in *Roma* 18 July 1953.

General Guzzoni now established Sixth Army headquarters near Randazzo, on the north slope of Mount Etna, where he was shortly joined by General Hube and XIV Panzer Corps headquarters. On 17 July Colonel Bogislaw von Bonin flew in with oral orders directly from Colonel General Jodl, chief of the operational staff of the German High Command. The gist of these was: —

"It is not to be contemplated that we can continue to hold the island. It is, however, important to fight a delaying action to gain further time for stabilizing the situation on the mainland. The vital factor, however, is under no circumstances to suffer the loss of our three German divisions. At the very minimum, our valuable human material must be saved." [8]

General Guzzoni, whose supreme command was more nominal than real after the arrival of General Hube, acted in complete accord with the Germans. Even the fall of Mussolini failed to disturb the good relations within the Axis at the tactical level. And the German concept of the Sicilian campaign, a delaying action followed by the salvage of "valuable human material," was carried out to the letter despite Allied superiority in land, naval and air forces.

2. *On to Agrigento, 11–18 July*

Since D-day, General Truscott's 3rd Division had been exploiting its initial success by thrusting north and west. To stop it, General Arisio of the Italian XII Corps made new dispositions. The Fulriede Regiment of the 15th Panzer Grenadiers, Italian infantry units including two Bersaglieri regiments, with artillery and armor, were formed into one tactical group (*ragruppamiento*) of about division strength under the command of General Scheiber of the 207th Coastal Division, and deployed on a semicircle from Canicattì to a point southwest of Agrigento. United, the Scheiber Group might have been a formidable barrier; but 3rd Division never gave them a chance to get together. As one Italian account says, "The

[8] Bonin p. 8.

enemy having landed imposing reinforcements of armor and artillery, supported by his own aviation and the fire of 15 to 20 naval vessels, forced the XII Corps to retire to the line of the river and towns of Naro and Campobello." [9] And the Northwest African Tactical Air Force, at last, gave substantial help. On the 11th, it attacked Italian units of the Scheiber Group while they were moving into position, reduced one infantry battalion to about 100 men, and left two artillery groups with only 10 pieces between them.[10] On 12 July the 3rd Division captured the important road junction of Canicattì, thrusting a wedge into the Scheiber Group, dividing it into two parts which were unable to maintain contact.

General Patton was now eager to profit by this situation and take Agrigento and Porto Empédocle, the good artificial harbor 25 miles west of Licata, in order to feed his anticipated cross-island drive. General Alexander had ordered him not to attack these places, fearing lest he become involved in a heavy battle and so afford no flank protection to the Eighth Army. So Patton hit upon the expedient of a "reconnaissance in force" – an advance which can be accepted if it succeeds, or dismissed as inconsequential if it does not. Elements of the 3rd Division under Lieutenant Colonel Harry B. Sherman were assigned to carry it out; and the movement started on the night of 14–15 July.[11]

Cruisers *Birmingham* and *Brooklyn* had been trying since 12 July to clear the way for Truscott's left flank, by delivering deep supporting fire. They were forced to fire at long range, owing to a German-laid mine field off Porto Empédocle. H.M. monitor *Abercrombie* moved over to help on 14 July with her 15-inch guns, and next day *Philadelphia* with two destroyers joined the gunfire group. By the end of the day she had fired on some fourteen targets, including an Italian railway battery at Porto Empédocle. On the 15th, *Birmingham* covered minesweeping operations by U.S.S. *Strive*, *Staff*, *Skill* and *Speed*. Next morning heavy fog lay over the waters, but as soon as it lifted, at 1300, *Birmingham* resumed shoot-

[9] "Operazioni Juglio 1943 in Sicilia" p. 30; "Operazioni in Sicilia" p. 31.
[10] General Faldella in *Roma* 17, 18 July 1953.
[11] Truscott *Command Missions* pp. 218–21.

ing at field batteries, shore batteries and troop concentrations designated by shore fire-control and spotting planes. The most persistent and troublesome battery, on the edge of the harbor, was served by German sailors of a fortress battalion.

As the afternoon waned on the 16th, Admiral Davidson decided to make a peaceful approach instead of pounding Porto Empédocle to a point where it would be useless to us. Shortly after 1800 two *Philadelphia* SOCs were launched, flying white flags; and in one of them the chief of staff, Captain Ransom K. Davis, bore a message from the Admiral demanding "unconditional surrender." The planes landed in the harbor inside the jetty – where, much to their discomfiture, they were greeted by a group of Rangers who had entered the city about four hours earlier. But Captain Davis's mission did some good, after all. The Rangers, who had run ahead of their supplies, were very hungry; they sent a major on board *Philadelphia* by one of the returning planes, to see what he could pick up; and, as soon as darkness fell, two motor whaleboats set forth from the flagship, loaded down with good Navy chow and medical supplies.[12]

In the meantime the four large minesweepers, helped by nine YMS, were doggedly disposing of the mine field. None was hit by gunfire, but *Staff* exploded a mine under her forward engine room on 15 July. Owing (says her C.O.) largely to the courage and initiative of Boatswain's Mate William H. Koch USNR, severe fires were brought under control and she was towed to Gela, where 20 members of her crew, suffering from frightful burns, were turned over to British hospital ship *Leinster*.[13]

On a hilltop a few miles inland from Porto Empédocle stands Agrigento, the ancient Akragas, Pindar's "loveliest city of mortals," the "eye of Sicily." Akragas, which once had a quarter of a million

[12] *Philadelphia* and *Birmingham* Action Reports and deck logs. The German gunners abandoned their pieces intact and surrendered to the Rangers.

[13] Com. Mindiv 17 (Cdr. W. L. Messmer) War Diary; *Staff* Action Report 7 Aug. 1943. The C.O. of *Philadelphia* pays a tribute to the minesweepers, "plugging along under constant and frequently uncomfortably close fire."

inhabitants, was notorious throughout the ancient world for her pleasure-loving and hospitable gentry. They grew rich by selling olives to the Carthaginians, who decided to take them over in 406 B.C. Akragas appealed to Syracuse for help, and put on a show of resistance, having lately hired a Spartan to train her militia. But an order of the Spartan general, to the effect that nobody on guard duty during the siege should bring to the walls more than a tent, a bed, a blanket and two pillows, so disgusted the luxurious citizenry that they surrendered their city to Hannibal and fled to Gela. Three ruined temples now remain on a terrace facing the sea, as sole evidence of Agrigento's former opulence; but the modern town commands both Porto Empédocle and the two main roads to Palermo. Truscott and Patton were as eager to capture it as Hannibal and Himilcon had been; and the Italian high command, placing slight trust in Agrigentian valor, had ringed the city with artillery strong points commanding every approach. On the map, it looked like a tougher proposition than Catania.

Nevertheless in a bold enveloping movement executed by the 7th Regiment and 3rd Rangers, carried out with speed, skill and energy and supported by naval gunfire, both Porto Empédocle and Agrigento were captured; the former (as we have seen) at 1430 July 16, and the latter at 0300 next morning — almost exactly one week after H-hour of D-day. The Italians fought manfully for Agrigento. A strong counterattack, by a motorized column rolling along the road from Aragona, was broken up by divisional field artillery; and *Birmingham* disposed of a small troop concentration near Empédocle. Together with the two cities, 50 fieldpieces, more than 100 vehicles and over 6000 prisoners were captured. Within two days Serridafalco, Raffadali and San Cataldo were taken by other units of the 3rd Division.

Porto Empédocle on 18 July became a port of entry for reinforcement,[14] the naval gunfire ships departed, and JOSS Force dissolved on 18 July, its work well done. The 3rd, 2nd Armored and

[14] During the rest of July 17,305 tons of supplies and 1130 vehicles were landed there.

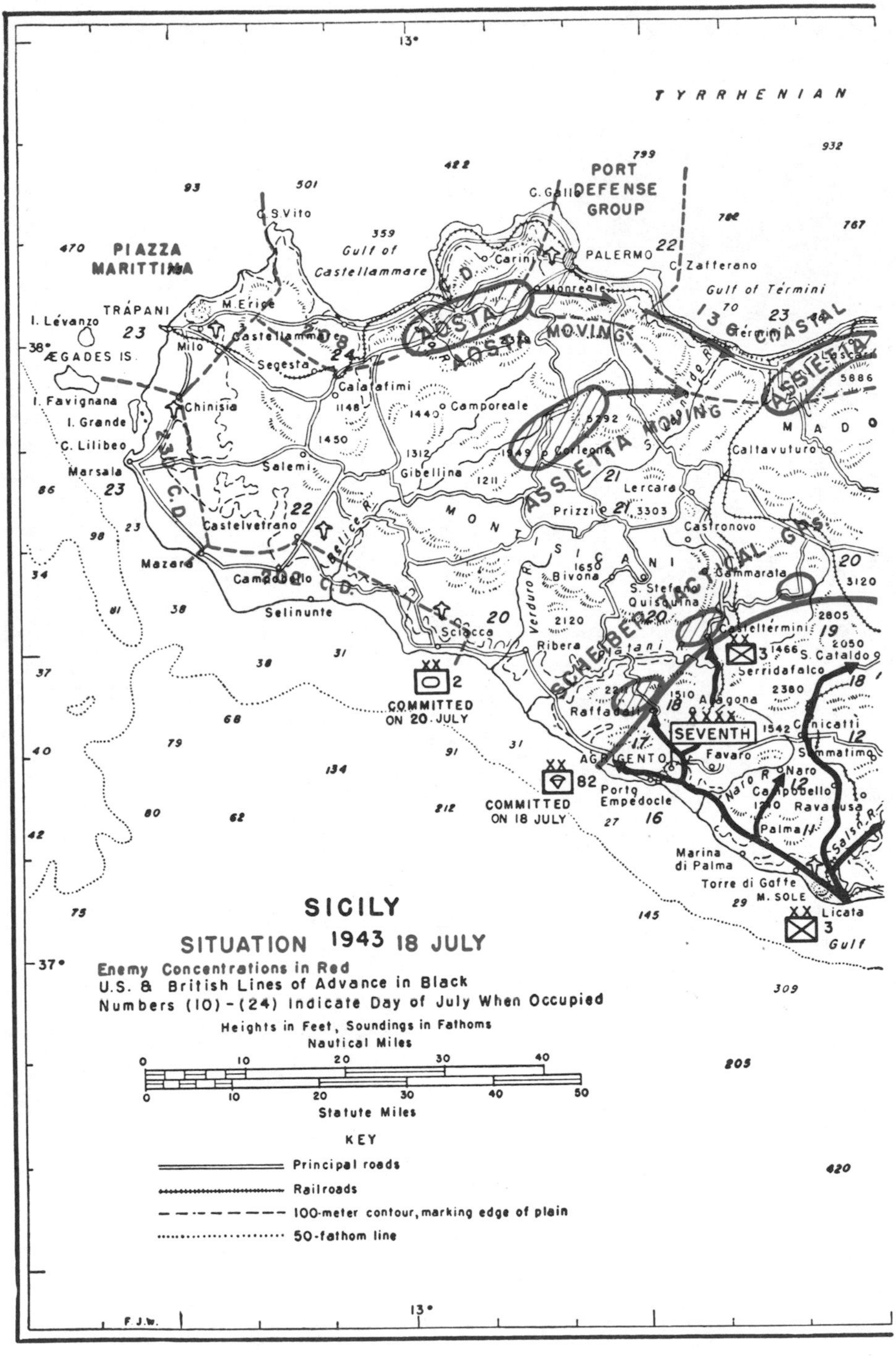

SICILY

SITUATION 1943 18 JULY

Enemy Concentrations in Red
U.S. & British Lines of Advance in Black
Numbers (10) - (24) Indicate Day of July When Occupied

Heights in Feet, Soundings in Fathoms

Nautical Miles: 0, 10, 20, 30, 40

Statute Miles: 0, 10, 20, 30, 40, 50

KEY

Principal roads

Railroads

100-meter contour, marking edge of plain

50-fathom line

F.J.W.

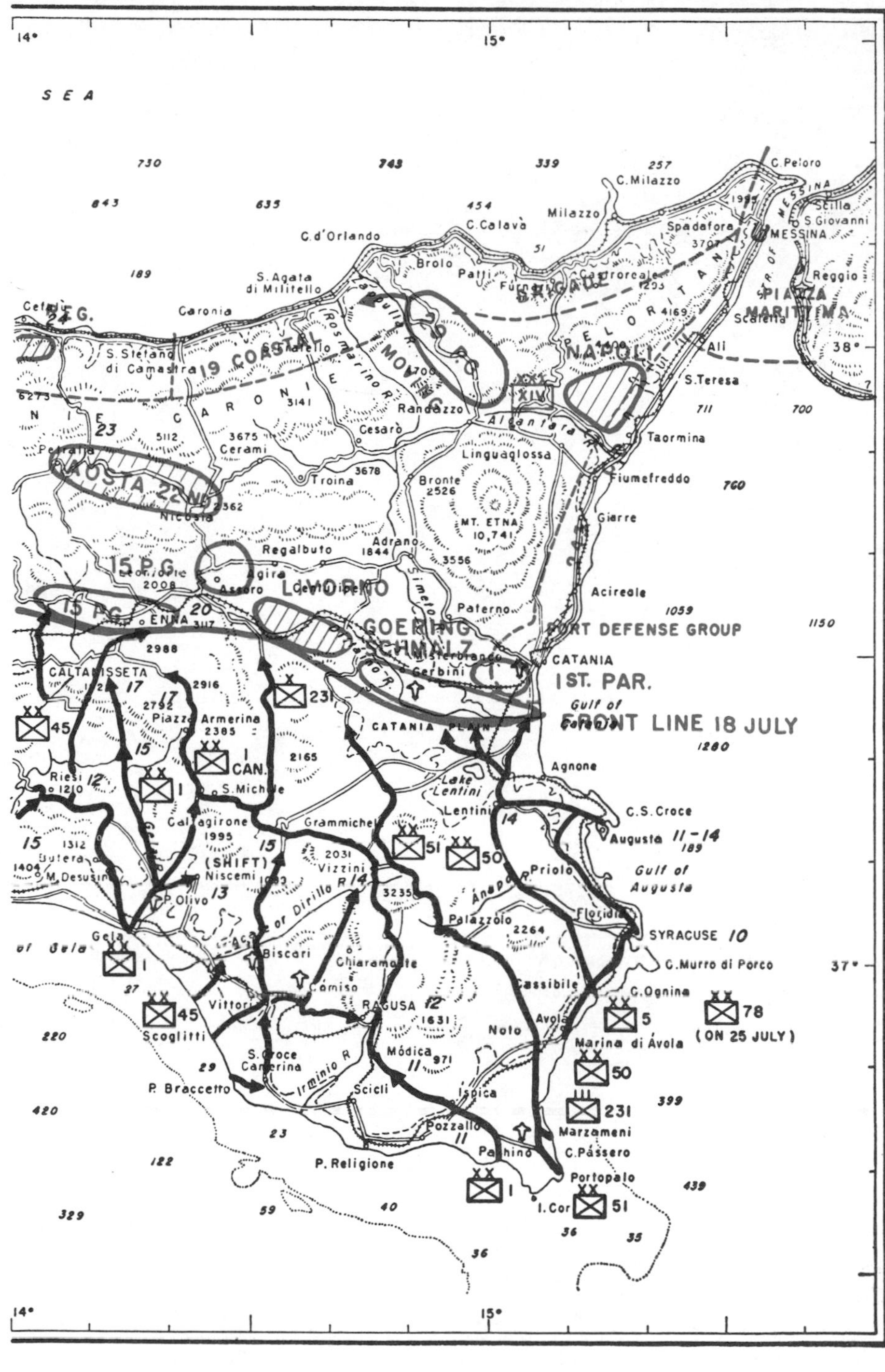
14°
15°
SEA
C.Peloro
C.Milazzo
Milazzo
Scilla
S.Giovanni
MESSINA
STR. OF MESSINA
Spadafora
C.Calavà
C.d'Orlando
S.Agata
di Militello
Brolo
Patti
Furnari
Castroreale
BRIGADE
Reggio
PIAZZA
MARITTIMA
Scaletta
Alì
38°
Cefalù
Caronia
S.Stefano
di Camastra
19 COASTAL
29 P.G.
MOVING
NAPOLI
S.Teresa
XIV
Randazzo
Cesarò
Alcantara R.
Taormina
Linguaglossa
Fiumefreddo
Petralia
AOSTA
22ND
Cerami
Troina
Bronte
MT. ETNA
10,741
Giarre
Nicosia
Regalbuto
Adrano
15 P.G.
Leonforte
Agira
Assoro
LIVORNO
Centuripe
Acireale
15 P.G.
ENNA
20
Paternò
GOERING
SCHMALZ
PORT DEFENSE GROUP
CATANIA
Misterbianco
Gerbini
1ST. PAR.
CALTANISSETTA
17
17
Piazza Armerina
231
45
FRONT LINE 18 JULY
Gulf of Catania
CATANIA PLAIN
15
1
CAN.
Agnone
Riesi
12
1
S.Michele
Lake Lentini
Lentini
Caltagirone
Grammichele
14
C.S.Croce
15
Butera
M.Desusino
(SHIFT)
Niscemi
15
Vizzini
51
50
Augusta 11-14
13
Gela R.
P.Olivo
14
Acate or Dirillo R.
Anapo R.
Priolo
Gulf of Augusta
Palazzolo
Floridia
Gela
Biscari
SYRACUSE 10
Gulf of Gela
1
Chiaramonte
C.Murro di Porco
37°
Comiso
Cassibile
C.Ognina
45
Vittoria
RAGUSA
12
Avola
5
78
(ON 25 JULY)
Scoglitti
Noto
Marina di Ávola
S.Croce
Camerina
Módica
11
Irminio R.
50
P.Braccetto
Scicli
Ispica
231
Pozzallo
11
Marzameni
Pachino
C.Pássero
P.Religione
Portopalo
1
I.Cor
51

82nd Airborne Divisions were now formed into a Provisional III Corps under Seventh Army command.

Patton, Truscott and Conolly were justly pleased with the progress they had made in a week's time. The Seventh Army commander flew to Algiers on 17 July, as soon as Agrigento was captured, and presented General Alexander with a plan for an enveloping attack on Palermo, which the Army Group Commander gladly accepted. On the 18th he ordered Patton's army to mop up the western half of Sicily. But before we follow the dash to Palermo we must examine the far less favorable situation on the Eighth Army front, which forced a vital change of plan.

3. *The Battle of the Catania Plain, 14–20 July* [15]

The Plain of Catania proved to be a major obstacle to Montgomery's Eighth Army.

Directly inland from Augusta, the town of Lentini lies on the edge of an escarpment from which an arid and almost barren slope descends to the plain; one can look directly across to Mount Etna and the city of Catania, tucked in between mountain and sea. The plain extends some twenty miles inland to include Gerbini, at and around which the Italians had built their largest airdrome in Sicily. The Dittáino and other rivers that water the plain join the largest of them, the Simeto, some three or four miles from its mouth; and a little more than a mile from its mouth the main coastal highway crosses the Simeto by a long bridge, the Ponte di Primosole. Before reaching this "Sunrise bridge" the highway, descending from Lentini, crosses a smaller stream by the Ponte dei Malati. Highway and both bridges had to be taken; the Malati by a Commando landing and the Primosole by airborne troops. The 50th Division would then rush the plain and take Catania.

So, as part of the airborne operation so severely fired on by Allied

[15] Alexander Despatch; Montgomery *El Alamein to River Sangro* ch. xi; Senger pp. 42–3.

troops and ships, 200 men of the 1st Parachute Brigade, with five antitank guns, glided down near the Primosole bridge at 0215 July 14, removed the demolition charges, and established a bridgehead. Unfortunately for them, a battalion of German paratroops had already dropped nearby; these men "fought with fanatical savagery,"[16] and outnumbered the British, who defended the bridge all day but had to retire at nightfall. The Commandos landed at Agnone, reached the Malati bridge at 0345 and removed demolition charges; but within two hours were forced by an Italian combat group to retire. The 50th Division, too, ran into strong resistance at Lentini, where Colonel Schmalz fought a stubborn rear-guard action to cover his and the Hermann Goering Division's retirement to the north edge of the Catania plain.

The time thus gained for him and lost for us was put to very good use by the enemy. It gave the Goering Division time to make its flanking movement; it enabled two more battalions of German paratroops, the Schmalz armored group, elements of the Italian Napoli Division, and two German fortress battalions to occupy strong positions along the southern and western foothills of Mount Etna.

The British recaptured Primosole bridge on the night of 15–16 July, and by the end of the 16th held a bridgehead some 3000 yards deep on the north bank of the Simeto. Catania was in sight, less than five miles north. On 16 July General Alexander ordered a frontal attack on the city. It was launched on the night of 17–18 July. Two brigades of the 50th Division pressed forward but ran into strong opposition, suffered heavy losses, and gained no ground. In the hope of broadening his front, General Montgomery on the 19th ordered the 5th Division to cross the Simeto by a bridge upstream and march around the 50th's left flank in the direction of Misterbianco. But this thrust was thrown back on the 21st. Montgomery, who had already ordered his reserves, the 78th Division, to be rushed over from Africa, now informed Alexander that the frontal attack would mean casualties too heavy to be borne, and that

[16] De Guingand *Operation Victory* p. 298.

he preferred to try a "left hook" against the Mount Etna line. "To persist in the thrust toward Catania," he wrote, "would have meant very heavy casualties and I was by no means convinced that success would follow the expenditure of life." [17] Alexander consented.

His humanity does "Monty" credit; and it is not surprising that he chose to make a flank attack, the maneuver so brilliantly successful at El Alamein, rather than incur heavy casualties in a frontal assault. But his change of plan had a vital effect on the entire campaign. It required shifting the pressure from a flat terrain, where he could have used his tanks, to a rugged, tangled interior, perfect for defense; from a seaboard where the Navy could have helped, to mountains that naval gunfire could not reach. It meant a static defense at the plain for almost two weeks while the Seventh and most of the Eighth Armies fought their way into new positions north of Mount Etna. Most important of all, it gave the enemy time to deploy another armored division (the 29th) and prepare an eventual evacuation to the mainland when he could no longer hold the Etna line.

The Royal Navy was ready to give close support to troops on the Catania plain; yet few calls were made upon it. With the naval gunfire power available, Montgomery should have been able to blast the tank and infantry counterattacks against his Simeto bridgehead, as Patton had done on the Gela front. But he seems to have distrusted naval gunfire unless laid down at a great distance from friendly troops. Battleship *Warspite's* bombardment of Catania on the evening of 17 July was loudly acclaimed, but it failed to achieve any military object; and on the 18th, a crucial day of the land battle, H.M.S. *Laforey* and *Lookout* were busily pounding Aci Castello and Misterbianco.

In retrospect, it would have been worth heavy ground casualties

[17] *El Alamein to the River Sangro* pp. 86, 92. The casualties of the Catania plain fight apparently have not been computed; but the Eighth Army lost 700 killed, 877 missing and 2239 wounded between 10 and 21 July, and the greater part of these must have been on the Catania front. An element in Montgomery's decision, according to his then chief of staff Maj. Gen. F. W. de Guingand (*Operation Victory* p. 307) was the fact that the 5th and 50th Divisions were tired and stale after their strenuous African campaign.

to have pushed the enemy out of Catania. If only he could then have been thrown off balance and pursued to Messina, his mobile forces would have been bottled up and compelled to surrender.

It was some consolation that good progress was being made on the British left flank, adjoining the American right. On 16–17 July the Canadians had a stout fight for Piazza Armerina. Enna, the road center and military capital of Sicily, was left to the United States 1st Division to take, which they did on the 20th.

On that day General Alexander, taking cognizance of Montgomery's reluctance to persist in the thrust on Catania, issued a new directive.[18] Since it was now evident that Eighth Army alone would not be strong enough to put the pincers around Mount Etna, the new plan was to hold the enemy before Catania, and get around the mountain to Messina by a three-pronged "left hook." The southern prong would consist of the Canadians and other XXX Corps elements. They were now ordered to turn east at Leonforte toward Adrano, in order to leave room for the Seventh Army. The addition of two more prongs to the left hook was entrusted to Patton. He fell in with the new plan by ordering his 1st Division to turn east at Petralia toward Troina, parallel to the Canadians; while the 45th and 3rd Divisions, in echelon, advanced along the coastal road parallel to the other two.

Since it was obvious that all three prongs would not be in their chosen positions to assault the Etna line until about 1 August, "the last week of July was characterized by a comparative lull on the Eighth Army front. . . . General Montgomery wished to rest his troops . . ." [19] During this rest the battered 5th and 50th Divisions suffered many casualties from malaria, for which the Catania plain and Lake Lentini are notorious. But the last ten days of July were anything but restful on the American front. In less than that time the Seventh Army overran the entire western half of Sicily.

[18] Despatch p. 1020; *cf.* General Bradley *A Soldier's Story* p. 145.
[19] Alexander Despatch p. 1021.

4. *The Race to Palermo, 18–22 July*

"I want you to be in Palermo in five days," was the word received by the 3rd Division from General Truscott on 18 July when they were taking a brief rest after the capture of Agrigento. The city was a hundred miles distant, by two roughly parallel roads over country almost devoid of water and studded by several strong points. Yet they did it on foot, in four days. To beat the record of the "Truscott trotters," one would have to go back to Stonewall Jackson's "foot cavalry."

And, let us add, the 45th Division, folded back because "Monty" wanted its planned road of advance, and placed on the right flank of the 3rd, also made fast time. It had a head start over the 3rd, reaching Santa Caterina on the eastern road to Palermo on 18 July; five days later one of its columns made the north coast at Términi Imerese. "Fighting First" entered Enna, General Guzzoni's former headquarters, on the 20th and Petralia on the 23rd; it then turned east along the road to Nicosia, in accordance with General Alexander's new plan. The 15th Panzer Grenadiers, after heavy losses of their armor "owing to continuous attack by fighter-bombers, artillery, and low-level aircraft," now withdrew to a north–south line through Regalbuto, tying in with the Hermann Goering Division on the south and the 29th Panzer Grenadiers on the north.

These advances into the interior of Sicily had to be carried out without benefit of Navy, and a fourth thrust which might have enjoyed seaborne assistance did not need it. This was a movement of the 82nd Airborne Division (now fighting as infantry), a unit of the 3rd Division – designated "X" Brigade – and the 2nd Armored Division to mop up the western end of Sicily. The paratroops took Sciacca and Menfi 20 July and reached the road junction at Castelvetrano next day. On the 23rd, "X" Brigade took Marsala, and the 82nd captured Trápani, whose *piazza marittima* surrendered to General Ridgway, after resisting for three hours. The 2nd Armored, rolling fast on wheels and tracks, turned 90 degrees at Castelvetrano and reached Monreale on the edge of the Concha d'Oro, ready to enter Palermo, on the evening of the 22nd. This movement encountered slight resistance, since the Italian mobile divisions had been sent east and the coastal divisions faded. It was unaccompanied by naval escort; no naval gunfire was required. Admiral Hewitt's cruisers and most of his destroyers, in the meantime, proceeded to Algiers for a little upkeep. They would be wanted soon enough on the north coast.

And now for Palermo. That noble city, metropolis of western Sicily, lies along a spacious waterfront, spreading inland, ringed by a crescent of golden orange orchards, toward the magnificent Norman-Byzantine cathedral of Monreale. The seat successively of Carthaginian, Arab, Norman, Hohenstaufen and Bourbon dominion, Palermo had been conquered so many times that even the historians lost count. Since Garibaldi's almost miraculous victory over the Neapolitans in 1860, the city had enjoyed its longest peaceful period in 2600 or more years. But it was now an important air, naval and supply center for the Axis, and had to expect trouble.

Allied air bombs began falling on the waterfront and the Roccadaforte airport in the spring of 1943; unfortunately many of them missed their marks, gutted medieval palaces and knocked twelfth-century mosaics off the cathedral and other churches. Von Neurath reported to Hitler on 20 May that Palermo was already "badly flattened," and that the British had got the harbor into such a state that it would be useless to them.[20] He couldn't have been more wrong.

The local Axis command woke up late to the fact that the city was doomed. "From one day to the next, transport operations had to be reversed, with meager results," recalled Admiral von Ruge. "Very few steamers got away, probably only two." But most of the German antiaircraft gunners and supply troops were evacuated in time by railway, truck, or lighters, three of which were sunk by Allied aircraft. Reichsmarschall Goering, in one of his whims,

[20] Felix Gilbert *Hitler Directs His War* p. 30.

ordered the Admiral to evacuate the porphyry sarcophagi of the Emperors Henry VI and Frederick II from the cathedral; but this order was quietly ignored, and the ashes of the splendid prince whom contemporaries named *Stupor Mundi*, the World's Wonder, still rest in the city that he loved and adorned.[21]

Spectacular was the advance of the 3rd Division along the two Agrigento–Palermo roads, both of which wind up to 2500-foot elevations, with barely 400 yards of level going at a time. Truscott's men encountered demolitions in the shape of blown bridges, tunnels and tank traps. Wheat stubble and harvested beanfields bordered the roads, and springs of sweet water were few and far between. And the dust! A compound of cattle dung and pulverized chalky rock, it penetrated the throat and made men desperately thirsty. Old desert hands swore it was worse than the dust of Africa.

Speed in military operations, as in everything else, is relative; and although Truscott's trotters were fast, the Italian XII Corps was faster. On 15 July General Guzzoni decided to pull all his mobile forces out of western Sicily. The Scheiber tactical group, still fighting the 3rd Division near Agrigento, covered the movement. By thus joining his western forces to the German divisions which (as we have seen) had already withdrawn to the Etna line, he hoped to make an orderly withdrawal from the island.

This flanking operation was carried out in masterly fashion. The Aosta Division, which had been located southwest of Palermo, had to be moved 166 kilometers to the Petralia–Nicosia road; and the rest of the Assietta Division was shifted to the north coast between Términi Imerese and Cefalù. The movement started on the 17th and was completed in five days.

On 19 July, a day of terrific heat, the 15th Regiment of the 3rd Division advanced along the eastern road from Agrigento to Palermo; while the 30th Regiment, taking the Raffadali road, marched 27 miles in daytime and pushed forward after dark to the heights overlooking San Stéfano Quisquina. There Mobile Group B of the Scheiber tactical group, all Italian, made a vigorous attempt to halt

[21] Rintelen *Mussolini als Bundesgenosse* (1951) p. 209.

the advance. The 3rd Battalion 30th Infantry marched 54 miles cross-country, carrying all their rations and water, in 33 hours, to reach their assembly area for the attack on the little gray town with the long name. A coördinated assault on it from three different directions, launched at 1330 July 20, continued through the afternoon. San Stéfano Quisquina, strongest point on the road to Palermo, was entered at 1700. A hundred more vehicles, some of them intact, and 750 prisoners were captured.

At 1840 July 21 the 7th Infantry entered Corleone, the last important place between Agrigento and Palermo. The 15th and 30th Regiments followed, and by the afternoon of 22 July most of the 3rd Division was poised on the rim of the Concha d'Oro, looking down into Palermo, across to spectacular Monte Pellegrino, and out over the indigo-blue Tyrrhenian Sea. It was a great moment in military history, recalling the day when General Winfield Scott's army first beheld Mexico City; or that 27th of May, 1860, when Garibaldi's ragged Thousand stood on the rim of the same "Golden Shell."

In the face of the irresistible American advance, all Italian coastal troops and naval units charged with port defense faded away. According to General Truscott, General Patton ordered the 3rd Division to hold back so that he could make a triumphal entry with the 2nd Armored. This plan was somewhat spoiled by a delegation of the municipality insisting on surrendering the city to the infantry, so that it could obtain troops to keep order. The GIs got there first.

Nevertheless, General Patton had his day. Picking up a guide near Monreale, he "started down a long road cut out of the side of a cliff, which went through an almost continuous village. The street was full of people shouting, 'Down with Mussolini!' and 'Long live America!' . . . The Governor had left, but we captured two Generals, both of whom said that they were glad to be captured because the Sicilians were not human beings, but animals." [22] Patton set up Seventh Army headquarters in the palace of

[22] Patton *War as I Knew It* pp. 61–2.

the Norman kings, from which, like old Roger II in the twelfth century, he directed the campaign along the north coast of Sicily.[23]

Calatafimi and Castellammare, last Italian strongholds in western Sicily, surrendered on 24 July; over 20,000 prisoners were captured, and others simply put on civilian clothes and blended with the local populace. At the same time, the 45th Division emerged on the north coast at Términi Imerese and turned east to capture Cefalù. Now the "Thunderbirds" were in a position to spearhead the drive on Messina.

Before we follow them along the north coast, let us see how the Axis dictators were taking these events.

5. *Decline and Fall of Mussolini, 19–26 July*

The negative success of defeating Montgomery's initial thrust on Catania was small consolation to the Axis dictators. One week of the Sicilian campaign had brought them little but woe. The assault, instead of being stopped "at the water's edge" as the Duce had once predicted, had been uniformly successful. Syracuse, Augusta, Gela, Licata and Agrigento had fallen; almost one third of Sicily was in Allied hands. On 19 July, Hitler met Mussolini at the Villa Feltre, somewhere in northern Italy. The Duce, coming as a beggar, had to listen to a long and rambling discourse by Hitler, who remarked, among other things, "It's really tragic how the English always get the jump in matters of organization. The prompt activation of the Pantelleria air base, and recent photographs of their fields near Gela and Licata, prove it." [24]

Mussolini wanted more armored divisions and 2000 more planes to defend Sicily; Hitler declared he could spare neither troops nor

[23] One of the General's aides was sent to the Grand Hotel delle Palmi in the center of the city, to demand quarters for 60 officers. He was greeted by a major-domo in cutaway coat and striped trousers, who said, "So sorry – you've come at the wrong season!"

[24] Two contemporary accounts of what went on are printed in *Hitler e Mussolini: Documenti* (V. Zincone ed. Milan 1946) pp. 165–90; and résumé in Bernotti *La Guerra sui Mari 1943–45* pp. 81–4.

planes, except for the 29th Panzer Grenadiers and the 1st Parachute Division, which were already streaming into Sicily. Put all your civilians to work! he shouted at the Duce. Sicily needs infantry, not armor; if you fight at all, you must fight fanatically! Reinforce Sicily with your fast cruisers that can beat off air attack, as the British reinforced Malta with their fast minelayers! Your immediate necessity is to guarantee absolute security of the Strait of Messina! The Fuehrer was certainly right on that point.

Hitler's discourse was interrupted by an officer bringing news that the Allies had just launched their first bombing attack on Rome, and that the central railway station, the Corso, and the University city had all been hit. Although the report was exaggerated, the 1000 tons of bombs dropped from 560 planes made a mess of the Littorio marshaling yards, damaged a number of historic monuments, killed over 2000 civilians and wounded as many more.[25] This first air raid on Rome, with the promise of more to come, proved to be the straw that broke the back of Fascism.

On 20 July Victor Emmanuel III told Mussolini, "We cannot go on much longer. Sicily has gone." Five days later the Grand Council of the Fascist Party voted that Victor Emmanuel should save his country. Mussolini called on the King, who told him he was out and Marshal Badoglio in; and the Duce was placed under "protective custody." So ended a dictatorship of twenty-one years' duration.

The Badoglio government, formed immediately, issued a statement that Italy held true to her ally and would prosecute the war with renewed vigor. This deceived nobody, least of all Hitler. The German command in Rome knew that Badoglio, a few days before,

[25] Gen. Lewis H. Brereton USA *The Brereton Diaries* pp. 194–6, and information from Historical Division Italian Air Force. Although every precaution, it was thought, had been taken to spare all but military objectives, and leaflets had been dropped the day before giving the hour of the raid and advising civilians to take cover, the bombers seeking the yards at the central railway station missed them, hitting the ancient basilica of San Lorenzo, plowing up graves in the Campo Verano cemetery, and badly damaging the Department of Public Health, the Instituto Regina Elena, and other public buildings.

had told the King that the war was *perduto, perdutissimo* – absolutely and completely lost.[26] Everyone suspected that Badoglio was looking for an opportunity to make peace without too much loss of face. On 26 July Hitler excitedly discussed with his generals the possibility of withdrawing divisions from the Russian front to hold down Italy; but the Russians were too strong in the Orel sector to make that possible. He proposed to take over Italy immediately by a *coup d'état*, but was dissuaded. The Fuehrer decided to tolerate the Badoglio government temporarily, and to use the time gained to rush more divisions into northern Italy from France and Germany. For two weeks the rails in the Brenner Pass and along the Riviera hummed with passing troop trains. Some of his generals proposed the immediate evacuation of Sicily, but Hitler could not make up his mind. So the war continued in Sicily; and at the tactical level the Italian command gave the Germans loyal coöperation to the end.

The check of Montgomery on the Catania plain, and the comparative lull there until 1 August, gave the Germans and Italians the time and opportunity to form a strong, continuous line from Catania to Monte Fratello and to prepare for an orderly evacuation.

6. *Naval Operations on the North Shore*

When Seventh Army began entering Palermo on the afternoon of 22 July, they were relieved to recognize as American a number of destroyers and minecraft steaming into the Gulf. These were Captain Wellborn's Desron 8 (*Wainwright*, flag) and a part of Commander Messmer's Mindiv 17 (*Strive*, flag) which had been patrolling and sweeping the waters around the northwestern capes of Sicily for several days. But the first American sailors actually to enter Palermo harbor were the high-spirited lads of Motor Torpedo Boat Squadron 15.

[26] Rintelen *Mussolini als Bundesgenosse* p. 224.

On the evening of 22 July, Lieutenant Commander Stanley M. Barnes, with four of his boats, departed Bizerta. According to his own narrative: —

> At dawn the next day we were off Ústica. First thing we saw a fishing boat putt-putting toward Italy. Going over, we found a handful of very scared individuals crawling out from under the floor plates, hopefully waving white handkerchiefs. This was the staff of the Italian Admiral at Trápani. The only reason we didn't get the Admiral was that he was late getting down to the dock and his staff said to hell with him. In addition to a few souvenir pistols and binoculars we captured a whole fruit crate of thousand-lira notes which we reluctantly turned over to the Army authorities later. While this was going on, one of the other boats spotted a raft with seven Germans on it feebly paddling out to sea. We picked those up too.[27]

At 0800 Barnes led his little flotilla inside Palermo breakwater. At first glance, everything seemed to be in ruins. Owing to attrition bombing by the Allies, last-minute demolition by the Germans, and scuttling by die-hard Fascists, over 50 vessels and craft, from destroyers down to floating cranes, cluttered the harbor. Moles were blasted, quayside buildings shattered, and most of the repair shops and cranes destroyed. The city was without water, light, power or sewerage. But the underground oil tanks on Monte Pellegrino, with a capacity of almost a million barrels, were intact, as was the pipeline thence to the harbor; and Palermo was a reservoir of labor, both skilled and unskilled, eager to work for us. Commodore Sullivan, the salvage expert, and Army Engineers, sailors, soldiers and civilians set about clearing up the mess, restoring services for the city and the armed forces, repairing the drydock, and constructing a staging area for 15,000 troops. General Eisenhower and Admiral Cunningham wished to make Palermo an advanced naval base where troops and supplies for the final act of the Sicilian drama

[27] Quoted in Cdr. R. J. Bulkley "History of Motor Torpedo Boats" Part II pp. 371–2; information from Capt. Barnes in 1953. The rest of Squadron 15 (total 18 boats) was later brought to Palermo. Lt. H. R. Manakee USNR, the squadron's Intelligence officer, adds that Barnes towed the fishing boat at 25-knot speed, which so opened the seams of the old craft that the staff officers had to bail for their lives with steel helmets.

might enter directly from the wings instead of from the rear across the island; and already they were planning to mount there a part of the next operation. On 28 July Naval Operating Base Palermo was established, with Captain Leonard Doughty in command. By the 30th, half the shipping berths in the harbor were cleared.[28] On 1 August, when transports bearing the 9th Infantry Division entered, twelve ships were able to unload simultaneously. During that month, 44,878 soldiers and sailors, 116,369 long tons of supplies and 6361 vehicles were landed in Palermo.[29]

August seemed a long way ahead, on 23 July. Three PTs of Squadron 15, on the night after their arrival, patrolled to the Strait of Messina and beyond. In the early hours of 25 July off Cape Vaticano – "the wart on the toe of Italy" – these boats, under the command of Lieutenant E. C. Arbuckle USNR, encountered the 8800-ton Italian merchant steamer *Viminale* being towed stern-first toward Naples, and managed to sink both ship and tug despite a natural confusion in aim owing to their strange posture.[30] This was the first occasion that the U.S. Navy made itself felt in the Tyrrhenian Sea. The event warned Italy that she could no longer supply Sicily except across the Strait of Messina.

On the night of 26–27 July three PTs, commanded by Lieutenant J. B. Mutty, made the acquaintance of armed lighters which the Germans called MFPs (*Marine-fährprähme*, literally "Naval perambulators") – we called them F-lighters. These were a formidable class of beaching craft, 163 feet long, making 10-knot speed with diesel engines, carrying up to 100 tons of cargo, partly armored, and heavily armed to repel air or surface attack. Their batteries included at least one 75-mm or 88-mm cannon. An MFP could hold its own with a destroyer, let alone a PT which had nothing more powerful than a 20-mm machine gun to shoot with. The PT carried torpedoes, to be sure, but the MFPs, drawing only four and one-half feet, were immune to the PT boats' torpedoes

[28] Engineer Report HQ Seventh Army 2 Nov. 1943 pp. 21–2; Lt. C. L. Molineaux USNR "Report of Survey of Port of Palermo 15 Aug. 1943."

[29] Seventh Army *Report of Operations* pp. e–15, 16.

[30] MTBron 15 War Diary; Ruge p. 27; *Marina Italiana, Navi Perdute*, II 81.

which, designed for the submerged tubes of the old battleships, would not run true at less depth than eight feet. The equipment of PTs here, as in the Pacific,[31] proved that these boats, designed as small giant-killers, must be armed and armored for protection in gunfire actions with vessels nearer their size.

This first scrap of PTs with MFPs took place off the volcanic island of Stromboli on the night of 26–27 July. The PTs fired six torpedoes and thought that they saw two of their adversaries explode; but German sources indicate that all torpedoes missed, and the ensuing gunfire duel resulted in slight damage to either side. On the night of 28–29 July, three boats under Lieutenant Arbuckle's command attacked off Cape Orlando what they supposed to be three MFPs, but what were really Italian MAS boats – motor torpedo boats somewhat smaller than ours. Again, torpedoes that ran hot, straight and true slid under the enemy keels without exploding. In a brisk exchange of gunfire, *PT–218* was punctured in some 60 places, one engine was disabled and two officers besides Lieutenant Arbuckle were badly wounded; but she made Palermo with all hands alive, and 18 inches of water below decks.

As a result of this engagement, and on orders from Admiral Hewitt, the PTs were instructed to avoid action with MFPs. Apparently the enemy now concentrated all his "marine perambulators" in the Strait of Messina for troop-ferry purposes, as no more were encountered off the north shore.[32]

While Barnes's motor torpedo boats prowled far afield, Charlie Wellborn's destroyers hovered near Palermo in case the Italian Navy came out. Here was the last chance for the Regia Marina to assert itself. But only the Luftwaffe challenged Palermo. The German Air Force carried out a series of heavy air raids on American forces in and around the city; attacks relatively more skillful and devastating than those during the opening days on the south coast.

[31] See Vol. VI pp. 209–12.

[32] Efforts to arrange joint operations between PTs and DDs were unsuccessful. On one occasion, when they tried a joint patrol, the destroyers fired on the PTs and spattered their decks in the first salvo. Since the PTs were 5 knots slower than the DDs, they actually ran for protection under *enemy* shore batteries on Cape Rasocolmo, which fired on the DDs and drove them seaward!

The Northwest African Tactical Air Command was unable to provide protection. First of these raids was on the morning of 26 July. At 0932 three Ju-88s attacked destroyer *Mayrant* on patrol ten miles off Palermo. She was so damaged by near-misses that she had to be towed into harbor by minesweeper *Strive*.[83]

On 27 July, when Palermo harbor was first open to shipping, Admiral Hewitt organized the few United States warships left in Sicilian waters into a Support Force. Task Force 88, as it was designated, was, in effect, General Patton's Navy; just as the Seventh Fleet in the Southwest Pacific was General MacArthur's Navy. It was set up to give support to the Seventh Army, and for no other purpose. As such, its mission was: (1) the defense of Palermo; (2) gunfire support to the Seventh Army as it advanced along the coast; (3) providing amphibious craft for "leapfrog landings" behind enemy lines; and (4) ferry duty for heavy artillery, supplies and vehicles to relieve congestion on the railway and the single coastal road.

Rear Admiral Davidson commanded the Support Force.[84] This tall, lanky flag officer, firm in decision and quiet of speech, never lost his temper under the most trying circumstances, and inspired confidence in everyone around. A gunnery expert, he had handled gunfire support off the south coast admirably. His flagship *Philadelphia*, together with cruiser *Savannah* and destroyers *Gherardi, Nelson, Jeffers, Murphy, Trippe* and *Knight*, steamed into Palermo harbor during the forenoon watch 30 July. There was no danger of their collecting barnacles on their bottoms. General Patton asked for gunfire support next day and was obliged with a vigorous bom-

[83] *Mayrant* had just arrived as escort to a convoy from Licata.

[84] Lyal A. Davidson, b. Iowa 1886; Naval Academy '10, M.S. Columbia 1917. Asst. engineer officer *New Hampshire* 1914, Engineer officer *Kansas* in World War I. Training duties N.O.B. Hampton Roads 1920–23; gunnery officer *Raleigh* 1924–7; duty in Washington bureaus to 1929; "exec" *Melville* 1929; aid to Com-Eleven 1937. Comdesdiv 9, 1934–6, duty at Newport torpedo station; C.O. *Relief* 1938 and *Omaha* 1939. Taught naval science at U. of Michigan 1940; promoted Rear Admiral Nov. 1941. Comcrudiv 8 and task force commander during Operations TORCH, HUSKY, AVALANCHE and ANVIL. Duty in office of C.N.O. Oct. 1944, retired 1946, died 29 Dec. 1950. His Action Report, "Naval Ops. of TF 88 in North Sicilian Waters in Support of Seventh Army," 5 Sept. 1943, is my principal source for north coast operations.

bardment of shore batteries near San Stéfano di Camastra. During the afternoon watch two Focke-Wulfs passed over the ships, dropped bombs, and were chased away by two R.A.F. Spitfires. Next, eleven dive-bombers attacked *Philadelphia* and two escorting destroyers. One bomb, miraculously a dud, missed the cruiser by 15 yards. Admiral Davidson, now deprived of fighter cover (because the Spitfires hadn't the gas to stay), sent a TBS call to *Savannah* in Palermo 40 miles away, asking her to request the Army airfield there to send out fighter protection. But "this message was relayed through three stations with consequent delay and additional fighters did not arrive in the area until all attacks were over."

Adequate air cover was never provided to the ships operating along this coast. Northwest African Tactical Air Command did furnish combat air patrol from its newly occupied Sicilian fields, but under conditions that greatly limited its usefulness to the Navy. The Air Force reserved the right to withdraw C.A.P. without warning, and it refused to permit naval vessels to communicate directly with the planes, lest some naval commander attempt to control them. Consequently, there could be no coördination between ships and planes in an enemy air attack. The Luftwaffe evidently got on to this strange state of affairs, for it adopted the tactic of sending a decoy plane ahead of a strike. The decoy would lead the entire C.A.P. away in pursuit, while the attack, the approach of which had been detected by ships' radar but could not be communicated to friendly planes, struck in. Fortunately the antiaircraft gunners in Task Force 88 became very expert, through abundant experience; beating off enemy air attacks without benefit of C.A.P. became almost daily routine.

A few minutes after the morning watch was called on 1 August, the Luftwaffe nearly enacted a Mediterranean version of Pearl Harbor. Forty-eight planes evaded Allied radar detectors and jumped the harbor and city. They first dropped flares, then about sixty very large bombs, which exploded with more noise and violence than any observed in the Sicilian campaign. Damaged *Mayrant* at that time was moored alongside sweeper *Strive*, which was

Illustrations

U.S.S. *Monrovia*, flagship of the Western Naval Task Force, before she left the United States

Admiral Hewitt greets General Patton on board

Eve of Departure

U.S.S. *Birmingham* passing Gibraltar

Photo by Major J. C. Hatlem USA

The Lake of Bizerta, 7 July 1943
(Note large number of JOSS Force LSTs)

Forward in the Mediterranean

Rear Admiral Lyal A. Davidson USN *and Flagship U.S.S.* Philadelphia

From a painting by Benjamin T. Stephenson

U.S.S. *Buck*

Group on bridge of *Buck* after sinking of submarine *Argento* LEFT TO RIGHT: Lieutenant Commander Millard J. Klein, Lieutenant Gremonini, Lieutenant Commander George L. Lambert, Commander Leo Masina, Italian Navy

Buck *Sinks* Argento

Photo by Major J. C. Hatlem USA, *Feb. 1944*

Licata and the Salso–Falconara Landing Beaches

Falconara Castle and Mount Gallodoro at right. Punta Due Rocchi in middle distance. Licata and Mount Sole at left, rear

U.S. Army Signal Corps photo

D-day on Beach Red
LCT discharging truck, another coming in

U.S. Coast Guard photo

S.S. *Robert Rowan* erupts, 11 July

Licata

LIFE *photo by Bob Landry*

Tanks advancing over the Gela plain, 11 July
Seen from Colonel Darby's observation post

U.S. Army Signal Corps photo

Air attack on roadstead
Beach Green 2 in foreground

Gela

U.S. Army Signal Corps photo

U.S.S. *Boise* firing on tanks from off Gela, 11 July
LST in foreground

U.S. Army Signal Corps photo

Italian prisoners embarking in *LCI–221*

Gela

Rear Admiral Alan G. Kirk USN

Photo by Major J. C. Hatlem USA, *Feb. 1944*

Scoglitti and the Camerina plain
Punta Zafaglione in left background; Wood's Hole beyond

Scoglitti

Bailey's Beach, D-day
LCVP riding the surf over a false beach; another broached on the beach; antitank gun ashore

Scene in Wood's Hole
Lee, *Wood*, *Dix* and other transports on horizon. Italian prisoners seated at left, LCM on beach at right. Engineers laying steel mat on beach exit

Scoglitti Landings

British Admiralty photo

Admiral of the Fleet Sir Andrew Cunningham RN

British Admiralty photo

Admiral Sir Bertram Ramsay RN

Flag Officers of the Royal Navy, at Sicily

British Admiralty photo

Rear Admiral Sir Philip Vian RN
Commanding Force "V"

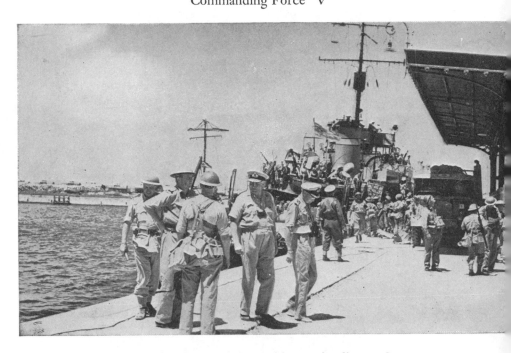

Rear Admiral Thomas Troubridge RN landing at Syracuse

Flag Officers of the Royal Navy, at Sicily

Photo by Major J. C. Hatlem USA, Feb. 1944

Agrigento and Porto Empédocle

U.S. Army Signal Corps photo

Palermo, 22 July 1943

Cathedral at right, Monte Pellegrino at left

Photo by Major J. C. Hatlem USA

Brolo, Scene of the Amphibious Landing 11 August 1943

The town is in the middle distance, obscured by cloud shadow; Monte Creole rises behind it

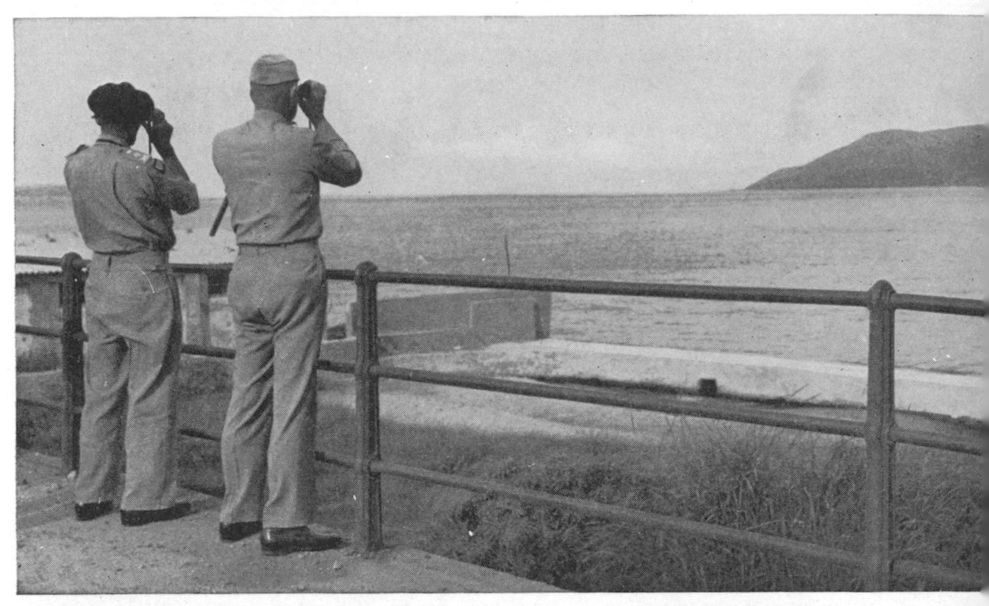

Generals Eisenhower and Montgomery at Messina, 30 August

Major General Hawkesworth, British Army, and Rear Admiral Richard L. Conolly USN on board U.S.S. *Biscayne*

Savor of Victory

Photo by Major J. C. Hatlem USA, *early 1944*

Air View of the U.S. Landing Beaches, Paestum

Tower at right center; Salerno and Sorrento Peninsula in background

The Temple of Neptune and adjacent Army hospital tent

U.S. Army Signal Corps photo

Squad of 143rd RCT landing from LCVP, D-day

Paestum

U.S. motor torpedo boat laying smoke

U.S.S. *Savannah* hit by radio-guided bomb

Scenes in Salerno Roadstead

Commodore William A. Sullivan USN *and Admiral Sir John Cunningham* RN

Discussing salvage problems at Naples

Rear Admiral Frank J. Lowry USN

LIFE *photo by Robert Capa*

Roadstead during an air attack

Anzio Beachhead

U.S. Army Signal Corps photo

Landings on X-ray Beaches
Dukws rolling ashore from LSTs over pontoon causeways

Photo by Major J. C. Hatlem USA

Beachhead from the air. Artificial harbor at right. Villa Borghese rises above the trees; part of Nettuno at right rear; Alban Hills in background

Anzio Beachhead

giving her light and power and keeping her pumped out. When railway cars containing 900 tons of ammunition caught fire from a bomb hit 50 yards distant, both ships were showered with shell fragments over a period of four hours. On the bridge of *Mayrant* Coxswain Nunzio Cammarata, as he expressed it, had his leg "took off" and "laid beside me on the bridge." Lieutenant Franklin D. Roosevelt jr., the "exec," applied a tourniquet and carried the man down the ladder and across the brow to *Strive*, where a pharmacist's mate administered first aid and saved his life. An LST was damaged, and a British freighter in the harbor received a direct hit and sank.

The 9th Infantry Division, off shore in five converted passenger vessels and seven Liberty ships, were interested if somewhat anxious spectators of this raid. They had arrived from Oran after dark, escorted by six destroyers of Desron 17 (Captain Madeira) and had been ordered not to go alongside until morning. The formation stood off-and-on all night, and fortunately escaped the attention of the bombers. The 9th disembarked at Palermo 1 August and pushed right on in vehicles to an assembly area at Cerami near Troina.

The Luftwaffe chose the morning watch of 4 August for another air attack. This time radar gave ample warning, and a fiery cone of antiaircraft missiles greeted the planes. They hesitated, then swooped in and hit destroyer *Shubrick* with three bombs which exploded in the forward engine room, killed nine men and burned eight others so badly that they died. Friendly fighters arrived at 0526, half an hour after the battle was over.[85]

Within twenty-four hours, four or five Italian motor torpedo boats attempted a raid on Palermo. Destroyer *Plunkett*, on patrol, picked them up on her radar; *Gleaves* illuminated, opened fire and forced the boats to retire.[86] There was a small air attack at 0430 August 6 and a few bombs were dropped; on this occasion a timely interception by friendly night fighters beat off the enemy.

Palermo escaped a naval bombardment only by a fortuitous en-

[85] *Philadelphia* and *Savannah* Action Reports.

[86] At about 0045 Aug. 5. Desron 7 War Diary; Admiral Davidson calls them E-boats, but from the failure of Ruge to mention this attack I conclude they were Italians trying to prevent U.S. naval interference with their evacuation.

counter. On 5 August, two Italian light cruisers, *Raimondo Montecuccoli* and *Eugenio di Savoia*, left their lair at La Maddalena, Sardinia, with orders to bombard American forces in Palermo. They might well have got within range, since Admiral Davidson's cruisers were many miles up the coast, supporting the Seventh Army. According to a German account, the Italian cruisers were "intercepted about 0430 on the 6th by two Allied motor torpedo boats, and a short battle ensued. A few shots and flares were fired by the Italians, the torpedo boats sought to close, then contact was lost." [87]

It was no motor torpedo boat that stopped the cruisers, but *SC–530*, engaged in escorting a lowly motor barge carrying water and provisions to the Italian fishermen at Ustica, a small island about 30 miles north of Sicily! [88] The subchaser's men, unterrified by two large warships looming up, opened fire, escaped damage, and went on their way rejoicing; while the Italian cruisers, discouraged at being detected, reversed course and headed for Naples.

After the 5 August raid, Palermo enjoyed comparative peace until almost a week after the last enemy troops had evacuated Sicily. At 0405 August 23 the harbor was attacked by about 20 Ju–88s. Destroyer *Wainwright*, patrolling outside the harbor, received two near-misses and was slightly damaged. Subchasers *SC–694* and *SC–696*, moored to a pier, were hit by 550-pound bombs and set on fire. A fuel compartment in one and a magazine in the other exploded, showering the area with steel and burning oil which spread to a British freighter and to U.S. naval tug *Narragansett*, moored to the other side of the pier. The tug's crew, who were trying to fight the fires in the SCs, had to confine attention to their own ship; she was badly damaged and more men were killed. This raid, which was not intercepted, cost the United States Navy two subchasers, 30 men blasted or burned to death, and 35 painfully injured. By this Parthian shot the Luftwaffe served notice that it was still a force to be reckoned with in the forthcoming invasion of Italy.

[87] German Naval Command Italy War Diary 5 Aug. 1943.

[88] Ústica had capitulated to DDs *Plunkett* and *Gleaves* and *LCI–213* on 5 August.

7. *The Three-Pronged Eastward Thrust, 29 July–7 August*

We have now reached the point where we must pick up General Alexander's directive of 20 July,[39] and see how the Seventh Army fitted into his "left hook" against the Etna Line. His directive, supplemented by a second after he had conferred with Generals Patton and Montgomery at Cassibile on 25 July, outlined a three-pronged thrust, to start 1 August. It assigned to Seventh Army the two topmost prongs – the coastal road and the Nicosia–Randazzo road (No. 120) – while the British XXX Corps continued along the Leonforte–Adrano road.

The Germans now had three reinforced divisions in Sicily – the Hermann Goering, the 15th and 29th Panzer Grenadiers, and two regiments of the 1st Parachute, which had been incorporated in the Goering. Of the Italian mobile divisions, the Aosta and the Assietta were still formidable; but the Napoli and Livorno had been pretty well cut up. General Hans Hube, as we have seen, arrived in Sicily with XIV Panzer Corps headquarters about 15 July, and, two days later, received orders from General Jodl "to fight a delaying action to gain further time for stabilizing the situation on the mainland," and "under no circumstances" to fail to extricate the German divisions. He also had secret orders from Hitler to take over the island defense as unobtrusively as possible, which the aged and discouraged General Guzzoni appears to have been very glad to let him do. On 2 August Hube formally took over tactical command of all Axis combatant forces in Sicily; actually he had been running things since his arrival.[40]

During the last week of July General Middleton's 45th Division, the north prong of the hook, had been pushing along the north coast from Términi Imerese. The Assietta Division, which had been moved out of western Sicily, and the Ulich Combat Group, consist-

[39] See above, p. (14).

[40] Bonin "Considerations" p. 8; information from Historical Office of the Italian Army.

ing of two regiments of the 29th Panzer Grenadier Division, blocked them. Beyond Cefalù, the "Thunderbirds" found the going very difficult. In most places the troops were confined between sea and cliffs to a narrow coastal road, heavily mined. Enemy artillery, mortar and machine-gun fire were very severe. The Germans intended to make a prolonged stand at San Stéfano,[41] but the 45th, supported by gunfire from Admiral Davidson's cruisers, was too much for them, and that town was captured on 31 July. General Truscott's 3rd Division, which had enjoyed over a week's rest in Palermo, entrained in cars of the railroad, which Army engineers had placed in operation, and began relieving the 45th on the 31st. By midnight 1 August the entire 3rd Division was concentrated on the Torremuzza Plain west of San Stéfano, on the edge of the Tyrrhenian Sea.

On 1 August the Axis line ran from Caronia on the north coast, a few miles east of San Stéfano and Sant'Agata, south around Troina and Regalbuto, east to include Adrano, and thence to Acireale on the coast, although Catania was still held by forward elements.

For a week the 3rd Division made slow progress against ingenious delaying tactics and determined rear-guard stands. The weather was desperately hot, temperature rising above 100° F. every noon under a cloudless sky, and the problem of getting water to the American troops was exceedingly difficult. Most of the watercourses were dried up, and the Germans had a nasty habit of heavily mining every spot where a spring or pipe of water issued from the hills. This road, the ancient Via Valeria, bordered by pink and white oleanders and lemon orchards, is a joy to tourists; but it was a curse to the GIs as they slogged along with only the strident creaking of the cicadas as martial music. Every few miles a river (dry at that season) made a small plain between steep mountain ridges, each of which commanded the road for miles on either side. A few mobile guns and riflemen on a ridge could hold up infantry for hours. Each time, troops had to work around and behind the strong point, and

[41] Fries "Ops. of 29th Panzer Grenadier Division," pp. 7, 11, especially mentions the "heavy naval guns."

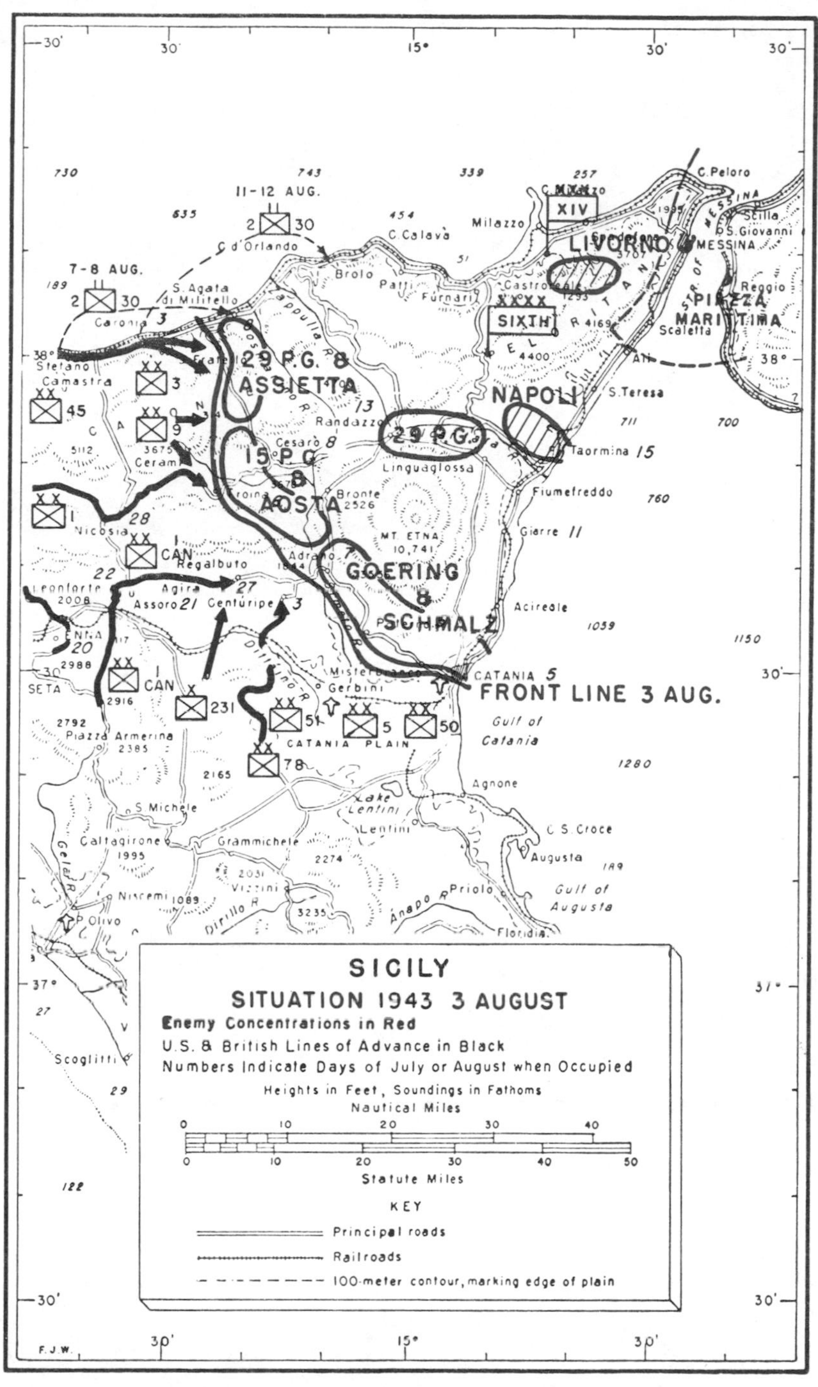
SICILY
SITUATION 1943 3 AUGUST
Enemy Concentrations in Red
U.S. & British Lines of Advance in Black
Numbers Indicate Days of July or August when Occupied
Heights in Feet, Soundings in Fathoms
Nautical Miles
Statute Miles
KEY
Principal roads
Railroads
100-meter contour, marking edge of plain
FRONT LINE 3 AUG.
11-12 AUG.
7-8 AUG.
LIVORNO
NAPOLI
29 P.G. 8 ASSIETTA
15 P.G. 8 AOSTA
GOERING 8 SCHMALZ
29 P.G.
PIAZZA MARITTIMA
XIV
SIXTH
MESSINA
CATANIA
Gulf of Catania
Gulf of Augusta
MT. ETNA 10,741
CATANIA PLAIN
F.J.W.

generally when they got there the enemy had moved on to the next ridge.

Owing to a lucky encounter by part of Task Force 88, the number of land mines available to the Germans was somewhat diminished. A two-destroyer patrol, *Gherardi* and *Rhind* with Commander J. B. Rooney as O.T.C., were making an offensive night sweep along the coast on the night of 3–4 August. At 2215, when a few miles off Cape Calavà, they picked up a small convoy consisting of one of the German MFP lighters escorted by two motor torpedo boats. At a range of 4000 yards the destroyers illuminated the convoy with star shell and opened up with main batteries. The F-boat blew up at 2225 and disappeared, and one of the escorting boats was sunk; the other fired at least one torpedo, which missed. Later it was ascertained that the MFP had been loaded with land mines.[42]

Other destroyers, as well as *Savannah* and *Philadelphia*, were busy all that week with bombardment missions along the coast between San Stéfano and Cape Orlando. For reasons not altogether clear, the troops did not ask for much call fire, and the ships confined their attention largely to coast defense batteries and fixed positions.

General Hube, after the 29th Panzer Grenadiers were forced out of San Stéfano, intended his right flank to make a stand on the San Fratello–Cesarò–Troina line until Kesselring should decide to evacuate Sicily. This was a very strong position, with its anchor on Monte Fratello, a 2400-foot mountain that dominates both the coastal road and the road to Cesarò. Here the German reserves had time to construct field fortifications, which they and the Assietta Division served so well that the 3rd Division was held up for five days. If the German withdrawal thence was not quite "according to plan," it was because Patton had the good sense to use the sea power at his disposal.

At his request Admiral Davidson drafted a plan for a "leapfrog" amphibious operation. A task group composed of two LSTs, seven

42 Comdesdiv 34 (Cdr. Rooney) Action Report 5 Aug. 1943.

LCTs, and *LCI–217*, commanded by Lieutenant Commander R. G. Newbegin USNR, embarked the 2nd Battalion 30th Regiment, with a platoon of tanks and a battery of field artillery, at the beaches west of San Stéfano, late in the afternoon of 7 August. *Philadelphia, Savannah* and six destroyers covered the movement. In calm midsummer weather the ten beaching craft landed every soldier and vehicle on a beach near Sant'Agata, nine miles east of Monte Fratello, by 0408 August 8.[43] "It's the chance that few outfits get, so let's cut the rug and knock them all the way back to Messina," was the word of the troop commander.

Shortly before midnight 7 August, Cincmed sent Admiral Davidson a dispatch warning him that two Italian light cruisers with two destroyers were on the prowl and probably heading for Palermo. These were *Garibaldi* and *Duca d'Aosta*, and Palermo was indeed their target; but no destroyers were with them. Davidson immediately led *Philadelphia, Savannah, Bristol* and *Ludlow* in the right direction to intercept.[44] Surface battle with the Italian Navy at last! Again, hopes were dashed. The Italian cruisers ran into a dense fog bank; and, having neither radar nor screen, prudently retired after 0200, when a German reconnaissance plane reported Davidson's force on an intercepting course.[45]

Either just before the cruisers took off or during their absence, one of the destroyers contributed greatly to the success of the Sant'Agata landing by a lucky hit. The Germans were withdrawing along the coastal road. They had mined the highway bridge over the Rosmarino River, east of the Monte Fratello position, in order to blow it up after their own columns had crossed. But an American warship, wrote General Fries, commander of the 29th Panzer Grenadiers, "which had been shelling the coastal road in the rear

[43] CTG 88.3 (Lt. Cdr. Newbegin) Action Report 16 Aug. 1943; Taggart p. 67. This is sometimes referred to as the Torrenova landing, as it took place between that town and Sant'Agata. It would have taken place a day earlier had not *LST-3*, one of the two participating, been so damaged in an air raid that departure had to be postponed.

[44] Four destroyers remained to support the landing. *Savannah* returned to Algiers and was relieved by *Boise.*

[45] Information from Historical Office of the Italian Navy, in letter to Admiral Hewitt of 19 Jan. 1954.

of the German front continuously during the afternoon and evening, succeeded in hitting the bridge . . . in such a way that, unfortunately for us, the charge was set off and the bridge blown into the air prematurely." The Germans had already mined the nearest crossing of the dry river bed hoping to harass the pressing Americans; now they had to extract the mines in order to clear a crossing for themselves. The delay made a long traffic block of stalled vehicles, and just as the traffic jam was about to break it was hit by the American landing force, "causing confusion and great difficulties."[46] The landing force killed 250 and captured 100 Germans, disabled four tanks, and captured a number of vehicles. After daylight an American infantry battalion, advancing overland, occupied Monte Fratello; and the Axis defense line was thrown back to the Zappula River and the Cape Orlando–Randazzo road.

As soon as Admiral Davidson was satisfied that the Italian cruisers had fled, he brought *Philadelphia* back to Sant'Agata roadstead. She commenced firing at 0807 August 8, with a shore fire-control party and an Army artillery plane spotting. Enemy bombers attacked her at 0947, were chased off by antiaircraft fire and friendly fighter planes, returned at 1025, were thwarted by the quick, violent maneuvers at 31 knots in which Captain Hendren was adept, and were finally intercepted and driven off by friendlies. *Philadelphia* then returned to Palermo.

Actually the Sant'Agata landing accomplished little, because General Fries had already begun to evacuate Monte Fratello. The capture of Troina by the 1st Division on 6 August had laid the Fratello position open to attack from the south and forced the General's decision. If only Patton could have put the landing on a week earlier, the rôles would have been reversed; the Germans would have been pinched out of Fratello and then forced to evacuate Troina and Regalbuto. As it was, the 1st Division had a terrific fight for the one, and the British XXX Corps for the other.

Twenty miles south of the coast, across the Nebrodi range, Gen-

[46] Fries pp. 16–17; he says it was a cruiser, but destroyer *Plunkett* probably did it.

eral Allen's 1st Division had been slowly pressing Axis forces eastward along the road to Troina since 23 July, when it entered Petralia and, in accordance with the Alexander plan, turned 90 degrees right. Nicosia was taken on the 28th, and by 1 August the Fighting First was within striking distance of Troina, a highly defensible hill-town. The attack, bloodiest of the campaign for the Seventh Army, opened promptly. Fifteen full battalions of field artillery supported the infantry. From strong natural positions the 15th Panzer Grenadiers and the Italian Aosta Division offered stout resistance, counterattacking no fewer than 24 times. With excellent aërial and artillery support the 1st Division finally overcame the enemy and entered Troina 6 August.

Seventh Army reserve, the larger part of the 9th Infantry Division (Major General Manton S. Eddy) landed at Palermo on 1 August; and, after relieving the 1st at Troina, pushed ahead and captured Cesarò on 8 August.

While General Montgomery awaited the deployment of his reserve infantry division, the 78th (which began landing south of Syracuse on 25 July), and while all remained quiet on the Catania front, the Canadians thrust a third spearhead along the next road south of the 1st Division's prong. They had been allotted the most rugged country in all Sicily and the enemy defended it well. After taking Leonforte (22 July) and Agira (27 July) the Canadians, helped by the 231st Brigade, wrested Regalbuto from the Hermann Goering Division, which had been ordered to hold it "at all costs," on 2 August. The newly arrived 78th Division took Centúripe the same day, and entered the town of Adrano on 7 August.

Adrano was the central anchor to the Etna Line. The Germans were holding it only long enough to make an orderly evacuation from Catania, behind which, at Acireale, they had established an eastern anchor on the sea. On 5 August the 5th and 50th Divisions, after a rest of over two weeks, crossed the plain and entered Catania, Misterbianco, and Paterno without opposition.

CHAPTER X

Sicily Conquered—and Evacuated

3–17 August

1. *On to Messina, 7–16 August*

MILITARY operations in Sicily during August can be understood only in the light of what has come out since the war from former enemy sources. The Allied generals imagined that they were driving the enemy back by a series of brilliant offensives. Actually the Axis was conducting a series of rear-guard actions to cover an orderly evacuation of Sicily, which was carried out with complete success.

Hitler, immediately upon hearing of the fall of Mussolini, directed Kesselring to prepare for the possibility of evacuating all German troops from Sicily. But, in consequence of strong arguments against it by Admiral Doenitz, he could not bring himself to give the order. Marshal Kesselring, without waiting for Hitler to make up his mind, ordered the operations officers of the divisions then in Sicily to fly to his headquarters at Frascati to plan Operation LEHRGANG, the evacuation of Sicily.[1]

While the question of whether or not to evacuate was being threshed out at Fuehrer headquarters, and while Marshal Badoglio also vacillated, General Guzzoni made the decision independently, for the forces of his own nation. On 31 July he directed Rear Admiral Pietro Barone, commanding at Messina, to prepare to evacuate Italian troops starting 3 August.

[1] Rintelen *Mussolini als Bundesgenosse* p. 224; "Sicilian Campaign, Information from German Sources" p. 10.

Hitler's headquarters were still arguing when Kesselring, wishing to avoid another débâcle like that of Tunisia, authorized General Hube to use his own judgment as to when to begin getting the German troops out. The XIV Corps commander had already laid out five lines of resistance converging on Messina, which would be held and relinquished in successive nights, while 8000 to 10,000 men a day crossed the Strait. Line No. 1 started at Monte Fratello, ran through Troina, Bronte, and Adrano, and around Mount Etna to Acireale. The only Allied disturbance of Hube's schedule, and that not serious, was the American capture of Troina and Sant'Agata a few days before Hube was ready to evacuate them. Colonel von Bonin, Hube's chief of staff, intimates that the taking of Regalbuto, Sant'Agata and Troina within one week (2–8 August) determined Hube to start the evacuation on the 10th. And Operation LEHRGANG began that night.[2]

The terrain was perfect for an orderly withdrawal. The huge bulk of Mount Etna prevented the Allies from maneuvering their superior numbers, and the Peloritan range of mountains, continuing almost to the tip of the peninsula, canalized all military movements to the coastal roads. There were any number of Thermopylae where Axis units could, and did, fight tough rear-guard actions while the main part of their forces retreated across the Strait.

But the Allies had two superior elements, sea and air power, which might and should have more than compensated for the terrain. These they failed to use intelligently. General Hube had no air reconnaissance, and was completely in the dark as to Allied troop concentrations, or as to the intentions of the Seventh and Eighth Army commanders.

General Patton, who by 5 August correctly estimated enemy intentions,[3] made good use of sea power at his disposal, which General Montgomery did not. Highly pleased over the success

[2] Bonin "Considerations" pp. 17–18. Ruge states that it began at 0200 Aug. 13, but Kesselring informed Army headquarters at Berlin on the 10th, "Evacuation has started according to plan." "Sicilian Campaign, Information from German Sources" pp. 15–16; compare Rintelen p. 240.

[3] Seventh Army *Report of Operations* pp. C-39–40.

of the Sant'Agata landing, Patton planned a second leap to Brolo for 9 August.

This small amphibious operation was mounted at Caronia, about 12 miles west of Sant'Agata, where a pebbly peninsula affords protection from the prevailing westerly wind and a good beach for embarkation. The movement was postponed to the night of 10–11 August by a Luftwaffe raid which damaged *LST–318* beyond repair. One LST, two LCIs and six LCTs lifted the 2nd Battalion 30th RCT for its second leap in three days. According to the war correspondent who accompanied this small expedition, the troops felt that they were tempting fate to risk an amphibious landing behind the enemy's lines a second time.[4] Their instinct was correct. A hundred of them never got beyond Brolo.

For a few hours the Caronia–Brolo movement went well. *Philadelphia* and six destroyers covered the transports, the sea journey was short, two night fighter planes flew ahead, moonlight and a prominent offshore rock helped locate the planned landing beach west of the town, and no opposition developed as the troops stepped ashore in quiet darkness between 0243 and 0400 August 11. In the tiny town, clustered around a Norman castle on a rocky outcrop at the edge of the sea, everyone appeared to be asleep. *Philadelphia* commenced supporting fires on Cape Orlando, west of the beach, at 0538. Inaccurate return fire was received from a shore battery. Four Italian torpedo-bombers flew very low over the water, but apparently did not like the looks of the United States ships and sheered off without attacking. At 0930, since calls had ceased from the shore party and all prearranged targets had been attended to, the warships started back to Palermo. But, shortly after noon, just as he was about to enter the port, Admiral Davidson received an urgent order to return to Brolo and break up a counterattack.

Back came *Philadelphia*, *Bristol* and *Ludlow* at 31 knots. Before 1400 they were off Brolo beach and in contact with shore fire control. The flagship fired 15-gun salvos on enemy targets for 40

[4] Belden *Still Time to Die* p. 272.

minutes. She then ceased fire because the radio voice from shore became erratic and then silent. Ships cannot bombard a coast where friendly troops are fighting, except on specific call, and Allied planes appeared to be taking care of the situation; they were observed to be dropping bombs on the area. So, at 1500, Admiral Davidson took it on himself to withdraw his support force. An hour later, Seventh Army headquarters asked him to return a second time, which he promptly did. While he was delivering gunfire support, at 1656, eight Focke-Wulf 190s showed up. There followed a half-hour battle of guns against planes, with rapid maneuvering by the ships, bombs missing them by feet only, and spirited interception by friendly fighter planes. One only of the German planes got away. Captain Hendren claims that *Philadelphia* shot down five, and credits *Ludlow* and an Army fighter plane with one each.

After taking on board some troops who, chased off the tiny Brolo beachhead by enemy tanks, had put out to sea in dukws, the ships retired for the third time; since, deprived of shore communications, plane spot and air cover, there seemed to be nothing for them to do. From the rescued troops details of the sad plight of the 2nd Battalion were obtained. If the landing had taken place opposite the town of Brolo, several good beach exits would have been available; but, probably from a wish to avoid street fighting, whoever planned this operation selected a beach west of the town, where tanks and vehicles were held up by a high railway embankment. At this point both beach and road are dominated by a steep conical hill of almost 1000-foot elevation.[5] The troops seized this hill by 0530, leaving their vehicles parked in a lemon grove below. By that time enemy troops in Brolo had recovered from their surprise and, at 0700, began a series of counterattacks which continued until noon. A strong German thrust from the east was broken up shortly after 0900 by *Philadelphia's* gunfire, friendly airplanes, and the battalion's own artillery. Later tank-supported attacks also were

[5] In Action Reports this is called Monte Creole; on the official map of Sicily, Monte Cipolla; the natives call it Monte Brolo or simply La Montagna. It can be identified by a large luminous cross at the turn of the road to Sinagra which winds up the eastern slope.

repulsed. Everything might have gone well if the Army radio had not conked out so that the troops could no longer ask for supporting gunfire or direct air-bombing. Their worst misfortune was an attack by seven Army A-36s from Ponte Olivo field. The American aviators, unable to communicate with ground forces but eager to help, took a long chance at identification and planted two bombs on the American command post on the hill, and several more on the artillery parked below, destroying all four fieldpieces. Surviving gunners in the plain now withdrew to the hill; and the 2nd Battalion, battered more by friend than by foe, set up a defensive perimeter for the night.[6] Being on the defensive, they were unable to prevent the main body of the Germans, then west of the hill, from rolling along the coastal road to safety, around 2200.[7]

Rescue arrived early next morning, 12 August. At 0600 the soldiers on the mountain saw the 1st Battalion of their regiment approaching along the highway from the west, and made contact with them at 0830. The 2nd Battalion had lost 99 men killed or missing, and 78 wounded; German casualties were about the same.

The German naval commander for Italy regarded the Brolo exploit as unimpressive. He was unable to understand why the Allies, with their overwhelming sea power, had not done this sort of thing earlier, more often, and on a bigger scale. And we must admit that he was right. The Sant'Agata landing did upset the enemy in the midst of a withdrawal, and the Brolo one resulted in his pulling out of Cape Orlando a day earlier than he had intended; but no German troops were trapped on either occasion.

Now let us see what was happening on the other prong of the "left hook." The fresh 9th Division United States Army, even before taking Cesarò on 8 August, had divided into two combat teams. The 60th Regiment, for which there was no room on the road to Randazzo, marched cross-country from a point north of Cesarò to Floresta, for a large part of the way making its own road. There

[6] Taggart pp. 69–71, and information from the evacuated troops in Adm. Davidson's Action Report.

[7] Fries pp. 20–25.

was no opposition here but the terrain. On this main road the enemy still covered his retreat with mines and demolitions, and the 9th did not enter Randazzo until 0930 August 13.

After the capture of Adrano on 6–7 August, by the 78th Division, General Montgomery withdrew the Canadian 1st Division to reserve. The 78th now turned north to Bronte, seeking to help the United States 9th Division to take Randazzo. But the Germans held at Maletto until the 12th, and the 78th was unable to coöperate. The 51st Division crossed the Dittáino Valley into Biancavilla on the 7th. None of these units exercised any appreciable pressure on the Axis retirement after the fall of Adrano, and all contact was lost with enemy forces on the 15th.

General Montgomery missed another opportunity to rush forces into Messina along the eastern slope of Mount Etna. On 5 August, as we have seen, the 5th and 50th Divisions entered Catania and the towns west of it. This was his last chance to seize and close the Strait, the only Axis escape route. He had command of the air and sea, more than enough naval gunfire to blast out coast defense batteries, and sufficient troop-lift to perform a series of amphibious landings. Good landing beaches are not wanting on this coast.

Admiral Cunningham goes far, for a British sailor, in criticizing Generals Montgomery and Alexander. Subsequent to the capture of Augusta, he says: —

> . . . No use was made by the Eighth Army of amphibious opportunities. The small LSIs were kept standing by for the purpose, at the call of Rear Admiral McGrigor, and landing craft were available on call; but the only occasion on which they were used was on the 16th August, after the capture of Catania, when a commando landing was made, but fell short of the flank of the retreating enemy.
>
> There were doubtless sound military reasons for making no use of this, what to me appeared, priceless asset of sea power and flexibility of manœuvre; but it is worth consideration for future occasions whether much time and costly fighting could not be saved by even minor flank attacks, which must necessarily be unsettling to the enemy. It must be always for the General to decide. The Navy can only provide the means and advise on the practicability from the naval angle of the

projected operation. It may be that had I pressed my views more strongly, more could have been done.[8]

What were these sound military reasons? Neither Alexander nor Montgomery has explained. The one "amphibious opportunity" that Montgomery embraced was sending the 40th Royal Marine Commando to land near Ali and Scaletta on 16 August, the day after the 50th Division entered Taormina. But by that date the enemy had withdrawn the greater part of his army across the Strait. The General ascribes his slow progress to the fact that the United States 9th Division did not capture Randazzo until 13 August. But the capture of Randazzo could have been expedited by an amphibious landing at Fiumefreddo at the end of the Randazzo road. That would have turned the German left flank.

The amount of naval gunfire used to support the seaward flank of the Eighth Army is not impressive. Light cruiser *Mauritius* and two destroyers bombarded Giarre on 8 and 12 August, as did *Uganda* and *Flores* on the 10th; three destroyers bombarded the lower town of Taormina on 7 August. That is all that I can find recorded in the way of naval gunfire support *after* the fall of Catania.

Montgomery was not the only general to stage a leapfrog operation too late to leap the frog. "Old Blood and Guts" Patton, impressed by the Brolo landing, planned with Admiral Davidson his biggest amphibious assault for 15 August, with an entire regimental combat team and a battalion of paratroops. As a preliminary, *Boise* bombarded the town of Milazzo, which the enemy was reported to be evacuating, on the afternoon of the 14th. But the Germans had already passed that point. Accordingly, the target for the landing was shifted east at the last minute, to Spadafora. Again the enemy eluded us; by the time this amphibious force started to land, at 0050 August 16, he had retired beyond Spadafora and in fact had got most of his troops across the Strait of Messina. Here, as in the Eighth

[8] Despatch in *London Gazette* 25 Apr. 1950. Admiral McGrigor twice had a sizeable Commando force embarked in LSIs, and once actually got them under way for an amphibious landing, but both times Montgomery called it off.

Army sector, the Germans retreated at their own pace and with insignificant losses.

Nevertheless, Admiral Davidson's Task Force 88 had done a great deal to help conquer Sicily. Admiral Cunningham compliments both General Patton for his sagacious use of sea power and Admiral Davidson for his "rapid planning and execution of outflanking operations." Besides performing two useful amphibious landings, TF 88 had hauled hundreds of tons of artillery, ammunition and rations from one point to another along the coast, bypassing road blocks, land mines and blown bridges and tunnels that held up Army trucks. Combatant ships based on the uneasy roadstead of Palermo constantly patrolled the coast, denying it almost completely to the enemy, and furnished gunfire support to the Seventh Army. Motor torpedo boats prevented Axis ships from entering the Strait of Messina, but they were unable to prevent Axis use of the Strait itself.

"On all occasions," wrote General Patton in his summary of the campaign, "the Navy has given generous and gallant support." [9] And, when speaking of Admiral Davidson, he would use his highest commendation: "There is a real fighting so-and-so!"

A memorable chapter in the war was closing, and another beginning; for there was little rest in the Mediterranean war. Few men of the Seventh Army, or for that matter the Eighth Fleet, suspected in mid-August that on 9 September they would be fighting in the thunderous assault on Salerno, which was to make the Sicilian landings seem like a summer picnic. In Algiers, staff planners had so long taken the fall of Sicily for granted that its only interest lay in betting between British and Americans as to whether Montgomery or Patton would reach Messina first.

Patton won the race. On the morning of 17 August his foremost infantry patrol entered the battered and deserted city of Messina. Two hours later a column of Eighth Army tanks rumbled in from the south amid shouts from GIs of "Where you tourists been?"

[9] General Order No. 18, Aug. 22, 1943.

To which the Tommies replied with a grin, "Hello, you bloody bastards!" [10]

Sicily was ours; but the savor of victory was tainted by the enemy's escape to the mainland.

2. *The Enemy Evacuation* [11]

The final episode in this campaign has never received proper attention; partly for want of information, partly because nobody on the Allied side has cared to dwell on it. This is the Axis troops' evacuation of Sicily across the Strait of Messina, an outstanding maritime retreat of the war, in a class with Dunkirk, Guadalcanal and Kiska. The main reasons for its success were long practice in the reverse direction and the Allies' failure to make any serious attempt to stop it.

The Italian evacuation began slowly on 3 August, by means of two or three small steamers. About 7000 men had crossed by 9 August, when Guzzoni received a positive order from Rome to evacuate all Italian troops from Sicily, and the movement speeded up. A day or two earlier General Hube had ordered the German evacuation to begin on 10 August.

For months the Northwest African Air Force had been trying to bomb the train ferries out of business. Two of the four had been

[10] Hal Boyle in *Rome Daily American* 10 July 1953; George Biddle *Artist at War* p. 113. Biddle protested that this was not a nice term to apply to one's allies, to which a Tommy retorted, "It don't mean nothing. That's the way we call each other!"

[11] Adm. von Ruge "Report on the Evacuation of Sicily" (1948) with Cdr. Liebenstein's Report as enclosure; Liebenstein's War Diary for 1–15 Aug. 1943 (Tambach docs. T-191A); Col. Baade's Operation Order for the evacuation (Gen. Mil. Doc. Sec. War Dept. No. 35746) with chart; Ammiraglio di Squadra Pietro Barone "Estratto della Relazione sull' Occupazione della Sicilia" (1946, courtesy of Historical Office Italian Navy) pp. 25–30; Gen. Walter Fries "Operations of 29th Panzer Grenadier Division"; documents by Bonin and Senger cited in chap. iii, footnote 1; Bernotti *La Guerra sui Mari* pp. 90–3, and chapter "La Nostra Dunkerque" in Bragadin *Che ha Fatto la Marina?*

knocked out, together with their slips at Reggio and Villa San Giovanni; but the Axis did not confine troop-ferrying to regular means of transport, or to the usual termini. In May and June the German Navy had brought in numerous Siebel ferries,[12] MFPs and other small craft, and placed the responsibility of organizing and operating the transit of the Strait upon a very efficient reserve officer, Commander von Liebenstein. In order to side-step air attacks Liebenstein frequently changed the embarkation and landing places, shifting pontoon landing stages from one point to another; by 10 August some twelve different crossings were practicable. General Hube appointed an equally capable and energetic Army officer, Colonel Baade, as Commandant of the Strait, with complete responsibility for approaches, defenses, and sea traffic, as far as the Germans were concerned. Since each division had to leave in echelons, each was assigned a specific assembly area in Calabria.

The Italian evacuation, organized by Rear Admiral Barone, also was carried out with complete success.[13] The Italians used several different routes, independent of the German ferries; one started from the port of Messina, and one from a beach north of Cape Peloro. They used their own craft exclusively.

From the start of the German evacuation, on the night of 10–11 August, the one coastal road along each side of the Strait, serving all embarkation and debarkation points, was jam-packed with men and vehicles. All hands were apprehensive of being bombed out of the approaches and exits. The Northwest African Air Force frequently tried to do it and claimed that it had been done, but the roads were never interrupted for more than two hours. Barrage balloons were used on some ferry craft to good effect, and all were provided with excellent antiaircraft batteries and trained gunners.

[12] Originally designed for the invasion of Britain in 1940, these were double-ended, pontoon-supported motor rafts which could carry 10 trucks, or 60 tons, and make a speed of 10 knots. A Siebel ferry could be loaded with 9 to 12 trucks in 20 minutes. They were taken to pieces and transported through France to the Mediterranean.

[13] Admiral Barone, the Italian Naval commander in Sicily, together with General Guzzoni, left Sicily 10 Aug. by order of Comando Supremo. Major General Bozzoni, commanding the Piazza Marittíma of Messina, and Rear Admiral Parenti, carried on.

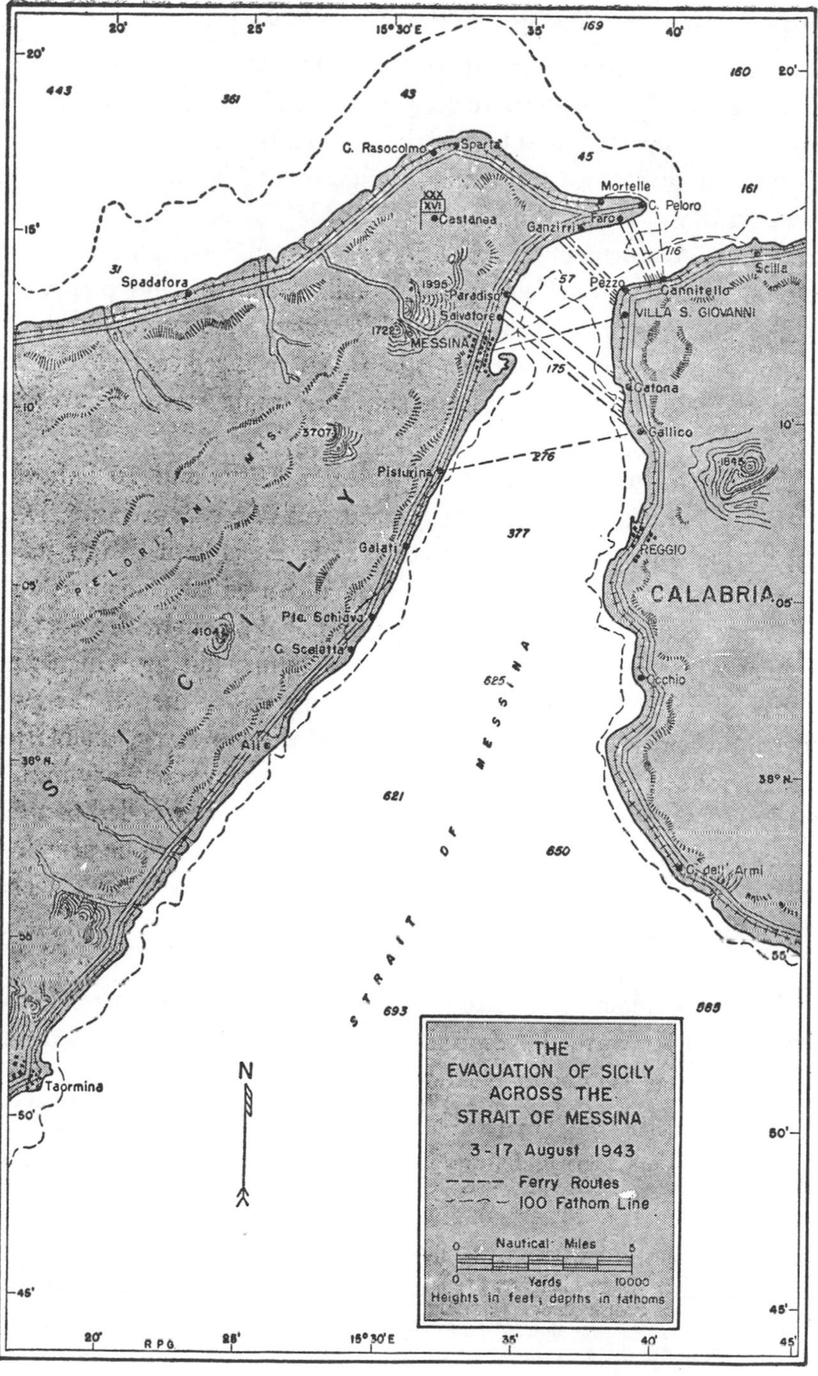
THE
EVACUATION OF SICILY
ACROSS THE
STRAIT OF MESSINA
3-17 August 1943
Ferry Routes
100 Fathom Line
Nautical Miles
Yards
Heights in feet; depths in fathoms
C. Rasocolmo
Sparta
Mortelle
C. Peloro
Faro
Ganzirri
Castanea
Spadafora
Paradiso
Salvatore
MESSINA
Pezzo
Cannitello
Scilla
VILLA S. GIOVANNI
Catona
Gallico
Pisturina
Galati
REGGIO
CALABRIA
Pta. Schiavo
C. Scaletta
Occhio
Ali
C. dell' Armi
Taormina
PELORITANI MTS.
SICILY
STRAIT OF MESSINA
RPG

In addition, the ferry routes were covered by batteries on both sides of the Strait. By 22 July, 30 long-range antiaircraft batteries had been there emplaced; and before the evacuation began two batteries of 170-mm guns with an effective range of 17 kilometers had been sited on both sides of Villa San Giovanni.[14] Altogether there were about 150 German 88-mm and Italian 90-mm dual-purpose guns divided between the Calabrian and Sicilian shores, and plenty of smaller pieces and machine guns.[15] All routes were protected by a patrol of motor minesweepers, and Italian midget torpedo boats were on hand to attack any large ship that might venture into the Strait.

The Germans used 13 Siebel ferries, 7 MFPs and 16 L-boats (artillery barges similar to the Siebels) in their evacuation.[16] The Italians had their 932-ton train-ferry *Villa*, capable of lifting 3000 men, in operation by 11 August. They also used two small steamboats and four navy-manned motor rafts. *Villa* caught fire on the 12th and was out of commission for 48 hours, during which the motor rafts saved the situation, transporting 20,000 men at the rate of a thousand a trip. *Cariddi*, the 2800-ton train ferry, unable to move under her own power, was loaded with heavy artillery in the roadstead north of Messina. The Italian command intended to tow her across, but no tugboat was available and she had to be scuttled as the Allies entered Messina. That, and one motor raft sunk, were the only serious losses in the Italian crossings.

Allied Intelligence reported promptly what was going on. General Alexander warned Admiral of the Fleet Cunningham and Air Chief Marshal Tedder on 3 August that the Germans were making preparations for an evacuation, which might start any day. "We

[14] "The Sicilian Campaign, Information from German Sources" p. 9; Col. Baade War Diary; Bonin "Considerations." The big guns belonged to the 15th Panzer Grenadiers.

[15] Barone p. 10.

[16] Ruge's figures; Liebenstein in his War Diary gives different figures: 11 Siebels, 5 MFP, and 10 L-boats available 11 Aug.; 9 Siebels, 7 MFP, 12 I- and S-boats, and 50 assault boats (landing craft) available by 16 Aug. The Allied aviators reported having sighted 80 Siebel ferries, according to Richard Tregaskis *Invasion Diary* p. 74.

must be in a position to take immediate advantage of such a situation by using full weight of Navy and Air Power. You have no doubt coördinated plans to meet this contingency. . . ." [17]

Cunningham and Tedder had no plans ready for that eventuality; but, according to R.A.F. records, they conferred, upon receipt of Alexander's signal, and agreed that the Air Forces, to begin with, would operate by day over the Strait north of lat. 38° N and east of Milazzo on the north coast, and that the two navies would intensify surface patrols by night.[18] Admiral Cunningham "gave the matter very careful thought," but decided that there was "no effective method" of stopping the enemy, "either by sea or air." [19] The British motor torpedo boats and small gunboats did what they could, but no larger warships were brought into the picture; and, so far as I can ascertain, Rear Admiral Davidson, in command of TF 88 on the north coast, was not even informed that the evacuation was on. Commander Barnes's PTs knew that it was taking place, but received no orders to do anything about it, and were forbidden to go south of the latitude of Cape Rasocolmo.

The British boats, based on Augusta, did their gallant best, but whenever they approached the narrows they were brilliantly illuminated by searchlights and driven out by shore batteries. On the night of 11 August, second of the German evacuation, three British MTBs, boldly patrolling under Allied flare-dropping planes, engaged about six small craft with torpedoes and gunfire, chased them into Messina and knocked out one Italian motor raft. This was the only occasion when Allied light forces managed to halt the ferry traffic. On the night of 15 August, H.M.S. *MTB-665* was hit by coastal gunfire and sunk with all hands. Two more British boats

[17] Signal communicated by Historical Section Canadian Army; cf. Craven and Cate II 472 and *El Alamein to River Sangro* pp. 89–90. Gen. Patton's G–2 on 4 Aug. stated that the Germans were fighting a delaying action with a view to evacuation, and next day was positive about it and correctly estimated three of the five withdrawal lines. Seventh Army *Report of Operations* pp. C–39, C–40. According to Tregaskis *Invasion Diary* p. 70, the evacuation plan of the Goering Division was in the hands of Allied generals on 8 Aug.

[18] Letter from Marshal of the R.A.F. Sir John Slessor, who kindly looked into the records for me, 19 Feb. 1954.

[19] Letter from Rear Adm. Roger Dick RN 4 Dec. 1953; *A Sailor's Odyssey* p. 550.

were badly damaged and had to withdraw on the night of the 16th. And, although monitors and destroyers were ordered to penetrate as far up the Strait as possible, they never went far enough to do anything useful; Admiral von Ruge declares that they always turned away when sighted by his motor minesweeper patrol.

Apart from these brave but ineffectual attempts by small craft, the entire burden of interception fell on Northwest African Air Force, which, to its great credit, did what it could. Strategic as well as Tactical bombers got into it, by night as well as by day, from 8 August on,[20] although the Germans did not observe any increase until the third day of the evacuation. Until the night of 13–14 August, "night-flying Wellingtons worked almost exclusively on evacuation beaches" – unfortunately the wrong beaches. "Thereafter, they bombed ports along the Italian shore" – the wrong ports. The Wellingtons flew an average of 85 nightly sorties against the Straits, and medium and fighter-bombers by day "flew 1170 sorties from the 8th to the 17th" against floating targets and termini. During the last three days, 15–17 August, the air effort continued "round the clock." It did succeed in sinking one MFP and two Siebel ferries, and in stopping the Italian ferry runs across the narrows at night; but the German timetable was never seriously interrupted.[21] The ferry craft were too agile and well defended to be greatly endangered by high-level bombing, and the brave attempts of fighter-bombers to dive-bomb were often fatal to the pilots, for the cone of antiaircraft they had to fly through was worse even than in the Ruhr. The Italians observed that they could count on peace in the Strait for an hour each side of first light, after the night bombers had retired and before the day bombers put in an appearance. And Admiral von Ruge remarks with some malice that, "knowing Anglo-Saxon habits," he found the lunch hour also a quiet time for crossing. The Axis ferries had absolutely no protec-

[20] Craven and Cate II 472; Tregaskis *Invasion Diary* p. 71 reporting conversations with pilots.

[21] Liebenstein War Diary and Bonin "Considerations" pp. 14, 18. "Much more trouble was caused us," he adds, "by the gradually increasing destruction of roads and railways in south and central Italy by attacks of heavy bombers." Norman Macmillan *The Royal Air Force in the World War* (1949) III 225.

tion by their own air forces, nor were the Allied planes ever attacked in the air.

A superb pyrotechnic display was put on by the air attacks. Nightly under a bright moon (full on the 15th), flares and bombs dropped from planes; lines of tracer and antiaircraft bullets from boats and shore crisscrossed the sky; sinuous wakes of dodging barges reflected the light; an occasional plane that tried to dive-bomb fell flaming into the Strait. The Allied Air Forces claimed the destruction of 23 boats, direct hits on 43, and near misses on 204, which was more than the enemy possessed.[22] Actual losses were six German boats and one Italian sunk or damaged beyond repair, and seven or eight others damaged.[23] At dawn 17 August, General Hube and staff, with the last of the German rear guard at Messina, made the final trip, unchallenged by their enemy.

Operation LEHRGANG took out no fewer than 39,569 German troops (including 4444 wounded), 9605 vehicles, 47 tanks, 94 guns, over 2000 tons of ammunition and fuel, and about 15,000 tons of gear and stores — all in six days and seven nights.[24] Even most of the German evacuation craft were saved. They pulled out of the Strait on the night of the 17th and, unchallenged by Allied planes or motor torpedo boats, made their way north, hugging the shore. After reaching Naples in safety these ferry craft were used to withdraw German troops from Sardinia and Corsica.

The Italian evacuation was concluded at noon 16 August when a motor raft took on board the last Italian troops and sailors and

[22] Craven and Cate II 473.

[23] Ruge p. 52, and 3 more Italian motor rafts were sunk 18 Aug.

[24] Figures from "Secret, Urgent (Marshal Kesselring's) Report" to the German high command 17 Aug. 1943, except the last two which are from Cdr. Liebenstein. He states (Ruge p. 18) that 38,846 German troops, 10,356 vehicles, and 14,946 tons of supplies were evacuated. The troop figure does not include 13,500 casualties evacuated since 15 July. He adds that the German ferry service brought 17,773 troops into Sicily in June, 40,116 in July, and 1687 in August — a total just short of 60,000. The same figures are in Liebenstein's War Diary. To this we should add at least 1000 troops flown in, and 15,000 for the 15th Panzer Grenadier Division already in Sicily on 1 July. Eighth Army took 3163 German P.O.W.s; Seventh Army, about 2360; and the lowest estimate of Germans killed is 5000. The Germans left behind 78 tanks and armored cars, 287 guns, and about 3500 vehicles on the beaches, according to British accounts. All Axis authorities insist that not one passenger was lost in the evacuation.

landed them safely on the mainland. According to Admiral Barone, who supervised the operation, about 62,000 Italian officers and men, 227 vehicles, 41 artillery pieces – and 12 mules – were transferred from Sicily to the mainland.[25]

General von Senger rightly called this evacuation a "glorious retreat."

Why could not the Allied forces, then absolutely supreme in the air, and with abundant floating gunfire power available, have made an all-out effort to stop it?

Admiral Cunningham believed, and still believes, that beyond what was actually attempted "there was no effective method" of stopping the evacuation, "either by sea or air." "The passage across the Strait of Messina, no more than three miles, could be made in less than one hour, and was covered by batteries and searchlights on both sides. The Germans sent their troops across by night, which ruled out serious interference by our aircraft. And though our MTBs made almost nightly sallies well into the Straits at great risk to themselves, they could not really interrupt the enemy's traffic." [26] Shore batteries and searchlights were indeed formidable hazards, especially the two German 170-mm batteries sited on each side of Villa San Giovanni. But could not these guns have been located by air reconnaissance, and knocked out by battleships and monitors firing over the land from waters north and west of Cape Peloro, at ranges between 8000 and 16,000 yards, or from the southern entrance to the Strait southwest of Reggio? Once these big guns had been silenced, a bold thrust of light cruisers and destroyers up the Strait from the south should have been able to silence most of the 88-mm and 90-mm batteries, and clear the way for MTBs, motor gunboats and even destroyers to operate effectively against the

[25] Barone p. 30. The small number of guns and vehicles saved, he explains by the fact that most of them were seized by the Germans.

[26] *A Sailor's Odyssey* p. 556. Admiral Hewitt agrees. These senior flag officers believe that naval gunfire, with such means of spotting and ranging as our ships then had, could only have temporarily silenced the shore batteries, which could have sunk any naval vessels or craft that might have ventured into the Strait. It is not true, however, that the Germans crossed by night only; and it was only at night that Allied aircraft seriously interfered with the process.

Siebel ferries and other evacuation craft. Ships could hardly have ventured into the narrows, where Allied Air Forces did manage to halt the evacuation by night; they could not have stoppered the bottle completely; but it would have been worth extensive damage to naval vessels to have prevented even one of the German Panzer divisions from leaving Sicily.

Any such attempt would have been highly hazardous for Allied ships, which would be urgently needed at Salerno. But the employment of them during the fortnight when the Strait was swarming with evacuation craft seems, in retrospect, to have been little short of frivolous. When the movement reached its height, on 14–16 August, Admiral Davidson's TF 88 was covering Patton's useless amphibious operation to Spadafora, in the enemy's rear. On the night of 15–16 August, destroyer *Trippe* and three PTs were sent north to take the surrender of the Æolian Islands. On the following night, after the evacuation was over, *Philadelphia*, *Boise* and four destroyers bombarded Palmi and Gioia Tauro, and did not even catch the Siebel ferries that were escaping to Naples. The British battleships and carriers at this time were safe in port. Light cruiser Force "Q" sailed from Bizerta 9 August to carry out an operation misnamed ANNOYANCE, in which it bombarded Castellammare in the Gulf of Naples and made a sweep along the coast of Campania. The cruisers returned to Bizerta, departed again in two divisions on the 12th and 14th, swept the Italian coast between Paola and the Gulf of Sant'Eufémia, and bombarded Vibo Valéntia and Scalea, a town on the Calabrian coastal road over a hundred miles north of the Strait of Messina. Nothing was accomplished except an encounter with a small Italian coastal convoy from which two tiny escort vessels were sunk. Vibo Valéntia received another working-over from cruisers in the early hours of 16 August, while the German evacuation was reaching its climax. There were no ships to be seen in the harbor; the only consolation for Force "Q" before returning to Bizerta was the fact that it missed two big German air raids on that important Tunisian harbor, late at night on [illegible] and 18 August. About fifty planes attacked, each time; several were shot down by Beaufighters, an LCI was sunk and a Liberty ship damaged.

"In the following days," wrote Colonel von Bonin, "we could hardly understand that the evacuation had been such a complete success."

The bulk of the German forces in Sicily – three good divisions – got away in good order with all their weapons and most of their matériel, "completely fit for battle and ready for service." [27] General von Vietinghoff declared this evacuation to be "of decisive significance for the entire later course of the campaign in Italy." His most valuable forces in the latter part of 1943 came from Sicily.[28]

It is some consolation to find that Hitler did not regard the evacuation as a success, for it marked the first loss of Axis territory in Europe. General Hube, the officer responsible, received neither promotion nor praise; and Admiral von Ruge, who had overseen the naval part, was dismissed from his command.[29]

3. *Conclusion to Operation* HUSKY

Writers on military subjects are in danger of contracting the occupational disease of omniscience. Years after a campaign they necessarily know more than the generals, admirals and statesmen did who had to make decisions on imperfect knowledge, and too readily conclude that everyone at the time made mistakes. Nevertheless, I cannot avoid the conclusion that the entire HUSKY plan was wrong; that we should have attacked the Messina bottleneck first. After a severe and prolonged air bombing of both shores, the Western Naval Task Force might have sailed around the western end of Sicily and landed the Seventh Army near Milazzo, while the Eastern Task Force landed the Eighth Army on both sides of the

[27] Kesselring Report p. 15 of translation.

[28] "Feldzug in Italien" ch. vi p. 230.

[29] Bonin pp. 21–2. Hube, says his chief of staff, "was a brave soldier, calm, well balanced, equal to any situation, never in doubt and always ready to take over responsibility." He met an accidental death on 20 Apr. 1944.

Strait, which was not nearly so strongly defended on 10 July as it eventually became a month later. The enemy, whose dispositions had been made to meet landings elsewhere, would have been completely surprised and his communications with the mainland severed. His forces could then have been rolled up into western Sicily and forced to surrender, and in less time than it took to push them out of Sicily into Italy, where they "lived to fight another day." More than one of the then top Allied commanders in the Mediterranean have agreed with me in conversation that this could have been done; and the postwar German commentators on the campaign could not understand why it was not done.

Even if a landing on the Strait seemed too risky, the whole weight of the Eastern Naval Task Force might have been shifted northerly, and a landing made near Catania. Eighth Army would then have had only the Schmalz Group and Italian coastal troops between it and the Gerbini airdrome; or, for that matter, between it and Messina.

Nevertheless, no blame should be attached to the Allied commanders because they did not follow some such plan. Air power was then the fetish. Enemy air forces had given such convincing demonstration of their ability to blast ships, both in Europe and in the Pacific, that no general dared project an amphibious landing beyond the range of friendly fighter planes, and no admiral cared to risk a lengthy exposure of his ships to air attack. Even Catania was beyond fighter-plane range, and the two Navies enjoyed no protection at this time from carrier-based planes.

Perhaps an equally powerful deterrent to a bolder plan, at the upper levels of naval command, was British memory, and American knowledge, of the Gallipoli campaign in World War I. The topography of the Dardanelles is roughly similar to that of the Strait of Messina, amphibious assaults there were a costly failure, and battleships were unable to cope with mobile artillery and coastal batteries. Admirals who as junior officers had spent the better part of a year dodging Turkish and German shellfire around the Gallipoli peninsula were not eager to get into a similar scrape again.

In the Sicilian campaign itself, the turning point was Alexander's change of plan on 20–21 July, at Montgomery's request, from a direct advance via Catania toward Messina, to a "left hook" around Mount Etna. That shift, which played into Axis hands, was due to heavy losses by two British divisions on the Catania plain. Alexander had given the British Eighth Army what he knew to be the hardest mission in HUSKY because it had proved its worth in Africa, as the American troops (in his opinion) had not. An American historian may be pardoned for wishing that the Seventh Army, under leaders like Patton, Truscott, Terry Allen and Middleton, had been given the tougher assignment.

When it came to stopping the Axis evacuation, the same considerations applied that precluded Allied landings nearer Messina. The Strait looked too much like the Dardanelles to British commanders who had been there, and to Americans who had studied the Gallipoli campaign in their war colleges. And, by the time the evacuation started, it was known in highest command circles that an invasion of Italy was in the cards, and that the Italians were about to surrender. Available United States and British warships were few enough to cover an invasion of the mainland, and the damage that they might inflict on the evacuating enemy seemed not worth the risk of their destruction in narrow waters whose banks were bristling with heavy ordnance. Above all, this seemed to be a proper task for the Air Forces, who were not only willing but eager to take it on.

The opinion of a defeated enemy is always interesting. Here is what Marshal Kesselring has to say in criticism of Allied strategy and tactics: —

> The absence of any large-scale encirclement of the island or of a thrust up the coastline of Calabria gave us long weeks to organise the defence with really very weak resources. The slow advance of the main attack and the remarkable dissipation of their other forces over the island allowed the Axis Command to bring sufficient reinforcements into the defence areas as they were threatened. The enemy failure to exploit the last chance of hindering the German forces crossing the Straits of Messina, by continuous and strongly co-ordinated attacks

from the sea and the air, was almost a greater boon to the German Command than their failure immediately to push their pursuit across the straits on 17 August.[80]

On the positive side, a notable achievement in Operation HUSKY was the genuine comradeship between the United States and Royal Navies. Perhaps the best tribute to the two Navies came from General Sir Harold Alexander: —

> I must at this point try to make clear the debt which land operations owed to the sister services. On Admiral Cunningham fell the weight of what was in some ways the most arduous, detailed and vital part of the operation, the actual conveyance of the troops to their objectives. . . . I must mention only in passing the assistance of naval gunfire on the beaches and the silent strength of the covering forces waiting, and hoping, for the appearance in defence of its native soil of that fleet which once claimed to dominate the Mediterranean. It is a theme . . . of which the Royal Navy and the United States Navy are justly proud.[81]

The same applies to relations between the United States Navy and Army. Mutual recriminations that marred their joint action in TORCH were notably lacking. Sailors admired the soldiers' courage on shore; soldiers were grateful, not only for gunfire support, but for the hospitality of Navy transports — the quality of the food, the last hot meal before the troops debarked, the plates of thick sandwiches and gallons of hot coffee handed out to soldiers as they were waiting for the signal to lower boats. It had rightly been dinned into every sailor that the Navy was there for one purpose only — to land the Army at the beaches of its choice, and to help protect it there as far as the Navy could shoot.

In estimating the technique of the Western Task Force landings, we must remember that this was only the second amphibious operation of World War II for the United States Atlantic Fleet; that it came only eight months after the first, preceding Tarawa in the Pacific by four months and the brilliantly conducted landings in the Marianas and Normandy by a full year. Moreover, all the assault landings here were at night, whilst those in the Pacific, and in Eu-

[80] *Memoirs of Field Marshal Kesselring* (English trans. of his *Soldat bis zum Letzen Tag*, 1953), p. 165.

[81] Despatch p. 1017.

rope after Anzio, were by day. Even with its imperfections, the amphibious phase of Operation HUSKY was well and gallantly carried out; and there was little to choose in performance between the two Navies concerned. The British showed more flexibility in landing procedure than the Americans; if they could not find the planned beach in the darkness, or if the planned beach proved to be unsuitable, they quickly shifted their landing craft to another, or even to a rocky shore, to effect what they called a "scramble landing." But very few of the British landings were troubled by surf. The Americans were the more ingenious in thinking up ways to surmount false beaches, and were better at handling the new beaching craft and the dukw, which they had invented. The British "beach bricks" were more efficient at getting supplies off the beaches than were the American Army engineer shore parties, which could hardly have been worse.

Although both Navies were magnificent in their gunfire support, the United States ships, off Gela and Scoglitti, had better opportunities. Undoubtedly the greatest contribution of Operation HUSKY to amphibious technique was the demonstration of what naval gunfire could do in support of troops fighting within a few miles of the shore.[32] Again and again I have been told by soldiers of the Seventh Army that the sight of "those beautiful ships" standing by, or spouting fire from their big guns, gave them a sense of security and a feeling of invincibility. Nicias, addressing the Athenians about to launch an amphibious assault on Syracuse in 413 B.C., warned them that Sicily would be difficult to conquer unless they made themselves master of the country the very day they landed; that the enemy could otherwise counterattack in superior force. His warning held good for over 2350 years; only the range and weight of naval artillery made it invalid in A.D. 1943.

Lessons in the employment of air power in HUSKY were numer-

[32] Statistics for the Royal Navy are lacking; but the six light cruisers under Rear Admiral Davidson expended 7,537 rounds of 6-inch 47 cal. in shore bombardment of the south coast, and 5,651 rounds on the north coast of Sicily; and 24 United States destroyers expended 6,912 rounds of 5-inch 38 cal. on the two coasts. Vice Admiral Hewitt to Admiral King, 23 Jan. 1944. These figures do not include ammunition expended in antiaircraft actions.

ous. The air marshals and generals continued firm in their belief that the war could be won by strategic bombing, but General Eisenhower saw to it that they provided close support to ships and ground troops in the next operation; and the two Navies firmly resolved to have carrier-based airplanes near the next target. The lamentable accidents to the second air drop obscured for a time the really great accomplishments by airborne troops in Sicily: the blocking of a tank attack near Gela and the seizure of strategic bridges near Syracuse and Catania. But General Eisenhower was deeply impressed. With his own hand he interpolated in the first draft of his official Dispatch the following: —

> Our losses were inexcusably high, with blame about equally distributed among the several services, and with a large measure falling on me because of my failure to make better provisions against misunderstandings, particularly in the follow-up operations. . . . But in spite of all this the airborne troops contributed markedly to success, in both sectors.

The casualties in the air drops have never been accurately computed; those of the United States Army Air Force were about 28 killed, 88 missing, 41 wounded.[83] Casualties of all Allied forces were commendably low, considering the tough opposition that they encountered at sundry points. Those of the Seventh Army through 17 August were 2237 killed in action, 5946 wounded in action, 598 captured, out of about 203,000 engaged.[84] Casualties of the Eighth Army were 2062 killed, 7137 wounded, 2644 missing, out of a peak strength of 250,000. The United States Navy lost 546 killed or missing, and 484 wounded. The Royal Navy lost 314 killed, 411 wounded, and four prisoners.[85]

[83] Information from Dr. Albert F. Simpson, U.S. Air Force Historian.

[84] Dept. of the Army *Army Casualties and Non-battle Deaths in World War II, Final Report* (1953) p. 93. This includes those to the Army Air Force since 14 May. Seventh Army *Report of Operations* p. b–8 states that its total strength 15 July was 203,204. I do not know whether or not this includes the 9th Infantry Division, not yet committed. If not, 14,000 should be added. The Medical Statistics Division of the Surgeon General's Office, Washington, informs me that the total number of Seventh Army in Sicily, 20 Aug., was 201,000. By that time most of the wounded and a number of combat units had evacuated.

[85] U.S.N. figures from *History of Medical Department U.S. Navy World*

Leadership in the Western Naval Task Force, as in the Eastern, was superb. Admirals Hewitt, Kirk, Hall, and Conolly, to mention only the force commanders, showed intelligence in planning and suppleness in execution that marked them for honors and promotion. Yet the heroes of the western landings, so it seemed to one flag officer at least, were the crews of the landing craft and beaching craft.[36] These were mostly very young reservists, many of whom had not even smelled salt water before the year 1943. They were the last link in a chain consisting of naval and military bases painstakingly developed in North Africa, of three reinforced Army divisions, trained for months, with all their supplies, vehicles, armor, and equipment; of transports costing millions of dollars apiece. All these lives and the bulk of all this matériel were dependent on beaching craft or small landing craft, to get ashore safely. The ensigns or enlisted coxswains who commanded the landing craft negotiated five miles or more of strange waters, often with no scout boats to guide them; they located their targets in the darkness, beached their craft, and provided their own support against enemy gunfire, while discharging troops and equipment. Some mistakes were made, but surprisingly few. The beaching craft, with slightly more experienced leadership, had even more complicated and difficult tasks. If landing and beaching craft crews had failed, the entire American part of Operation HUSKY would have failed, and the British would have been left to carry the war into Sicily unsupported. They did not fail; these young sailors performed marvels of valor and miracles of judgment. All honor, then, to these lads of the last link, since they proved themselves to be strong, brave and resourceful. And if their names may not be recorded in tablets of bronze, let their deeds be kept in fresh memory by the Army, the Navy, and the nation that they served.

War II p. 170; British from Historical Section Canadian Army, figures which include casualties from "named" ships 10 July–19 August, and from coastal craft or naval units ashore through 7 September 1943. Kesselring in his official report claims the capture of 1152 Allied prisoners.

[36] Rear Adm. Biesemeier "*Charles Carroll* in Operation HUSKY" p. 11.

PART III

Salerno[1]

(*Operation* AVALANCHE)

[1] Admiral of the Fleet Cunningham's Despatch of 8 Mar. 1945 in *Supplement to London Gazette* 28 Apr. 1950; Gen. Alexander's Despatch of 19 Apr. 1947 in "Allied Armies in Italy 3 Sept. 1943–12 Dec. 1944" in same for 6 June 1950; Vice Adm. H. K. Hewitt *The Italian Campaign. Western Naval Task Force. Action Report of the Salerno Landings* (Jan. 1945) and "The Allied Navies at Salerno," U.S. Naval Institute *Proceedings LXXIX* (Sept. 1953), pp. 959–76; Action Reports of Rear Adms. Hall and Conolly, and of units and ships concerned; British Admiralty documents; *Fifth Army History* Vol. I (1945); [Chester Starr and Roy Lamson] *Salerno* (1944), a pamphlet in the American Forces in Action Series, is excellent. General Eisenhower *Crusade in Europe* (1948); General Mark W. Clark USA *Calculated Risk* (1950); Winston Churchill *Closing the Ring* (1951).

Principal German sources are Gen. Heinrich von Vietinghoff's chapter vi of "Feldzug in Italien," a report by several generals prepared for the U.S. Army in 1947; Marshal Albert Kesselring *Soldat bis zum Letzen Tag* (1953) and Gen. Siegfried Westphal *The German Army in the West* (1951). *The Fuehrer Conferences, Navy, 1943; The Fuehrer Directives;* "War Diary of the German Naval Staff, Operations Division"; "War Diary, German Naval Command Italy" and numerous documents in the Adjutant General's Office, U.S. Army, Washington, including War Diaries of Tenth Army and the 16th Panzer Division.

CHAPTER XI

Preliminaries to Salerno[1]

May–September 1943

1. *Discussion and Decision, 12 May–26 July*

WOULD Sicily prove to be "a sofa or a springboard?" asked Mr. Churchill. Nobody had the answer when the operation started, because American and British strategists could not agree. The Joint Chiefs of Staff regarded HUSKY as little more than a logical conclusion of TORCH. They were fearful lest another commitment in the Mediterranean provide our Ally with a reason for again postponing the cross-channel operation. Mr. Churchill and the British Chiefs of Staff, on the contrary, wished to exploit the conquest of Sicily to "knock Italy out of the war," and obtain a foothold on the Italian mainland that would make possible a direct communication with resistance forces across the Adriatic. They believed that this could be done before the cross-channel attack on *Festung Europa* started, and argued that it must be done in order to draw German forces away from France. Italy was supposed to have between 25 and 35 divisions in Greece and the Balkans; if she surrendered, German divisions would have to fill the vacuum or let southeastern Europe go by default. Just as England had first got at Napoleon by a peninsular campaign, so now, it seemed, a strong movement against the Italian peninsula was the logical preliminary to a frontal attack on Germany.

In order to resolve this fundamental disagreement and bring about a firm decision, Churchill persuaded Roosevelt to call another

[1] Col. E. A. Peterson USAF ms. History of the J.C.S. sec. III "The War Against Germany and Satellites" (1951) ch. viii, part D, and papers of the J.C.S.; compare Sherwood *Roosevelt and Hopkins* chap. xxix.

plenary conference of the Combined Chiefs of Staff, to meet at Washington in May. This conference not only decided on the next step forward but firmed up several matters that had been glossed over or left vague at Casablanca.

TRIDENT Conference, as it was called, convened on 12 May in a different atmosphere from the happy get-together at Casablanca. Each Allied delegation eyed the other warily; both were primed for wordy battles of planetary scope. Fortunately the war news was good. On the opening day word of the Axis surrender in Tunisia arrived. And this meant that a decision on the next step must be made promptly. In the Atlantic the U-boat situation was much easier; the hunters were now becoming the hunted. On the Eastern Front, Russia had driven the Germans back to the Donetz River basin. In the Pacific movements against the Central Solomons, the Bismarcks Barrier and the Western Aleutians were about to begin.

Composition of the Combined Chiefs of Staff at Washington was the same as at Casablanca, except that Admiral Leahy, too, was present, and Lieutenant General J. T. McNarney USA represented the United States Army Air Force. Ordinary sessions were held at the Federal Reserve Building on Constitution Avenue; plenary sessions in the White House.

Admiral Leahy set the tone the first day, by declaring that global strategy must be discussed before proposals for the next operation were taken up, and that the entire Pacific problem must be reviewed. The British Chiefs, surprisingly, agreed. President Roosevelt observed "that the keynote of our plans at the present time should be an intention to employ every resource of men and munitions against the enemy"; to which Mr. Churchill added that "it was our duty to redouble our efforts and grasp the fruits of our success." Again he set forth the "great prize" of eliminating Italy from the war, which he predicted "would cause a chill of loneliness over the German people," [2] and reiterated his firm intention of using a Mediterranean operation to further, not to postpone, the execution of OVERLORD. The great bombing attack on Germany

[2] *Hinge of Fate*, p. 791.

would start as soon as enough big bombers were assembled on British airfields. The President expressed gratification over this assurance but said that he "had always shrunk from the thought of putting large armies in Italy. This might result in attrition for the United Nations and play into Germany's hands." And Admiral King expressed deep concern lest an Italian operation "cause a vacuum into which our forces would be sucked," as had happened in TORCH, and so force a postponement of OVERLORD beyond 1944; he and General Marshall wished that the British would pay more attention to knocking *Germany* out of the war. Sir Alan Brooke seemed to confirm the worst fears of the Americans by dropping the remark that a major operation on the Continent appeared impossible until 1945 or even 1946. General Marshall observed that if the British continued to insist on a strategy which required an indefinite postponement of OVERLORD, planning for that operation should cease and the United States should redeploy its main military, naval and air forces toward the Pacific.

It really came down to this: the British believed that another major operation in the Mediterranean was an indispensable preliminary to OVERLORD, while the Americans were equally firm in maintaining that any such operation should be subordinate to requirements for invading Normandy. The deadlock was broken because the majority, on both sides,[8] wanted to get on with the cross-channel operation as soon as possible. The British agreed to set 1 May 1944 as target date and to aim at a total of 29 divisions. The Americans refused, despite Mr. Churchill's arguments, to agree to any specific invasion of Italy; but the Prime Minister succeeded in obtaining the substance of what he wanted in securing their assent, on 25 May, to the following directive to General Eisenhower. He was "urgently instructed" to plan operations in exploitation of HUSKY, with the double object of eliminating Italy from the war and en-

[8] Eisenhower ***Crusade in Europe*** pp. 167–8 states that, as far as he could see, Mr. Churchill was always loyal to the cross-channel concept but that Brooke, in private conversation, admitted that he was in favor of eliminating it altogether, believing that Germany could be defeated by air bombing, naval blockade and peripheral land attacks.

gaging as many German divisions as possible. When his plans were made the Combined Chiefs of Staff would decide which should be executed.

That put the initiative in General Eisenhower's hands. But his hands were tied by another clause of this directive which required him to count only on the forces under his command, and not on all of them. Four American and three British divisions, and perhaps some landing craft too, would have to be withdrawn to the United Kingdom about 1 November. Moreover, at the same time the C.C.S. firmed up the amphibious assault directed at Burma for November 1943, and a large proportion of the assault shipping and landing craft for them would have to be pulled out of the Mediterranean.

The strategic thinking at TRIDENT was more realistic than at Casablanca; differences were both strong and clean-cut. But the decisions as to the Mediterranean were still vague and subject to different interpretations. As Sir Alan Brooke said at closing, both the British and the American strategists had "achieved a clearer appreciation" of each other's outlook and conceptions. They parted better friends than they had met, and now began to see the end of the war. Mr. Churchill well said in the House of Commons on 8 June 1943, immediately after his return to England: —

> At Washington the entire expanse of the world war, on which the mellow light of victory now begins to play, was laid open to the British and American leaders. We have shown that we can work together. We have shown that we can face disaster. We have still to show that we can keep ourselves at the height and level of successful events and be worthy of good fortune.[4]

[4] Hansard *Parliamentary Debates* 5th ser. CCCXC 562.

Implicit in the compromise, although outside the scope of this volume, were (1) the decision to start SICKLE, the big bomber offensive against Germany, at once, and to build it up to 2700 heavy and 800 medium bombers; and (2) the decisions about the Pacific War. The J.C.S. finally were given complete control over the Pacific. When I wrote my earlier Pacific volumes I supposed that this had been done at Casablanca, but the directive adopted there was so vague as to raise different interpretations. Admiral King (as related in *Fleet Admiral King* pp. 416, ff.) argued for the better part of one session, against the British Chiefs of Staff, in favor of leaving the determination of measures in the Pacific War to the judgment of the J.C.S., within the limits of the major strategic decision to beat Germany first. Finally Marshall drafted an amendment that King wanted — the

The next few months were very onerous for General Eisenhower. He was asked to plan an invasion of Italy just before that of Sicily began; to do it with such forces as would be left after Sicily was conquered, minus those to be abstracted for OVERLORD and the Indian Ocean; and to conduct delicate diplomatic negotiations with the Italian government.

At a conference at Eisenhower's headquarters in Algiers on 3 June, "Mr. Churchill was at his eloquent best in painting a very rosy picture of the opportunities that he foresaw opening up to us with the capture of Sicily." [5] The Prime Minister, knowing that the Americans regarded his desire to strike here, there and everywhere in the Mediterranean as hopelessly romantic, declared emphatically "that he was not advocating sending an army into the Balkans now or in the near future." But he pressed hard for a firm commitment as to Italy. None was then made, since Marshall backed up Eisenhower. Both insisted that the end of Sicily must be in sight before making any decision as to what we could or would do in the matter of invading the Italian peninsula. But staff studies for the next move were begun at once.

On 30 June the Supreme Commander informed the C.C.S. that his choice of future operations would depend on the speed and success of HUSKY and the chances of Italy's getting out of the war. He thought that if the invasion of Sicily were unduly prolonged and Italian morale improved, an invasion of Sardinia in October would be the best thing that his command could undertake in 1943. If, on the other hand, Sicily fell quickly and Italy tottered, he

---

italicized part of (2) below, which they accepted. And the final decision on overall strategy was as follows: (1) Unconditional surrender of the Axis at the earliest possible date. (2) To maintain and extend unremitting pressure against Japan with the purpose of reducing her military power and attaining positions from which her ultimate surrender can be forced. *The effect of any such extension on the overall objective to be given consideration by the Combined Chiefs of Staff before action is taken.* (3) Upon the defeat of the Axis, in coöperation if possible with Russia, to direct the full resources of the United States and Great Britain to bring about at the earliest possible date the unconditional surrender of Japan.

[5] *Crusade in Europe* p. 167. Admiral Cunningham, General Alexander, Air Chief Marshal Tedder and others took part.

would propose a two-pronged invasion of Calabria at or near Gioja and Crotone. This was currently known as the "toe-and-ball" project, with reference to the foot of the Italian boot.

HUSKY was less than a week old when the promise of a speedy victory caused Allied commanders to raise their sights. On 20 July the C.C.S. asked General Eisenhower to consider a direct assault on Naples instead of the "toe-and-ball." Before a prolonged argument between British and Americans could start about ways and means, news of the fall of Mussolini on 25 July brought them into agreement. The British Chiefs, anticipating the surrender of Italy, now consented to the American concept of "do the best with what you've got." The J.C.S., as a concession, allowed the Royal Navy to contribute one light carrier and four escort carriers to augment air cover at the beachhead. On 26 July they joined the C.C.S. in giving Eisenhower the green light for Salerno: "You should plan forthwith landings in the Bay of Salerno, to be mounted at the earliest possible date, using the resources already available to you."

Discussions of this operation, now named AVALANCHE, did not end here. Eisenhower wanted all he could get and the British wished him to have it, but the J.C.S. were still acting as stern guardians of OVERLORD, that vestal virgin of Allied strategy. They were shocked at the General's request for 40 more transport types to launch AVALANCHE, at a time when Admiral Nimitz was woefully short of troop-lift.[6] Air Chief Marshal Portal, head of the R.A.F., was willing to lend Eisenhower several heavy bomber squadrons for the Italian invasion because he wanted the Foggia airdrome to help his big bomber offensive against Germany. General Arnold, on the contrary, thought Foggia would be useless and opposed the diversion of bombers from England to the Mediterranean.[7] Running

[6] See Vol. VII pp. 108–10.

[7] A main object of this bomber offensive was to weaken the Luftwaffe before OVERLORD; but 50 per cent of German fighter planes were being produced in South Germany factories, almost inaccessible from England but within fair range of Foggia. Gen. Arnold, however, was right; the air planners reckoned without the Alps. Even in summer the Alps could not be safely traversed by big bombers on most days, and the South Germany targets were eventually bombed from British bases.

through all this debate was the British doubt whether OVERLORD could succeed in 1944 unless Italy were occupied first, and the American suspicion that the British were trying to divert military strength to the Mediterranean in order to get out of OVERLORD.

Nevertheless AVALANCHE, with Salerno as target, was authorized on 26 July. When the next plenary conference (QUADRANT) met at Quebec in mid-August, it confirmed the decision that Eisenhower must invade Italy with what he had, unless the C.C.S. decided otherwise – which turned out to be a very important exception.

2. *First Mainland Landings, 3–9 September*

Only once before in her long history had Italy been invaded the hard way, from the toe up the boot. That was fourteen centuries earlier, when the Emperor Justinian's General Belisarius, leaving "sufficient garrisons in Palermo and Syracuse, embarked his troops at Messina, and landed them without resistance on the opposite shores of Rhegium." And "from Rhegium to Naples, the fleet and army of Belisarius, almost always in view of each other, advanced near three hundred miles along the coast." [8] How simple were logistics in those days! No vehicles except a chariot for the general, no weapons save what the soldiers could carry, no ammunition replenishment except a supply of arrows. And Belisarius's system of advancing his fleet parallel with his army was a forerunner of modern combined operations.

On 26 July 1943 the Eighth Army was given the mission to cross the Strait of Messina on 30–31 August, secure a bridgehead on the toe of Italy, and engage the Germans vigorously in the hope of drawing their forces away from Salerno. General Montgomery acted with his customary caution and deliberation. Troops could easily have been ferried across within a week of securing Messina,

[8] Gibbon *Decline and Fall of the Roman Empire* V chap. xli; see also Charles L. Lewis "The Byzantine Invasion of No. Africa, Sicily, and Italy," U.S. Nav. Inst. *Proceedings* Nov. 1943 pp. 1435–42.

and General Eisenhower pressed him to hurry; but "Monty" would not move until he had hundreds of guns lined up to support the crossing. He did not even have an outline plan ready for Rear Admiral Roderick McGrigor RN, who was to conduct the crossing, until 23 August; so late that it had to be postponed. "The halt called by the Allies until 3 September," wrote Marshal Kesselring, "was again a gift to the Axis." Nor was it the last of their gifts, even in this theater.

On 3 September the XIII Corps British Army, under cover of a furious (and unnecessary) artillery bombardment, was set ashore by landing craft between Reggio and Villa San Giovanni. Italian coast defense batteries fired a shot or two and surrendered; the landing was practically unopposed. The one German regiment at the Strait, covering a front of 17 miles, promptly retired.[9] During the night of 3–4 September, British Commandos landed unopposed at Bagnara, about six statute miles east of Scilla.

On the 8th, in order to speed the advance of XIII Corps, and in the hope of trapping German units, a "leapfrog" operation was put on to Pizzo on the Gulf of Sant'Eufemia, the narrowest part of the "foot." Like Patton's leapfrogs, it came too late. The 231st Infantry Brigade, lifted in beaching craft, escorted by two gunboats and H.M. monitor *Erebus* and commanded by Rear Admiral McGrigor in *MTB–77*, steamed into Pizzo roadstead just as the 29th Panzer Grenadiers were rolling along the highway a few yards from shore. German artillery and dive-bombers blasted the British flotilla, and a shell burst close aboard the torpedo-boat flagship; Admiral McGrigor had the experience, unusual for a flag officer, of being tossed high into the air. He was wounded, but not severely. H.M.S. *LST–65* (Lieutenant Commander L. J. Smith RNR) saved the day. She charged the beach full speed when heavily hit and burning furiously; a bulldozer burst open the jammed bow doors, the ramp was dropped, and mobile guns rushed ashore, completely changing the situation. Fighting at Pizzo continued until late that night,

[9] Gen. von Vietinghoff, ch. vi of "Feldzug in Italien."

when the Germans pulled out eastward along the coastal road. *LST-65* had to be abandoned on the beach.[10]

This landing took place on the very day that the Italian armistice was announced, and one day before Fifth Army landed at Salerno. Also on 9 September, a few hours after AVALANCHE started, there took place an improvised occupation of Taranto.[11]

This was Admiral of the Fleet Cunningham's idea; he had suggested it to General Eisenhower only a few days earlier. Cunningham said he would furnish the ships if Eisenhower could produce the troops, and Operation SLAPSTICK was put on. Commodore W. G. Agnew RN, flying his broad pennant in H.M.S. *Aurora*, with three other light cruisers and the 2600-ton fast minelayer *Abdiel*, was ordered to lift the British 1st Airborne Division from Bizerta to Taranto. At the last moment it became evident that some of these troops would be left on the beach unless another cruiser were provided. Cunningham appealed to Rear Admiral Davidson, already leading a column of light cruisers toward Salerno. Davidson at 1914 September 7 signaled the C.O. of *Boise*, "Return at once to Bizerta, report to Cincmed." This sounded so like a reproof that Captain Thébaud replied, "Please repeat"; and Davidson, in repeating, put the Captain at his ease by adding, "Hope this makes you an admiral!" On arriving at Bizerta Thébaud reported to Admiral Cunningham, who led him to a command car, and on its dust-covered side traced a chart of Taranto with his finger and ordered *Boise* to take station astern of Commodore Agnew's disposition. That was all the "op. plan" Thébaud ever saw. *Boise* embarked 788 officers and men, including a curious mixed unit commanded by Lieutenant Colonel Vladimir Peniakoff and called, after him, "Popski's Private Army." Planes were sent ashore so that *Boise's* hangar and fantail could be stacked with 60 or 70 jeeps,

[10] Information from Admiralty and conversation with the First Sea Lord (Admiral McGrigor) in 1953. This was called Operation FERDY.

[11] Cunningham *A Sailor's Odyssey* pp. 563–4; *Boise* Action Report and conversations with Rear Adm. Thébaud in 1953; George Biddle *Artist at War* chap. iii.

and the force for Taranto sailed from Bizerta on the evening of 8 September.

Admiral of the Fleet Cunningham, observing that if the Italian warships then at Taranto got "mixed up" with Commodore Agnew's convoy, they could be a "jolly nuisance," ordered Vice Admiral Power RN at Malta to join Operation SLAPSTICK with battleships *Howe* and *King George V* and six destroyers. As the British ships and *Boise* approached Taranto in the afternoon of 9 September, they met two Italian battleships and three cruisers, standing out. Every Allied ship went to Action Stations, and for a few minutes the atmosphere was very tense; one trigger-happy gun pointer on either side might have set off a minor Jutland. But, as General Eisenhower expressed it, "The final challenge by Admiral Cunningham, delivered with the same cold nerve that had characterized all the actions of that great sailor, went unanswered. The Italian Fleet passed out of sight on its way to surrender." [12]

At dusk, as the cruisers steamed into the harbor of Taranto, an Italian pilot boarded each ship. The one in *Boise* indicated a mooring which Captain Thébaud declined in favor of a berth at the mole. There "Popski's Private Army" first to debark, drew up alongside in rigid formation and marched off smartly, left arms swinging wide and boots smacking the ground. H.M.S. *Abdiel* unfortunately accepted the berth declined by *Boise*. Shortly after midnight a moored contact mine exploded under her when she was discharging troops, and in a few minutes this beautiful new ship sank, with a loss of 48 members of her crew and 101 soldiers.

There was no opposition to the Taranto landing, and the harbor became very useful to the Allies. The cruisers were promptly sent through the Strait of Messina to support the Fifth Army at Salerno. And for the British Army it was a short march across the heel of the boot, to occupy the important city and harbor of Bari.

[12] *Crusade in Europe* p. 189.

3. *Italy Joins the Allies*[13]

Italy, after the fall of Mussolini, had fallen into the state so poignantly described by Dante: —

Nave senza nocchiere in gran tempesta.
Ship without helmsman in a mighty tempest.[14]

And the business of dealing with a country that wanted desperately to get out of the war, but also to have a seat in the car of victory, gave General Eisenhower one more heavy responsibility.

King Victor Emmanuel III on 25 July entrusted his government to Marshal Badoglio, an elderly soldier who had lost the capacity to make quick or firm decisions. The Marshal loudly declared that Italy would stick to her ally; but he was only waiting for a good opportunity to break loose from the Axis. There then developed a negotiation which had comic aspects, but in truth was deplorable for misunderstandings and lost opportunities.

The Marshal waited for an offer from the Allies; but they, ignoring the national love of bargaining and sentiment of *honore*, expected Italy to come on her knees crying *mea culpa*. Each side really wanted the same thing: no mere surrender and sulky neutrality, but an active alliance against Germany; yet they found it almost impossible to agree, because each was the victim of its own propaganda. The President and Prime Minister had adopted the Unconditional Surrender slogan, and were afraid of the political consequences of conceding anything to an Axis member; the hullabaloo over the "Darlan deal" in 1942 still rang in their ears. And Badoglio had been sounding off so frequently about "prosecuting the war with renewed vigor," that his own people doubted his intentions; and the Allies, when he offered to change sides, suspected that they,

[13] This subject is dealt with by all the leading writers who cover the Italian campaign — Churchill, Eisenhower, Alexander, Butcher, Sherwood, Cunningham, Kesselring, Westphal, Rintelen, Bernotti, Badoglio, Maugeri; also Jane Scrivener *Inside Rome with the Germans* (1945), David Brown in *Sat. Eve. Post* 9 and 16 Sept. 1944, G. Salvemini in *Il Ponte* IX No. 7 (July 1953).

[14] *Purgatorio* vi. 77.

not Germany, might be the victims of a doublecross. In this atmosphere of mutual suspicion and distrust, it is surprising that anything was accomplished. Before the end of July the Italian government inquired of the British ambassador to the Vatican, and of the personal representative of President Roosevelt to the Pope, whether they would transmit secret peace proposals to their governments. Each refused, on one pretext or another, and two weeks were wasted. On 15 August General Castellano of Comando Supremo staff arrived incognito in Madrid, and presented the British ambassador with a letter from Marshal Badoglio indicating his willingness to surrender unconditionally — provided Italy could join the Allies. This caused a great sensation at Quebec, where the President and Prime Minister were holding the QUADRANT Conference. Everyone at the Château Frontenac cried with one voice, "Let Ike handle it!" Unfortunately, they tied his hands by dictating the terms.

General Eisenhower sent his chief of staff, Major General Walter Bedell Smith USA, and his Intelligence Officer, Brigadier Kenneth W. D. Strong of the British Army, to meet General Castellano at Lisbon. Their first conference on 19 August was chilly. Castellano conveyed Badoglio's desire to switch from enmity to alliance without the ignominy of a formal surrender. This was received in icy silence. General Smith read the terms, which had been radioed from Quebec: Armistice to be proclaimed in Rome at the same time it is announced by Eisenhower; prompt dispatch of the Italian Air Force and Fleet to Allied ports; immediate release of Allied prisoners; and so forth. Badoglio could take them or leave them. If he accepted, and Italy proved amenable, we would discuss terms of an alliance later; but she must "work her way back." But first Badoglio had to be told what the conditions of the unconditional surrender were; and that took time, as Castellano had no means of communication with Rome and had to wait at Lisbon for a slow diplomatic train which got him to his capital only on 25 August. Another week had been lost. Badoglio, after some demur, accepted the terms by secret wireless, and another meeting was arranged to take place in Sicily.

On the last day of August Castellano and Bedell Smith met again, this time at General Alexander's headquarters near Cassibile. The Italian announced that he came not to sign but to bargain, which revived suspicions of his sincerity. The situation had changed, he said. Germany was pouring troops into Italy and had his country by the throat; Badoglio, before surrendering to the Allies, must have guarantees that they could and would break the German grip. In particular, he wanted them to land in fifteen-division strength north of Rome and drop a parachute division on Rome, to secure the capital. Castellano again was told "take it or leave it," again returned to Rome, flew back to Cassibile, and after more fruitless bargaining signed an armistice with Bedell Smith, in the presence of Eisenhower, on 3 September. Eisenhower felt that the terms were "unduly harsh"; that the Allied governments intended "to make a propaganda Roman holiday." [15]

From that date Italy was officially out of the war, but as yet not one dozen people knew it. For, among the agreed terms, the armistice was to be kept secret, to give the Allies time to land in Italy and secure key points before the Germans could seize them. Choice of time for the announcement was left to General Eisenhower. He chose 1830 September 8, nine hours before the scheduled landing at Salerno. But no hint of where that landing would occur was conveyed to the Italians. Still fearing a gigantic hoax, we made the same mistake as in North Africa, withholding full confidence from our new friends. Consequently, they were unable to help us as they wished.[16]

Castellano finally convinced the Allied negotiators of his personal integrity. As earnest of it, he proposed to coöperate in receiving an Allied parachute drop on Rome. General Eisenhower thought well of the idea and Admiral Cunningham promised to send LCTs or even destroyers up the Tiber with ammunition and supplies. The 82nd Airborne Division was already alerted for an air drop near Naples. Why not switch it to Rome?

[15] Butcher *My Three Years with Eisenhower* p. 405.
[16] See Vol. II of this History, pp. 65–70.

So it was decided at Allied headquarters. But definite arrangements for the paratroops' reception on Roman airfields must be made, if only to ensure that the Italian antiaircraft batteries would not fire, and that Italian troops would keep the Germans off. A secret mission was quickly arranged. Brigadier General Maxwell Taylor, Commanding General of the 82nd Airborne Division, and Colonel William Tudor Gardiner, an air intelligence officer, made rendezvous off Ústica with an Italian corvette at daybreak 7 September, and that very night were in Rome.[17]

Time was running out; within twenty-four hours the armistice would be announced, just before the landing at Salerno. General Carboni, commander of Italian troops in Rome, talked with Taylor and Gardiner. He threw cold water on the paratroop plan. The Germans had 12,000 troops around Rome, on both banks of the Tiber, and 36,000 more were not far away, so he said; Italian soldiers had only a few rounds of ammunition left and no gasoline; he could not even guarantee to hold the airfields necessary to receive a parachute drop. General Taylor, dismayed, demanded to see Badoglio. The Marshal, routed out of bed at 0200 September 8, confirmed everything Carboni had said, and pled for delay, both in the drop and in announcement of the armistice. His government must have time to make the necessary arrangements. He must know where the Allied amphibious forces were about to land. Taylor had strict orders not to tell him that; we could not risk a leak. After a short palaver, Taylor concluded that without Italian coöperation an air drop on Rome, with so many Germans in the neighborhood, would be suicidal. He radioed his recommendation to Eisenhower to call it off, and it was canceled only an hour before the time the planes were to fly.

Badoglio, too, radioed to the Supreme Commander begging for a delay in the armistice announcement. Eisenhower sternly refused, and the surrender of Italy was broadcast at 1830 September 8. Badoglio followed suit an hour and a quarter later. Having fulfilled

[17] Accounts of this mission are in Tregaskis *Invasion Diary* pp. 103–8 (from Col. Gardiner direct); Maj. Thruelsen *et al. Mediterranean Sweep* (1944) pp. 144–60; and *Sat. Eve. Post* 16 Sept. 1944.

the letter of his agreement, the Marshal fled that night with the King to Brindisi, leaving no authority in Rome, no orders for the defense of Rome, nothing but a vacuum that the Germans were well pleased to fill.

Here was a great opportunity lost. General Carboni had grossly exaggerated the strength of the Germans near Rome and minimized that of the Italian Army in Rome.[18] An air drop on Rome was what the Germans most feared. Actually they had only two battalions in a position to challenge Italian control of the Roman airfields. Kesselring, bombed out of his Frascati headquarters on 8 September, kept his binoculars trained on the sky all next day, watching for enemy transport planes that never came; and on the same day, the 9th, he heard that the Allied landings were at a comfortable distance southward. By nightfall the Marshal breathed easier and decided to occupy Rome.

Citizens cognizant of the situation believed that so spectacular a move as a thousand paratroops dropping on Rome would have rallied the people, who were only waiting for some gesture to rise against their oppressors. The local garrison of five Bersaglieri divisions, deserted by their King, by Badoglio and by hundreds of their own officers, managed nevertheless to beat off the Germans for two days. Obviously, with resolute direction, they could have protected the two airfields necessary for the drop, helped American paratroops to secure the city, and established a bridgehead at the mouth of the Tiber.

Badoglio was not unreasonable in demanding time to issue orders and make troops dispositions to safeguard the drop. On the other hand, General Taylor, an airborne specialist, saw the difficulties only too readily and had neither the wit nor the information to call Carboni's bluff. We should resolutely have gone ahead with the drop; Badoglio would not have dared not to coöperate, since he knew that if he did not, his government and his king would be over-

[18] Westphal p. 150 and Kesselring *Memoirs* p. 182 give the German dispositions; the 3rd Panzer Grenadier Division was deployed around the Lake of Bolsena near Orvieto (66 miles from Rome), the 2nd Parachute Division was south of Rome, and some antiaircraft units close to the city.

thrown. It might have failed, as all such operations are very risky; but the certain benefits from its success were vast, out of all proportion to the possible damage from failure. For not only is Rome the heart of Italy; it was then the vital communications center for the Germans in Italy and had to be in German hands if their forces in the south were to be supplied. A successful air drop might even have forced the enemy to fall back to the Po and the Adige. As it was, Rome underwent a brutal German occupation for eight months, and the Allies had to "crawl up the boot" fighting Germans, until the end of the war.

Hitler executed his plan to rescue Mussolini on 12 September and set up the Duce as chief of a puppet Fascist state in Northern Italy. But the Fuehrer was not in time to force the Italian Fleet to strike or to scuttle. That was one good result of Eisenhower's insistence on announcing the armistice on 8 September; most of the Italian Navy got away to join the Allies. It was, in fact, the only branch of the Italian armed forces that carried out the armistice terms. Badoglio was powerless to do more, and the Italian Army and Air Force simply melted away.

The procedure for the Italian Navy to follow when the armistice was announced had been carefully worked out at Cassibile and brought by General Castellano to Rome. Admiral Sansonnetti telephoned instructions to the appropriate naval commanders on the night of 8–9 September. All warships on the west coast of Italy were to proceed to Corsica and pass down its western coast and that of Sardinia; thence sail to Bône in North Africa for orders. Those in Taranto and on the east coast were to sail directly to Malta; those in the Ægean, to Haifa. Merchant shipping was to make for Gibraltar or Alexandria. All were given recognition signals, and assured that they would be received honorably in Allied ports.

The main battle fleet was at Spezia. Admiral Bergamini, the commander, a few minutes after receiving word from Rome, summoned his commanding officers to a conference. "Tell your men," he said, "to accept this great sacrifice. . . . Our ships, which an hour ago were ready to sail against the enemy, are now able, because the country requires it, to meet the victors with the flag flying; the men can hold their heads high. This is not what we imagined would be the end, but this is the course by which we must now steer, without hesitation, because what counts in the history of a people is not dreams and hopes and negations of realities, but the consciousness of duty carried out to the bitter end. . . . The day will come when this living force of the Navy will be the cornerstone on which the Italian people will be enabled to rebuild their fortunes." [19]

At 0230 September 9 battleships *Roma, Vittorio Veneto, Italia,* and light cruisers *Attilio Regolo, Montecuccoli, Eugenio di Savoia,* sortied from Spezia with eight destroyers, just as German soldiers were breaking into the city. Off Calvi in Corsica, they were joined by ships from Genoa – light cruisers *Abruzzi, Aosta,* and *Garibaldi* and two more destroyers. All headed for Maddalena, Sardinia, to pick up other ships. Just as they were about to enter the Strait of Bonifacio, Admiral Bergamini received word that the Maddalena base had been occupied by German troops. He reversed course and headed for sea. He had no air cover; the Italian Navy possessed none and Allied air forces were too busy covering the Salerno landings to furnish any. So, when a heavy squadron of German bombers attacked at 1552, the ships had only their antiaircraft batteries for defense; and these were little use against the new guided bombs that some of the German planes carried. *Roma* was sunk with great loss of life: 66 out of her 71 officers, including Bergamini and another admiral, and over 1300 men. In the meantime the Genoa squadron was running the gantlet of the Maddalena batteries, losing two destroyers to their gunfire. Three destroyers and cruiser *Attilio Regolo,* after rescuing survivors, made for the nearest neutral harbor, Port Mahon in Minorca, to land their wounded, and were there interned; the rest proceeded to Bône and thence to Malta. The

[19] Admiral Fioravanzo *The Italian Navy's Struggle for the Country's Liberation* (1946). My account is based on this, and on a mass of signals and data collected by Lt. Reck at Palermo in 1944.

Taranto fleet arrived safely at Malta, as did battleship *Giulio Cesare* from Pola.

On the night of 8–9 September a light squadron under Rear Admiral Pollone, consisting of 12 torpedo boats, four corvettes, a number of subchasers and other small vessels, with the Duke of Aosta on board flagship *Aliseo*, broke out of Bastia, Corsica, under fire from German shore batteries and E-boats. Pollone decided to return and beat up his new enemies, which he did to such good purpose that the port was soon in Italian hands. After making temporary repairs, this squadron shoved off again and on the morning of the 11th put in an unheralded appearance off the port of Palermo, to the consternation of the Americans there, who had just received a copy of Admiral Cunningham's signal to the Admiralty: "Be pleased to inform Their Lordships that the Italian Battle Fleet now lies at anchor under the guns of the fortress of Malta." Captain Leonard Doughty, commanding N.O.B. Palermo, felt like observing, "Be pleased to inform Their Lordships that Palermo lies under the guns of an Italian fleet!" He and a couple of junior officers boarded *Aliseo*, where they were received with more than usual honors by the Admiral and the Duke, heard their story and arranged that the ships would be furnished with food and medicaments before proceeding to Malta.

Thus, most of the Italian Navy was saved for "co-belligerency" with the Allies against the Germans; but 49 combatant ships were destroyed – some by air attack when evacuating Italian garrisons from Albania and the islands; some by shore batteries; some, under repair in northern Italian ports, by seizure. The only Navy left for Mussolini's puppet government was a squadron of motor torpedo boats commanded by Prince Borghese.

Admiral de Courten, now Supermarina, met Admiral Cunningham at Taranto on 22 September and arranged for the participation of the Italian Navy and merchant marine in the war with Germany, against which the royal government formally declared war on 13 October. Italy's co-belligerency was now complete. The larger Italian vessels for the most part were laid up in ordinary; but the destroyers, MAS boats and some of the light cruisers coöperated loyally with Allied forces in the Mediterranean.

In the Ægean and Ionian Islands, where the Allies were unable to render much assistance, the Italian naval units and army garrisons fared very ill. Mr. Churchill was eager to send an infantry division of the Indian Army into Rhodes, but this division and its trooplift had been earmarked by the Combined Chiefs of Staff for the elusive Burmese operation that never came off. On 9 September the German garrison in Rhodes forced the Italian troops there to surrender to them. After the C.C.S. belatedly authorized it, a company of British infantry parachuted into Cos, but was overwhelmed by German paratroops on 3 October. Winston Churchill pled in vain with Eisenhower and Roosevelt for "small aid," such as lifting an infantry division in beaching and landing craft to recapture Rhodes, but they rightly refused to be drawn into another diversion.

Against Leros, the principal Italian base in the Ægean, now occupied by three battalions of the Malta garrison, the Germans on 26 September launched an attack with air forces and continued for 50 days with increasing violence. A German convoy thither was destroyed by combined British air and naval action on 7 October, a few Allied reinforcements were sent in by submarine, but on 12 November 1943 strong German ground forces from the Piraeus landed and after a stout fight captured the island on the 16th.[20] As a final indignity, two Italian admirals, the one commanding in

[20] Churchill *Closing the Ring* pp. 203–25. Writing in 1951, Mr. Churchill still felt bitter because Eisenhower refused to be drawn into these Ægean operations; he seems to feel that Ike owed it to him. "I had cleared the way for his successful campaign in Italy" (p. 224). He has not however indicated what forces could safely have been withdrawn from the touch-and-go Italian campaign for dispatch to the Ægean, nor shown how an Allied capture of these islands could have shortened the war. (Cf. the Alexander Despatch on AVALANCHE p. 2881*n*.) In overall strategy, enemy possession of the Dodecanese was no more important than the Japanese retention of most of the Marshall and Caroline Islands. At the adjourned SEXTANT Conference in Cairo, 3–6 Dec. 1943, the British Chiefs of Staff again tried to swap the Burmese operation for a full-scale invasion of Rhodes. The Joint Chiefs and President Roosevelt set their faces firmly against the Rhodian project, but the President was persuaded by the P.M., against the advice of the J.C.S., to drop Burma altogether, on the fallacious argument that Russia's entry in the Pacific war would render it superfluous.

the Ægean and the other commanding the Leros garrison, were captured, tried for treason by a court of Mussolini's puppet government, and executed.

Admiral Bergamini's speech to his officers, on the night before he went down with his flagship, was prophetic. The living force of the Italian Navy did prove to be the cornerstone on which that nation rebuilt her fortunes.

4. *Commands, Plans and Approach, 30 August–8 September*[21]

Commanders were chosen and the basic organization of AVALANCHE was decided by 1 August. General Eisenhower remained Supreme Allied Commander in the Mediterranean. In the next echelon were the same three service commanders as in HUSKY: – Admiral of the Fleet Sir Andrew Cunningham RN, General Sir Harold Alexander, and Air Chief Marshal Sir Arthur Tedder. Immediately under Cunningham were the Western Naval Task Force, Vice Admiral H. Kent Hewitt, including all amphibious forces in AVALANCHE, and the Royal Navy covering forces. Under Hewitt were a Northern Attack Force (mainly British) commanded by Commodore G. N. Oliver RN, and a Southern Attack Force (mainly American) commanded by Rear Admiral John L. Hall. Rear Admiral Richard L. Conolly was given an amphibious group on the left flank of the northern assault, corresponding to his former JOSS.[22] Rear Admiral Kirk, after a visit to Pearl Harbor to give the Pacific Fleet the benefit of his Mediterranean experience, was sent to London to plan and prepare for OVERLORD.

Ground forces for AVALANCHE, organized as the Allied Fifth

[21] Vice Adm. Hewitt *Action Report of Salerno Landings* has the fullest details on these phases.

[22] Conolly volunteered to command this task group, although senior to Commodore Oliver, and in his Action Report said it was an honor to have served under Oliver's command. Similarly, Admiral Cunningham had waived rank when volunteering to serve under Eisenhower.

Army, were under the command of Lieutenant General Mark W. Clark USA. Fifth Army was divided into two corps: – the United States VI, Major General E. J. Dawley USA, comprising the 36th and 45th Infantry Divisions with the 3rd and 34th in reserve; and the British X Corps, Lieutenant General Sir Richard M. McCreery, comprising the 46th and 56th Infantry Divisions, and reserves.

Planning for AVALANCHE was even more dispersed, hectic and exasperating than for HUSKY. And it started late, since "toe-and-ball" had the precedence. The forces were dispersed between Oran and Alexandria, including the newly won ports of Sicily. Hewitt, Hall and Oliver, fortunately, were together at Algiers; but General Clark's headquarters were at Mostaganem.

Under these circumstances, it is not surprising that General Alexander did not have a firm plan to submit to Eisenhower until 30 August, only ten days before D-day. He had considered three possible targets for AVALANCHE: north of Naples, the Gulf of Naples, and the Gulf of Salerno. The first was discarded because the beaches were poor and the area too distant for cover by long-range Spitfires based on Sicilian fields. A frontal assault in the Gulf of Naples was ruled out as too hazardous, owing to the strong coast defenses all along the shore. So it had to be in the Gulf of Salerno. This had the disadvantage of being some thirty miles from Naples at the other end of an easily defended mountain pass, and also of being too far for effective fighter cover. But it was estimated that a Sicily-based Spitfire could remain about twenty minutes over the Gulf before having to turn back, and the Royal Navy had made five carriers available to augment local air protection. Many changes had to be made in the plans, owing to "the inability of the Army command to reach a final decision as to what troops should be employed in the operation and how they should be distributed between the two task forces." A troublous factor was the late discovery that the Gulf of Salerno was mined. This meant that, in order to give the minesweepers a chance to remove the mine field, British and American transports would have to lower their landing craft nine and twelve miles, respectively, off the beaches. That entailed a complete revision of the intricate timetables for assault waves.

The C.C.S., very reluctantly, slightly relaxed their requirement that General Eisenhower make-do with what he had. As early as 28 July he asked that the VIII Army Air Force in Great Britain lend him four full groups of B–17s (140 planes) for six weeks; but he did not get them. On 17 and 18 August the Luftwaffe showed its hand heavily, in the shape of two 80-plane raids by Ju-88s on Bizerta, where there was a great landing-craft concentration for AVALANCHE. An LCI was sunk, three other vessels damaged, some oil installations destroyed, 22 men killed and 215 wounded,[23] including the commanding general of the British X Corps, who had to be relieved; a pleasant prospect for the approach convoys, indeed! Eisenhower promptly pressed the C.C.S. to be allowed to retain three squadrons of Liberators which he had previously been ordered to send to England, pointing out he would not have enough bombers to keep enemy airfields pounded down during the week preceding the invasion. This was refused. Admiral Cunningham sounded off in no uncertain terms about this meticulous insistence on the letter of the agreement. "I believe that we can and shall succeed," he said in a signal to the First Sea Lord, "but only if we go flat out. If we whittle away our resources now to build up OVERLORD our chances of success will be greatly reduced, and if AVALANCHE fails OVERLORD may be stillborn." All that Eisenhower could get was the retention of three squadrons of Wellington heavy bombers, which had been earmarked for return to the United Kingdom, and of beaching craft at his discretion.[24] Fortunately the losses of landing and beaching craft in HUSKY had been much less than expected; 65 per cent of the overall number were available for AVALANCHE, and Cincmed detained 48 LCTs previously ordered to Britain, 30 of them for the "singularly inappropriate" use of handling anti-torpedo nets at Scapa Flow. But the Admiral was

[23] Craven and Cate II 510, 518. The Germans lost 14 planes.

[24] He also managed to get back under his command ten large troopships which had been sent to the United Kingdom after employment in HUSKY.

ordered to dispatch to India the American LSTs allotted to the Burma operation, which he had detained at Oran.

The result of this uncertainty about forces was a spate of last-minute amendments, addenda and annexes to the operation plans, rendering them obscure in many particulars and very difficult for harassed troop and ship commanders to digest. Admiral Hall, commanding the Southern Attack Force, was not certain – even when approaching Salerno on the eve of D-day – of the exact number and designations of the beaching craft under his orders, or of what units were embarked in them. Reliance had to be placed on personal briefing of commanding officers and flotilla leaders; and many did not get the word. Six LSTs supposed to load stores for the Royal Air Force at Milazzo went elsewhere, and LCTs had to be diverted from the Reggio ferry service to do the job. Two follow-up convoys scheduled to arrive off Salerno 10 September got there a day in advance and had to mill around until wanted. Yet nothing really important went awry. As Admiral Hewitt remarked, a great deal of credit for the success of AVALANCHE must be accorded the hard-working planners.

Of all decisions about AVALANCHE, the most unfortunate was the Army command's insistence on no preliminary gunfire support, in order to obtain tactical surprise. Admiral Hewitt argued against this in vain, as he had before HUSKY. He pointed out that the Germans knew something was on, as evidenced by their August air raids on Bizerta; that any officer with a pair of dividers could figure out that the Gulf of Salerno was the northernmost practicable landing place for the Allies; that reconnaissance planes would snoop the convoys; in short, that it was fantastic to assume we could obtain tactical surprise. He was right in every particular. Implicit in the denial was the fear that preliminary bombardment would attract German forces to Salerno. But on 6 September the Germans had already sent the 16th Panzer Division into the Salerno plain. The enemy had several days in which to set up 88-mm and other guns, cut down trees, build strong points, site the Italians' Breda machine guns and fieldpieces on the beaches and their exits, bring up tanks, and cram nearby airfields with their planes.[25] As it turned out, a good selective shoot on strong points on the edge of the Salerno plain, for a day or two before D-day, would have rendered the landings much less arduous.

"The logistics of this operation reached tremendous proportions," states the official British account. That was true for the European area; but the relative proximity of Salerno to Allied ports like Malta, Palermo and Bizerta rendered unnecessary the formidable array of tankers, "reefers," ammunition ships, and replacement-plane carriers that were required for the Pacific. Ammunition and fuel of all kinds were accumulated in Sicilian ports such as Messina, Palermo, Términi, and Castellammare for speedy forwarding to the battle area by the LSTs and LCTs after these had discharged their assault loads. It was hoped to be able to use the port of Salerno by 10 September. Follow-up convoys of Liberty and other merchant ships were planned to arrive on 11 September and at frequent intervals thereafter, and a troop convoy of 13 transports on 21 September; the latter, it was expected, would land at Naples. As the event proved, the AVALANCHE plan was unduly optimistic.

Air support was better organized than in HUSKY, partly because General Eisenhower insisted that the Northwest African Air Force coöperate with the other armed forces, and partly because of the presence of escort carriers. An efficient fighter-director team under Brigadier General Edward J. House USA was installed in Admiral Hewitt's flagship, and two standby fighter-director ships were provided. Coastal Command of Northwest African Air Force took care of the convoys until dark 8 September, when Tactical took over. During the landings Tactical assumed fighter cover within 50 miles of the beaches while Coastal patrolled outside that arc; P–38s and R.A.F. Spitfires were the types commonly used. Naval aircraft were furnished by H.M.S. *Unicorn*, *Attacker*, *Battler*, *Hunter* and *Stalker* until the morning of 12 September, when they had to retire for fueling; and it was arranged that the two fleet carriers with the British battleship force provide C.A.P. for the escort carriers.

[25] War Diary of 16th Panzer Div.

The general plan of air defense was to box-in the assault area with a constant daylight patrol of fighter planes stacked between 6000 and 20,000 feet.

The Royal Navy again provided the covering forces. Force "H," commanded by Vice Admiral Willis in *Nelson*, included three other battleships, fleet carriers *Illustrious* and *Formidable*, and 20 destroyers. The mission of this force was to provide air cover against surface attack for assault convoys, and C.A.P. for the second covering force, "V," which included the escort carriers. Rear Admiral Vian's cruisers departed Malta on the morning of 8 September and threaded the Strait of Messina; churches on both sides were floodlighted and, through binoculars, the populace could be seen dancing in the squares to celebrate the end of the war – for them. H.M.S. *Scylla* and *Charybdis*, in the Admiral's words, "made a bowing acquaintance with their famous forebears," and reached the Gulf of Salerno at dawn on D-day. The carriers, operating 30 or 40 miles off shore, flew morning and evening combat air patrol to fill in for the Army Air Forces.[26]

Assault convoys started from Oran, Algiers, Bizerta, Palermo, Términi and Tripoli. The principal convoy of the Southern Attack Force, lifting the 36th Infantry Division from Oran in 13 U.S. transports, 3 British LSIs and 3 British LSTs, escorted by *Philadelphia*, *Savannah*, *Boise* and 12 destroyers, departed Oran at 1700 September 5 – but *Boise*, as we have seen, was temporarily diverted. Admiral Hall in *Samuel Chase* sailed with his convoy; Vice Admiral Hewitt, who had taken over the well-equipped *Ancon* as his flagship, sailed with H.M.S. *Palomares* and destroyers

[26] There was also a Diversion Group (TG 80.4) under command of Capt. C. L. Andrews USN in DD *Knight* (Lt. Cdr. Joel C. Ford), comprising the gunboat H.N.M.S. *Flores*, 4 U.S. SCs and 1 PT, and 6 British armed motor launches and 10 air-sea rescue boats. At 2315 Sept. 8 they arrived off the island of Ventotene 20 miles west of Ischia and directed a recorded broadcast to the Italian garrison, demanding their surrender; but German troops present fouled things up, and 60 paratroops had to be landed to occupy the island. *Knight* was sent to Salerno for reinforcements, but by the time she returned, with 65 more troops, the Germans on Ventotene had surrendered. A detachment of TG 80.4 at 0330 Sept. 9 simulated a landing near the mouth of the Volturno, but failed to impress the natives. CTG 80.4 (Capt. Andrews) and *Knight* Action Reports.

Bristol, Nicholson and *Edison* from Algiers on the 6th. There was no general assembly point, but all convoys passed north of the Ægades and from somewhere off Palermo shaped courses directly to their release points in the Gulf of Salerno.[27]

Enemy air attacks en route turned out to be not so bad as had been anticipated. The heaviest was delivered by about 180 aircraft on a slow convoy when it was anchored in Bizerta roads on the night of 6–7 September. A smoke screen was quickly laid and no damage was done. There were several attacks on 8 September (D minus 1) as the convoys were steaming north of Sicily. A slow convoy of American LCTs suffered some damage by FW–190s at 1355; three hours later, the same convoy, 15 miles off Capri, was pounced on by five Focke-Wulfs and five Ju-88s, which managed to sink *LCT–624*. Between 2015 and 2230 the Luftwaffe obligingly lighted up the route to Salerno with brilliant flares, and disobligingly dropped numerous bombs and torpedoes. Fortunately only one, and that a dud, hit a ship: *LST–375*. This, intended to be the big effort, aborted, largely because the torpedo-bombers made the mistake of concentrating on Vice Admiral Willis's battleships and cruisers, which were more than able to take care of themselves.

At 1830 September 8, as both Northern and Southern Attack Forces were approaching the Gulf of Salerno by parallel routes, a broadcast was heard, in the familiar voice of General Eisenhower, announcing the armistice with Italy. In justice to the Italians the armistice had to be announced before we landed on their soil, but it was singularly ill-timed with reference to embarked troops. These, naturally assuming that they were to have a walk-over at Salerno, proceeded to relax, mentally and otherwise. Senior officers

27 "Release point" is the British term for the location in a transport area where troops enter landing craft. The LCT convoys and those containing PTs and SCs staged through Términi or Castellammare for refueling. H.M.S. *LST–417* was torpedoed by a U-boat off Términi 7 Sept. and had to be beached. British Force "K," a close cover force of 3 light cruisers and 5 destroyers, sailed from Augusta 7 Sept. Most British troops were staged through Tripoli, whence a slow convoy sailed 3 Sept.

tried to undo the mischief by warning the men by loud-speaker that they would still have to fight Germans; but Admiral Cunningham states "that many took no heed of these warnings and viewed the proceedings with a sense of complacency." Complacency is hardly the word for it; the general impression seemed to be that the war was over. We were landing in Italy, and the Italians had quit, hadn't they?

So the tenseness that one usually feels just before an amphibious landing dissipated; the approach continued under a sort of spell. It was a beautiful, calm, bright night. To many of the ships Capri was visible, swimming in a silver sea; the jagged outline of the Sorrento peninsula made a dark cut-out against a "floor of heaven . . . thick inlaid with patines of bright gold"; and beyond lay the Bay of Naples, redolent with history, beauty and romance. Lookouts in the Northern Attack Force could even see the twinkling lights of Positano, and the flares of the Amalfi fishermen. "In such a night" it seemed fantastic to approach Italy in hostile array. One should have been sitting with a dark-eyed girl in the stern sheets of a rowing barge, singing "*O Sole Mio*!"

This illusion lasted even after the beacon submarine – H.M.S. *Shakespeare* – flashed her guiding light seaward, and until the transports began easing into their release points at one minute past midnight. Then orders rang out, boatswains' whistles shrilled, and the clang and clatter of lowering landing craft broke the spell.

CHAPTER XII

D-day on the Salerno Beaches[1]

9 September 1943

1. *Paestum, the American Sector*

DAYLIGHT revealed to lookouts in the crow's nests a superb panorama, unsurpassed even on the west coast of Italy. The Gulf of Salerno, Longfellow's "blue Salernian bay with its sickle of white sand," loosely embraced by a jagged mountain wall, stretches 30 miles from the Sorrento peninsula to Cape Licosa. Between mountains and sea lies a plain shaped like a second-quarter moon, with the bright little city of Salerno at the upper and the small town of Agrópoli at the nether tip. The Naples–Reggio coastal highway and railway pass through Salerno, skirt the plain, and at the town of Battipaglia are met by another road and railway from southern Italy.

This plain is very unlike those of Sicily where the Seventh Army had landed in July. It is well watered by several rivers, of which the largest, the Sele, is too wide and deep for vehicles to ford. In 1943 the lowlands were intensively cultivated with tobacco, olive and walnut groves, truck gardens and a few dairy farms, but were virtually uninhabited; a thousand years ago the farmers had discovered that dwellers near the sea were exposed to malaria and to pirates, and so built their houses in small towns and villages in the foothills, where they could retire at night after cultivating their crops.[2] Thus, the plain offered a rare opportunity for deploying

[1] For principal authorities see bibliographical note at head of Part III.

[2] In the last ten years there has been a great change in this respect, owing partly to D.D.T., partly to the De Gasperi policy of building houses for agricultural workers near their fields, and partly to a discovery by the burghers of Salerno

troops on a grand scale. If only key points in the mountain gap could be promptly seized and the Germans kept out, there seemed no reason why the entire Fifth Army should not pivot on its left flank and pour through the Cava and Mercato gaps into the classic Phlegræan Fields and the Gulf of Naples.

On the seaward rim of this fertile plain is the 20-mile "sickle of white sand," most of it suitable for amphibious landings. Beach gradients are somewhat more favorable than those of Sicily, but the approaches here, as there, are obstructed by sand bars. Along the shore are a number of conical stone watchtowers, built centuries ago to warn the people of Saracen attacks; they now made convenient landmarks for Allied landings.

The planners for AVALANCHE decided to put the British X Corps ashore near the northern end of the gulf, for prompt capture of Salerno, Montecorvino airport and Battipaglia; while the American VI Corps landed opposite the temples of Paestum in order to protect the Allies' right flank and make contact with Montgomery's Eighth Army marching up from Calabria. It may seem odd that the two sets of beaches should have been eight miles apart, instead of contiguous; but the beaches near the mouth of the Sele are more obstructed by sand bars than those farther away, and the exits are not good.

As one approaches Paestum from seaward, the scene is completely dominated by 3556-foot Monte Soprano, and by the perfect cone of 2079-foot Monte Sottane to the right of it. From the eastern edge of the plain a long slope covered with wheatfields tilts up to the cliffy base of Soprano and sweeps right around Sottane; between the two mountains a dirt road winds up to the town of Capaccio, one of the prime American objectives. Three miles from the shore one can see clearly from a ship's bridge two almost perfect Greek temples and a few columns of a third, rising over scrubby vegetation at the water's edge. These, with a surrounding wall of Cyclopean masonry, are all that is left of Poseidonia, the

---

that the beaches of the Gulf make excellent seaside resorts; there is now (1953) even a little Lido opposite Paestum; and the plain, by American standards, seems fairly well populated.

Panorama of the Salerno Beachhead

KEY:

1 Naples
2 Sorrento peninsula
3 Amalfi
4 Maiori
5 Vietri
6 Salerno
7 Uncle Beaches
8 Sugar Beaches
9 Roger Beaches
10 Montecorvino Airport
11 Battipaglia
12 Beach Red
13 Beach Green
14 Beach Yellow
15 Beach Blue

—*Courtesy of Office of Chief of Military History*

16 Paestum
17 Agrópoli
18 Monte Soprano
19 Capaccio
20 Monte Sottane
21 Altavilla
22 Persano
23 Ponte Sele
24 Eboli
25 Cava Gap
26 Avellino
27 Tobacco Factory
28 Fork of Sele and Calore Rivers

Greek City of Neptune founded in the sixth century B.C., famous for its roses in the Augustan era, and destroyed by Saracens a thousand years ago. After weathering the wars and changes of twenty-four centuries, the temples of Paestum, serene in the silent plain, still looked out over the Tyrrhenian Sea. A fierce battle was about to rage around their walls, and an advanced dressing station would be set up by VI Corps medicos adjoining one of them. But, except for a few chips knocked off by shell fragments, the temples were untouched by this latest and most violent of all the battles that have rolled around their stately Doric columns.

We are running ahead of the story. Let us see what happened between midnight and daylight in the American sector opposite Paestum. Here, Rear Admiral Hall's Southern Attack Force was to land two regimental combat teams (141st and 142nd of the 36th Infantry Division) in six boat waves as assault troops, to overrun the railway behind the temples and seize positions in the foothills. The 36th Division (Major General Fred L. Walker USA), originally a Texas National Guard outfit, had been intensively trained at Arzeu; this was its first experience in combat. Two RCTs of the 45th Division, the "Thunderbirds" who had fought all through the Sicilian campaign, were held in floating reserve, to land next day.

At 0001 September 9 the leading transports, three British LSIs, were in position. *Marnix van St. Aldegonde* had her landing craft in the water in 20 minutes. She and four United States transports carried the 142nd RCT, which was to land on the two northernmost beaches (Red and Green) at H-hour, 0330. Simultaneously, five U.S. transports were to land the 141st RCT on the two southern beaches, Yellow and Blue. Five other U.S. transports and one LSI carried the 143rd RCT, which was destined to follow up on Beaches Red and Green at 0630.[8]

The same Scouts and Raiders who had functioned in HUSKY

[8] See Appendix II for Task Organization. The LSIs were converted English Channel steamships, formerly under the Belgian flag.

were embarked in four scout boats (LCS),[4] one for each beach. Using a radar fix on Monte Soprano obtained by *PC–624*, reference vessel for the Southern Attack Force, each of the four scout boats took a position a few hundred yards off its assigned beach, and started blinking seaward, to guide the boat waves. The boat commanded by Ensign G. Anderson USNR arrived at a point 400 yards off Beach Red at 0230 and began blinking red. That of Lieutenant (jg) Grady R. Galloway USCG located Beach Green by sighting, against the starlit sky, the Torre di Paestum – a medieval stone watchtower that adjoins the road exit between the two pairs of beaches. Galloway started blinking green at 0310 from 100 yards off shore. Ensign J. G. Donnell's boat found the center of Beach Yellow from a bearing on the tower, and took station 600 yards off shore. (During the hour of waiting, the men in this scout boat heard clanking and clattering ashore and saw the lights of vehicles; German troops were moving down to the water's edge.) Ensign Ross E. Schumann USNR, commanding the guide boat for Beach Blue, found that beach by a bearing on Monte Sottane.

Next after the scout boats came Commander Richards's minesweepers to clear a channel through the mine field reported to lie between the line of departure (6000 yards off shore) and the transports. This was done by the same group of fleet minesweepers (*Seer*, flag) that had been used in Sicily, and ten small motor minesweepers (YMSs). According to Admiral Hewitt, the sweep plan was too ambitious, requiring not only the boat channels but fire support areas to be swept by 0330. That was more than the available craft could possibly accomplish. Several boat waves were held up by reports of floating mines, and one LCVP was blown up.

The American beaches were well selected for an orderly night landing. There would have been no trouble if tactical surprise had been obtained, or if the enemy had been lukewarm fighters, as

[4] Fast motor boats with some armored protection and gasoline engines, well muffled. One each was carried in *Barnett*, *Dickman*, *Carroll* and *Jefferson*. Lt. Cdr. Harrie A. James USNR "Observations during Operation AVALANCHE" and conversations with him at the beaches in Jan. 1945.

had happened on the coast of Sicily. Unfortunately for us, the Germans were almost as well prepared to contest landings at Salerno as the Japanese would be at Tarawa two months later.

General von Vietinghoff, commanding the German Tenth Army, had been expecting a landing in the Salerno Gulf for several days. On 7 September, when he heard that large convoys were heading thither, the 16th Panzer Division and the Italian 222nd Coastal Division were already busy installing mine fields along the beaches, building strong points at the most likely landing places, digging tank traps and preparing bridges for demolition. By D-day there was a series of strong points along the shore between Salerno and Agrópoli, armed with light and heavy machine guns, quads of antiaircraft 20-mm, and either 75-mm or 88-mm cannon. In the hills and along the Salerno-Battipaglia road were several batteries of 88-mm mobile artillery, and the Germans were in process of taking over all Italian coastal and fieldpieces. The commanding general of the coastal division, who objected to taking German orders, was quietly taken out and shot. By D-day all beaches between Salerno and Agrópoli had been mined, and pioneers were preparing the port of Salerno for demolition.

When Vietinghoff got the word of the Italian surrender, during the evening of 8 September, he ordered the 26th Panzer Division, then delaying Montgomery's advance in Calabria, to break contact and hasten north. Still uncertain of the main Allied target, Vietinghoff made no further troop dispositions until daylight revealed that the Allies had made a *Grosslandung*, not a Commando raid.

The higher levels of German command also were well prepared. Hitler's headquarters as early as 1 August had drawn up a plan for Operation ACHSE, to start when and if Italy surrendered. This involved the swift occupation of Genoa, Leghorn, Venice and Trieste by Marshal Rommel, now commander in northern Italy; of central and southern Italian ports by Marshal Kesselring, commander in those parts of Italy; the evacuation of Sardinia and Sicily by German troops, and a brisk transfer of German divisions to Italy. At 1950 September 8, Kesselring ordered Operation ACHSE to be executed. When news of the Salerno landings reached him, the Marshal was apprehensive of an American air drop on Rome; but when nightfall came, with no paratroops, he felt confident enough to issue a grandiloquent proclamation: –

> The invading enemy in the area Naples-Salerno and southwards, must be completely annihilated and in addition thrown into the sea. Only by so doing can we obtain a decisive change of the situation in the Italian area. I require ruthless employment of all the might of the three army units. Every commanding officer must be aware of his historical responsibility. British and Americans must realize that they are hopelessly lost against the concentrated German might.[5]

As first light broke on D-day, at 0330, the initial waves for the four American beaches were nearing the ends of their eight- to ten-mile runs over a calm sea. All hit their respective beaches within seven minutes of one another (0335 to 0342) and the second and third waves followed at the proper intervals. Both waves were guided to the line of departure by patrol craft; but, unlike the British, they had no close fire support from that point to the beaches. Admiral Hewitt offered to furnish rocket craft or small gunboats, but the U. S. Army would have none of them; the soldiers imagined that they could obtain complete surprise if they landed silently. This decision was unfortunate; for want of close support, many men in landing craft were killed by German gunners ready and waiting behind the beaches. And, what made matters worse, the Luftwaffe at the same time began to bomb and strafe the beaches, on a scale never before or since equaled in a Mediterranean landing.[6] Fortunately this did not long continue.

Colonel John D. Forsythe's 142nd Infantry went ashore on Beaches Green and Red. Heavy fire from mortars, 88-mm cannon, and machine guns, descended on and around his landing craft, and the troops, even when wading ashore, came under machine-gun fire from the Torre di Paestum. Relentlessly they worked

[5] War Diary German Naval Command Italy 10 Sept. 1943.
[6] Vice Adm. Hewitt *Action Report* p. 143.

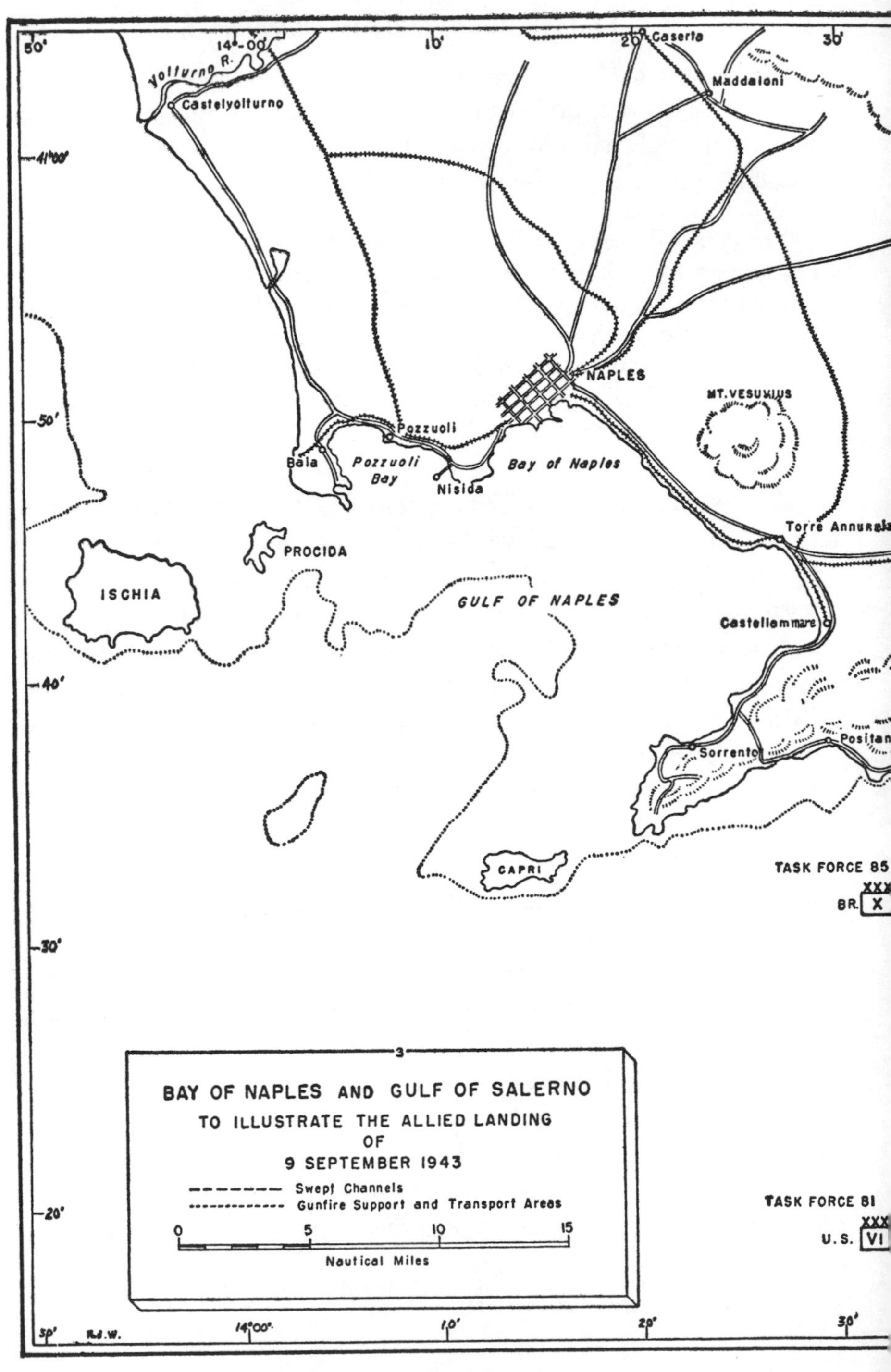

Volturno R.
Castelvolturno
Caserta
Maddaloni
NAPLES
MT. VESUVIUS
Pozzuoli
Baia
Pozzuoli Bay
Nisida
Bay of Naples
Torre Annunziata
PROCIDA
ISCHIA
GULF OF NAPLES
Castellammare
Sorrento
Positano
CAPRI
TASK FORCE 85
XXX
BR. X
TASK FORCE 81
XXX
U.S. VI
BAY OF NAPLES AND GULF OF SALERNO
TO ILLUSTRATE THE ALLIED LANDING
OF
9 SEPTEMBER 1943
Swept Channels
Gunfire Support and Transport Areas
0 5 10 15
Nautical Miles

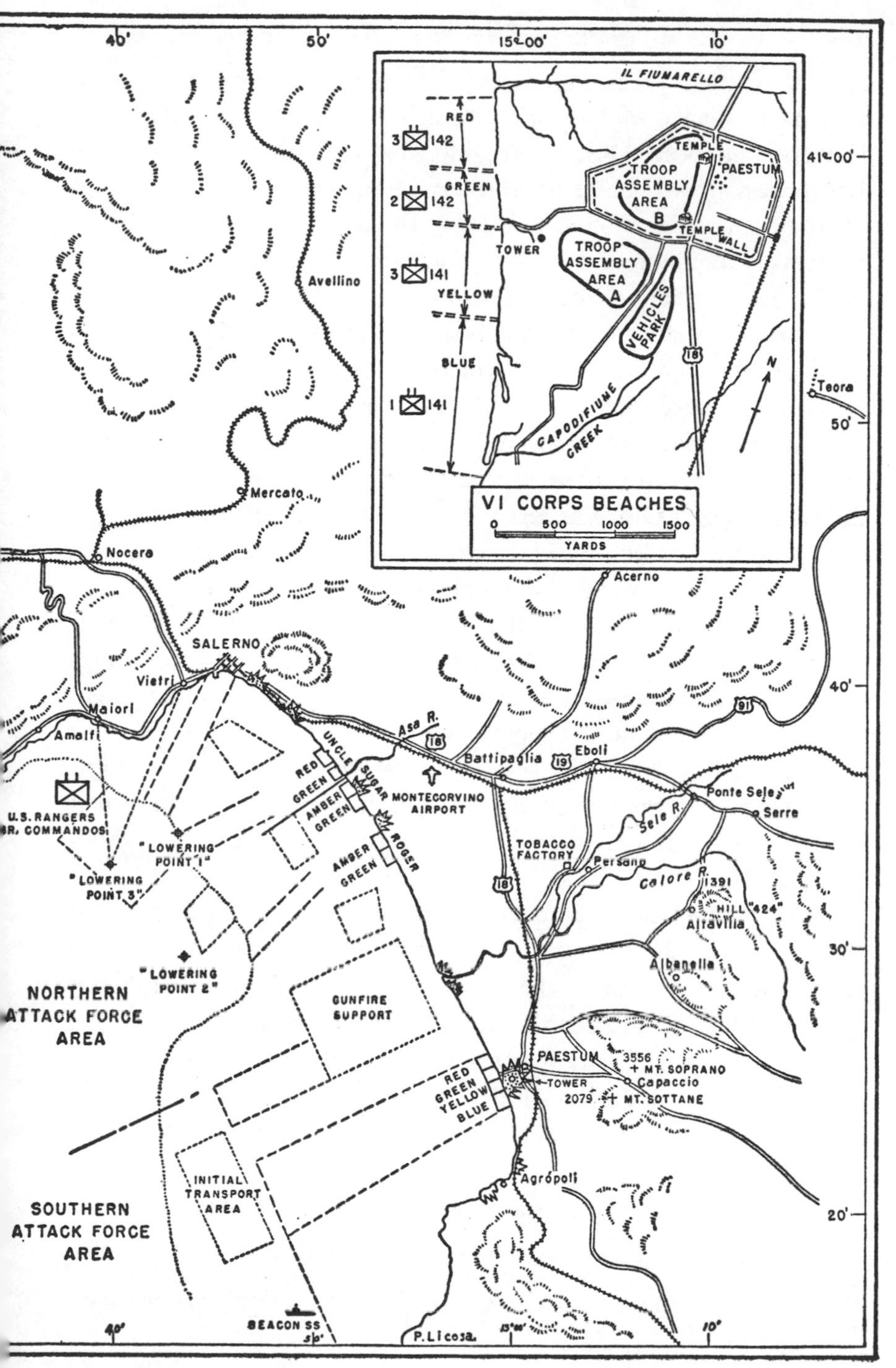

VI CORPS BEACHES
0
500
1000
1500
YARDS
IL FIUMARELLO
RED
GREEN
YELLOW
BLUE
3 142
2 142
3 141
1 141
TOWER
TEMPLE
PAESTUM
TROOP ASSEMBLY AREA B
TROOP ASSEMBLY AREA A
TEMPLE
WALL
VEHICLES PARK
CAPODIFIUME CREEK
18
N
40'
50'
15°00'
10'
41°00'
Avellino
Teora
Mercato
Nocera
Acerno
SALERNO
Vietri
Maiori
Amalfi
U.S. RANGERS
BR. COMMANDOS
"LOWERING POINT 1"
"LOWERING POINT 3"
"LOWERING POINT 2"
UNCLE
SUGAR
ROGER
RED
GREEN
AMBER
GREEN
AMBER
GREEN
Asa R.
18
Battipaglia
19
Eboli
91
MONTECORVINO AIRPORT
Ponte Sele
Serre
Sele R.
TOBACCO FACTORY
Persano
Calore R.
1391
HILL "424"
Altavilla
Albanella
NORTHERN ATTACK FORCE AREA
GUNFIRE SUPPORT
PAESTUM
3556
+ MT. SOPRANO
TOWER
Capaccio
2079
+ MT. SOTTANE
RED
GREEN
YELLOW
BLUE
Agropoli
INITIAL TRANSPORT AREA
SOUTHERN ATTACK FORCE AREA
BEACON SS
P. Licosa
40'
50'
10'
30'
20'

around to their prearranged assembly area, and made it by sunrise, 0436. Plenty of Germans were left near the beach for later arrivals to mop up. Dukws carrying fieldpieces arrived from three Killer-class British LSTs at 0530. An hour later, the 143rd Regiment began to land on Beach Red. By 0800 that beach had become very congested, owing to the usual failure of Army shore parties to do their job of stevedoring.

Lieutenant Galloway's scout boat for Beach Green was, by exception, provided with a few rocket launchers which were used to silence gunfire directed at the first wave. The second wave of landing craft for this beach was delayed by mines and became mixed up with subsequent waves, beaching only at 0630. Thirty dukws hit Beach Green as early as 0525, one in every twelve bringing much-wanted 105-mm howitzers, and the others, ammunition. They unloaded in good order behind the dune line and most of them returned to the transports. No fewer than 123 dukw landings were made on the American beaches between 0530 and 0730 — a remarkable achievement.[7] The 2nd Battalion of the 142nd Regiment here had a hard time getting through barbed wire and lost men from exploding land mines; but it managed to reach the same assembly area as the battalion from Beach Red. The southern half of Beach Green was interdicted by enemy gunfire throughout D-day.

Much of the trouble here and on the next beach (Yellow) came from machine guns mounted on the 50-foot stone tower and from one or two tanks that lurked behind the farm buildings attached to it. This tower was too near the beach for naval gunfire to take on. It was finally captured, the tanks put out of business, and all German defenders killed or made prisoner by the 531st Shore Engineers, who had already lost a number of officers and men in the early air attacks.[8]

[7] Rear Adm. Hall Action Report p. 9, most of these, according to Lt. Cdr. James, had landed by 0530.

[8] Company D of this engineer regiment, commanded by 1st Lt. G. L. Shumaker USA, did fine work preparing the beaches with bulldozers and steel mat, under heavy fire from the tower. Disparaging remarks directed at Army shore parties do not apply to the 531st Shore Engineers.

The two southernmost American beaches, Yellow and Blue, were the most difficult for the invaders to negotiate. Behind them, the Germans had constructed a strong point, and both beaches were within range of coastal batteries near Agrópoli. As the landing craft approached, a loud-speaker blared in English "Come on in and give up. We have you covered!"[9] The first three assault waves of the 3rd Battalion 141st Regiment were indeed covered. Tank fire from behind the stone tower stopped them, but there was no giving up; and a reserve battalion came in at 0500 to help them get off the beach. From 0830 to 1330 Beach Yellow was completely interdicted, and on Beach Blue the 1st Battalion was pinned down for 20 hours. Heavy gunfire prevented six tank-laden LCTs from landing there at about 0640. Four of the six were hit by 88-mm shell; in *LCT–244,* Ensign S. J. Cavallaro USNR, guiding the formation, was killed, and the tank nearest the bow started to burn; the crew promptly lowered the ramp and shoved the tank overboard. The LCTs retired out of range, awaited orders, started in again about noon with gunfire support from a destroyer, and at 1330 discharged their tanks on Beach Red. Tank-laden *LST–389,* which also carried pontoon units, beached at Blue at 1241. Her crew bravely rigged this pontoon under enemy fire and at 1354 her tanks began to roll off. Within twenty minutes enemy gunfire forced another closing of Beach Blue, but it was reopened at 1600 and became the principal beach for discharging tanks.[10]

Thus, the 36th Division had very little armor ashore on D-day, but German Mark IV tanks had been active from 0700, maneuvering both in the open and behind the old Greek city walls, on which machine guns were mounted. The GIs, with the aid of a dismounted cavalry reconnaissance troop, bazookas, 105-mm howitzers and naval gunfire, prevented these tanks from reaching the beaches, and by noon forced them to retire; but some of their fire still reached Red and Green. At 1020 thirteen more Mark IVs

[9] *Fifth Army History* I 32.
[10] Vice Adm. Hewitt *Action Report* pp. 139–40; Lt. Cdr. James "Observations."

rumbled down the highway from the north, threatening the 142nd Regiment's command post which had just been set up in the Capaccio railway station, a few miles north of Paestum. A dukw hauling a 105-mm howitzer arrived just in time to shatter two of the tanks; a third was destroyed by an Invader (A-36) dive-bomber; gunfire from a naval vessel, probably H.M.S. *Abercrombie,* accounted for two more, and the rest retreated.

The landings at Paestum and the British sector were among the most fiercely contested in World War II. Few soldiers suffered so severe a baptism of fire on landing as did those of this yet untried division, or came through it so well. Like the Sons of Tola, the 36th "were valiant men of might." Yet even they could not have carried on without naval gunfire.

Rear Admiral Lyal A. Davidson in *Philadelphia,* tempered by his experience in North Africa and Sicily, commanded naval gunfire support in the American sector. He also had *Savannah* at his disposal, and four destroyers, while H.M.S. *Abercrombie,* screened by Dutch gunboat *Flores,* stood by to serve when 15-inch shell was wanted.[11] The monitor was the first to get into action. Between 0825 and 0915 she fired 11 rounds at an enemy battery, with aircraft spotting. At 1025, as we have seen, she fired on a tank concentration, and again at 1112. Next, she bombarded the town of Capaccio. All at ranges of over 25,000 yards. This hard-hitting monitor, whose help had already been appreciated in HUSKY, struck a mine that afternoon, took a 10-degree list, reached an even keel by counterflooding, but was so badly damaged that she had to steam to Palermo.

Delays in passing through mine fields and in establishing communications with harassed shore fire-control parties prevented the other fire support vessels from functioning as early as they wished. In Admiral Hall's opinion, they did not do so well this day as on D-day in Sicily; but there was no complaint from the troops.

[11] *Boise,* diverted to Taranto, was much missed on D-day. There is a careful diary of naval gunfire support in both sectors in Vice Adm. Hewitt *Action Report* pp. 234-47, and additional details in those of Rear Adms. Hall and Davidson, and in the action reports of the ships mentioned.

At 0914 *Savannah* established communication with her shore fire-control party, which wanted a railway battery silenced. That was accomplished with an expenditure of 57 rounds. For more than an hour, beginning at 1132, *Savannah* fired on a concentration of tanks at the good range of 17,450 yards, yet (so it was reported from shore) forced them to retire. Other targets were German infantry, artillery batteries, observation posts, and the town of Capaccio. The cruiser answered eleven calls for fire support on D-day and expended 645 rounds of 6-inch ammunition. For spotting she used her own SOC observation planes, as well as Army Mustangs; for the 111th Fighter Reconnaissance Squadron had been trained to spot naval gunfire. These P–51s, flying in pairs, turned in an excellent performance at Salerno; one would spot while the other covered against enemy air attack.[12]

Flagship *Philadelphia's* work on D-day, the first of ten spent off the Salerno beaches, began at 0943 when, on call from shore fire-control party, she opened on an enemy battery. At 1033 she launched an SOC spotting plane, and two minutes later took a bridge under fire to hold up approaching panzer units. At 1057 she launched a second spotting plane and then followed a minesweeper through a swept channel to close the beach. From 1220 to 1309, with destroyer *Ludlow*, she fired at a German battery which was shelling beached LSTs on Beach Blue, then recovered her planes. Shortly before 1400 she launched another plane which, simultaneously with one of *Savannah's*, discovered a covey of German tanks concealed in a thicket adjacent to Beach Red. *Philadelphia's* 6-inch salvos flushed 35 of these birds and kept them under fire as they scurried to the rear; about seven were destroyed. Continuing almost to midnight, this cruiser expended 305 rounds of 6-inch shell on D-day.

Outstanding performance in gunfire support was given also by the destroyers. *Philadelphia* was now monitoring the calls from shore fire-control parties and parceling them out. *Bristol's* share was a couple of bridges over the Sele River, including the one

[12] Vice Adm. Hewitt *Action Report* pp. 230–1.

whose destruction helped to halt the German counterattack four days later. *Edison,* having threaded the mine field by noon, operated with *Bristol* about 5000 to 6000 yards off shore. Both destroyers fired on artillery, trucks and tanks, and were counterattacked, without success, by German shore batteries which they were unable to locate. Between them they expended 1400 rounds of 5-inch shell on D-day. One destroyer, probably *Edison,* was credited by a shore fire-control party with having knocked out eleven German tanks. *Ludlow* at 1010 started to escort LSTs to the beach, but was held up by floating mines. By 1145 she had passed through the field and taken position about 1600 yards off Beach Blue, the dangerous right flank of VI Corps. There she gave vitally important support to the LSTs that were going in to the beach. Lieutenant Commander Creighton of *Ludlow,* observing that the leading LST was under fire from a shore battery, quickly laid his main battery on that target and silenced it. At 1255 a two-gun mobile battery took some other LSTs under fire; *Ludlow* detected its position from the gun flashes and destroyed it. The same performance was twice repeated that afternoon, except that the last target proved to be beyond 5-inch range, so the coördinates were passed to *Philadelphia.* In this timely and accurate firing, almost entirely without air spot or shore fire control, "Lucky Lud," as the men called her, expended 465 rounds in 15 separate shoots.

Woolsey, arriving inside the mine field at about 1100, took a crack at an observation tower which the troops were then trying to capture. While waiting to get in contact with her shore fire-control party, at 1313, she was straddled several times by fire from an enemy battery. Unable to locate it, she retired beyond range. Communication with her shore fire-control party was finally established at 1625; but *Woolsey* received only one call, to help *Bristol* shoot up some enemy tanks. Her skipper complained that all the "plums" in gunfire support went to the cruisers, "that destroyers are not being employed to their full advantage." But there were no complaints on that score from the other "cans."

Owing to the interdiction of Beaches Yellow and Blue by

enemy gunfire, Beach Red became horribly congested after noon. A veritable mountain ridge of boxed ammunition and baled supplies lined the water's edge and extended several feet into the sea. Landing craft could not even find room to let down ramps. Troops detailed to unload drifted away, as usual, leaving boat crews to do the stevedoring. Admiral Hall at 1036 appealed to General Clark to assign 200 men to each beach to clear up the mess, and the General gave him about that many from his headquarters troops in *Duchess of Bedford;* but they were untrained for such work and were unable to cope with the sea-wall of supplies.

Landing craft crews functioned even better here than in HUSKY; discipline and seamanship alike were excellent. And although the sea was much calmer than it had been off Sicily, enemy fire on the boats was far heavier. The crews stuck by their craft, and worked around the clock to unload transports. When the operation was over, the incredibly small number of eleven boats had to be abandoned, and all but one of these had been knocked out by enemy action.

Despite this fine boat performance, the unloading of transports and assault cargo ships was unduly delayed. Distance of the transport area from shore (10 miles for some ships), beach congestion, lack of LCTs,[13] and defective combat loading at Oran were responsible. Disregarding the lessons of TORCH and HUSKY, the Army had again taken charge at that port, stowing equipment urgently needed for the assault where it could not be got at, and piling in stuff that would not be needed for days — as if the expedition were bound for some far-off Pacific island. At the end of D-day, the transports of the Southern Attack Force were only partially unloaded, the percentage ranging from 17 to 65. They would not have done even this well but for an extensive use of cargo nets which enabled bulk cargo to be hoisted out of landing craft by portable cranes onto trucks and dukws.[14]

[13] Only 16 out of 54 LCTs promised from the Northern Attack Force area actually turned up on D-day.

[14] Vice Adm. Hewitt *Action Report* pp. 93–101, 110; Rear Adm. Hall Action Report p. 34 and narrative of 11 Sept.

Surmounting all difficulties, the 36th Division reached important objectives by the end of the day. It had taken the 459-foot hill called Templo San Paolo, two miles inland from Capaccio railway station; another hill south of it; and the town of Capaccio, from which the Germans had already retired. One company had fought its way almost to the summit of Monte Sottane. On the right flank, the 141st Regiment was still pinned down on Beach Blue. These fell short of D-day objectives, but General Clark was on the whole satisfied; he "felt that we had achieved as much as could be expected." [15]

If anyone then imagined that the Germans had shot their bolt, he was destined for a great disappointment. They were still able to challenge from the air; they now had full control over the roads and railways of southern Italy, and of communications with the north. Reinforcements were rolling in from the mountains, and the Hermann Goering Panzer Division was coming south from Naples; leading elements of the 29th Panzer Grenadiers had reached the Salerno beachhead at 1900, less than 24 hours after they had been ordered north. During the three following days, the issue was continually in doubt.

That the Army achieved so much was, in some measure at least, due to the quality of naval gunfire support; the boldness of the destroyers driving in through mine fields to deliver accurate shoots was especially praised. It inspired a generous message from the divisional artillery commander of the 36th Division, Brigadier General John W. Lange, which was relayed to every fire support ship and joyfully entered in their logs: —

> Thank God for the fire of the blue-belly Navy ships. Probably could not [otherwise] have stuck out Blue and Yellow beaches. Brave fellows these; tell them so.[16]

[15] *Calculated Risk* p. 191.

[16] *Ludlow* Action Report. The Naval gunfire liaison officer attached to 36th Division Artillery reported that several tank formations had been broken up by naval gunfire alone.

2. *The British Sector* [17]

"What's the weather like at Salerno?" wrote Horace to a friend, about the year 20 B.C.; "and what sort of people shall I encounter there?" [18] That's just what the Northern Attack Force wanted to know in A.D. 1943. The weather could not have been better for an amphibious landing; but the people, instead of the friendly Italians whom the troops expected to find on the beach, turned out to be very tough and uncoöperative Germans of the 16th Panzer Division.

The general plan for this northern sector was for Commodore Oliver to land Lieutenant General McCreery's X Corps on beaches between three and six miles south of the city of Salerno. On the northernmost pair, designated "Uncle," the 46th (North Midland) Division, Major General Hawkesworth, was to swing left after landing and secure control of the high ground behind Salerno. One column was to capture Salerno and then move through the Cava gap toward Naples; the other to move up the valley of the Picentino and through a pass to Mercato, north of Salerno. The 56th (London) Division, Major General Graham, would land on the "Sugar" and "Roger" pairs of beaches south of Uncle, capture Montecorvino airfield and then drive toward Ponte Sele, apex of the desired beachhead line, ten miles inland. None of these objectives, unfortunately, were attained for many days.

On the Sorrento peninsula, whose astonishing beauty – a unique combination of rugged mountains and sophisticated building and planting – must be seen to be believed, two subsidiary landings took place. At Maiori, two miles east of Amalfi, there is a shingle beach with a gradient so steep that small cruising yachts anchor within a stone's throw of the shore. Maiori is the terminus of a road from Naples through the Chiunzi pass, and it was to seize this pass that three United States Ranger battalions were landed

[17] Vice Adm. Hewitt *Action Report*, Rear Adm. Conolly Action Report, and sundry British Admiralty documents.

[18] *Quod coelum, Vala, Salerni; quorum hominum regio, et qualis via?* (*Epistles* I xv).

under Lieutenant Colonel Darby, the hero of Gela. A few miles farther east, and very near Salerno, the Marina de Vietri, with a short sand beach, lies at the foot of the Cava gap, through which the main road and railway run to Naples. British Army and Royal Marine Commandos under Brigadier R. F. Laycock RM, augmented by an American mortar battery, landed here to destroy nearby coast defenses and seize the gap.

Darby's Rangers, embarked in two LSIs and five American LCIs, began landing at Maiori at 0320. Unexpectedly, for Rangers, they met no opposition; succeeding waves and supply runs were sent in smoothly; by 0615 all supplies and equipment were ashore and the landing was completed. By this time the troops had reached the height of the Chiunzi pass, and the ridges which overlook the main road and railway running from Salerno to Naples. And their positions also dominated the defile of Nocera, a bottleneck where a network of roads converged.

At Vietri the British Commandos (embarked in *Prince Albert* and three British LCIs) were less fortunate. The first wave landed unopposed at 0330 after H.M.S. *Blackmore* and a gunboat had silenced a shore battery. For the next two and a half hours the landings continued "according to plan." But Vietri was too near Salerno for the Germans to ignore the threat. They infiltrated the town, mounted mortars and machine guns on several houses which overlooked the beach, and drove off landing craft attempting to come in after 0630. After almost two hours' fighting the enemy was driven out. As early as 0600 the Royal Marine section of the Commandos had reached the defile of La Molina about a mile inland, where they were counterattacked by a German force supported by tanks, and were pinned down for some time.

All these landings were subsidiary to the main operation. The main body of the Northern Attack Force sighted the outer ship of a string of reference vessels at 2317 September 8. Six fleet minesweepers of the Royal Navy and seven American YMSs preceded Admiral Conolly in *Biscayne*, commanding "Uncle" group, on its final run-in. By 0150 September 9 they had swept a channel through the mine field. Next after the minesweepers came three Hunt-class destroyers, which took fire support positions only one mile off the beaches — a bold plan, the wisdom of which was soon proved. Conolly received word from Admiral Hewitt at 2341 that shore installations were not to be engaged unless they opened fire — hoping that all would be abandoned, owing to the armistice.

The enemy soon canceled this restriction. At 0121, as the 15 six-davit American LSTs bearing assault troops were deploying in their allotted area, gunfire was observed on the beach ahead. Shortly after 0200, *Biscayne* and the LSTs were subjected to severe shelling by 88-mm guns. One LST had several members of her crew and 25 soldiers put out of action by the first three salvos.[19] Admiral Conolly immediately ordered the supporting destroyers to return fire, while *Biscayne* stood across the inshore boundary of the transport area to lay a smoke screen. At 0225, when shore fire slackened, Conolly ordered the landing to proceed. As the first boat wave for the two Uncle beaches, Red and Green, made its run for the beach, gunboats picked up the ball from fire support destroyers and, just before the boats touched down, an LCR discharged 790 rockets onto Beach Red. The first wave landed precisely at H-hour, 0330, met stiff resistance and quickly overcame it. Artillery and ammunition followed, and at 0645 the Brigadier Commanding was on the beach with his staff.

Unfortunately the rocket barrage intended for Beach Green was almost half a mile off in deflection, and fell on Beach Amber of the Sugar pair. Guide boats were stationed off Beach Green and the commander of the first wave could easily have landed there; but, as rockets were considered necessary to explode beach mines, General Hawkesworth and Admiral Conolly had agreed that, if they went wild in the darkness, the boats must follow the rockets and not the plan. So the first wave destined for Beach Green landed at Amber instead, and three more waves followed at 15-minute intervals.[20]

[19] *LST-357* Action Report.
[20] Adm. Conolly Supplementary Action Report p. 6, and conversation in 1953.

Landing behind the rockets may have saved some soldiers from being blown up by beach mines, but it crowded the 56th Division off Beach Amber, left intact an enemy strong point near Beach Green, and forced two assault battalions of the 46th Division to the wrong side of the Aso River. These battalions, working north to link up with the rest of their brigade, encountered German troops and, without vehicles or supporting weapons, suffered many casualties. And when their vehicles and artillery finally landed on the correct Beach Green, heavy 88-mm fire pinned them down.

German artillery and the Luftwaffe concentrated on the Uncle beaches and roadstead, and made things very hot afloat as well as ashore. "We were straddled by near-hits on all sides," quaintly recorded one skipper of an LCI. Between 0417 and 0537 the entire transport area was under attack by enemy planes. Two or three bombs exploded close aboard U.S.S. *Nauset*, setting her on fire, knocking out her power and causing extensive underwater damage. Her crew, assisted by that of another tugboat, attempted to beach her, but a violent explosion broke her in two; 59 of her crew of 113 were casualties.

The LSTs unloaded under heavy gunfire, and four of them were badly damaged. *LST–386*, carrying a pontoon causeway, was approaching Beach Green under artillery fire when she sideswiped a floating mine. The explosion demolished the pontoon and caused 43 casualties. *LST–385* was hit thrice coming into Beach Red; and twice more when discharging vehicles. Her skipper, Lieutenant Jerome Brock USNR, although fighting fires and harassed by German machine-gunners, succeeded in landing her entire load of vehicles and equipment, with only nine casualties to his crew and the same number to embarked troops. *LST–375* suffered the worst mishaps. Approaching Beach Uncle Red at 0715, she received two direct hits, and more while unloading, which started gasoline fires and severed the elevator cable so that she could not discharge vehicles from the main deck. After two hours' struggle she pulled out into the roadstead, patched up the elevator, and managed to get about half the vehicles onto the tank deck before a heavy truck collapsed the jury rig. At 2155 she received a direct hit from an air bomb, which exploded below her bottom. Yet she managed to land her remaining vehicles next day and departed with a convoy that night. At Beach Uncle Green *LST-336* had a similar experience. She beached at 0745 when the front lines were only 150 yards inland, and for the next hour and a quarter was subjected to heavy fire from enemy batteries. But "their positions were not discoverable from this ship and we were unable to retaliate," reported the skipper. The ship received 11 direct hits, lost 3 killed and 19 wounded among embarked troops.

These are samples of the landings in Uncle sector. It would be difficult to say whether or not these were more vigorously contested than those of the 36th Division at Paestum. LSTs drew the heaviest fire, but many small beaching craft also were damaged. When Admiral Conolly ordered unloading to break off at Beach Green at 0851, all Uncle craft were diverted to Beach Red. But by 1040 that beach too was under heavy enemy fire, and an effort was made to reopen Beach Green. This had to be abandoned at noon because of artillery fire. At 1241 reports were received off shore that the Germans had retaken Green and were threatening Red. Actually the hard-pressed Hampshires still held a narrow strip of Green, but it was not reopened for unloading until the following day.

Commodore Oliver directed the landing of General Graham's 56th Division in the Sugar and Roger sectors: 169th Brigade, two battalions abreast, on the Sugar pair; 167th Brigade, two battalions abreast, on the Roger pair. The first wave of landing craft hit these beaches at 0340. At Sugar the troops were more bothered by their fellows crowding in from Uncle, owing to the misdirected rocket barrage, than by the enemy. The LST convoy arrived at 0600 with heavy equipment preloaded in dukws, which were launched off shore as the troops were calling for antitank weapons; after which, at 0900, the LSTs beached dry-ramp.

In Roger, southernmost pair of the British beaches, the first two waves carrying assault troops of the 167th Brigade landed 1500 yards too far south; a fortunate mistake since the correct beach was directly under the guns of an unsuspected 88-mm battery. At daylight this battery became active and sank an LCT that was waiting to beach. A support boat from *Princess Astrid* closed the shore at full speed, firing machine guns and mortar, and silenced the battery, which was later knocked out for good by a destroyer. At no time was there serious enemy fire on the Roger beaches; but, owing to a poorly trained Beach Brick (shore party), a serious congestion of vehicles and supplies developed during the day.[21]

Throughout D-day, fire support ships were blazing away in reply to aërial bombing and enemy artillery fire. Rangers and Commandos each had a destroyer and an LCG (converted beaching craft armed with 4.7-inch guns) to cover their landings on the Sorrento peninsula. Three British destroyers and three LCGs were assigned to support the 46th Division in Uncle, and the same number, with one more LCG, were assigned to the 56th Division in Sugar and Roger. Cruiser Squadron 15, commanded by Rear Admiral C.H.J. Harcourt RN in H.M.S. *Mauritius*, with *Uganda*, *Orion*, monitor *Roberts* and two destroyers, operated directly under Commodore Oliver in support of the entire X Corps, but the cruisers had such difficulty communicating with their F.O.O.s and ascertaining the relative positions of friend and foe that they were unable to do much on D-day.

The destroyers more than made up for the cruisers' silence. Off Uncle beaches, H.M.S. *Mendip* and *Brecon* and three small gunboats were busily engaged from 0215 on. They found it easy to silence enemy batteries temporarily, but the German 88s for the most part were mobile and constantly shifted position. When daylight made direct observation possible, enemy fire increased. The German artillery was so well camouflaged that gun flashes and smoke could seldom be detected by ships lying off shore. Admiral Conolly, from the bridge of flagship *Biscayne*, spotted a battery firing into the transport area from a hill southeast of Salerno. Unable at that moment to raise the destroyers by radio, he ordered

[21] L. E. H. Maund *Assault from the Sea* p. 226.

his flagship to take care of the battery; she moved in and silenced it with 12 rounds from her two 5-inch guns.[22] Soldiers and sailors had begun to call this flag officer "Close-in-Conolly" after his performance off Licata; this incident confirmed his nickname.

The same destroyers, together with H.M.S. *Blankney*, throughout the morning carefully pounded every German battery that that they could detect. Liberal use was made of smoke to cover both transports and ships approaching the beach. Smoke provided good protection, since enemy artillery did not fire on floating targets unless they were clearly visible. When Beach Uncle Green was (falsely to be sure) reported overrun by the enemy, during the mixup over Green and Amber, these destroyers steamed so close to shore that they even came under rifle fire. *Loyal* had a boiler knocked out by an 88-mm shell. After *Laforey* had blown up the ammunition dump of a troublesome battery, a second battery nearby straddled her, but she silenced it at 0600, after receiving five hits. Her crew made temporary repairs in the roadstead, and she returned to action within an hour. The 56th Division reported that her fire had reduced several German guns to scrap and inflicted many casualties on their crews. *Lookout* closed Green Beach and put out of action a battery which had sunk an LCT. She remained off the Roger beaches all day, firing at every target seen, although she had but one contact with her F.O.O.

When a strong enemy tank column attacked the 167th Brigade on the right flank of the 56th Division, gunfire from *Nubian* was decisive in breaking up and driving off the assault.[23]

Air defense of the beachhead, controlled by Brigadier General E. J. House USA from his fighter-director center in Admiral Hewitt's flagship *Ancon*, was adequate on D-day because the Luftwaffe put in but few and feeble appearances after the early morning attacks. The British escort carriers, operating well out to sea, placed Seafires over the transports and beaches from dawn to 0745, when fighter planes from the Sicilian fields took over. They started

[22] *Biscayne* War Diary Sept. 1943.
[23] *Fifth Army History* I 34.

"home" at 1800, when the Seafires resumed combat air patrol and continued until after dark. There were only four "Red" alerts on D-day; and during the first three days, 10–12 September, only 156 enemy air raids were plotted by fighter-director control. Most of them were intercepted by Allied fighters and broken up before entering the assault area. Allied pilots had begun to feel that their activities were wasted, and top air force officers were beginning to suggest using them for "offensive missions," when the Luftwaffe disclosed a new secret weapon that made necessary an increase rather than a decrease of fighter support.

With the exception of the Uncle area, landings in the British sector were less strongly opposed than at Paestum. But the X Corps became just as heavily engaged ashore as did the United States VI Corps at the same time. By evening the left flank of the 46th Division was about three miles from Salerno, whence its front ran east to a line about two miles inland, where the 56th Division took over. Its right flank joined the coast four miles northwest of the Sele River mouth, leaving a gap of about seven miles between the British X and the United States VI Corps. The Salerno harbor, Montecorvino airfield and Battipaglia – three important D-day objectives – had not been attained.

The pattern of assault in the British sector was very similar to that in the American. Amphibious technique was almost identical, troops were equally aggressive, landing craft crews as skilled and industrious and gunfire support ships equally bold. Commodore Oliver reported that "there was not enough space to bring into action all the artillery landed; naval gunfire filled the gap." Admiral Hewitt concluded that "without the support of naval gunfire, the assault of the beaches could not have carried and the Army could not have remained ashore without the support of naval guns and bombing aircraft."

CHAPTER XIII

The Battle for the Salerno Beachhead[1]

10–17 September

1. *Ground Fighting and Naval Gunfire, 10–12 September*

ALTHOUGH the German command in Italy found D-day both confusing and critical, it quickly recovered balance. On 10 September the Hermann Goering Division and part of the 15th Panzer Grenadier Division began to move toward Salerno. With Rome secured, the 3rd Panzer Grenadier Division was able to start south from near Orvieto; and in Calabria the whole LXXVI Corps was hastening north, after disengaging Montgomery. At 1000 September 10 Kesselring received a cheerful report from the 16th Panzer Division at Salerno that the beachhead front was stabilized; half an hour later General Herr, commanding LXXVI Corps, arrived from the far south and took over. He promptly ordered the 16th Panzers to counterattack VI Corps from Eboli down the Sele Valley toward Paestum, and, as a diversion, to launch a tank attack from Battipaglia against the British X Corps. Both movements started at 1610, but neither succeeded.

Action ashore during the first four days, 9–12 September, is difficult to follow because almost nothing was "according to plan." Heavy fighting started even before the first landing waves beached, and continued with little let-up. We shall attempt to describe the

[1] Authorities cited at beginning of Part II, especially *Fifth Army History* I, Clark *Calculated Risk;* Admiral Hewitt *Action Report;* Action Reports of Admirals Hall and Conolly.

ground action in a general way in order to lay the foundation for our account of the vital part that naval gunfire support played. The intensity and volume of naval gunfire delivered in direct support of troop operations here set a new high in that aspect of naval warfare; one that would not be exceeded in the Pacific until Iwo Jima and Okinawa. Unfortunately no accurate or complete log was kept of these shoots, or even of the calls. On the basis of incomplete reports it has been estimated that during the Salerno operation the ships delivered more than 11,000 tons of shell in direct support of troops ashore. This was the equivalent of 72,000 field artillery 105-mm high-explosive projectiles, and in total weight greatly exceeded that of the bombs dropped by the Northwest African Air Force on the Salerno beachhead, which amounted to only 3020 tons.[2]

In the American sector of the beachhead, VI Corps met slight opposition, enabling it to reorganize, to get the floating reserve (two regiments of the 45th Division) ashore, and to consolidate positions. The gunfire support ships had a rest — few calls came. On the 11th the beachhead was expanded by nightfall against mounting opposition and VI Corps had reached a line starting at Agrópoli [3] on the coast, running thence inland through hilly country and high ground for about ten miles, through Albanella and Altavilla, and to a point near Persano on the Sele River. The 179th Infantry of the 45th Division very nearly reached Ponte Sele, apex of the desired beachhead line, but was stopped short of it by German tanks and artillery. For the 29th Panzer Grenadier Division arrived that day in the foothills behind the Salerno plain, tipping the balance of forces in favor of the Germans; it attacked down the Sele River, on the 45th Division front, while the 16th Panzer Division thrust outward from Battipaglia toward Salerno, in order to clear the way for the Hermann Goerings to reach the plain through

[2] Vice Adm. Hewitt *Action Report* p. 233; *Fifth Army History* I p. 56. The Air Forces during the same period dropped many more bombs than this on strategic targets far afield.

[3] On 10 Sept. a small fishing boat flying a white flag hailed *Ludlow;* and three Italians who came from Agrópoli asked for troops to occupy that town, as the Germans had evacuated.

the passes north of Salerno and Maiori. The 157th Regiment, just committed from Fifth Army reserve, moved up the right bank of the Sele River to help the rest of the 45th Division, but was held up by German troops who had occupied a large stone tobacco factory on the other bank of the river. The best the 45th could do by nightfall was to dig in along a line seaward of Persano.[4]

Heaviest fighting on 10 and 11 September occurred in the British sector. Facing a long, 2000-foot ridge which dominated the beach and accommodated a strong concentration of enemy artillery, X Corps made little progress. From Salerno southeastward, Highway No. 18 skirts the base of this ridge and leads past the Montecorvino airfield to the rail and road center of Battipaglia, nearly five miles inland from the beach. On the right flank of X Corps, patrols of the 56th Division were in Battipaglia early on the 10th. Intense fighting continued there throughout the day. At dusk a counterattack by German tanks drove the British out. During the 11th, the 46th Division beat off several enemy counterattacks, and by nightfall it had captured Montecorvino airfield. But this important airdrome, the only one on the plain, remained under German artillery fire for several days. And X Corps had only a weak contact on its right flank with the American VI Corps to the south.

Toward Salerno itself the 46th Division had to fight on a narrowing strip of plain dominated by German artillery on the long ridge. The city was captured on the 10th. A British naval port party entered soon after to open the harbor, but their efforts were countered by the German gunners, who continued to range so accurately on the harbor that Salerno remained useless to the Allies for another two weeks.

At least 37 calls for naval gunfire were answered on 10 September in the British sector. Destroyers *Tartar*, *Lookout* and *Loyal*, which had been in the thick of the action on D-day, continued their active support on the 10th. *Loyal* departed for Palermo at 1030 to replenish ammunition, but was back on the job by dawn 12 September. Typical of the support rendered was that of H.M. destroyer

[4] *Fifth Army History* I pp. 34–35, and Map No. 5.

Nubian, which fired 341 rounds of 4.7-inch shell on that day. In the early morning she broke up a German tank concentration, between 1000 and 1145 she bombarded and destroyed an enemy battery, besides demolishing a building which her F.O.O. thought to be a German strong point; for half an hour from 1250 she engaged an enemy battery that was firing on British troops, and destroyed it. Next targets were an ammunition dump and a concentration of enemy vehicles; at 1648 she shifted again to tanks, and closed a busy day at 1951. Cruiser *Mauritius,* flagship of Rear Admiral Harcourt, answered 17 calls for fire and expended nearly 500 rounds on a variety of targets ranging through enemy troops, artillery and tanks to road intersections. Cruisers *Uganda* and *Orion* and monitor *Roberts* joined in some of these shoots, which were very accurate — "Target destroyed" or "Battery silenced" being the usual closeout comment on a specific target.[5] The cumulative effect of naval gunfire in checking German attacks and helping the hard-pressed British troops to hold their positions cannot be precisely assessed, but there can be no doubt that it was very important.

Commandos and elements of the 46th Division moved north through the pass from Vietri against mounting resistance, and held a good position against a heavy infantry and tank attack in which the Royal Marines suffered 198 casualties out of a total strength of 350. On the heights of Mount Chiunzi the Rangers held firm against determined German attacks. Dug in as they were in positions as high as 4000 feet, supply was their major problem; they fought on with skeleton rations and little water. Even mules collapsed when bringing water and ammunition up from the beach by the steep path. From observation posts high in the hills, the Rangers directed artillery and naval gunfire onto the roads below.

On 11 September, the 4th Battalion seized Monte Pendolo, far to the left of the 3rd Battalion, with a gap of several miles between.[6] In order to strengthen their lines on these important positions overlooking the passes between Salerno and Naples, General Clark on

[5] Vice Adm. Hewitt *Action Report* pp. 237–38.
[6] Altieri *Darby's Rangers* pp. 54–9.

11 September lifted a battalion of the 143rd Infantry, reinforced with artillery, tanks, tank destroyers and engineers, in beaching craft, from the VI Corps sector to Maiori.

By nightfall 11 September, Fifth Army beachhead at deepest penetration reached about ten miles inland, but on the northern flank it tapered to about a mile. There was a lightly held gap between VI and X Corps north of the Sele River that was in the course of being plugged with the 157th Regiment.

Enemy air attacks on troops ashore on 10 and 11 September were little more than nuisance raids. But the Luftwaffe made serious raids on the roadstead, using the new radio-controlled glide-bomb. Two types of radio-controlled bombs, fitted with fins and with rocket-boosters, had been developed, one with a range of about 8 miles and maximum speed of 570 m.p.h.; the other with a range of 3½ miles and maximum speed of 660 m.p.h. Both were guided visually by radio from a high-flying plane which released them at a safe distance from the target; each carried a warhead explosive charge of 660 pounds. The existence of these bombs was already known to Allied naval commanders, since they had been used to a limited extent earlier in the war. Their employment in this theater was anticipated, but as yet no good defense against them had been devised.

Savannah was put out of action by one of these bombs. She was lying-to in her support area, awaiting calls for gunfire support, at 0930 September 11, when 12 Focke-Wulf 190s were reported approaching from the north. The cruiser rang up 10 knots' speed, which she increased to 15 knots after a heavy bomb had exploded close aboard *Philadelphia*, nearby. Ten minutes later, *Savannah* received a direct hit on No. 3 turret. The bomb, which had been dropped by a Dornier–217 from 18,000 feet, detonated in the lower handling room. The blast wiped out both the crew of the stricken turret and the No. 1 damage-control crew in central station, blew a large hole in the ship's bottom and opened a seam in her side. Fires were extinguished in several boilers, and for a short time the ship had no power. She settled by the bow until the forecastle was nearly awash. Surviving damage-control parties worked smartly to seal off the flooded and burned compartments; salvage tugs *Hopi* and *Moreno* moored alongside to assist. *Savannah* was kept on an even keel by shifting her fuel oil. At 1800 she retired under her own power, screened by four destroyers, and arrived safely at Malta.[7]

Although enemy resistance had been so strong that several D-day objectives had not yet been reached, the beachhead seemed secure by the evening of 11 September. After a visit to X Corps, General Clark reported to General Alexander that he would soon be ready to launch an attack northward through Vietri toward Naples.[8] The Germans, despite their rapid reinforcement and partial success in counterattacks, were none too happy. The commanding general of the 16th Panzer Division reported to General Herr that the situation was critical. His troops were under heavy pressure at Battipaglia and his lines had been breached by American tanks near Persano. But the tables were soon turned.

Ominous reports began to flow in to General Clark's headquarters ashore, shortly after 0930 September 12. Elements of the Hermann Goering Division moving south from Naples had been identified opposite X Corps, and the presence of the 15th Panzer Grenadier Division in the same area was ascertained. Elements of the 26th Panzer and 29th Panzer Grenadier Divisions arrived at the beachhead from Calabria and went right into action against VI Corps. The Eighth Army was supposed to be hot on their trail; Alexander on the 10th ordered Montgomery to hurry, and on the 12th sent his chief of staff "to explain the full urgency of the situation." [9] But Montgomery's advance patrols did not make contact with VI Corps until 1400 September 16, after the crisis had passed.

On the right center of VI Corps, a battalion of the 142nd Infantry occupied Hill 424 behind Altavilla early on 12 September. Before it could organize this position, an important one to deny the

[7] *Savannah* War Diary 11 Sept. 1943 and Buships publication "U.S.S. *Savannah* Bomb Damage." After temporary repairs she proceeded to the United States.

[8] *Fifth Army History* I p. 36; *Calculated Risk* p. 195.

[9] Alexander Despatch p. 2896. On p. 2898, however, he refers to Eighth Army's "splendid gallop through Calabria, Lucania and Apulia."

enemy since it commanded a complete view of plain and beaches, the Germans counterattacked and forced them to abandon Altavilla. On the left of VI Corps, elements of the 45th Division drove the enemy out of the tobacco factory, with the help of gunfire from *Philadelphia*, captured Persano and advanced inland. General Dawley regrouped his troops during the night of 12–13 September to strengthen and tighten his lines; but there was still a wide gap between VI Corps and the British. General Dawley planned to drive against Hill 424 on the 13th.

On the extreme left flank of Fifth Army, the Rangers captured several more heights overlooking Castellammare on the 12th and sent a night patrol into that town, where they ran into stiff resistance. This thrust was little to the Germans' taste, as it threatened to break a way for the Allied forces to enter Naples. But the élan of the Rangers gave the enemy an exaggerated idea of their strength and he decided to reinforce before launching a major counterattack. The Rangers were strong enough to dominate the Sorrento peninsula and control the road-railway gap at Nocera, but too weak to exploit their positions.

No significant gains were made by X Corps on 12 September, although it was well supported by the gunfire of monitor *Roberts* and several destroyers. The 167th Brigade 56th Division was driven out of Battipaglia, sustaining such heavy losses that it had to be relieved. Despite comparative quiet in the British sector, X Corps had suffered some 3000 casualties – from 5 to 7 per cent of its strength – by the evening of 12 September, and the troops were exhausted.

Thus Fifth Army lost Battipaglia and Altavilla on 12 September, a day of more intense fighting than any that had preceded. It became obvious that the Germans were rapidly and dangerously building up their strength in front of Salerno beachhead. By the 12th, Kesselring had at his disposal 600 tanks and mobile guns, on which he relied to throw Clark into the sea before Montgomery could come up to relieve him[10] The day closed for the Allies on a very

[10] Jacques Mordal *Cassino* (1952) p. 36.

different note from that on which it had opened. General Clark began to think that he would have to evacuate the southern beaches and concentrate his entire army north of the Sele River.[11]

2. *The Crisis of 13–14 September*

Although the Montecorvino airport had been in British hands since 10 September, it was still dominated by German artillery fire on the 13th, and unusable. Army Engineers met the emergency by constructing a strip on the plain two miles north of the Greek temples at Paestum, and had it ready 12 September. On that day the British escort carriers had to retire to fuel at Palermo, but 26 of their Seafires were flown in to the Paestum airstrip from which they operated until replaced by planes of the Northwest African Air Forces. By 13 September a second strip was ready near the first, work had been begun on a third, and the British sappers, not behindhand, had two emergency strips ready in X Corps area.[12]

To strengthen the VI Corps left flank and also to close the dangerous gap between it and the British, General Dawley ordered many front-line units shifted during the night of 12–13 September. When news reached him that night of the German recapture of Battipaglia, he withdrew two more infantry battalions from the right flank of the 36th Division and sent them to the threatened left.

A tactical group, called the Martin Force from the Colonel commanding, composed of three battalions from the 142nd and 143rd Infantry, counterattacked Altavilla and Hill 424 at 0600 September 13. It did very well during the morning, but later in the day a German column isolated the Martin Force and stopped its offensive. It had to withdraw during the night of 14–15 September.

The crux of the German counterattack on 13 September came on the VI Corps left flank, especially in the angle formed between the Sele and the Calore River that empties into it.

[11] *Calculated Risk* p. 198.
[12] Vice Adm. Hewitt *Action Report* pp. 197–98; Craven and Cate II 526–27.

At 1542, one column of six German tanks attacked the left flank of the 1st Battalion 157th Infantry, which was dug in on the north slopes of the tobacco factory hill, and at the same time 15 more tanks rolled down the road from Eboli, followed by a battalion of the 79th Panzer Grenadier Regiment and towed fieldpieces. They captured the tobacco factory and drove the 1st Battalion back to the railroad. Another force of infantry-supported tanks hit the 2nd Battalion 143rd posted on the road to Ponte Sele and forced it to retire across the Calore, with a loss of 508 officers and men.

Then, fortunately for us, the German commander made a bad tactical error. At 1715 he sent his main body of tanks right down into the fork between the Sele and the Calore. His intention, obviously, was to cross the Calore where the maps showed a bridge, and drive through the VI Corps to Paestum and the beach. But the bridge had been burned, the dirt road chosen by the tanks was lined by deep drainage ditches, so they could not deploy, and, on the rolling open grassland south of the burned bridge, two battalions of United States field artillery, the 189th and 158th, were posted. Lieutenant Colonels Hal L. Muldrow and Russell D. Funk USA stripped their batteries of all but minimum gun crews, commandeered every stray GI and truck driver they could pick up on the road, put headquarters company and band into line, and posted these improvised infantrymen, armed with rifles and machine guns, on the slope between the batteries and the river. The fire of these men, added to that of the artillery, crossed the tanks' "T" as neatly as Admiral Togo did that of the Russian fleet, and forced all surviving tanks to retreat.[13]

Although *Philadelphia* and several destroyers were available, they were not called upon for gunfire during this critical battle. Probably there was no shore fire-control party among the impromptu defenders at the river fork. *Boise*, arriving off the beachhead that afternoon to replace stricken *Savannah*, divided 36 rounds of 6-inch between a German tank concentration and a battery at the

[13] *Salerno* pp. 62–66 with good maps; Gen. Clark *Calculated Risk* p. 302; personal reconnaissance in 1953. The artillery fired 3950 rounds in this action.

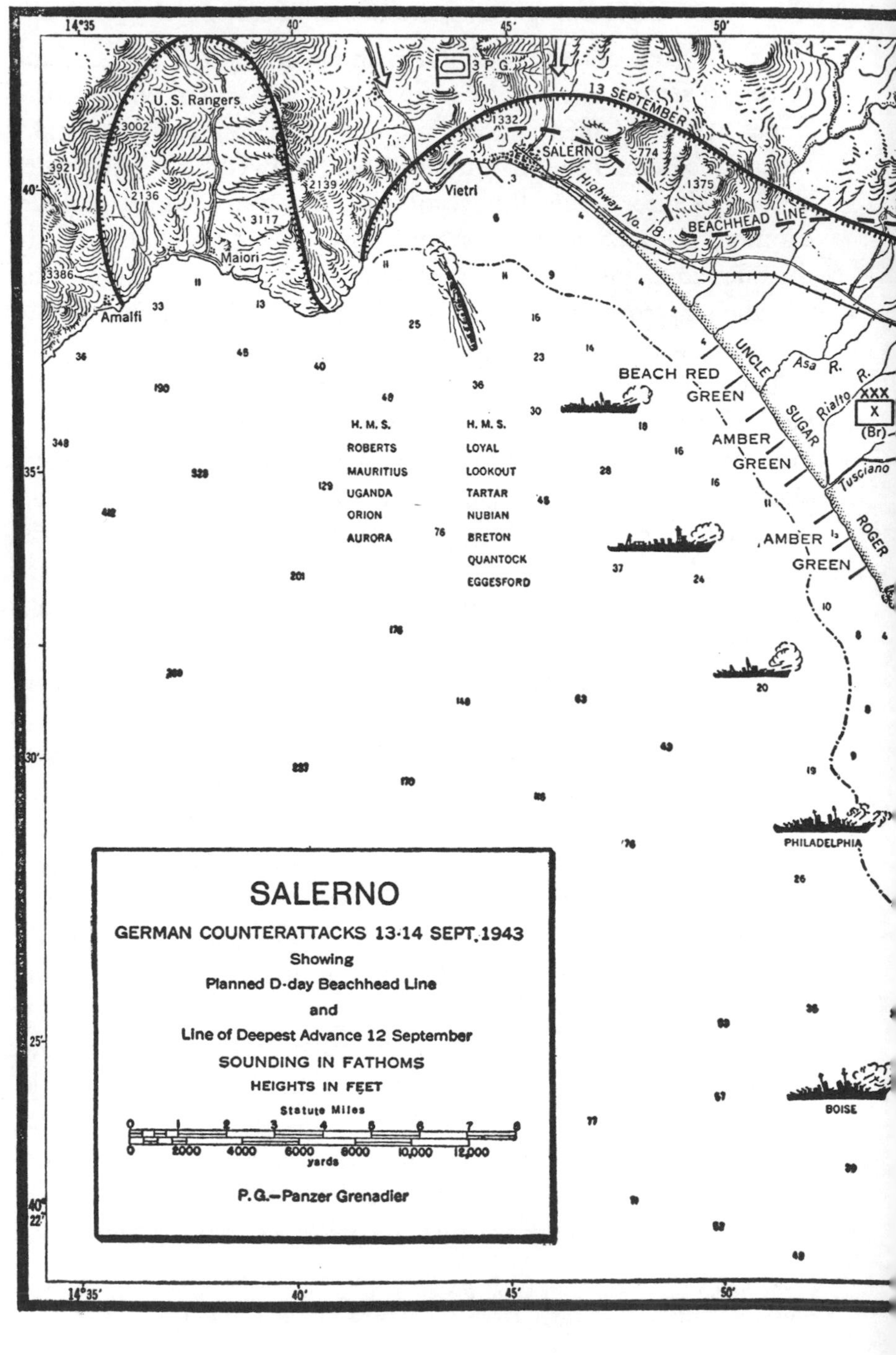

SALERNO
GERMAN COUNTERATTACKS 13-14 SEPT. 1943
Showing
Planned D-day Beachhead Line
and
Line of Deepest Advance 12 September
SOUNDING IN FATHOMS
HEIGHTS IN FEET
Statute Miles
yards
P. G.—Panzer Grenadier
U. S. Rangers
Amalfi
Maiori
Vietri
SALERNO
3 P.G.
13 SEPTEMBER
Highway No. 18
BEACHHEAD LINE
BEACH RED
GREEN
AMBER
GREEN
AMBER
GREEN
UNCLE
SUGAR
ROGER
Asa R.
Rialto R.
Tusciano
XXX
X
(Br)
H. M. S.
ROBERTS
MAURITIUS
UGANDA
ORION
AURORA
H. M. S.
LOYAL
LOOKOUT
TARTAR
NUBIAN
BRETON
QUANTOCK
EGGESFORD
PHILADELPHIA
BOISE
14°35'
40'
45'
50'

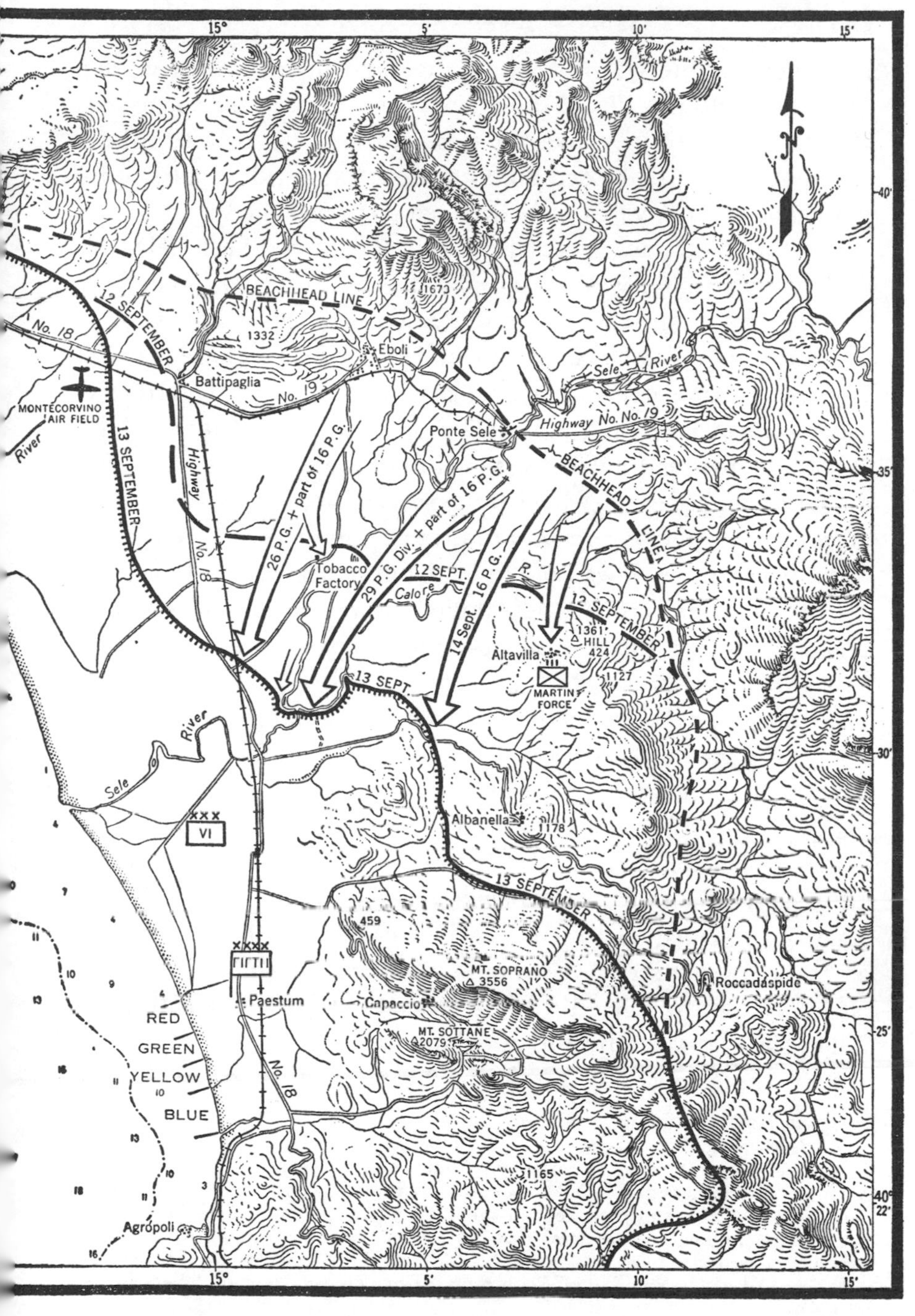

15°
5'
10'
15'
40'
35'
30'
25'
40°
22'
BEACHHEAD LINE
12 SEPTEMBER
No. 18
1332
1673
Eboli
Battipaglia
No. 19
Sele River
MONTECORVINO AIR FIELD
River
13 SEPTEMBER
Highway
Highway No. No. 19
Ponte Sele
26 P.G. + part of 16 P.G.
29 P.G. Div. + part of 16 P.G.
14 Sept. 16 P.G.
BEACHHEAD LINE
No. 18
Tobacco Factory
12 SEPT.
Calore R.
12 SEPTEMBER
1361
HILL 424
Altavilla
MARTIN FORCE
1127
13 SEPT.
River
Sele
VI
Albanella
1178
13 SEPTEMBER
459
FIFTH
MT. SOPRANO
3556
Roccadaspide
Paestum
Capaccio
MT. SOTTANE
2079
RED
GREEN
YELLOW
BLUE
No. 18
1165
Agropoli

rear, checking fire when her shore fire-control party reported the battery demolished. *Philadelphia* was busy brushing off enemy air attacks. Two of the new radio-controlled bombs were aimed at her, but nimble "Philly" eluded both and they exploded harmlessly in the water, one 100 yards, the other 100 feet from the ship.[14]

Even after the tank attack in the river fork had been defeated the situation ashore was still critical. Several American units had been decimated, and there were few reserves to throw in next day. When the ground commanders assembled at VI Corps headquarters at Paestum that evening, things looked bad. Only the two artillery battalions had prevented a complete break-through, and X Corps was still heavily embroiled.[15] General Clark, as a precaution in case the Germans had worse things in store for the morrow, sent Admiral Hewitt an urgent request to prepare plans to evacuate the VI Corps from the beachhead and re-land it north of the Sele to aid the X Corps, or vice versa.[16] The Admiral did not like the idea – but, as the Navy was there to support the Army by any and every means, he went ahead with the plans.

Although the main strength of the German attack on 13 September was directed at the weak left flank of VI Corps, there was heavy fighting on the British X Corps front as well, especially near Battipaglia. To support the troops, H.M.S. *Roberts*, three cruisers and six destroyers delivered shoots on troops, batteries, tanks and road intersections, as called for by their F.O.O.s. Cruiser *Uganda* was struck by a guided bomb at 1440 when no alert was on; the attacking plane was not seen.[17] The bomb penetrated seven decks and exploded below the ship. Although flooded with some 1300 tons of water, she was saved by prompt shoring of threatened bulkheads, and left the combat area early next morning under tow of U.S.S.

[14] *Philadelphia* Action Report p. 7.

[15] *Salerno* p. 66.

[16] Admiral Hewitt letter to writer 14 Aug. 1953 correcting his *Action Report* p. 88, and article in the U.S. Naval Inst. *Proceedings* Sept. 1953 p. 972. The Admiral here says that this occurred on the 14th, but his message recalling *Ancon* was sent at 0315 Sept. 14, indicating that his meeting with Gen. Clark had occurred some hours earlier.

[17] Vice Adm. Hewitt *Action Report* pp. 34–35. *Uganda* lost 16 killed and 7 wounded.

Narragansett, escorted by three destroyers. Within an hour of *Uganda's* hit, destroyers *Nubian* and *Loyal* were narrowly missed by guided bombs. Now that two light cruisers were out of action, and other ships running low on ammunition, Admiral of the Fleet Cunningham ordered H.M.S. *Aurora* and *Penelope* up from Malta. They arrived off Salerno by sunrise 14 September.

Important reinforcements arrived on the 13th – the 82nd Airborne Division which would have performed the drop on Rome had it not been canceled. Some of the paratroops were landed at Maiori to reinforce Darby's Rangers; the rest, standing by on Sicilian fields, were requested by General Clark, at 1330, to fly in that very night.[18] General Ridgway, equal to every emergency, organized the drops at an hour's notice. Mindful of what had happened in Sicily, he asked that all antiaircraft guns on the beachhead or in the roadstead be forbidden to fire that night; General Clark and Admiral Hewitt so directed. The first planes took off at 1930. Led by three Pathfinders with paratroops and ground signaling equipment, 82 C–47s and C–53s, starting from Cómiso and Trápani–Milo fields in Sicily, dropped over 600 paratroops exactly where they were wanted behind the VI Corps lines south of the Sele; only one man was injured. The following night 1900 more paratroops were dropped successfully in the same zone.[19]

Throughout the night of 13–14 September weary Army officers worked to arrange a new defensive line, starting at the crossroads west of the tobacco factory, along the rise whence the artillery had stopped the tanks, and around the east edge of a line of foothills, almost to the hill town of Roccadáspide. At dawn 14 September the Germans renewed their attack with probing tank and infantry thrusts; but, thanks to the night time regrouping, VI Corps held its ground. In the X Corps sector the 46th Division was well dug in on hills near Salerno, but the 56th was still in the open plain

[18] Clark *Calculated Risk* pp. 196–97.

[19] A third drop during the night of 14–15 September at Avellino was less successful, because the mountains forced it to be made from altitudes between 3000 and 5000 feet. Only 15 of the 40 planes carrying 600 paratroops hit the right place; the rest dropped their men from 8 to 25 miles away in small groups. Most were captured; some worked their way south and made contact with the Fifth Army.

southwest of Battipaglia, under enemy observation from the nearby hills. The Coldstream Guards and the 9th Royal Fusiliers repulsed a strong enemy tank attack during the night of 13–14 September, and on the 14th moved over to close the dangerous gap between the X and VI Corps. Although the rest of the 26th Panzer Division from the south, and a regimental combat team of the 3rd Panzer Grenadier Division from the north, arrived in the battle area that day, these were the last reinforcements available to the German command, and when darkness descended over the Salerno plain on 14 September the situation of the Fifth Army had greatly improved.[20]

Naval gunfire support was a material contribution to this result. Of the 14th Vietinghoff wrote: "The attack this morning pushed on into stiffened resistance; but above all the advancing troops had to endure the most severe heavy fire that had hitherto been experienced; the naval gunfire from at least 16 to 18 battleships, cruisers and large destroyers lying in the roadstead. With astonishing precision and freedom of maneuver, these ships shot at every recognized target with very overwhelming effect." [21]

Philadelphia, as usual, was to the fore. She continued to shoot at targets designated by her shore fire-control party throughout the night of 13–14 September, firing 921 rounds of 6-inch on tanks, batteries, road intersections and massed troops, and receiving such messages as: "Very good – we are under attack – stand by," and "Thank you – stand by." Between 0844 and 1345 September 14, *Boise* relieved her, firing almost continuously at tanks and troops – 18 different targets – and expending nearly 600 rounds. Shore fire-control party reported "Very well!" after a tank concentration had received 83 rounds. At 1503 *Philadelphia* returned for a two-hour session. There followed another lull in naval gunfire support; then, at 2130, *Boise* was called on for rapid fire on troops. With shore fire-control party reporting "No change" and "Straddle, straddle!" she unloaded 72 rounds in short order. An hour later she was called on again, and after firing 121 rounds got the word, "Cease firing;

[20] *Salerno* pp. 68–73.
[21] "Feldzug in Italien" chap. vi pp. 34–35.

thank you, stand by." At 2310 she delivered interdiction fire on German troops marching down from Eboli; "You are doing well," said the shore party. All night 14–15 September she continued firing on call. In the British sector the pattern of gunfire support was much the same. Four light cruisers and four destroyers got into the shooting, with good results.[22]

Although Fifth Army and supporting fleets were successfully beating off German attacks on 14 September, the situation still seemed grave to the higher Allied commanders. Admiral Hewitt, it will be remembered, had been making plans for a possible shifting of VI Corps to X Corps sectors, or vice versa, at General Clark's insistence. That afternoon he sent an urgent message to Admiral of the Fleet Cunningham: "The Germans have created a salient dangerously near the beach. Military situation continuing unsatisfactory. Am planning to use all available vessels to transfer troops from southern to northern beaches, or the reverse if necessary. Unloading of merchant vessels in the southern section has been stopped. We need heavy aërial and naval bombardment behind enemy positions, using battleships or other heavy naval vessels. Are any such ships available?" [23]

Admiral Cunningham reacted promptly to the request for naval reinforcements. At 1732 September 14 he ordered Admiral Vian to expedite the loading of troops at Philippeville and to sail immediately with H.M.S. *Euryalus, Scylla* and *Charybdis* to Salerno. An hour later he ordered battleships *Valiant* and *Warspite* to depart Malta with six destroyers and report to Admiral Hewitt as soon as possible after daylight next morning. Unfortunately Hewitt's dispatch reached an important addressee, General Eisenhower, in a garbled form which suggested that he and General Clark were contemplating a complete evacuation of the Salerno beachhead.[24] There was consternation at headquarters over what appeared to be going on, and consternation at the beachhead over what Hewitt thought

[22] Vice Adm. Hewitt *Action Report* pp. 241–42.
[23] Paraphrase of the actual message, sent at 1445.
[24] *Crusade in Europe* p. 187; Butcher pp. 417–18.

he might have to do, if General Clark insisted. Both Commodore Oliver and General McCreery, in no uncertain terms, opposed the idea of transferring troops from one part of the beachhead to another, insisting that they should fight it out where they were, with all the gunfire support the Navy could provide.

General Alexander, after reviewing the situation on the spot, killed the plan for shifting troops.[25] It was fortunate that the shift never had to be made, since a reverse amphibious operation under hostile fire is exceedingly difficult to carry out. But neither General Clark nor Admiral Hewitt at any time contemplated a complete withdrawal from the beachhead.

Northwest African Air Forces were not idle through all this. On 13 September General Eisenhower ordered Air Chief Marshal Tedder to send every plane that could fly against sensitive spots in the German formations. This great air attack was delivered on the 14th. Although in part ill-directed, owing to the lack of ground air-control units with the troops, it badly disrupted German mobility and communications, and materially helped the Allies to regain the initiative.

In retrospect, it appears that the German drive to the beaches was defeated not only by the stout resistance of all three Allied arms, but by the German dual command in Italy – Rommel in the north, Kesselring in the south. A single commander could on 9 September have sent south to Salerno several divisions of the Army group stationed around Mantua, and they could have arrived by the 13th. But Rommel, who never believed in the southern Italy campaign, would not let them go. Even two divisions more would have enabled Kesselring to make good his threat, and wipe out the beachhead.[26]

[25] Conversation with Admiral Conolly 24 Sept. 1953.

[26] Jacques Mordal *Cassino* p. 36; Kesselring *Memoirs* p. 186 complains of Hitler's "almost obsequious submissiveness to Rommel."

3. *Ground Fighting and Naval Gunfire, 15–17 September*

The successful defense of the beachhead on 14 September convinced General Clark that the crisis had passed. Now that reinforcements were pouring in, it was time to draft plans for taking his main objective, the port and airfields of Naples. As the plan evolved, the British 46th Division would attack through the Cava Gap between Vietri and Nocera while the 56th Division drove due north from Salerno toward Mercato San Severino. VI Corps, in the meantime, would sweep around the right flank and make for Avellino and Teora. But first it would be necessary to break out of the beachhead.

During the night of 14–15 September *Boise* delivered call fire, mainly on enemy troop movements around Persano. At 0042 her shore fire-control party signaled: "We need support. When able, give four minutes' rapid fire." She did just that and, after responding to several more calls, at 0336 received the word: "Your firing has won our praise. It has Jerry puzzled. Well done. Will be back in 20 minutes for more." Only four minutes later that "more" was asked of *Boise*, and gladly given. At 0530 September 15 she ceased firing, having expended 893 rounds during the night. *Philadelphia* relieved her an hour later and was soon pounding German tanks near Persano; by 1015 she had expended 70 per cent of her ammunition. Fortunately, the U. S. Naval Commander at Palermo, Captain Doughty, anticipating an ammunition shortage at Salerno, had loaded 780 rounds of 6-inch — his entire available stock — in *Ancon*, about to leave for Salerno to resume duty as Admiral Hewitt's flagship; and the Admiral sent destroyer *Gleaves* to Malta to borrow bullets from damaged *Savannah*.[27]

At 1000 September 15 naval gunfire support was augmented by the arrival off the southern beaches of H.M. battleships *Valiant* and *Warspite*, escorted by six destroyers. It took so long to brief their

[27] Vice Adm. Hewitt *Action Report* pp. 39–40.

gunnery officers and to send F.O.O. parties ashore that they did not open fire until 1720. *Warspite* then fired 29 rounds of 15-inch shell at targets around Altavilla, at the same time that *Philadelphia* and *Boise* were plastering that unfortunate town. As the war diary of the German naval command in Italy records, "Our attack had to stop for reforming because of the great effect of the enemy sea bombardment and continuous air attacks." And Alexander, from the beachhead, signaled Eisenhower that, although "not actually happy about the situation," he was happier than he had been twenty-four hours earlier.[28]

General von Vietinghoff, from his headquarters at Sant'Angelo di Lombardi in the Apennines, now issued orders for one more try. It began all along the line at 0900 September 16. Colonel Schmalz's combat group, now in the Hermann Goering Division, attacked toward Salerno from the Naples road, ran into heavy fire from British field artillery, cruisers and destroyers, and quickly came to a halt. Another attack on X Corps sector was stopped by British tanks. On the extreme right of the American sector, the Germans gave indications of retiring. Paratroop patrols walked into Roccadáspide, eight and a half miles east of Paestum, before noon on the 16th. In the afternoon two battalions of the 504th Parachute Regiment marched along the Albanella ridge, and at 1630 launched an attack from the south against Hills 424 and 315. Darkness and German artillery fire forced them to halt for the night a mile and a half short of Altavilla.

That ended the Germans' hope of winning back Salerno. And will the reader please note the reason given by Marshal Kesselring? "On 16 September, in order to evade the effective shelling from warships, I authorized a disengagement on the coastal front. . . ." [29]

No wonder that the Luftwaffe concentrated on gunfire support ships. At 1427 September 16, H.M.S. *Warspite*, after completing her second shoot of the day on Altavilla, was put out of action by two direct hits and two near-misses from guided bombs. She headed

[28] Despatch p. 2897.
[29] *Memoirs* p. 187.

for Malta under her own steam but soon went dead in the water and was taken in tow by U.S. tugs *Hopi* and *Moreno.* Captain Packer, with engine rooms flooded and U-boats known to be about, and in expectation of fresh air attacks, described the situation of his ship as "unattractive." But she had ample protection from five destroyers and three cruisers, and she made Malta safely at the end of a towline, on the 19th. Battleship *Valiant,* after firing one short bombardment, was released by Admiral Hewitt on the evening of the 16th and returned to Malta.

At 1400 September 16, elements of Montgomery's Eighth Army finally made contact with Clark's Fifth at a village about 15 miles southeast of Agrópoli. That evening Clark felt justified in reporting to Eisenhower: "We are in good shape now. We are here to stay. This morning we have restored the salient between the Sele River and the Calore. . . . I am prepared to attack Naples. We have made mistakes and we have learned the hard way, but we will improve every day and I am sure we will not disappoint you." [30] On the 17th, General Eisenhower flew to Palermo, there embarked in a British warship in which Admiral of the Fleet Cunningham temporarily wore his flag, visited the Salerno beachhead and conferred with General Clark.

The Salerno campaign now enters its final phase, the drive that swept Fifth Army through Naples and to the Volturno River.

4. *Build-up and Diversion*

Admiral Hewitt's operation plan assumed that the Fifth Army could be maintained and reinforced over the beaches until the ports of Salerno and Naples were available. That assumption, based on Hewitt's experience in Sicily, was put to a severe test, yet proved valid.[31] Fifth Army plans had scheduled the port of Salerno for occupation on D-day, and that of Naples by 21 September, together

[30] Clark *Calculated Risk* pp. 208–10.
[31] Vice Adm. Hewitt Op Plan 7–43, Annex I, and *Action Report* pp. 160–7.

with smaller harbors like Amalfi. But Salerno, though captured on 10 September, did the Allies no good until the 25th because it was under constant observation and fire by German artillery; and Naples was not taken until 1 October. The planned build-up of the Fifth Army to 225,000 troops, 34,000 vehicles and 118,000 tons of supplies by 4 October had to be somewhat modified in the light of these circumstances.

Assault shipping was supposed to be unloaded by the end of 10 September, and, except for a few LSTs at the southern beaches, that was done, by working holds and landing craft throughout the night. Commodore Oliver's ships and beaching craft were formed into convoys and routed south as fast as they were unloaded, to pick up more troops and supplies. Rear Admiral Hall in *Samuel Chase* sailed for Oran with 15 unloaded transports and assault freighters, escorted by ten destroyers, at 2215 September 10.[32]

Shortly after midnight, destroyer *Rowan* of the transport screen sighted a torpedo wake about 100 feet distant, on the starboard bow. Commander Ford ran down the track and promptly made radar contact on a surface target about two and a half miles northwesterly. As the range increased rapidly, *Rowan* turned up 27 knots, gave chase, and, when the range had decreased to 4800 yards, opened fire with her forward 5-inch guns. But the target, a couple of German E-boats, increased speed still more and pulled away. *Rowan* ceased firing and changed course to rejoin the convoy. Within five minutes a new radar contact was made on the port quarter at 2800 yards, and the ship's course was changed to bring all her guns to bear. By the time they did, the range had decreased to 2000 yards, a distance which would offer the enemy so good an opportunity for torpedo attack that Commander Ford, in anticipation, ordered Full Right Rudder to put the expected torpedo astern. *Rowan* did not answer the helm quickly enough; a torpedo hit her during the turn. There was a tremendous explosion, probably in

[32] Rear Adm. Conolly in *Biscayne* replaced him in command of all naval support for VI Corps, Conolly's place in the northern sector being taken by Capt. Rupert M. Zimmerli. Unloading in the southern sector, according to Rear Adm. Hall, was done in about half the time that the transports required in Sicily.

the after magazine, and she sank in 40 seconds. *Bristol*, detached from the transport screen, managed to rescue only 71 members of the crew; 202 officers and men went down with the ship.[33]

This deed was done by one of three German E-boats whose division commander was making a sweep off Salerno Gulf on his own initiative. He thought that he had sunk a 10,000-ton freighter, and was evidently deterred by *Bristol* from trying another shot.[34]

The same quick follow-up of merchant-ship convoys was tried at Salerno as in Sicily. On 11 September 16 Liberty and other ships laden with troops, vehicles and supplies arrived off the southern beaches. Although these vessels were 42 per cent unloaded by the end of the 12th, they were not completely emptied until the 17th. One of them, S.S. *Bushrod Washington*, was hit on 14 September by a radio-guided bomb whose explosion set the gasoline in the cargo afire. The master, Jonathan M. Wainwright V, the last to jump overboard, returned on board with several members of the crew and armed guard, to help salvage-tug *Hopi* fight the fires. They rescued a number of wounded who were still on board, but had to quit when the flames got beyond control, and *Washington* was a total loss. Next day S.S. *James Marshall*, when discharging cargo with an LCT, was hit by a guided bomb which killed a large number of merchant mariners and soldiers, started fires and also a panic among the survivors. Salvage tugs alongside extinguished the flames, but as most of the survivors skulked on the beachhead, *Marshall* was unloaded by Captain Wainwright and members of *Washington's* crew, with other volunteers. Towed to Bizerta and eventually to England, she ended her career as part of a "Mulberry" artificial harbor in the Normandy operation.[35]

Again, as in Sicilian waters, British hospital ships found that white paint, red crosses and bright lighting gave no immunity from the Luftwaffe. The *Leinster* was bombed at 1327 September 12, but

[33] Rear Adm. Hall and *Rowan* Action Reports.

[34] War Diary German Naval Command Italy 10 Sept. pp. 37–38.

[35] Rear Adm. Conolly Supplementary Report p. 11, survivors' statements; letter 1 Feb. 1954 from Capt. Wainwright, son of the late General Jonathan M. Wainwright USA.

not hit. The *Newfoundland* was bombed in the early hours of the 13th and had to be abandoned and sunk by gunfire. The *Somersetshire* was bombed at night while lying ten miles west of the beaches, but she also escaped.

The planned build-up of Fifth Army was complicated not only by lack of port facilities but by the rushing in of reinforcements that had been urgently called for when the situation seemed desperate. On 18 September Major General Truscott's 3rd Infantry Division and the third regiment of the 45th were brought up from Sicily in LCIs and LSTs. Shore parties, now relatively efficient, worked hard to keep the beaches cleared, and the fleet of dukws was a gift from Heaven; but supplies piled up again at the water's edge between 19 and 23 September when 32 merchant ships were unloading over the beaches. On the 21st, nine big transports brought up the 34th Infantry Division U. S. Army. Some of these vessels required a week to unload. By 27 September 90 merchant ships had arrived, together with countless shuttles of beaching craft, the most valuable workhorses of the build-up. So far the weather had been fair; but on the 28th a sudden gale of wind with gusts up to 80 knots hit the beachhead. Sixty landing craft and 27 beaching craft were driven ashore and broached. Unloading was seriously disrupted, but there were enough supplies already on shore to keep the troops moving toward Naples, and excellent salvage work by the Navy soon had enough craft working so that full-scale unloading could be resumed.

During this period Captain Andrews's heterogeneous Diversionary Group was active in the north. On 11 September his forces comprised Lieutenant Commander Barnes's Motor Torpedo Boat Squadron 15, two flotillas of British MTBs and a British gunboat flotilla. Their main mission was to stop enemy coastal traffic north of Naples and to capture islands in the famous Gulf. On 12 September Ponza surrendered to Captain Andrews. His flagship (U.S. destroyer *Knight*) was boarded by an Italian officer who requested him to occupy Capri. Next day he did so, and established his headquarters in Countess Edda Ciano's villa. Ischia and Procida were occupied 14 September.

Lieutenant Commander Barnes's PT boats did not move up to Capri but spent their days in Salerno Bay and patrolled by night. Their main object was to protect the roadstead against attacks by their opposite numbers in the German Navy; and in this they were successful. In addition, they performed a variety of tasks, acting as couriers and passenger ferries between ships and the beaches, disseminating orders to ships and craft that could not otherwise be reached, laying smoke during air raids and supplying island garrisons. Their offensive capabilities could not be fully used for want of proper fuel; the tanker supposed to supply them with high octane gasoline failed to appear.

At noon 17 September, Captain Andrews's group was dissolved. British and American PTs and other small craft reverted to Admiral Hewitt's command, for operations against coastal traffic north of Naples.[36]

[36] Vice Adm. Hewitt *Action Report* p. 43; Com MTBron 15 (Lt. Cdr. Barnes) Action Reports.

CHAPTER XIV

"Avalanche" Concluded

18 September–13 October

1. *Breaking out of the Beachhead*[1]

MARSHAL KESSELRING, as we have seen, decided on 16 September to turn his back on Salerno. Two days later General Vietinghoff issued a field order for a delaying action up to the Volturno, with prolonged resistance at crucial points and thorough demolitions. Alert for possible new landings in the Bay of Naples, he ordered XIV Panzer Corps to hold the Salerno–Castellammare line and the passes between Salerno and Naples. Using this corps first as a hinge and then as right flank, LXXVI Corps would wheel left until it reached a line of defense from the Adriatic near Foggia, to the Volturno River mouth north of Naples. The movement would be completed in four weeks; Naples to be evacuated 1 October after removal or destruction of supplies. It was carried out almost exactly according to plan; the Germans were past masters at orderly retirement.

General Clark's order for Fifth Army to attack on 19 September was almost an exact complement to Vietinghoff's. The British X Corps, pivoting on its left in the high ground of the Sorrento peninsula, would seize the Nocera–Castellammare line; while VI Corps, now under command of Major General John P. Lucas USA, would drive up the Sele and a valley behind Eboli, linking up with Eighth Army on its right.

During the night of 16–17 September *Philadelphia* fired 302

[1] Lt. Gen. Truscott *Command Missions* (1954) and Clark *Calculated Risk* have the best accounts of this phase.

rounds of interdictory fire south of Battipaglia. She and destroyer *Niblack* were also called on for fire support several times next day. H.M.S. *Roberts*, five cruisers and two destroyers were called upon for fire support in the northern sector, on 17 September. *Philadelphia* was again narrowly missed by guided bombs on the 18th. Still luckily intact, she sailed to Bizerta for fuel and ammunition, and Admiral Davidson shifted his flag to *Boise*. The British cruisers and destroyers continued to fire in the northern sector; but they were unable to silence the German mobile batteries still shelling Salerno, as long as those batteries chose to stay.

On 22 September General Eisenhower received an accolade from Winston Churchill: "As the Duke of Wellington said of the Battle of Waterloo, 'It was a damned close-run thing,' but your policy of running risks has been vindicated." [2]

What the Iron Duke actually did say of Waterloo was "It has been a damned nice thing — the nearest run thing you ever saw in your life. . . . By God! I don't think it would have done if I had not been there!" [3] Eisenhower might have said the same. His headquarters were then at Amilcar near Carthage, but he had a finger on the Fifth and Eighth Armies, on the Northwest African Air Force, and on both Navies, and his decisions were prompt and resolute. This was his "finest hour" to date. And a large share of credit for the successful conclusion to AVALANCHE must be accorded to General Alexander, whom the testy Truscott well describes as a "charming gentleman and magnificent soldier."

The campaign for Naples and Foggia proceeded slowly and methodically. Montgomery's Eighth Army, sweeping around the right flank of the Fifth, crossed the Ofanto River near the Adriatic coast and, on 27 September, drove through Foggia into the hills that commanded that airdrome. In Fifth Army sector, advance elements reached Benevento on 2 October. General Truscott's 3rd Infantry Division, which had made such rapid progress in Sicily,

[2] *Closing the Ring* p. 148.
[3] John Gore ed. *Creevey Selected* (1948) pp. 141–42.

moved through a valley leading north from Battipaglia and advanced only 28 miles in eight days, to the heights east of Avellino; the 45th Division made little better time. For the terrain was mountainous and the Germans employed skilled delaying tactics. Rearguard detachments on selected hillsides, well provided with mobile artillery, forced the American troops to make slow enveloping movements. All bridges were blown; land mines were plentiful; the streets of towns were filled with rubble to second-story level. On the left flank the British X Corps, aided by the United States Rangers and elements of the 82nd Airborne, battled for eight days to break the hinge of the German movement and capture the passes. British cruisers and destroyers provided daily though diminishing gunfire support on this flank, until 28 September when the German hinge began to withdraw. Led by the British 7th Armored Division, X Corps debouched from the Sorrento peninsula on 29 September; and at 0930 October 1, the Dragoon Guards entered Naples on the heels of the Germans. The Americans, in the meantime, were pressing the German left flank beyond Naples, and by 6 October the enemy had reached his new defense line along the Volturno River.

The Allied command, up to this time, had assumed that the Germans intended to retire all the way to northern Italy,[4] which is what Rommel wished them to do. They were destined to a bitter disappointment. Kesselring's concept of defending Italy line by line won Hitler's favor, and in November he was entrusted with the unified German command in Italy.[5]

2. *Sardinia and Corsica*[6]

Sardinia and Corsica had a sentimental as well as a strategic value both for Allies and Axis in the Mediterranean. The larger island was

[4] Alexander Despatch p. 2899.

[5] *Memoirs* p. 191.

[6] Fritz Siebel "Operations in the Mediterranean of the Special Ferry Service, parts AI and II" (AGO doc D–159); War Diary German Naval Staff Operations

an ancient possession of the House of Savoy; and Corsica, French since the eighteenth century, was the cradle of the House of Bonaparte. When the surrender of Italy was announced it became a matter of great concern to the Germans to get their garrisons out of both islands, and to the Allies to get their troops in.

At that time, the 90th Panzer Grenadier Division and several German antiaircraft units were in Sardinia, and a storm-trooper brigade in Corsica. Hitler's ACHSE plan provided for the evacuation of all German troops from Sardinia to Corsica, and from Corsica to the mainland. The German naval command in Italy feared it would be unequal to the task, since Siebel ferries and other lighters had to be moved from Naples and other ports to Sardinia, with no artillery cover as had been the case in the Strait of Messina; and the operation might be interfered with by Italian troops in Sardinia. But it proved to be unexpectedly easy. "Thanks to the complaisance of the Italian army commanders there," says Kesselring, all German troops with their weapons, and an Italian paratroop division which decided to stay with the Axis – in all 25,800 men, 4650 vehicles, 4765 tons of supplies, 66 medium antitank guns, 78 heavy antitank guns, 62 tanks and 311 pieces of artillery – were ferried across the Strait of Bonifacio to Corsica by 18 September.

Sardinia with its airfields then fell into Allied possession, but the French had to fight for Corsica. And the German withdrawal from Corsica was equally successful as that of the evacuation of Sicily.

Twelve French submarines were being refitted at the French naval base of Toulon in November 1942, when the Germans took over. All but one were scuttled to prevent their falling into German hands; *Casabianca* (Capitaine de Frégate Jean L'Herminier) escaped and joined the Allied naval forces in North Africa.[7] Under General de Gaulle's direction, and with the full support of General Eisenhower, Commander L'Herminier began running agents, weapons and supplies into Corsica to build up French resistance to the Axis.

Division Sept. 1943 p. 278; War Diary German Naval Command Italy; records of French ships in the Service Historique de la Marine, Paris, especially *Collection des rapports mensuels addressés au Géneral de Gaulle aoû 1943–mai 1945* (494 pp.).

[7] Lt. Harold Wright USMCR "The Trojan Sea Horse," *Seapower* Apr. 1946.

At the time of the Italian armistice he had just delivered a contingent of French troops and brought back to Algiers a Corsican leader of the resistance who wished to recruit more. Allied shipping was then completely tied up with the Salerno operation, but a number of French warships were available to run French troops into Corsica. L'Herminier anchored at Ajaccio on 13 September and landed 109 men; the 3000-ton destroyers *Le Fantasque* and *Le Terrible* were released from screening Force "V" off Salerno to act as fast transports. Two more submarines and five torpedo boats were pressed into service, as were cruisers *Jeanne d'Arc* from Martinique and *Montcalm* from Dakar. During the remaining 19 days of September, 6600 French and North African troops, 1276 tons of matériel, and 208 guns and vehicles were safely landed at night.[8]

At the time of the armistice there were 76,000 Italian troops in Corsica. Except for a few blackshirt outfits, they welcomed the armistice, yet were unwilling to fight Germans. The German garrison of Bastia retook that town after Admiral Peloro's fleet departed to surrender, and held it. There followed one of the most curious naval operations of the war: the Germans' successful evacuation of Corsica from one end of the island while the French poured in troops at the other end.[9]

Hitler on 12 September ordered all German troops in Corsica, including those who had just crossed over from Sardinia, to be transferred to Leghorn. General von Senger und Etterlin was flown to Bastia to take command and organize the evacuation, which began on the 18th. Small craft and impressed Italian vessels shuttled back and forth, carrying troops and equipment; but most of the Germans were flown out in transport planes.[10] There was no interference with this movement by Allied surface ships at any time. But on the night of 20–21 September Wellingtons, Mitchells and Liberators of the Northwest African Air Force began to strike airfields, shipping and port installations at Bastia, Leghorn and

[8] *Collection des rapports mensuels* pp. 15–19.

[9] Lt. (jg) S. P. Karlow USNR "Notes on Corsica" (an O.S.S. Report).

[10] Naval Staff Operations War Diary pp. 308, 378; Siebel "Operations."

Pisa.[11] A second strike on Bastia the following night damaged the harbor and slowed up the embarkation. Air attacks were made on unoccupied Corsican airfields and on ferry traffic to the mainland on 25–26 September, and four transport planes were shot down by Allied fighters. H.M. submarine *Ultor*, sent to the waters off Bastia to do what she could, on 24 September hit with two torpedoes the converted tanker transport *Champagne* of 10,000 tons. She had to be beached; after refloating was again torpedoed on 27 September, and then had to be abandoned. Even during the gale of 28–29 September, traffic continued; and on 3 October the evacuation was completed. Exact figures are lacking; but between 30,000 and 40,000 troops with their arms and equipment were saved.[12]

The French troops, who had been landed at Ajaccio on the opposite coast, deployed in two columns. One, had it been stronger and moved faster, might have cut the east coast road over which the Germans were moving from Porto Vecchio to Bastia. But Senger held both road and town as long as he had need of them. A column of Moroccan *goumiers* entered Bastia four hours after the last German had departed by sea.[13]

"An exceptional feat," Hitler called this evacuation, whose successful completion "was hardly to be hoped." The Fuehrer's "fullest appreciation" went to General von Senger and his troops, as well as to the naval and air force escort and to the transports and their crews.

The failure of the Allied surface navies to attack this Bastia–Leghorn ferry route, covering 60 miles of deep water, is even more astonishing than their similar failure to halt the Sicilian evacuation; for there were no deterrents here such as narrow seas and powerful coastal batteries. September 21 was too early to spare destroyers from the troubled waters of Salerno, but the French warships

[11] Craven and Cate II p. 543.

[12] Naval Staff Operations War Diary p. 324; Gen. Senger in his ms. "Battle for Sicily" written in 1951, states that he got out "practically all the matériel"; Kesselring *Memoirs* says "nearly 40,000 men."

[13] Karlow "Notes on Corsica" pp. 4–5.

would have been better employed at that juncture in attacking the evacuation than in landing an occupation force on Corsica; and the smaller and faster Italian warships, which were now under Allied command, would have been only too glad to "oblige." As it was, the Germans with very little trouble recovered at least 30,000 troops and a first-rate general to augment their forces in Italy.

On the other side of the balance, American engineers were soon working on bomber bases in Sardinia and Corsica which became very useful in the invasion of southern France the following year. And the citizens of German-occupied France received a much-needed stimulus to their morale when they heard that the forces of General de Gaulle had secured the birthplace of Napoleon.

In the meantime, Sardinia was put to good use by Allied small craft. The Royal Navy established an advanced coastal forces base at Maddalena before the end of September, and Lieutenant Commander Barnes reported there in early October. United States Navy PTs operated thence with their British partners, under Royal Navy command, to the end of the war in the Mediterranean.[14] By October a second base was established at Bastia, Corsica, which brought the Ligurian Sea and the Gulf of Genoa within easy range of the PTs. For months these bases were primitive affairs; the proper repair and support equipment for Squadron 15 did not begin to arrive from Palermo until mid-November, so that Barnes's boys welcomed a windfall of galley equipment, cutlery and crockery from a mined and abandoned British LST, "to the incalculable improvement of their own primitive mess."

The Germans operated a large number of coasting vessels to supply their forces in central Italy from Genoa and ports on the French Riviera. To protect that traffic they assembled a fleet of small but heavily armed craft of their own, besides commandeering French and Italian types. The F-lighters with which we became familiar in Sicily, and R-boats — escort vessels 85 to 115 feet long, armed with 40-mm and bigger guns — were used in large num-

[14] MTBron 15 Action Reports, Cdr. Robert J. Bulkley ms. PT History chap vi; conversations with Capt. Barnes in 1953; War Diary German Naval Staff.

bers. Most of these craft were more heavily armed than the PTs, whose only lethal superiority lay in their unreliable Mark VIII torpedoes. Nevertheless, the PTs made valiant efforts.

Beginning in October 1943 the Germans laid a minefield barrier along the Italian coast to protect an inshore channel for their coastal traffic. While it proved effective against destroyers and larger vessels, motor torpedo boats could get through because of their shallow draft.

The first definite score for MTBron 15 occurred during the night of 22–23 October, south of Giglio Island. Lieutenant Edwin A. DuBose USNR, in tactical command of three PTs, made an undetected torpedo attack on a small cargo vessel escorted by four E- or R-boats. One of four torpedoes fired hit the ship, which disintegrated in a violent explosion.[15] Between Giglio and Elba on the night of 2–3 November, two PTs under Lieutenant Richard H. O'Brien torpedoed a converted tanker estimated to be of 4000 tons,[16] which, before disappearing, managed to put an incendiary bullet through a gasoline tank of *PT–207* and into the officers' country. The explosion blew a hatch, and flames shot up to the top of the radar mast. A quick-witted radioman grabbed a fire extinguisher, opened its nozzle, threw it below, and slammed shut the hatch cover; another sailor blanketed the tank compartment with CO_2, and the flames were smothered.

On many winter nights the boats could not go out because of heavy seas, but it took really foul weather to daunt the PTs. On one such night, 29–30 November 1943, when *PT–204* was about three and a half miles from Bastia, four German R-boats suddenly appeared about 75 yards away on an opposite course; then a fifth showed up crossing her bows. Lieutenant (jg) E. S. A. Clifford USNR, the C.O., called for hard left rudder, but was unable to avoid

[15] While the third boat, *PT–212*, Lt. (jg) T. L. Sinclair, was lining up its sights for a shot, a circling torpedo from one of the other boats just missed her. Shortly after, the O.T.C. radioed "How many have you fired?" "None yet," replied Sinclair, "I'm too damned busy dodging yours!" Bulkley Ms. PT History p. 382.

[16] War Diary German Naval Staff Operations Division Nov. 1943 p. 54 calls this craft "Subchaser 2206," and states that 69 of her crew were saved.

a glancing collision with the R-boat. As they sheered off, the boats exchanged machine-gun fire at about ten yards' range. *PT–204* was riddled with bullets, but all of them missed the gasoline tanks, and not a man was scratched.

In the fall of 1943 the Germans began to operate a number of Italian torpedo boats – fast coastal destroyers of 30-knot speed – which they had captured. The PTs had several brushes with this class. Two PTs ran into a pair of them one night when patrolling between Elba and Leghorn, and were glad to escape. Torpedo boats shelled Bastia for 15 minutes one night in December, at a time when the seas were too heavy outside for the PTs to sortie. Lieutenant Commander Barnes, expecting a return call a few nights later, led four PTs out of Bastia as a reception committee. Within ten minutes of getting on station they picked up two torpedo boats heading in at 20 knots. The Germans promptly reversed course. Barnes pursued, hoping to maneuver them into the arms of the Elba PT patrol. His hope was realized, and off Elba a mêlée took place, with shore batteries joining in; but no one was hurt. According to the German records the shelling of Bastia could not be carried out that night "owing to unfavorable weather conditions." [17]

Although this sort of naval warfare was inconclusive, it did serve to prevent the enemy from making best use of his control over the Italian coast from Gaëta northward.

3. *Naples Secured; Parthian Shots*

Naples, entered by Allied troops 1 October, proved to be another challenge to their ingenuity. Departing Germans left the harbor even more of a shambles than that of Palermo. Fires were burning along the waterfront, access to every pier and mole was blocked by wrecks, and on the bottom of the harbor vessels, cranes, trucks and even an occasional locomotive were obscenely piled. Ashore, Vietinghoff's army had set a new record for cruel and

[17] War Diary German Naval Staff Operations Division Dec. 1943 p. 222.

malicious damage. The spaghetti factories on which the people depended for their sustenance had been blown up and utterly destroyed. The water system had been deliberately polluted. A German demolition squad even sought out the villa whither the Italian government had transferred the Neapolitan archives, soaked them with gasoline and burned the entire deposit of precious documents. Furniture and bedding had been heaped up in the courts of the principal hotels, soaked with gasoline and fired; while Parker's Hotel, left intact and so selected for United States naval headquarters, was provided with an infernal machine walled into a wine cellar, which American engineers discovered just in time to prevent a catastrophe. Another delayed time bomb exploded in front of the central post office at an hour when the place was crowded with civilians.

Fortunately, the Allies were prepared to deal with this situation. From his experience at Bizerta and Palermo, Commodore William A. Sullivan knew what to expect. Designated principal salvage officer on the staff of the Allied Naval Commander, Mediterranean, he had collected a team composed of bluejackets and United States Army Engineers, and had his plans ready. Sullivan operated in complete harmony with the Royal Navy port command under Rear Admiral John A. V. Morse RN, with a U. S. Navy fire-fighter outfit under Commander W. L. Wroten USNR and a New Zealand Navy hydrographic unit. All these moved into Naples promptly. The waterfront fires were brought under control; salvage pumps delivered water for civilian consumption from pockets in the mains of the city water supply, while the engineers were repairing them; piers were cleared of heaps of destroyed equipment; if a wreck alongside could not be moved it was bridged over and became a pier; access roads were bulldozed through the ruins of buildings near the waterfront. Although the harbor presented a spectacle of utter desolation, the situation was not too bad, since the Germans had planned their demolitions rather for revenge, to wreck the economy of Naples, than to prevent Allied use of the port. Pyramided vessels presented no great difficulty to U. S. Navy salvage tugs and Royal Navy heavy-lift ships. While these wrecks were awaiting their turn, souvenir hunters and harbor thieves were kept off by signs: DANGER: POISON GAS! And to give convincing authority to these signs, stink bombs were broken out on each wreck. The larger of two graving docks, with a 5000-ton ship in it, had been demolished so inefficiently that in ten days' time both dock and ship were repaired and the space made available for unloading. By the end of the year, more Allied tonnage was being discharged in Naples than the maximum official capacity of the port before the war. And minor ports on the Gulf, such as Nisida and Pozzuoli, had been cleared and opened as beaching craft and fueling bases.[18]

Until the harbor of Naples was cleared, Salerno had to serve as the principal port of entry for the Fifth Army. Here a U-boat delivered the first Parthian shot of Operation AVALANCHE. Destroyer *Buck*, patrolling the Gulf on the night of 8–9 October, got a surface radar contact shortly before midnight. As she was tracking the submarine, one or two torpedoes struck forward of her single stack and exploded with great violence. Lieutenant Commander "Mike" Klein, the much beloved skipper, and most of the officers, were killed in the explosion, and the destroyer began to go down. The men launched all life rafts that were intact, put such wounded as they could find on board them, and abandoned ship. About four minutes after the hit, her stern stood straight up for 100 feet; she plunged down half way, shuddered, and then slid under. As there had not been time to set all depth charges on "safe" before they became inaccessible, some exploded, killing or wounding swimmers and blowing the bottoms out of all the balsa rafts. There were no other ships nearby. An Army transport plane spotted floating survivors at 1000 October 9 and dropped three rubber life rafts, a godsend to swimming survivors. As no other planes or vessels appeared, they attempted to row ashore, 45 to 50 miles distant. Finally, at 2000, as a second night was descending, a destroyer was sighted and her attention attracted by shots from a Very pistol. This was U.S.S.

[18] E. E. Hauser "Commodore of Sunken Ships" *Sat. Eve. Post* 7 Oct. 1944; memo. from Rear Adm. Sullivan (Ret.) Jan. 1954. A graduate of M.I.T., he had specialized in naval salvage work since 1917.

Gleaves. Shortly after, *Plunkett* and H.M.S. *LCT–170* arrived at the scene to help pick up the men still alive – only 94 out of a crew of 260.[19]

U–371 managed to approach within 1100 yards of a Salerno convoy returning to Oran off the coast of eastern Algeria, under a full moon in the early hours of 13 October, without being detected. Destroyer *Bristol* of the convoy screen was struck by this U-boat's torpedo only 10 seconds after its hydrophone effect had been picked up by her sound gear. The destroyer buckled near the forward stack and both bow and stern angled upward; but Patrick J. Phillips, torpedoman's mate 3rd class, had time to check all depth charges on "safe" with his flashlight before the fantail tilted so high that he lost his footing. Since Commander J. A. Glick, the skipper, was injured by the explosion, his "exec." ordered Abandon Ship a few minutes before she sank. Two other destroyers rescued and saved 17 out of 22 officers and 224 out of 271 enlisted men.[20]

Operation AVALANCHE was concluded. Salerno and Naples had been won, and at no excessive cost, as this table of casualties indicates: –

	Killed	*Missing*	*Wounded*
U. S. Navy [21]	296	551	422
Royal Navy [22]	83	–	43
U. S. Army [23]	788	1,318	2,841
British Army [23]	982	2,230	4,060

[19] Senior Surviving Officer, Lt. (jg) John A. Hoye USNR "Report on Sinking of *Buck*" 5 Nov. 1943. The submarine was *U–616;* its War Diary is in Tambach docs. T–420, PG–30647.

[20] C.O. *Bristol* "Report of Action with Enemy Resulting in Loss of Ship" 26 Oct. 1943; War Diary of *U–371* in Tambach docs. T–265–A, PG–30433. Cdr. Glick here commends as responsible for the orderly abandonment the "exec." Lt. Cdr. W. J. Lederer, in whose *All the Ship's at Sea* (1950) is a vivid account of the sinking. *U–371* was sunk by joint action of French destroyer *Sénégalais*, U.S.S. *Pride* and *Joseph E. Campbell* on 3 May 1944. Mediterranean convoys at this time were frequently attacked by German planes based on airfields in southern France. One such attack, off Algiers on 6 Nov. 1943, resulted in the sinking of U.S. destroyer *Beatty* by an aërial torpedo, with the loss of 11 men.

[21] Vice Adm. Hewitt *Action Report* p. 216 – casualties through 31 Dec., including those of *Buck* and *Bristol.* Most of the "missing," being crews of ships in actions with enemy, were killed.

[22] Figures from British Admiralty.

[23] *Fifth Army History* I 98; these are through 6 Oct.; the "missing" were mostly P.O.W.

The loss of ships also was less than had been expected, in view of the Luftwaffe's new weapon, and the three United States destroyers lost (*Rowan, Buck, Bristol*) were sunk by torpedoes. The U. S. Navy also lost a minesweeper, a tug and six LCTs. Two cruisers and numerous beaching and other small craft had been damaged; three Liberty ships had been sunk and two damaged. The Royal Navy lost H.M.S. *Abdiel* at Taranto, hospital ship *Newfoundland* and five LCTs at Salerno. And there is a long list of shipping damaged in varying degrees.[24]

For the naval historian recording these events, it is a pleasure to read a tribute from General Westphal, Kesselring's chief of staff. After outlining the difficulties the Germans had encountered, he wrote: "But the greatest distress suffered by the troops was caused by the fire of ships' guns of heavy caliber, from which they could find no protection in the rocky soil." [25]

Already the Salerno beaches had been closed to supply and build-up traffic, and although Salerno harbor continued in use, it was replaced by Naples as a major port of entry. Within a month of the great crisis in AVALANCHE there was not an Allied soldier or sailor to be met with on the Plain of Salerno. The native population was busily engaged in clearing up the debris of war and preparing for winter plowing. The temples of Paestum, gray in the morning light, golden brown in the setting sun, continued their millennial vigil over the Gulf.

[24] Vice Adm. Hewitt *Action Report* pp. 171, 206–10.
[25] *The German Army in the West* p. 151.

PART IV

Anzio[1]

(*Operation* SHINGLE)

8 November 1943–4 June 1944

[1] Sacmed *Report,* i.e., General Sir Henry M. Wilson *Report by Supreme Allied Commander Mediterranean to the C.C.S. on the Italian Campaign 8 Jan.–10 May 1944* (there is a British and an American edition, both 1946); Com VIII 'Phib (Rear Adm. F. J. Lowry) Action Report on Anzio 22 Feb. 1944, Supplementary Action Report 17 May and "The Naval Side of the Anzio Invasion" U.S. Naval Inst. *Proceedings* LXXX No. 1 (Jan. 1954); CTG 81.8 (Capt. R. W. Cary) "Action Report Establishment of Anzio Beachhead 21 Jan.–8 Feb." 14 Feb. 1944; Lt. Cdr. Charles Moran USNR "Anzio-Nettuno Landings" – a draft written for the Combat Narratives series but never published. Numerous Admiralty documents have been made available to me through the courtesy of Rear Adm. Roger M. Bellairs RN; among these, Rear Adm. Troubridge's Action Report was particularly valuable. Lt. Gen. L. K. Truscott Jr. *Command Missions, a Personal Story* (1954) chap. vi is a somewhat more personal account of the ground fighting than the Historical Division of the Army's pamphlet *Anzio Beachhead* (1947) which has a well-rounded narrative and excellent maps. Maj. Gen. John P. Lucas USA "The Code Name Was SHINGLE," a ms. narrative based on his private diary, completed 1946; *Fifth Army History* (published in the field 1944) Part IV *Cassino and Anzio;* "Anzio, Seizing and Holding the Beachhead 22 January–23 May," a document prepared in Fifth Army headquarters; Maj. D. J. L. Fitzgerald *History of the Irish Guards in the Second World War* (1949); "Mediterranean Allied Air Forces' Operations in Support of SHINGLE 1 Jan.–15 Feb. 1944"; Eric Linklater *The Campaign in Italy* (H.M. Stationery Office 1951) is a good comprehensive account. Works earlier cited, by Churchill, Eisenhower, Alexander, Clark, Butcher, Craven and Cate; Jacques Mordal *Cassino* (Paris, 1952).

On the German side: The works by Kesselring and Westphal earlier cited, and German Military Document Section of U. S. Army "The German Operation at Anzio," a study from German sources; "Situation Reports, Mediterranean, Adriatic, Ægean and Black Seas" in War Diary German Naval Staff for 1944 (a Tambach Document recorded on microfilm in Office of Naval History); Gen. Wolf Hauser's chap. xii of "Feldzug in Italien" (prepared for U. S. Forces in 1947).

CHAPTER XV

Winter Stalemate

November 1943–January 1944

1. *Alarums and Excursions*

OPERATION SHINGLE, the seizure of a beachhead at Anzio and Nettuno near Rome, is unique in the naval history of the European war. It was the only amphibious operation in that theater where the Army was unable promptly to exploit a successful landing, or where the enemy contained Allied forces on a beachhead for a prolonged period. Indeed, in the entire war there is none to compare with it; even the Okinawa campaign in the Pacific was shorter.

This Anzio campaign was originally planned as a "left hook" on the enemy's flank to break his hold on Allied troops in the Garigliano and Rapido river valleys. About the middle of November 1943, the German Army ceased fighting rear-guard actions and dug in on mountain slopes ideal for defense along a line from a point on the Gulf of Gaëta to a point near Ortona on the Adriatic. If Allied forces were to continue their conquest of the Italian peninsula and not be content with holding the enemy, they had better do something besides beating against this Winter Line, as it was called, or any subsequent defensive line the Germans might set up. Why not exploit their sea power to effect one or more "end runs" — amphibious landings behind the enemy's right flank, to divert his strength and cut off his routes from Germany?

Generals Eisenhower, Alexander and Clark began to think about end runs as soon as Naples was secured. In late October Eisenhower approved a plan of Alexander's for a landing south of the Tiber at a time when the Fifth Army had reached a point where landing force and main army could be mutually supporting. Note well this proposed timing; for the abandonment of it doomed Operation SHINGLE to long frustration and heavy casualties. Eisenhower then agreed to press the Combined Chiefs of Staff to retain enough LSTs in the Mediterranean to mount the left hook. He pointed out that the amphibious force must be joined by the armies advancing overland within 48 hours, owing to the uncertainty of maintaining it by sea during winter weather; he estimated that the Fifth Army, with the Eighth on its right (Adriatic) flank, would not be in the requisite position before mid-December.

On 8 November, Alexander issued a directive for continuing the advance up the spine of Italy, starting 20 November; and on the same day he entrusted to Clark the preliminary planning for Operation SHINGLE. Anzio was promptly selected as the target because of its proximity to the Alban Hills, which dominated the main roads to Rome. The initial plan, approved by General Alexander 25 November, provided that troops be landed there when Fifth Army had reached a line a few miles northwest of Frosinone.[1]

Thus the whole concept of the Anzio operation depended on a successful Allied advance up the spine. When (and if) the Army reached Frosinone, the amphibious landing would start, with the prime objective of capturing the Alban Hills ahead of the Fifth Army. Once in possession of that ancient home of Romulus and Remus, the landing force could cut the enemy's communications and move into the city that Romulus founded. But if the two Armies failed to carry their objectives, or at least to be in a fair way to reach them a week before the amphibious D-day, Anzio would have to be postponed or abandoned. So everyone assumed at that time.

Briefly, the operation as then conceived was to land Rangers at Anzio in the small hours of 20 December to secure the port, and to drop paratroops on the Anzio–Albano road to prevent the arrival of

[1] Alexander Despatch (Supplement to *London Gazette* 6 June 1950) pp. 2908–09.

enemy reinforcements.[2] Next, but before daylight, the 3rd U. S. Infantry Division would be landed with seven days' supplies and no follow-up, to hold the beachhead until the Fifth Army arrived at Frosinone to lock arms with the Anzio force and drive the Germans north of Rome.

On 28 November 1943, Montgomery's Eighth Army, six divisions strong, moved across the Sangro River, raising the curtain on the first act of a long battle for Rome. Bad weather, swollen rivers, impassable roads, exposure of troops to winter rains, and determined resistance checked this drive far south of the first objective, Pescara. And Mark Clark's Fifth Army, eight divisions strong, starting 1 December, enjoyed no better success.

Next day, a devastating air assault on the important supply port of Bari further delayed the planned advance. On the night of 2 December 105 Ju–88 bombers surprised the port of Bari, crowded with some 30 sail of Allied shipping and brilliantly lighted. Coming in behind planes that dropped "window" to confuse radar operators, the German bombers met little opposition. Direct hits on one or two ammunition ships started a chain reaction of explosions; a bombed tanker spouted burning oil which spread over the harbor a sheet of fire, so that in the end, although few ships were hit, 16 vessels carrying 38,000 tons of cargo were destroyed and 8 others were damaged.[3] One of the destroyed ships carried a quantity of mustard gas for retaliation in case the Germans started gas warfare. Some of this was released, but fortunately an offshore breeze carried it out to sea. There were many instances of heroic rescues. Ensign Kay K. Vesole USNR of the naval armed guard of Liberty ship *John Bascom*, twice wounded, went from gun to gun directing action, led a rescue party below to carry wounded men to the boat deck, supervised the loading of the only undestroyed lifeboat, and helped

[2] Sacmed *Report* p. 6. The paratroops' part was taken out later, as it was felt that the British division could take their objective.

[3] War Diary German Naval Staff Dec. 1943 pp. 22, 44; Craven and Cate II pp. 587–88, minimize the affair, state only 30 bombers attacked. Five ships destroyed, and one of the damaged, were U. S. Liberty ships; the rest were British, Polish, Norwegian, Italian and Dutch.

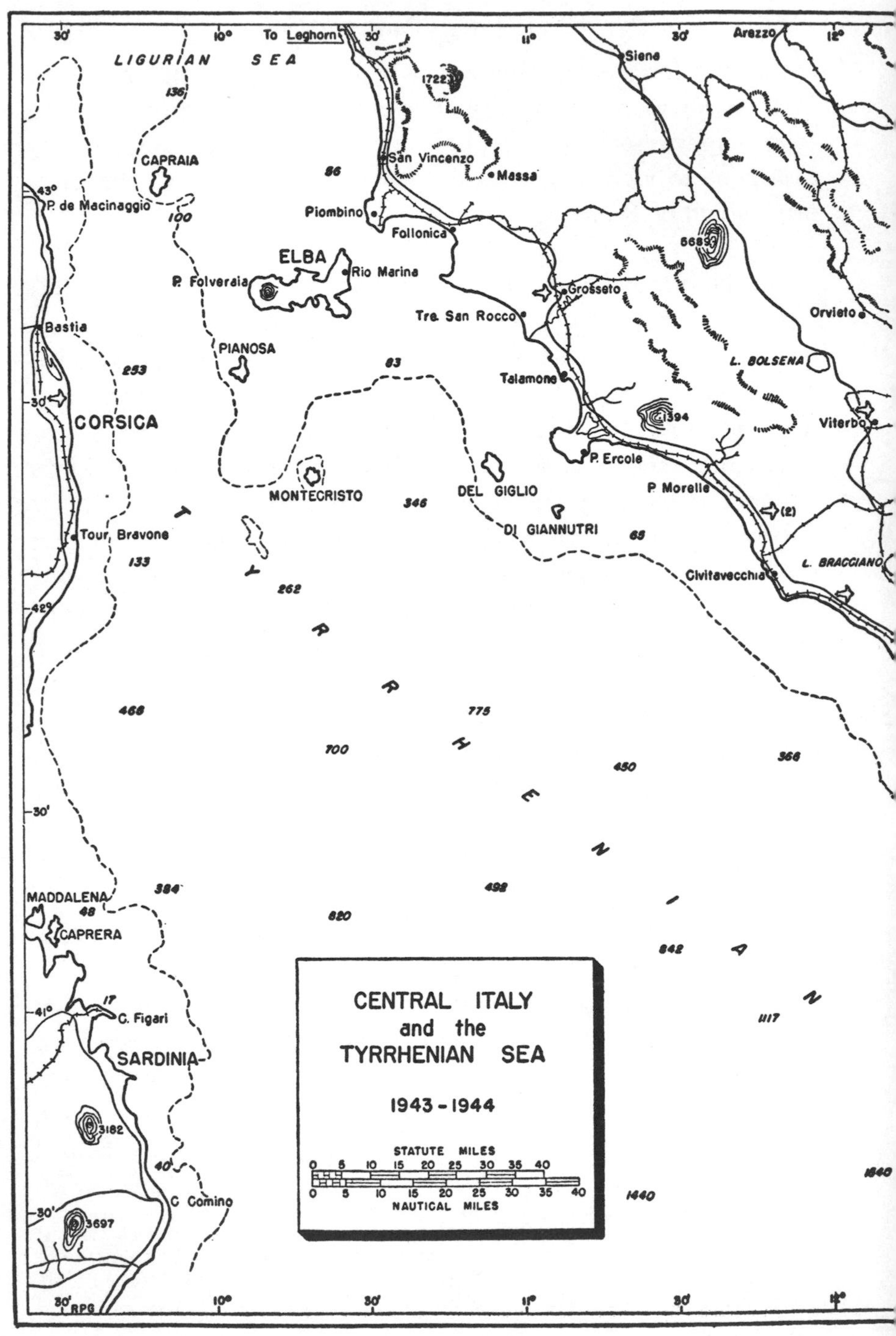
CENTRAL ITALY
and the
TYRRHENIAN SEA
1943-1944
STATUTE MILES
NAUTICAL MILES
LIGURIAN SEA
To Leghorn
Siena
Arezzo
San Vincenzo
Massa
CAPRAIA
P. de Macinaggio
Piombino
Follonica
ELBA
Rio Marina
P. Folveraia
Grosseto
Tre San Rocco
Orvieto
L. BOLSENA
PIANOSA
Bastia
Talamone
CORSICA
Viterbo
P. Ercole
MONTECRISTO
DEL GIGLIO
P. Morelle
DI GIANNUTRI
Tour Bravone
Civitavecchia
L. BRACCIANO
TYRRHENIAN
MADDALENA
CAPRERA
C. Figari
SARDINIA
C. Comino
RPG

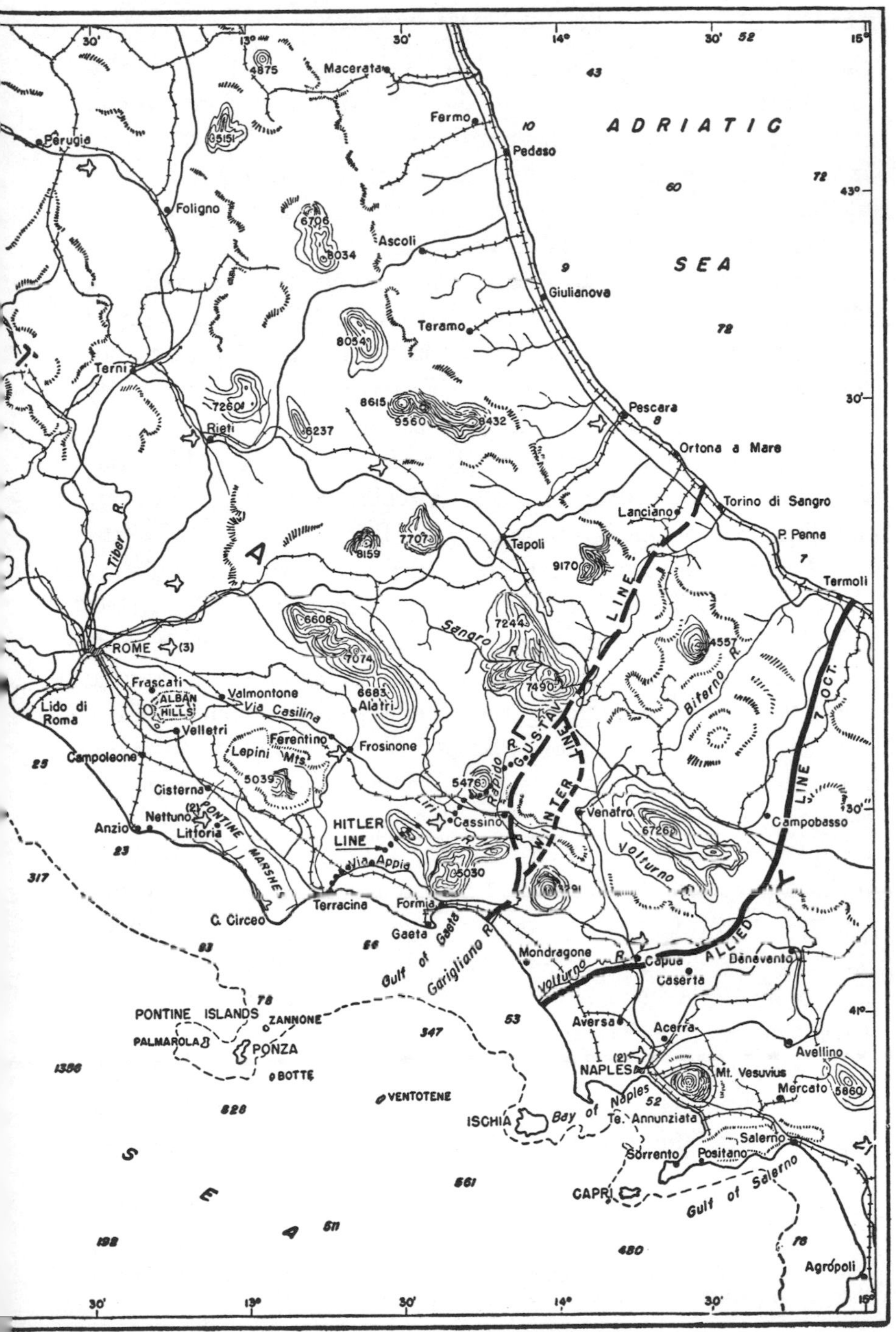

ADRIATIC
SEA
Perugia
Foligno
Macerata
Fermo
Pedaso
Ascoli
Giulianova
Teramo
Terni
Rieti
Pescara
Ortona a Mare
Torino di Sangro
Lanciano
P. Penna
Termoli
Tapoli
Tiber R.
Sangro R.
Biferno R.
ROME
Frascati
Valmontone
Via Casilina
ALBAN HILLS
Lido di Roma
Velletri
Ferentino
Frosinone
Alatri
Lepini Mts.
Campoleone
Cisterna
Nettuno
Anzio
Littoria
PONTINE MARSHES
HITLER LINE
Via Appia
Cassino
Liri R.
Rapido R.
GUSTAV LINE
WINTER LINE
Venafro
Volturno
Campobasso
LINE 7 OCT.
ALLIED
Terracina
Formia
Gaeta
C. Circeo
Gulf of Gaeta
Garigliano R.
Mondragone
Volturno R.
Capua
Caserta
Benevento
Aversa
Acerra
Avellino
NAPLES
Mt. Vesuvius
Mercato
Bay of Naples
Te. Annunziata
Salerno
Sorrento
Positano
ISCHIA
CAPRI
Gulf of Salerno
Agropoli
PONTINE ISLANDS
ZANNONE
PALMAROLA
PONZA
BOTTE
VENTOTENE
SEA

carry the wounded to a bomb shelter on shore, before he died from loss of blood. About 50 sailors of the U.S. naval armed guards and at least 75 American merchant mariners were killed in this raid.[4] It was three weeks before the harbor could be brought back to normal operation. This was the most destructive enemy air raid on shipping since the attack on Pearl Harbor.

At the time of the Bari disaster the SEXTANT conference of the Combined Chiefs of Staff was meeting with President Roosevelt and the Prime Minister at Cairo.[5] Although most of the sessions were devoted to Pacific and Far Eastern questions, the entire strategy of the war was once more overhauled.

The principal Mediterranean question at Cairo was, How far should the Allies attempt to push the Italian campaign? The same old difference of opinion prevailed: the British wanting to "nourish" Italian operations in the hope of reaching the River Po by spring, even if this meant a weakening or postponement of OVERLORD (the Normandy invasion); the Americans insisting that no new Mediterranean operation be undertaken unless as a supporting move for OVERLORD, and that the planned redeployment to England should proceed as rapidly as possible. Eisenhower, however, proposed that SHINGLE be put on as planned (for he still expected the occupation of Frosinone by Fifth Army in mid-December); and to that end he prevailed upon the Combined Chiefs of Staff to let him retain 68 of the 90 LSTs then in the Mediterranean, which were earmarked for prompt transfer to the United Kingdom. The Cairo Conference did not actually approve Operation SHINGLE, but assumed that it would take place if the Fifth and Eighth Armies advanced as anticipated.

At Cairo the long-planned amphibious operation against the Andaman Islands, as a preliminary to recovering Burma from the Japanese, was definitely canceled. The unfortunate South-East Asia

[4] Ms. "History of the Naval Armed Guard Afloat" pp. 166–69, Naval Administrative History Series.

[5] Inclusive dates 22 Nov.–7 Dec. 1943, the Teheran Conference with Stalin coming between the two sessions on 27–30 Nov. Eisenhower *Crusade in Europe* chap. xi, and Churchill *Closing the Ring* pp. 325–419.

theater commander, Vice Admiral Lord Louis Mountbatten, was first ordered to send about half his amphibious craft, and (on 7 January 1944) all the rest of them, to the Mediterranean and England. His loss was SHINGLE's gain; all the big British LSIs used to lift the British half of VI Corps to Anzio came from Mountbatten's fleet, as did 15 LSTs of the United States Navy.[6]

General Eisenhower was now appointed Supreme Allied Commander for Operation OVERLORD and, under him, Admiral Sir Bertram Ramsay RN of the Allied Naval forces, and Air Chief Marshal Tedder of the air forces. This decision removed several familiar figures from the Mediterranean, where General Sir Henry Maitland Wilson now became Supreme Allied Commander Mediterranean ("Sacmed"), Admiral Sir John Cunningham RN the naval commander (to relieve Admiral of the Fleet A. B. Cunningham, now appointed First Sea Lord), General Sir Harold Alexander the ground forces commander, and Lieutenant General I. C. Eaker USA air commander. These new appointments went into effect on or about 1 January 1944.

2. *Mr. Churchill Adopts* SHINGLE

Shortly after the Cairo Conference adjourned (7 December), the assumption upon which General Eisenhower had accepted the Anzio operation collapsed. Fifth Army, starting its drive 1 December, in ten days had not even reached the foot of Monte Cassino, a hopeless distance from the goal of Frosinone. Eighth Army, too, was bogged down. Thus it was impossible to start SHINGLE on schedule.

This situation inspired a striking revision of the proposed operation. On 10 December General Clark suggested that the attack on Anzio be launched "without waiting until the overland attack was within supporting distance. Once in, the landing force would con-

[6] Mountbatten *Report to the C.C.S. by Supreme Allied Commander South-East Asia 1943–45* (H.M. Stationery Office 1951) pp. 29–30; Churchill *Closing the Ring* pp. 431, 441.

solidate and make a stand until main Fifth Army came up. This conception would demand both a larger force and a resupply."[7] Fateful and prophetic suggestions! It was exactly what the Army was forced to do on Anzio beachhead — "consolidate and make a stand until main Fifth Army came up." But the LSTs were due to leave for the United Kingdom on 15 January, and without them no run into Anzio would be possible. Consequently, Clark on 18 December recommended to Alexander, with the concurrence of Eisenhower (who was then at Clark's headquarters), that SHINGLE be canceled; and canceled it was on 22 December.[8]

The Anzio operation should now have been allowed to die a natural death, as happened to many projected and planned campaigns in the course of the war.[9] On the contrary, it was revived the very next day, the 23rd.

Everyone cognizant of the situation in Italy felt very much discouraged at Christmastide 1943. The Allied line, starting near Ortona in the Adriatic, ran diagonally across Italy, following the east banks of the Sangro and Garigliano Rivers to the Gulf of Gaëta.[10] Troops who had not even cracked the German Winter Line were further depressed when they learned that the enemy was constructing, a few miles westward, the Gustav Line, to be rendered famous by its Monte Cassino anchor.

Mr. Churchill now stepped into the breach by summoning a special conference at Tunis for Christmas Day and presiding over it himself.[11] The Prime Minister was gravely concerned over the

[7] *Fifth Army History* Part IV p. 14; Truscott *Command Missions* p. 291.

[8] *Calculated Risk* pp. 250–1; Vice Adm. Lowry in U. S. Naval Inst. *Proceedings* LXXX (Jan. 1954) p. 25.

[9] Vice Adm. Oscar C. Badger in "Problems of Combined Logistics," U. S. Naval War College *Information Service* III No. 3 (Nov. 1950), states that some 28 different operations were approved by the C.C.S. at Cairo and submitted to the Combined Logistics Staff for a report on feasibility and timing; that they approved of only three in Europe — OVERLAND, DRAGOON (Southern France), and the continuance of the Italian campaign — and of two in the Pacific.

[10] Eisenhower *Crusade in Europe* p. 206.

[11] The conference was attended by the Prime Minister, General Eisenhower, General Wilson, Maj. Gen. W. Bedell Smith, Air Chief Marshal Tedder, and Admiral Sir John Cunningham.

Italian campaign. At Cairo he had remarked, "Whoever holds Rome holds the title deeds of Italy" [12] — a *non sequitur*, as the Vatican might have told him. He now harped on the theme that it would be folly to invade France with Rome in enemy hands and Italy only half recovered. With all his native eloquence he insisted that a jab in the enemy's flank at Anzio would cause him to withdraw forces from central and southern Italy and hasten the Allied capture of Rome. General Eisenhower protested, but was overruled. Alexander deferred to his Prime Minister. The operation disliked by the generals became Mr. Churchill's particular "baby." But he insisted that a British infantry division be added to the single American division provided by the initial plan.

Immediately after this Christmas Day conference, firm appointments for SHINGLE were made. Rear Admiral Frank J. Lowry USN,[13] who had relieved Rear Admiral Conolly as "Comlandcrabnaw" and Rear Admiral Hall as Commander VIII Amphibious Force, had been designated naval commander for SHINGLE in November. Shortly after the conference it was decided by General Clark that Major General John P. Lucas USA, who had relieved General Dawley as VI Corps commander at Salerno, would command the ground forces. SHINGLE was to be a really combined operation like AVALANCHE, with British and American forces intermingled; but the naval and military commanders were both to be American.

Thus at Tunis it was decided to hurl amphibious forces into Anzio, come hell or high water. Instead of being launched to link up with the main body of Fifth Army when it reached a line north of Frosinone, SHINGLE would now be carried out regardless, in the

[12] Sacmed *Report* (U.S. ed.) p. 4.

[13] Frank J. Lowry, b. 1888; Annapolis '11. Service in various ships until 1917; navigator and ordnance officer of *Raleigh* and "exec." of *Pittsburgh* during World War I; "exec." and C.O. of receiving ship, Mare Island, 1919–22; Naval War College course 1925–26; 1st Lt. *California* 1926–28; professor of naval science and tactics at Univ. of Calif. 1929; C.O. *Hale* 1931; training officer N.T.S. San Diego 1933; "exec." of *Tuscaloosa* 1936; C.O. *Minneapolis* 1940–42 when promoted Rear Admiral; commanded N.T.S. Great Lakes 1942; Cdr. Moroccan Sea Frontier Forces in Feb., "Comlandcrabnaw" 26 Sept., and Com VIII 'Phib Force 8 Nov. 1943. Subsequent to SHINGLE he commanded an amphibious group of the Pacific Fleet, served as head of Naval section General Board of U. S. Forces European Theater, and in office of C.N.O. Retired 1950 as Vice Admiral.

hope of drawing off Germans from the Fifth Army front. It would be a two-division instead of a one-division assault — eventually six divisions were needed to hold the beachhead. But where was the troop-lift to be found? A sufficient number of American LCIs and British LSIs were available for a two-division assault, but 56 LSTs were scheduled to sail for the United Kingdom on 15 January, leaving fewer than 30 in the Mediterranean — not half enough. A second appeal to the C.C.S. to stay them had to be granted. "Having kept them so long," wired Churchill to the President, "it would seem irrational to remove them for the very week when they can render decisive service. What, also, could be more dangerous than to let the Italian battle stagnate and fester on for another three months?" [14]

Mr. Churchill felt that he had conceded a great deal in abandoning another pet project, an Allied descent on Rhodes, in order to get enough LSTs for Anzio. President Roosevelt, in his reply to Churchill's announcement of the Tunis decisions, agreed to let Sacmed retain the 56 LSTs on the understanding "that OVERLORD remains the paramount operation," and "that Rhodes and the Ægean must be sidetracked." [15]

Even with this concession, there would not be enough beaching craft in the Mediterranean to provide more than seven days' supplies for the troops at Anzio beachhead. Planning for the operation proceeded under this distressing restriction, which, furthermore, made the land attack up the peninsula desperately urgent. What if troops could not hang onto the Anzio beachhead when the Navy had to withdraw its support? The result might be a second Dunkirk. General "Jumbo" Wilson, Eisenhower's successor as Supreme Allied Commander Mediterranean Theater, said on this point: "Should maintenance not be possible, the force would have to be withdrawn with total loss of equipment, some loss of personnel and serious risk to landing craft needed for the later assault against the

[14] *Closing the Ring* p. 437.
[15] *Closing the Ring* pp. 437, 441.

south of France. However, the prize to be gained was high enough to warrant the risk." [16] Admiral Sir John Cunningham enjoined Admiral Lowry, the naval task force commander for the operation, "to make clear to the Commanding General of the Army forces to be landed that no reliance can be placed on maintenance over beaches, owing to the probability of unfavorable weather, and your plans must allow for the disembarkation of the whole force immediately after the assault and the urgent need for withdrawal of LSTs for other operations." Pleasant prospect for Admiral Lowry and General Lucas!

A special conference on Operation SHINGLE was held by Mr. Churchill at the Villa Taylor in Marrakech, Morocco, where he was recovering from pneumonia, on 7–8 January 1944. Generals Wilson, Alexander and W. Bedell Smith, and Admiral Sir John Cunningham, were present; but Clark, Lucas and Lowry were not invited. Clark sent members of his staff, and Lucas was represented by his VI Corps operations and supply officers, Colonels W. H. Hill and E. J. O'Neill.

General Lucas, already feeling like a sacrificial lamb, thought he was "entitled to one bleat" as to the date, and instructed his colonels to press for a postponement of D-day from 20 to 25 January, to allow for a proper rehearsal; they finally obtained the 22nd, as a compromise. Alexander and Cunningham insisted that continuous maintenance, not a mere seven-day supply, must be provided, and that more LSTs must be allotted. Agreement was reached that gave Lowry enough LSTs for the first twelve days, after which the number would gradually be scaled down. The American colonels presented a plan for preloading trucks at Naples, driving them onto LSTs and, at the beachhead, driving them directly to supply dumps while the LSTs took empty trucks from the previous echelon and returned to Naples for more supplies. This procedure, which had been successfully followed by Seventh Fleet in the Southwest Pacific, was "completely disapproved" by the Prime Minister, Admiral

[16] Sacmed *Report* (British edition) pp. 12–13.

Cunningham and General Bedell Smith, and prohibited. Carried out nevertheless, it shortened the unloading time of LSTs at the beachhead from a full day to a single hour; without it, Operation SHINGLE would have been doomed to disaster.[17]

Churchill's report to Roosevelt that "unanimous agreement" had been reached about Anzio and that everyone was "in good heart" [18] doubtless represented what he, in his convalescence, felt; but it was far from being a fact. Actually he had imposed his will on the generals and admirals against their better judgment.

Admiral Lowry started for Anzio with a feeling that he had an even chance of success, but General Lucas was deeply discouraged. He did not see how his two divisions could be expected to contain the four German divisions reported to be in the neighborhood of Anzio. Nor did many others. General Patton flew from Palermo to Naples to say good-by. He blurted out, "John, there is no one in the Army I hate to see killed as much as you, but you can't get out of this alive. Of course, you might be badly wounded. No one ever blames a *wounded* general!" He advised Lucas to read the Bible when the going got tough, and then turned to one of the VI Corps commander's aides and said, "Look here; if things get too bad, shoot the old man in the backside; but don't you dare kill the old fellow!" [19]

3. *Anzio Plans and Preparations, 1–21 January*

Planners for the operation had assembled by New Year's Eve at Fifth Army headquarters in the imitation Palais de Versailles which an eighteenth-century king of Naples had built at Caserta. They were aided by a special group from Allied headquarters which had

[17] The Lucas Diary contains the gist of what the two colonels reported to him; and Truscott *Command Missions* pp. 298–301 summarizes their report of the proceedings to him. Compare Clark *Calculated Risk* pp. 259–60.

[18] *Closing the Ring* p. 447.

[19] Lucas Diary; but I have refrained from quoting Gen. Patton's *exact* words.

already lost four officers in making a study of the Anzio beaches.[20] Plans were completed and approved in record time, on 12 January 1944 – only ten days before D-day. Ground forces allotted to VI Corps were General Truscott's 3rd Division, the 1st British Infantry Division (Major General Penney), three battalions of Rangers and two of Commandos, and a regiment of paratroops. One regiment of the 45th Division and two of the 1st Armored were held in reserve at Naples.

Admiral Lowry was prevented, by his own involvement with the VIII Amphibious Force command, from putting in many personal appearances at planning deliberations. Captain E. C. L. Turner RN arrived to take charge of the Ranger spearhead; but he had to spend most of his time at Pozzuoli on the Gulf of Naples where Colonel Darby was training three of his veteran Ranger battalions. General Lucas and staff were at Maddaloni, not far from Caserta. He and Admiral Lowry were the same age – fifty-six; they coöperated perfectly; and the Admiral, said Lucas, was a "tower of strength" to him at Anzio beachhead.

A cover plan was devised to convince the enemy that our real intention was to attack Leghorn toward the end of January. To this end, a radio station in Corsica, purporting to be Advance Headquarters VI Army Corps, built up a plausible crescendo of traffic up to H-hour at Anzio. Fishing craft were collected in Corsican harbors, where Army Engineers made a great show of secret activity, compiling dummy dumps and constructing imitation landing craft. Information "leaked out" from Caserta that Fifth Army would not advance in January but that the British Eighth Army, with fresh troops, would make a big push up the Adriatic coast. A bombardment by H.M.S. *Dido* and two destroyers on Civitavecchia, and one by six cruisers and destroyers on Terracina, was expected to divert enemy troops from Anzio.[21] There is nothing in

[20] On the night of 30 Dec. 1943, Ens. K. E. Howe USNR and Ens. C. F. Pirro USNR were sent to make a silhouette and landmark reconnaissance of the beaches. They never returned to the PT from which they had launched their boat. The Royal Navy also lost two officers on a similar mission.

[21] Sacmed *Report* (British ed.) p. 16.

German records to suggest that all this whoop-de-do made even a faint impression. Marshal Kesselring, with fresh divisions in northern Italy and others promised from France and Germany, had plans all worked out in case the Allies attempted to land at Leghorn, Genoa, Ravenna, Istria or Anzio. He was ready to execute any one of them when and if the Allies acted, but not before.

The Allied assault plan called for only a show of force on the Eighth Army front (Adriatic side) where enough pressure was to be exerted to keep the enemy from transferring troops, while Fifth Army threw itself against Cassino once more in hope of drawing off whatever reserves the enemy might have around Anzio. The Fifth Army push was to precede the amphibious landing by five days, and by its ferocity to convince the enemy of a determination to burst through the Liri Valley and force the road to Rome.

General Alexander's Operation Instructions for SHINGLE, dated 12 January 1944, gave as the object of this operation "to cut the enemy's main communications in the Colli Laziali (Alban Hills) area southeast of Rome, and to threaten the rear of XIV German Corps," which was then engaged around Cassino.[22] General Clark's directive to General Lucas, dated the same day, was less explicit. The primary mission was "to seize and secure a beachhead in the vicinity of Anzio," and thence to "advance on the Colli Laziali." [23] In the earlier plan the main object of the Anzio operation was to capture the Alban Hills in order to cut the German line of communications south of Rome. And that is what General Alexander's instructions implied. But General Clark's order simply required VI Corps to "advance on" the Alban Hills – an important distinction. Obviously, Operation SHINGLE was now to be independent of main Fifth Army attack, not a projection of it as originally planned. As such, the only possible good it could do would be to divert German forces from the main front.

[22] *Fifth Army History* IV p. 196.

[23] Field Order No. 5, Hq. Fifth Army 12 Jan. 1944; quoted in Lucas Diary pp. 33–36. Gen. H. M. Wilson uses exactly the same wording in describing "our final plan," indicating that Clark's modification was approved by him, and, implicitly, by Alexander. Sacmed *Report* (U.S. ed.) p. 14.

Allied Air Forces were not idle. Fighter planes attacked targets around Civitavecchia, where we wished the enemy to think the landing would take place; bombers flew missions right up to the Franco–Italian border. Between 2 and 13 January 1944, rail communications in central Italy were systematically attacked to choke off supplies from the enemy's southern front, but they were never knocked out long enough to count. After the 13th, the process of "sealing off the beachhead" began in earnest. Airdromes around Rome and throughout central Italy were heavily attacked with demolition and fragmentation bombs. On 19 January Viterbo, Rieti and Perugia were visited by medium and heavy bombers. As D-day approached, air bombardment hammered Roman airfields and reached out to Florence and southern France. Strikes against railroads, bridges and marshaling yards were stepped up.

Although the usual brash claims were made by the air forces, such as that, by 19 January, "All communications from northern Italy to the Rome area were cut," [24] most of this bombing did no good to the amphibious forces bound for Anzio. Airfield craters can be filled in overnight; and, although marshaling yards made good targets, and impressive photos were taken of these bombings, German engineers were always able to keep at least one track open, all they needed for troop and supply trains; civilian supplies could wait. The air arm did force German reconnaissance planes, based on the Perugia airdrome, to stay aground just before the assault convoys sailed. And some of the 1200 sorties flown on D-day hit main roads leading to the beachhead.[25] But roads, too, were quickly repaired and wounds of the Luftwaffe soon healed; it returned to the line of duty for a frightful revenge at Anzio.[26] The beachhead never was sealed off, except by the Germans after the assault.

Both planners and assault forces worked at high pressure during

[24] "Mediterranean Allied Air Forces Operations in Support of SHINGLE" pp. 8–10.

[25] *Anzio Beachhead* p. 17.

[26] Between 2 and 22 Jan. the Mediterranean Allied Air Forces flew 22,850 sorties and dropped 12,238 tons of bombs. These figures, however, include strategic missions such as strikes on Sofia, Pola, Skoplje, Mostar, and the Piræus, and the Messerschmitt factory at Klagenfurt, Austria. The cost was 58 bombers and 84 fighters. "M.A.A.F. Operations" pp. 7, 10.

the first three weeks of January. Admiral Lowry paid tribute to the British planners, whose celerity and intelligence, he wrote, was "reflected in the outstanding and seamanlike manner in which their handling was carried out." The United States 3rd Infantry Division was moved to Pozzuoli, the British 1st Division to Salerno. Ships and beaching craft were so widely separated that many troops had no shipboard training. A spell of foul weather, with cold, driving rain, set in.

"Peter" Force, as the British half was designated, rehearsed on beaches about six miles south of Salerno with only partial success; but the American rehearsal on the same beaches was a fiasco. It was held on a night of very rough weather (17–18 January); the naval vessels did not close the beaches near enough, and forty dukws were swamped, with the loss of many 105-mm howitzers and a number of lives. "The accidents were so many," said Admiral Lowry, "that it appeared impractical on the face of it to make an assault without further training." [27] General Truscott, who also was present, remarked, "Of 37 LCTs assigned for the operation, only 11 went on the exercise. . . . No single battalion landed on time or in formation. . . . Transports were so far off shore that assault craft required three to four and a half hours to reach the beach. . . . No single element was landed . . . on its correct beach. . . . The rehearsal provided no test for communications, particularly with reference to naval gunfire." [28] But there was no time for another rehearsal.

Admiral Lowry, chagrined at the performance of VIII Amphibious Force, informed his ships' commanding officers in no uncertain terms that they were to heave-to within three and one half miles of the Anzio beaches, "the penalty for lagging to be a kick in a soft spot by a cruiser." [29]

Fifth Army reopened its offensive on 12 January with a hearten-

[27] Interview of 21 Dec. 1944 on sound track, Office of Naval History Recordgraph No. 320.

[28] Letter to Lt. Gen. Mark Clark 18 Jan. 1944, included in 3rd Infantry Division Operation Report Jan.–Feb. 1944.

[29] Lucas Diary p. 50.

ing advance of nearly ten miles by General Juin's French Army Corps. Five days later the British X Corps moved across the Garigliano with heavy loss, in the face of fast-gathering German reserves. It just managed to secure a bridgehead across the river. On 20 January, the United States II Corps attacked across the swollen waters of the Rapido River with the object of passing Monte Cassino and advancing along the Via Casilina (No. 6). Through torrential rain the Corps strove to keep supplies coming up. Casualties mounted, the push slowed down, and after two bloody days the Rapido bridgehead was abandoned, on the very day of the Anzio landings. All the valor and energy of this attack went for naught. The Gustav Line, the new German defense line from the bend of the Sangro to the Gulf of Gaëta, held.[30]

So many German reserves were thrown into this front that the actual landings at Anzio were a pushover; but Kesselring had sufficient forces to hold the Gustav Line and counterattack at Anzio. He held the entire country from Monte Cassino to Rome and northward, and was able to deliver right-and-left punches against the two widely separated Allied armies. Defeat on the Rapido doomed the Anzio beachhead to a long stalemate, if not to failure.

Ships and beaching craft of the American task force "X-ray" – which Admiral Lowry commanded in *Biscayne*, in addition to his overall naval command[31] – loaded their troops at four different points in the Gulf of Naples. All sortied early 21 January, rendezvoused and steamed off in proper order. Italian vendors sold picture post-cards of Anzio and Nettuno to the crews of LCIs at Pozzuoli, but that was their good guess; the Germans learned nothing.

Vessels of the British task force "Peter," commanded by Rear Admiral Thomas Troubridge RN in *Bulolo*, assembled on the afternoon of 21 January south of Capri. The British 1st Division was

[30] The Rapido action caused the 29th and elements of the 90th Panzer Grenadiers to be rushed south from around Rome to the Gustav Line, and the Hermann Goering Division was in reserve at Valmontone, with elements south of Frosinone.

[31] General Truscott (p. 302) thinks that this was a mistake; but it was the same dual command system that Admiral Turner successfully employed in the Pacific on several occasions.

embarked in three LSIs recently returned from Admiral Mountbatten's command, and in three "Killer" class LSTs.[32]

Routes from the Gulf of Naples to Anzio were laid out to pass four to twelve miles seaward of Ischia, Ventotene and the Pontine Islands, making a run of about 110 miles. LCTs, joining other beaching craft of Force X-ray south of Ischia, took the shorter inside course. As usual in amphibious operations, the final approach was made at right angles to the coastline in order to shorten the required swept channel and to prevent detection as long as possible.

There was no detection, no attack; and fair weather stayed with both forces all the way. Light airs barely ruffled a calm sea, and the sun shone faintly but cheeringly through stratocumulus and cirrus clouds. Temperature hovered around a brisk 55° F. With a ceiling of 6000 feet, participating air forces could work well over their targets. Aërologists predicted that these conditions would hold for four days. Neither daylight, sunset nor starlit darkness brought an enemy air attack. The approach to Anzio beachhead was uneventful — almost ominously so.

At 2211 January 21, Admiral Lowry's flagship *Biscayne* made a radar contact on Anzio lighthouse, and at five minutes past midnight she anchored in 18 fathoms, four miles southeast of the town.

[32] See Appendix III for Task Organization.

CHAPTER XVI

The Assault on Anzio-Nettuno

22–28 January 1944

1. *The Landings, 22 January*

ON THE MAP of Italy you may note two shallow bays, little more than scallops in the otherwise straight coastline, that extend southeast from the Tiber's mouth to Cape Circe, where the lady of that name is said to have detained Ulysses. On the point between these two scallops, 37 statute miles south of Rome by road or railway, lies Anzio, a town long famous in the history of Italy. It should also be memorable in the history of the United States and Great Britain as the place where many thousands of their sons suffered, and about five thousand were killed.

Ancient Antium, after serving disreputably for centuries as a pirates' lair, was cleaned up in the Augustan Era and became a fashionable seaside resort. The Emperor Nero, a native son, built his favorite palace there, together with a mole and artificial harbor where the imperial barge could moor in comfort. The harbor silted up during the decline of Rome, and the place reverted to piracy. Pope Innocent XII, the next Roman ruler to show an interest in Anzio, built a new mole east of Nero's, in the seventeenth century. This had been extended to make shelter from all winds but the east, and in conjunction with a smaller mole which forms a completely protected small-boat basin, a harbor for fishing craft. East of the clean, modern town is a 40-meter height crowned by Roman pines which half conceal the gardens of the Villa Borghese. East of that hill begins the town of Nettuno, similar to Anzio and connected with it by a sandy beach, the Riviera di Levante, and a coastal road lined with stone villas covered with bright-colored stucco. The two towns and the pine-clad hill between them make a singularly attractive picture, even in the dull light of a January morning.

A glance at our map will show why Anzio seemed the ideal entrance for a strategic beachhead. The town is on a blunted headland, the apex of a wide-angled triangle. The Riviera di Levante, next the apex, was reserved as a landing beach for the Rangers, to secure both towns. Northwest, a line of beaches runs to the mouth of the Tiber; a mile-and-a-half stretch of them was designated as the Peter beaches for the British task force. East of Nettuno a mile-and-a-quarter stretch of beach, designated X-ray, was allotted to the United States task force; and beyond that the Mussolini Canal is a natural barrier to the Pontine Marshes. Behind both sets of beaches the Anzio plain, dry, gently rolling and cultivated with corn, vineyards and small crops, rises by slow degrees to a railway embankment 13 miles north of Anzio, and thence tilts upward more sharply to the ancient Via Appia which skirts the southern and western slopes of the Alban Hills. If Allied troops could wrest road and railway from the Germans, they would be in possession of one of the two main lines of communication between Rome and Naples. But unless they took the Alban Hills themselves and dominated the second railway and the Via Casilina on the north side, they would not cut these communications; their beachhead would be a mere nuisance to the enemy, who might be expected to react violently against it. That was the fundamental weakness of Operation SHINGLE. Either it was a job for a full army, or it was no job at all; to attempt it with only two divisions was to send a boy on a man's errand.

At Anzio night landings made sense, as Intelligence reported the coastal defenses and defenders to be so few that a night assault offered a good chance to establish a wide beachhead quickly. H-hour was set for 0200 January 22, in order to give the landing forces four hours of darkness. A waning, last-quarter moon rose

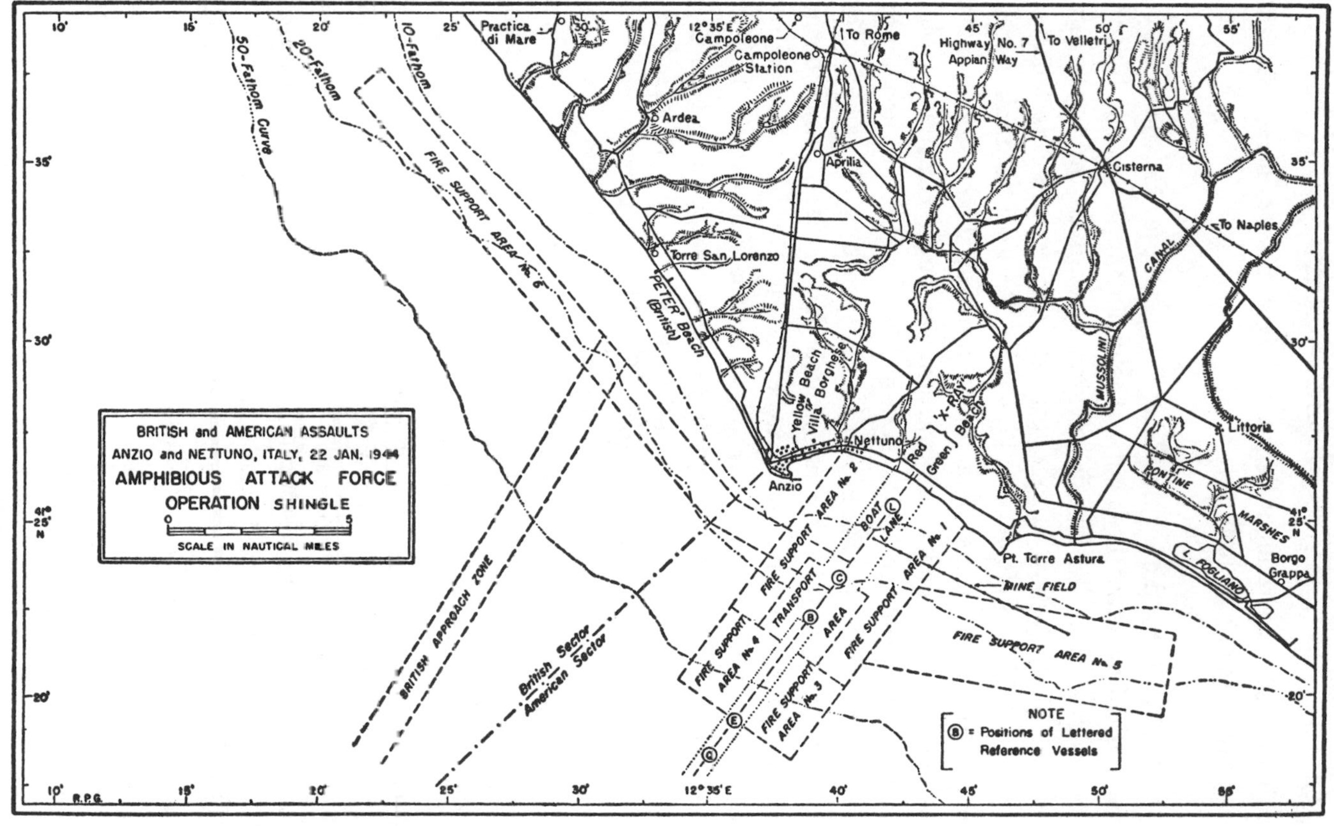
BRITISH and AMERICAN ASSAULTS
ANZIO and NETTUNO, ITALY, 22 JAN. 1944
AMPHIBIOUS ATTACK FORCE
OPERATION SHINGLE
SCALE IN NAUTICAL MILES
NOTE
(B) = Positions of Lettered Reference Vessels
Practica di Mare
Campoleone
Campoleone Station
To Rome
Highway No. 7
Appian Way
To Velletri
Cisterna
To Naples
Ardea
Aprilia
Torre San Lorenzo
'PETER' Beach (British)
Yellow Beach
Villa Borghese
Anzio
Nettuno
Red
Green
'X-RAY' Beach
CANAL
MUSSOLINI
PONTINE
MARSHES
Littoria
Borgo Grappa
L. FOGLIANO
Pt. Torre Astura
MINE FIELD
50-Fathom Curve
20-Fathom
10-Fathom
FIRE SUPPORT AREA No. 6
BRITISH APPROACH ZONE
British Sector
American Sector
FIRE SUPPORT AREA No. 2
FIRE SUPPORT AREA No. 4
TRANSPORT AREA
BOAT LANE
FIRE SUPPORT AREA No. 1
FIRE SUPPORT AREA No. 3
FIRE SUPPORT AREA No. 5
12°35'E
41° 25' N
R.P.G.

at 0300, morning twilight began at a few minutes before six, and the sun did not rise until 0731.[1]

We shall first take up the Rangers' spearhead. Colonel Darby's men, lifted in British LSIs under the command of Captain Turner RN, landed on the Riviera di Levante, now given the unromantic title of Beach Yellow, a mile-long strand between Anzio harbor and the Villa Borghese hill. The three British LSIs took station around midnight as the light offshore breeze died away to a flat calm. Haze cut visibility shoreward to 300 yards. The folbot which marked the beach for the Rangers had been paddled to its position 400 yards off the exact center of the beach by 0115; and Ensign Henry W. Noel USNR, the naval scout boat officer, turned on his yellow battle lamp ten minutes before H-hour, as a beacon for incoming assault waves.[2] That was also the moment for H.M.S. *LCT–147*, a craft mounting 798 rocket tubes, to deliver a lethal shower on the beach. By bad timing she arrived late and dared not fire for fear of hitting the Rangers. Their boat waves waited three minutes, fearing to get rockets on their necks, and then went right in. This contretemps turned out to be fortunate; Beach Yellow was neither mined nor defended, and the Rangers obtained complete tactical surprise.

There was no opposition. German engineers who had been sent from Rome to destroy the long mole were captured in the nick of time, a lucky encounter which saved days in preparing the harbor for Allied use. By 0645 all the Rangers were ashore, and their transports were ready to retire. Captain Turner awaited word that the town was taken, and at 0815 received it from Colonel Darby. The Captain then went ashore, located the Colonel and assumed the rôle of Naval Officer in Charge, Anzio.

Rear Admiral Troubridge's task force, carrying the British 1st Infantry Division, drew the worst beaches in any Italian land-

1 Rear Adm. Lowry Action Report 22 Feb. 1944.
2 Ens. Noel's letter to Com VIII 'Phib Force 23 Jan. 1944.

ing. Steep, sandy cliffs extend for some four miles northward from the lighthouse, so that Peter beaches had to be selected north of the cliffs. Their gradient was about 1:120, which caused even a mild chop to make up into surf; there were numerous false beaches on the approach, and the sand was too soft for vehicles, especially in the exits through the dunes. Troubridge declared them to be the worst in his experience.[3]

Task Force Peter arrived by midnight. A beacon submarine, H.M.S. *Ultor*, had been lying off shore since the day before, taking fixes on the beach and checking mine fields so as to help the minesweepers to begin clearing the approach channel at 2030 January 21. This sweep was only a qualified success. Owing to want of rehearsal or even proper briefing, there were fouled gear, near-collisions, narrow escapes from floating mines.[4] The few Germans behind Peter beaches must have suspected what was going on, since the rocket craft commenced firing at 0153 January 22; but they lay low.

Assault craft touched down on time, 0200, but the work of removing land mines caused heavy congestion at the water's edge, while soldiers waited for the word to advance. As one officer remarked, "It must be realized that no amount of shouting through loud hailers will induce troops to advance through a mine field." Neither dukws nor beaching craft could be accepted until the mines were cleared. At 0400 the dukws began to roll in, but the first LCT did not beach until 0645 and the first LSTs arrived even later. Lack of exits and serious delay in rigging pontoon causeways postponed the unloading of LSTs until 1045, while 18 LSTs and 24 LCIs, which arrived from Naples at 0715, impatiently milled about the roadstead. But the landing of troops was so uneventful as to be called "very gentlemanly, calm and dignified" by the Adjutant of the Irish Guards.

[3] Vice Adm. Lowry in U. S. Naval Inst. *Proceedings* LXXX 24–5.

[4] Cdr. C. H. Corbet-Singleton RN, who directed the sweep, respectfully submitted to the Admiral after the operation that, in future, officers in his position "be given some idea of the minesweeping plans, whenever possible, a little in advance."

H.M.S. *Palomares*, carrying the standby fighter-director crew, hit a mine and had to be towed to Naples. German artillery fired on the ships all day, and although only a few LSTs were hit, with minor casualties, this shelling, added to the unsatisfactory nature of the beaches, forced a decision to divert follow-up convoys to the American sector. Peter beaches were virtually abandoned after 23 January.

The X-ray beaches (Red and Green) allotted to the United States 3rd Division begin two statute miles east of San Rocco church, at the eastern end of Nettuno. These were similar in character to Peter beaches, with somewhat coarser and firmer sand, and an average gradient of 1:90. Except for the medieval Torre di Astura on the point of that name, there were no good landmarks; the soft profiles of the Alban Hills afforded no guide.

As usual, the sweepers showed the way, guiding on H.M. submarine *Uproar*, the beacon ship. Commander Alfred H. Richards in *Pilot* had charge of 23 minecraft, big and small, divided into three task units which reached the roadstead at 1930 January 21. These three units, executing crowded sweep patterns in assigned areas, were like so many platoons of infantry trying to avoid collision in a darkened drill hall. The small YMSs, slow in streaming their gear, could not be told to get a move on because they had no radio; "the unit commander could only sit, wait and pray." His prayers were answered and there were no serious mishaps, although the sweep was behind schedule and the assault convoy arrived 20 minutes early. Admiral Lowry called the operation "a most remarkable job." Only a few mines were found in the approach lanes. And, as yet, the enemy fired not.[5]

At 0153, seven minutes before H-hour, the two British LCTs attached to Force X-ray began firing 5-inch rockets, which were

[5] Cdr. Richards and Cdr. W. L. Messmer Action Reports. Eventually about 34 mines were swept up in the American sector, all between the 5- and 20-fathom curves, but large areas were unswept, for our own protection. Because of shortage of American minesweeping gear, French and even captured German gear was borrowed from the French Navy.

effective in destroying land mines on the beaches. LCVPs landed initial assault troops dryshod and standing up. These troops encountered no resistance. Enemy outposts on coast-watching duty were quickly overpowered; four intoxicated "Krauts" were caught riding in a staff car, and several others in a similar condition were found still asleep in spite of the sharp, crackling uproar of rocket fire. German batteries four miles inland kept silent.

The third and fourth assault waves were made up of LCIs. At 0239 *LCI–211*, in the third wave, grounded on a false beach, off a runnel too deep for troops to wade. LCVPs closed to help, and were taking off two boatloads of troops when heavy machine-gun fire opened from ashore, causing many casualties. The fifth wave, LCTs, hit the beach at 0315 and was followed at 0430 by a wave of 132 dukws. Seventh and eighth waves, all LCTs, were beached by 0634.

It still lacked one hour of sunrise. Morning twilight had stolen over the calm sea and was beginning to illuminate landmarks on the Anzio beachhead. The region seemed to be ours for the taking. General Truscott, always impatient to get ashore, left *Biscayne* with his staff at 0645, and established his command post in a wood a few hundred yards from the beach. General Lucas, who had already sent a signal congratulating all hands, boarded Rear Admiral Troubridge's flagship *Bulolo* shortly before sunrise, to see how the British were doing, but was back on board *Biscayne* by 0830. There, much to his annoyance, he had to play host to at least five general officers who had sailed up from Naples to see the show. His guests included Generals Clark and Alexander and "Wild Bill" Donovan of the Office of Strategic Services. Lucas did not establish his headquarters ashore, in Nettuno, until next day.

As light increased, D-day became more lively. *Mayo* initiated naval gunfire at 0748 by demolishing a military building with 60 rounds from her main battery, at the behest of her shore fire-control party. The first enemy air attack quickly followed. About six Messerschmitts broke through fighter cover to dive-bomb Beach Red, setting fire to loaded vehicles. Convoys of empty

LCIs formed up and sailed for Naples as others arrived with fresh troops.

About 1010 *Portent*, maneuvering inside the 20-fathom curve, struck a mine which exploded under her stern and sent up a 150-foot column of water. She sank within three minutes and lost 18 men. Then came another air raid. Focke-Wulf fighter-bombers swooped down over the harbor and dropped bombs among the LSTs and LCIs clustered around the two pontoon causeways at Beach Red. A 500-pound bomb smashed through *LCI–20* and exploded below her bottom, destroying her.

All day long the waters off Anzio and Nettuno witnessed a scene typical of an amphibious operation. Cruiser *Brooklyn* zigzagged, awaiting calls for fire support from her shore fire-control party; British cruisers were firing off Peter Beach to the northwest; myriad black puffs of ack-ack were exploding in the clear air, aimed at the enemy's hornet-like dive-bombers. Spitfires, P–51s and P–38s were patrolling and pursuing;[6] tiny YMSs mineswept under enemy shellfire, even into the port of Anzio; landing craft scurried between ships and beaches. General Truscott described enemy artillery fire of D-day as merely "slight and harassing," but when night closed in under heavy black clouds one could see flashes of artillery fire inland, and patterns of red tracers in the sky.

In Anzio town and harbor, Army Engineers plucked demolition charges from the walls of stone buildings, which, if blown up, would have toppled into the main street, and Captain Turner made a thorough survey of berthing spaces. *LST–410* and two LCTs entered the port at 1700, much to the relief of Colonel Darby, who needed their cargo of antitank guns and halftracks. Soundings were taken in the harbor and along the moles; it was found that two LST berths on the north "hard" (as the British call a firm beach) could be augmented by six along the big mole as soon as Army Engineers could shear off a few feet of it to take an LST's ramp. They did so, and LSTs began using Pope Innocent's mole at noon 24 January.

[6] Allied planes "flew more than 1200 sorties" on D-day in support of the operation (*Anzio Beachhead* p. 17), but only 140 enemy air sorties were counted.

At midnight of D-day 36,034 men, 3069 vehicles and large quantities of supplies, 90 per cent of the assault load, had been brought ashore. D-day casualties of VI Corps were only 13 killed, 44 missing and 97 wounded. Those of the Navy, from the sinking of *Portent* and *LCI–20*, were somewhat higher.[7] Troops were already moving slowly to the initial beachhead line, and all three assault units – British 1st Division, Rangers, and 3rd Infantry Division U. S. Army – were in contact with one another.

So far, Operation SHINGLE had been an unqualified success. "After the almost disastrous performance during the rehearsal," writes General Truscott, "our Navy comrades gave us one which was almost unbelievably smooth and accurate." [8] Good seamanship and experience were, at bottom, responsible for this unexpected result; both navies included a body of officers and enlisted men familiar with every aspect of the business, and for whom the process of landing troops and vehicles on a pitch-black night was no longer a novelty. But fair weather and the complete surprise of the enemy certainly helped. Marshal Kesselring had alerted his troops there, numbering not more than one thousand, for three nights earlier, but canceled the alert on the crucial night. There were no coastal defenses but land mines and scattered artillery pieces – a few 88s and several old Italian, French and Yugoslav pieces, most of which were not even fired.

The German Naval High Command, piecing together the Anzio picture in Berlin, was reminded of the invasion of Salerno. Their estimate of the size of the Allied naval force, however, was too flattering; for Admiral Lowry's task force was credited with having an aircraft carrier, four cruisers and twenty destroyers.[9] Marshal Kesselring's plans were already made; he had only to send out the code word "Richard" to have designated units move on Anzio. He believed that he could not only contain VI Corps in a narrow

[7] *Anzio Beachhead* p. 18.
[8] *Command Missions* p. 309.
[9] War Diary German Naval Staff 23 Jan. 1944. The "aircraft carrier" may have been *LST–16*, which was fitted with a flight deck to launch Piper Cubs for spotting.

beachhead, but hold Fifth and Eighth Armies at the Gustav Line as well. He was right. Failure to appreciate German skill in the rapid movement of troops to seal off any possible Allied beachhead, was a major lapse in Allied Intelligence. And the reason for this failure is clear; the Allied Air Forces imagined, and reported, that they had disrupted all rail and road communications in central Italy.[10]

2. *Establishing the Beachhead, 23–28 January*

On 23 January, D-day plus 1, eager *Brooklyn* was finally given a chance to interdict troop movements at a town well inland, Littoria (since renamed Latina), on the edge of the Pontine Marshes, which the enemy was using as an assembly point. She fired 27 rounds at 0859, which satisfied the shore fire-control party and broke up a counterattack.

The German Air Force, mildly active during the day, put in a deadly appearance at Peter beaches as twilight deepened under low clouds and mist. "Red Anzio, Red Anzio!" — the signal to send gunners to their antiaircraft weapons — passed over the voice circuit. Of 55 planes in the attack, 34 were driven off by Allied fighters, but the rest got in some deadly work. They picked on H.M. destroyers *Janus* and *Jervis*, which had carried the burden of fire support off the Peter beaches for two days. *Janus* was hit by an aërial torpedo, and *Jervis* by a radio-guided bomb. Vigorous countermeasures to this new and dreaded air weapon had been adopted, but as yet they did not work. *Jervis* suffered no casualties and made Naples under her own power, but the bridge and forecastle of *Janus* were demolished; the bomb explosion broke her apart, and she capsized with loss of 159 officers and men. *Jervis*, a patrol craft and three dukws recovered 93 survivors.[11]

This serious loss pointed up the question of retaining gunfire

[10] Truscott *Command Missions* pp. 305–7 is emphatic on this point.
[11] Admiralty Records; War Diary German Naval Staff Jan. 1944 p. 303. See Chapter XVII, for the countermeasures.

support ships at the beachhead when not immediately needed. It now seemed that ships without a definite prospect of fire mission should not linger. The reaction of the British was a move to retire their cruisers to Naples. Rear Admiral J. M. Mansfield RN, commanding Cruiser Squadron 15, had assumed the duty of gunfire support commander that morning, and in that capacity ordered *Penelope* to Naples after the evening air attack. He wished also to withdraw *Orion* and *Spartan* from the British sector, which he felt was adequately protected by two destroyers, two gunboats and the divisional artillery, almost all of which was now ashore. His order was transmitted by signal immediately after the air raid, and brought an instant challenge from Rear Admiral Lowry: "By whose authority?" This caused a cancellation of the signal and an agreement to release the British cruisers while *Brooklyn* remained at the beachhead, with her skipper in command of all gunfire support. There was acrimonious discussion later concerning the wisdom of an arrangement which reduced naval gunfire support on the third day of the operation.

In spite of increasing surf, unloading progressed satisfactorily during the day. There were few delays, and only one craft was lost through broaching.[12]

Fair weather ended on D-day plus 2, January 24, with a 20-knot westerly wind and high seas. Peter beaches closed down, after the two pontoons that served them had broached. All British amphibious craft now moved through the swept channel which connected their sector to X-ray, and were placed under the command of Admiral Lowry. This left Rear Admiral Troubridge without anything particular to do; so, after exchanging signals with Lowry, he returned to Naples.

During the afternoon and evening of 24 January, 33 LSTs steamed up to Anzio in time to be on the receiving end of a sensational twilight air raid. First 15 fighter-bombers, then 43 at dusk, and finally 52 after dark attacked the transport area repeatedly. One struck destroyer *Plunkett* with a 550-pound bomb, killing 53

[12] Moran "Anzio-Nettuno Landings" p. 41.

of her crew and disabling the port engine, but she was able to reach Palermo under her own power.[13] *Brooklyn*, which *Plunkett* was screening, was near-missed several times but escaped damage. A near miss forced *Prevail* out of action as she was making a much-needed sweep of a fire support area. The Luftwaffe then selected as targets three British hospital ships which bore the brightly illuminated markings of their type. These defenseless ships were severely shaken by repeated near misses, and *St. David* finally took a direct hit and sank with some loss of life.[14] This infuriated the assault forces as did no other act of the enemy during the operation.

This raid, prolonged until the air throughout the anchorage was saturated with the smell of powder, was subsiding about 1945 when there came a call for help from *Mayo*, about two and a half miles off shore. She had struck a mine. The explosion killed five men, ruptured her starboard side and propeller shaft, flooded after fire- and engine rooms, and caused loss of steering control; damage control coped with the flooding in time to avoid foundering. This was the fourth destroyer to be knocked out in 24 hours. At 2300 H.M. tug *Prosperous* passed a line and towed *Mayo* to Naples. She had been firing almost continuously for 17 hours and her speed and accuracy, said Admiral Lowry, "kept the Germans from counter-attacking across the Mussolini Canal." [15]

These first three days of the Anzio operation had been the most costly so far in the Navy's Mediterranean experience; but the job of landing troops and supporting them with gunfire had been very well done. On 24 January VI Corps was in possession of a roughly rectangular beachhead seven miles deep and fifteen long,[16] running up to important crossroads.

No time was lost in preparing the port for amphibious craft. On 23 January, D-day plus 1, eight LSTs unloaded there. On the 24th, the weather was so bad that the outside beaches were closed, but

[13] *Plunkett* War Diary and Action Report 25 Jan.; War Diary German Naval Staff Jan. 1944 p. 316.

[14] *St. David* had on board a crew of 144, 78 patients, 4 U.S. Army medicos, and 3 prisoners of war.

[15] Endorsement on *Mayo* Action Report 8 May 1944.

[16] *Fifth Army History* Part IV p. 65.

seven LSTs managed to unload in the port; and the next day 19 cleared for Naples. By the end of January there had been over a hundred LST unloadings at Anzio; an impressive record, considering the frequent attacks by artillery and aircraft; and it could never have been made without the preloaded truck plan thought up by General Lucas's staff. Always, however, remained the threat that "a lucky hit on a ship entering or leaving might block the channel, whilst a hit on an LST berthed might put that berth permanently out of action." [17] General Lucas afterward admitted that the protection of the port of Anzio was his greatest anxiety at this time.

While unloading proceeded, assault forces pushed inland, and the Germans prepared to roll them back. Parts of the 4th Parachute, 71st Infantry, and 3rd Panzer Grenadier Divisions were in the Anzio plain early on 23 January. That evening one regiment each of the Hermann Goering and 15th Panzer Grenadiers (our old friends!) reached the area, fought the 30th Infantry for the bridges over the Mussolini Canal, and lost them, owing partly to good fire support by destroyer *Trippe*.[18] Enemy resistance was still light that day, as VI Corps moved to deepen its beachhead.

British light cruiser *Orion* came up in the morning of the 25th, flying the flag of Rear Admiral J. M. Mansfield RN, who took over from Captain Cary command of all fire support ships.[19] A large convoy of reinforcements arrived, with those old faithfuls, H.M.S. *Royal Ulsterman* and *Princess Beatrix*, and 33 beaching craft. Other naval business for the day was the continued minesweeping of a fire support area, carried out under such accurate enemy gunfire that sweeper formations were thrown into confusion. The result was a swept area only 2000 yards wide, although 10½ miles long. In the course of the morning, destroyer escort *Frederick C. Davis*, with a United States Army radio intercepting team on board, passed the word that German reconnaissance planes had been detected reporting to their headquarters a successful coverage of the whole

[17] Capt. Turner Report.

[18] Her shore fire-control party radioed: "Jerry pulled out. You knocked off plenty of them on both problems. That stuff was beautiful."

[19] *Brooklyn* Action Report, Enclosure A p. 22.

anchorage area. This was ominous news, portending days and nights of air attack without respite.

At 0932 minecraft *Strive*, with a formation of 13 YMSs, started to re-sweep and extend the newly created Fire Support Area No. 5. *Trippe*, which had opened fire at 0803, kept it up with great effectiveness until 1232, when *Edison* relieved her. The enemy batteries did not take the little YMSs under attack that day, which was well for them, as they had a trying time sweeping a 1000-yard strip on the shoreward side. *YMS–30*, on the shoreward edge of the area, struck a mine herself. "There was a terrific wall of flame and an explosion instantaneously, and then the vessel disappeared." [20] Seventeen men perished.

Ludlow, *Gleaves* and *Edison* were assigned to fire support in X-ray area during the day. *Edison* got off 125 rounds at a road junction during the afternoon, and *Brooklyn* was called in for two bombardments.

Evening brought a rising west wind with mounting seas. Most of the ships got under way to ride out the storm; those that did not dragged anchors. On the morning of the 26th, H.M.S. *LST–422*, just up from Naples and loaded with troops and ammunition, drifted into unswept waters near Torre di Astura. She hit a mine at 0521 and burned fiercely, lighting up ships throughout the anchorage. Several vessels hastened to the rescue, playing searchlights over the ruddy waters; one of them, *LCI–32*, struck a mine near the blazing LST at 0540 and sank in three minutes, losing 30 of her crew killed, and 11 wounded. Daylight revealed scores of dead and survivors floating in the rain-lashed sea. *Pilot*, *Strive*, and YMSs, bravely steaming along the edge of the mine field where *YMS–30* had been blown to bits the day before, pulled about 150 survivors out of the water, up over their sides; for it was impossible to lower boats.[21]

Fog now closed down with intermittent rain and sleet squalls. Seas breaking high on X-ray beaches stopped unloading. By daybreak 26 January all pontoons, together with an LCI and twelve

[20] Cdr. Messmer Action Report, Enclosure A p. 35.
[21] Same p. 38.

LCTs, had broached. Nine or ten LSTs managed to unload in the port of Anzio. "Had not the port of Anzio been operated at three or four times its expected capacity for LSTs, the loss of pontoon causeways would have doomed the beachhead," wrote Admiral Lowry.[22] For most of the ships, this day was chiefly devoted to holding out against the storm and repelling five German bombing attacks. The dusk raid of FW–190s[23] damaged H.M.S. *LST–366*, seven patrol craft, two merchant ships and a rescue tug. Liberty ship *John Banvard* drew such a close near miss by a guided missile that her master ordered Abandon Ship; but some of the naval armed guard returned on board during the next alert and manned a gun against a second bomb attack.[24]

Under stress of weather and frequent broachings of landing craft, tempers became frazzled; and, in the absence of a central salvage authority, commanding officers of the beach battalion ashore and salvage group afloat indulged in vain recriminations. Most of the broaching was the result of weather rather than poor seamanship. LCTs, being nothing more than large motorized barges, are ungainly craft to handle in any kind of sea.

Poems are made by fools like me,
But only God can steer an LCT!

is the theme song of their sailors. Unloading greatly improved after Admiral Lowry had designated Captain Robert Morris his deputy for the unloading and coördination of salvage and beach parties.

Even more than LCTs, pontoon causeways are vulnerable in rough water; and a broached causeway is more difficult to salvage than any stranded boat. Admiral Lowry decided that the only way to save the precious pontoons from storm damage was to have them towed clear of the beach, either to be anchored in sheltered waters or to be kept under tow until the seas subsided. This required quick action, usually over Army objections, upon receipt of a

[22] Supplementary Action Report 17 May 1944 p. 10.

[23] War Diary German Naval Staff Jan. 1944 pp. 349, 361. The Germans lost 8 planes in this raid, and after dark raided again with 31.

[24] S.S. *John Banvard* Armed Guard Report.

storm forecast; and pontoons are difficult to maintain under tow in heavy seas or high winds.[25] Under winter conditions the worst harbor is better than the best beach.

During these first few days naval gunfire support at Anzio beachhead was much less effective than it had been at Salerno or Sicily. At first there was less need for it, and then the dusk air attacks with guided bombs became such a menace that Admiral Lowry ordered all cruisers and most destroyers to retire seaward every afternoon at 1600. By 26 January, when VI Corps began asking for fire on targets beyond 6-inch range, Admiral Lowry sent an urgent request to Admirals Hewitt and Cunningham for a heavy cruiser or a monitor. He was told that neither was available.[26]

By the morning of 27 January both wind and sea had abated, and 22 LSTs discharged that day in Anzio. But at X-ray the surf had formed new false beaches, and broached pontoons and stranded LCTs had been left so high and dry that salvage was uncommonly difficult.[27] Nevertheless, twelve LSTs were unloaded by LCTs on X-ray in the next 24 hours. Messages of congratulation were now in order. Admiral Sir John Cunningham commended all hands for "the very successful conclusion of the first phase. Having landed the Army, it now remains to support and supply them." [28]

General Mackensen, Commander Fourteenth Army, took over the German command on the 25th and set up his headquarters near Rome. Next day units of the 3rd Division, advancing along the Nettuno-Velletri road, on reaching the top of the rise that faces Cisterna, met increasingly strong opposition. The same day, patrols of the British 1st Division reached the outskirts of Campoleone Station on the nearest railroad. By this time the Germans had elements of ten divisions south of the Tiber, and four of them were closing in on Anzio beachhead. By the 28th, VI Corps had moved beyond the range of naval gunfire support except on its flanks, and much stiffer enemy resistance developed along the entire front. This day

[25] Rear Adm. Lowry Supplementary Action Report.
[26] *Brooklyn* Action Report p. 38.
[27] Cdr. O. F. Gregor Report p. 7.
[28] Capt. R. W. Cary Action Report, Enclosure A p. 28.

Edison was called on twice to give fire support to the VI Corps right flank near Littoria. "Very, very good," reported her shore fire-control party after 103 rounds on a troop concentration; "Brassed off a bunch of Krauts!" [29] But there were plenty more.

Although the Air Forces rendered valuable protection to ships in the roadstead, and support to troops on the beachhead, they were still fighting their own war. Admiral Troubridge, who had a fighter-director team in H.M.S. *Ulster Queen*, complained that virtually no movements of friendly aircraft were passed to this key vessel, and that no ships were given the code for friendly aircraft operations and movements. This resulted in wasted efforts investigating radar plots of approaching planes, unnecessary air-raid warnings, and exposure of Allied planes to ships' antiaircraft fire. And the senior Allied air officer afloat was not in *Ulster Queen* but in *Biscayne*, which had neither air plot nor direct communication with Air Force headquarters ashore. General Truscott is equally emphatic. "Air support was – and continued to be – the weak point in all beachhead operations." The Air Force still believed in the concept of "isolating the battlefield" by bombing bridges and the like beyond the battle area; yet these tactics never seriously deterred the enemy's movements of troops and supplies. Truscott had worked out an effective air support procedure with Rear Admiral Monroe Kelly in the assault on Mehedia in Operation TORCH, similar to the shore fire-control parties for naval gunfire support, and wished to apply it at Anzio, but the Army Air Force would have none of it.[30]

3. *General Lucas's Tactics*

It was now too late for VI Corps to capture the southern slopes of the Alban Hills or even the road and railway between Campoleone and Cisterna. The Germans themselves were puzzled by our

[29] *Edison* Action Report p. 2.
[30] Truscott *Command Missions* pp. 353–55.

slow motion. "Why didn't the enemy, in a daring quick dash to the Alban Hills, push through to Valmontone and cut the supply road to the south flank of the Tenth Army?" asked General Hauser after the war. In the next breath he answered: "He felt himself not strong enough and thereby missed his great chance." [31]

Many at the time and since have belabored General Lucas for not forming a mobile column at once to roll over the Alban Hills into Rome. Mr. Churchill put it vividly: "I had hoped we were hurling a wildcat onto the shore, but all we got was a stranded whale." [32] It is true that Lucas, not very fit physically, was not an aggressive personality; and General Clark certainly did not encourage him to strike quickly in telling him just before departure, "Don't stick your neck out the way I did at Salerno." General Fuller compares him to General Stopford who, at Suvla Bay in 1915, sat still while the Turks occupied the commanding heights; Lucas, he says, should have "created a scare epidemic in the rear of the German front on the Garigliano." [33] There is no doubt that the British Guards Brigade could have marched right into Rome where, on 23 January (if the doorman of the Hotel Excelsior is a reliable historical source), "You couldn't find one German officer; they had all packed up and got out." There is no doubt that elements of the 3rd Infantry Division, well provided with vehicles, could have rolled into Valmontone, on the second or third day. But there is nothing in the German military record to justify the assumption that they would have been thrown into a panic by Allied columns dashing north and northeast.

On the other hand, Anzio (says Horace) was dedicated to the goddess of Fortune,[34] and the whole operation was a gamble; a little more audacity might have scored a colossal success. But to play safe, await developments and consolidate while the enemy was spread thin, actually amounted to passing a good hand and giving your opponent another chance to draw. However, if Mr. Churchill

[31] "Feldzug in Italien" chap. xii.
[32] *Closing the Ring* p. 488.
[33] J. F. C. Fuller *Second World War* p. 271. Maj. D. J. L. Fitzgerald has put the case for a quick dash cogently in *History of the Irish Guards* pp. 214–22.
[34] He addresses her as *O Diva, gratum quæ regis Antium* (*Odes* I xxxv).

and General Alexander had wanted a bold gambler, they should have chosen a different general. If blame there be, Generals Clark and Alexander must share it with General Lucas; Commander Fifth Army for his woolly directive,[35] and Commander Fifteenth Army Group for his failure to correct Clark or prod Lucas when he had the opportunity. Alexander "in all his talks with me," wrote Mr. Churchill about five weeks after D-day, "envisaged that the essence of the battle was the seizure of the Alban Hills with the utmost speed." [36] Now, Alexander visited Anzio beachhead on D-day and again on D-day plus 3. He inspected the terrain, conferred with Lucas and many other officers, acquiesced in the corps commander's tactical dispositions, and described the operation as "a splendid piece of work," so far.[37] If he had wanted seizure of the Alban Hills "with the utmost speed," here were two opportunities for him to have done something about it. But he gave no orders, offered no suggestions, applied no heat. With access to top intelligence data, he must have had accurate knowledge of enemy dispositions, and agreed with General Lucas that the Germans were too formidable in that sector to risk spreading VI Corps any thinner. General Truscott's 3rd Division, reinforced by the Rangers and paratroops, was extended over a 20-mile front on 24 January, almost twice the safe length for a divisional front on an open plain against an alert enemy.

Although Anzio was dedicated to Fortune, Horace in the same ode admits that *sæva Necessitas*, stern Necessity, ever stalks before her; and General Lucas chose to follow the leader. He showed sound tactical sense in making consolidation of the beachhead paramount. He knew that the Germans were past masters at cutting off flying columns and pinching out salients. If Lucas had "stuck his neck out," he would in all probability have lost his neck, and the beachhead too.

[35] See above, p. 330. The operations officer of Fifth Army, who delivered this order in person, made it perfectly clear that much thought had been put into its wording, "so as not to force me," said Gen. Lucas, "to push on at the risk of sacrificing my corps. Should conditions warrant, however, I was free to move to and seize Colli Laziali." Lucas Diary pp. 33–34.

[36] To Field Marshal Smuts 27 Feb. 1944; *Closing the Ring* p. 493.

[37] Lucas Diary 25 Jan. 1944.

CHAPTER XVII

Beachhead Struggle

28 January–30 April 1944

1. *First Advance Halted, 28–31 January*

ALLIED advances during the last days of January were disappointingly slow. The 3rd Division was stopped three miles short of Cisterna by its old Sicilian antagonist, the Hermann Goerings. The Guards Brigade of the British 1st Division on the left flank wrested the town of Aprilia from the 3rd Panzer Grenadiers and advanced a short distance north on 28 January, but were brought up short before Campoleone, where the Germans had fortified every farmhouse.

It now became evident why the terrain between railway and hills was so important for us to take and for the enemy to hold. The people here, instead of crowding their houses in hill towns, built them in the open, well spaced, like farmsteads in England and New England; and each farmhouse, two or three stories high and with stone walls two to three feet thick, was a potential strong point. Aprilia, a modern community center clustered around a large stone and concrete "factory," as the Guards called it, was ideal for defense; and Cisterna, on the right flank, became a German stronghold comparable to Monte Cassino.

On 28 January Adolf Hitler issued an emphatic Order of the Day to his armed forces in Italy. He announced that "The landing at Nettuno is the beginning of the invasion of Europe planned for 1944." All German armed forces "must be filled with the fanatical will to emerge from this fight victorious, and not to rest until the last enemy has been destroyed or thrown back into the sea. The battle must be waged with holy hatred towards a foe who is fighting a merciless war of extermination against the German people." [1]

During the next four days the German armed forces came very near carrying out their Fuehrer's wishes. The Luftwaffe sent over the beachhead 30 fighter-bombers by day and 47 at night, on 29 January.[2] At Salerno the Navy had learned how to cope with the enemy's latest weapon, the radio-directed glide-bomb. Army fighter-director teams had been installed on board U.S. destroyer escorts *Frederick C. Davis* and *Herbert C. Jones*, and H.M.S. *Ulster Queen.* By monitoring all Luftwaffe frequencies they could even tell when the bombers were warming up at Rome, and from what direction an air raid would come. *Davis* and *Jones* also possessed jamming devices to disrupt the enemy aviator's control of his guided missile, and deflect it into the water. One or the other of these ships was constantly on duty at the beachhead. With practice they became almost perfect, but on 29 January they had not been at it long,[3] and that evening the enemy managed to pull off a severe guided-bomb attack on the anchorage. Flak rose in heavy streams to meet the planes, one of whose bombs hit H.M.S. *Spartan,* anchored close inshore. The cruiser capsized at 1905 and became a total loss. Another bomb hit Liberty ship *Samuel Huntington.* Her crew fought fires until 1930, when the master ordered Abandon Ship, as his cargo consisted largely of ammunition and gasoline. Salvage tug *ATR–1*, which had stood by *Spartan* until she was past help, closed *Huntington* and gamely started to fight the fires; but while so engaged was badly damaged by near misses in the next air raid. The Liberty ship continued to blaze until 0300 next morning, when she exploded and sank.

Admiral Lowry experienced the usual trouble in obtaining a

[1] *Fuehrer Directives 1942–45* pp. 121–22.

[2] War Diary German Naval Staff. It has no reports for the 30th, planes were grounded by weather on the 31st, and the Diary for Feb.–Apr. is not complete in our files.

[3] A German plane would circle over the roadstead at high elevation and let go the bomb, which was provided with vanes to check its speed. When the pilot saw a good target, he would attempt to guide the bomb to it by radio; and it was up to *Davis* or *Jones* to deflect it. Information from Cdr. R. C. Robbins USNR, former C.O. of *Davis,* in 1951.

quick unloading of Liberty ships, whose crews, as well as the Army shore parties detailed to help them, knocked off at every Red alert. Finally he arranged for the stevedores who had loaded the vessels at Naples to stay on board to help the unloading, and ordered the ships to run aground and anchor; an unusual procedure, but it saved time – emptying the ship floated her off. Dukws and LCTs proved to be the best means of getting the cargoes ashore quickly, and a floating drydock was constructed at Naples out of pontoon units to service and repair them on their frequent turnarounds.

Anzio, in the meantime, was undergoing a quicker change for the worse than it had ever known in its long history. German shelling of the town and harbor went on day and night. Buildings around the port disintegrated one by one; sumptuous villas were deprived first of their elaborate cornices, then of their roofs. Sailors who made the convoy runs from Naples to Anzio noted the progressive deterioration of the town, and laid bets whether this white apartment house or that pink villa would be standing on their return. The sturdy Italian stone construction stood up remarkably well. A direct 88-mm hit would burst a roof and gut one or two floors, but the walls still stood.

Operation SHINGLE was now a week old. Seven Liberty ships and 201 LST loads had been cleared at the beachhead, and 27,250 tons of stores landed. "With 68,886 men, 508 guns and 237 tanks ashore, and backed by the large credit in stores on the beachhead, VI Corps was now prepared, on 29 January, to launch its attack." [4] General Lucas had the equivalent of four divisions under his command; since the United States 45th Infantry Division (Major General Troy Middleton USA) had landed and the rest of the 1st Armored Division (Major General Ernest N. Harmon USA) would be up from Naples shortly. But four divisions were now not enough for a successful offensive.

On the night of 29–30 January the Rangers were ordered to steal across a treeless plain and seize Cisterna, at the junction of the Rome–Naples railroad with the Appian Way; while units of the

[4] Sacmed *Report* p. 20.

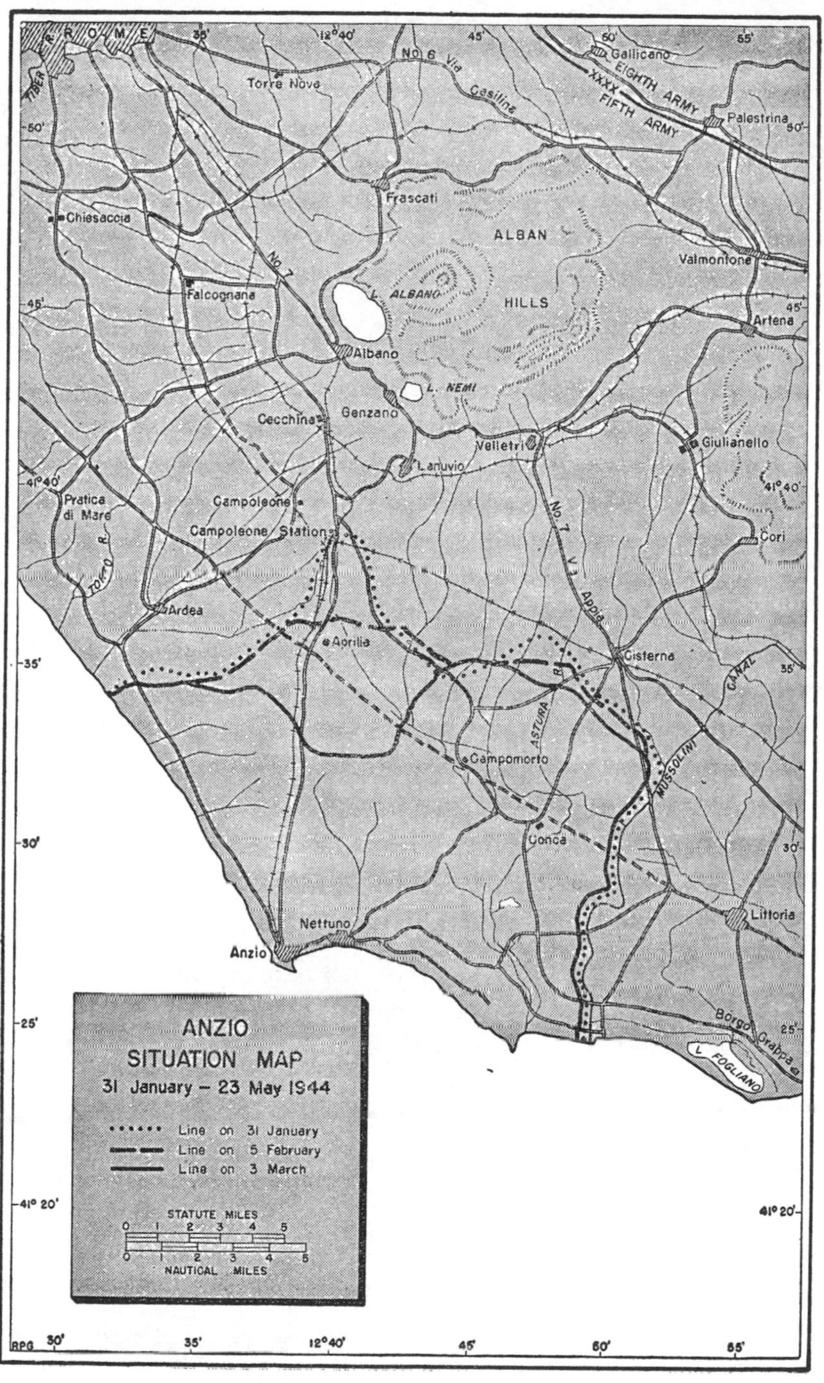

ROME
TIBER R.
Torre Nove
No 6 Via Casilina
Gallicano
EIGHTH ARMY
FIFTH ARMY
Palestrina
Frascati
Chiesaccia
ALBAN
HILLS
Valmontone
No 7
Falcognana
L. ALBANO
Artena
Albano
L. NEMI
Cecchina
Genzano
Velletri
Giulianello
Lanuvio
Pratica di Mare
Campoleone
Campoleone Station
Cori
TORTO R.
Ardea
No 7 Via Appia
Aprilia
Cisterna
CANAL
ASTURA R.
MUSSOLINI
Campomorto
Conca
Littoria
Nettuno
Anzio
Borgo Grappa
L. FOGLIANO
ANZIO
SITUATION MAP
31 January – 23 May 1944
Line on 31 January
Line on 5 February
Line on 3 March
STATUTE MILES
NAUTICAL MILES
RPG

3rd Division on the flanks cut railroad and highway in two places. At the same time, the British 1st Division attempted to take the crossroad north of Campoleone, which would have opened the way for a drive by the U.S. 1st Armored to Albano, halfway from Anzio to Rome.

Both attacks were frustrated. Instead of encountering delaying positions before Cisterna and Campoleone, VI Corps tangled with 30 German infantry battalions supported by armor and artillery. The 16th Panzer Division had come in; rain and soft ground bogged the offense. For two days the struggle for Cisterna continued. Two Ranger battalions were surrounded and captured — a loss of 761 fighting men; and as many more in other units were killed or missing. On the left flank, General Harmon's 1st Armored swung wide in the hope of reaching Albano behind the Germans, but was stopped by the mud. And the British ran into a hornet's nest of resistance from Germans firmly entrenched in stone farmhouses. General Lucas concluded that to continue these attacks would mean useless sacrifice.

There was little naval gunfire support in this major attack; *Edison,* however, distinguished herself by a shoot of 336 rounds which brought the signal, "Very effective. Many enemy troops killed by your fire. Good work." [5]

On 30 January H.M.S. *Dido* and *Delhi* departed for Naples with *Spartan* survivors, while cruisers *Brooklyn* and H.M.S. *Phoebe* relieved them in fire support duties. All that day low clouds and a thick haze shrouded the beachhead. General Clark arrived in a motor torpedo boat [6] and set up temporary Fifth Army headquarters in the Villa Borghese. "His gloomy attitude," noted General Lucas in his diary, "is certainly bad for me. He thinks I should have been more aggressive on D-day. I think he realizes the serious nature of the whole operation. His forces are divided in the face of an enemy who is operating on interior lines, and now neither of the

[5] *Edison* Action Report. There was also firing on the left flank by British cruisers, of which I have no record.

[6] It was mistaken for enemy, fired on by a minesweeper and badly damaged; there were several casualties.

parts is capable of inflicting a real defeat on the hostile troops facing it." On 1 February General Alexander called again. "He was kind enough," recorded Lucas, "but I am afraid is not pleased. My head will probably fall in the basket, but I have done my best."

Admiral Lowry departed in *Biscayne* at midnight February 1, after eleven days' command of the most thoroughly harassed naval operation yet launched in the Mediterranean. "I will miss him," noted General Lucas. "The work of the Navy under his direction has been one of the outstanding achievements of the operation." Admiral Hewitt notes in his War Diary for 2 February, "Assault phase of Operation SHINGLE completed."

On the same day, Cincmed (Admiral Sir John Cunningham RN) directed Rear Admiral Lowry "to hand over control of SHINGLE area to Flag Officer Western Italy," Rear Admiral John A. V. Morse RN. Although Admiral Lowry subsequently visited the beachhead twice, and as Commander VIII Amphibious Force was responsible for keeping the beaching and other craft sailing, he had nothing more directly to do with the Anzio operation. At the time of his departure, Rear Admiral Mansfield RN in H.M.S. *Orion* was senior officer afloat off the beachhead. But this local tactical command frequently changed as British and American ships rotated duty. Guided missiles had rendered Anzio roadstead so dangerous for cruisers that Admiral Cunningham ordered them to be sent there only "to resist serious threats to security of the bridgehead and to reduce strong points beyond the reach of Army artillery." [7]

On 1 February General Wilson, Supreme Allied Commander in the Mediterranean, conceded that "the first phase of the winter campaign had come to a close." The Eighth Army front, unchanged since 22 January, had become static. Men on the main Fifth Army front were terribly fatigued. Had it been practicable, the best of them would have been shifted to Anzio, making SHINGLE the main

[7] Comnavnaw (Vice Adm. Hewitt) War Diary; *Brooklyn* (Capt. R. W. Cary) Action Report, Enclosure A, pp. 37–39. Admiral Hewitt visited the roadstead 1 Feb. and returned to Naples in *Brooklyn*, which then proceeded to Palermo to pick up much-needed ammunition and supplies for the beachhead. Rear Adm. John A. V. Morse RN (FOWIT), with headquarters at Naples, had complete charge of shuttle convoys to Anzio.

show instead of a diversion; but there was not enough troop lift to effect any substantial transfer. So VI Corps went on the defensive, dug in south of the Campoleone–Cisterna line and prepared for a German counterattack.[8]

Marshal Kesselring must have experienced a rare feeling of elation. With his southern front holding firm, he was convinced that he could rub out Anzio beachhead with forces then available; but he was worried about naval gunfire and mounting Allied air superiority.[9] German units could be moved from the Adriatic to Anzio and Cassino because the Eighth Army offensive had come to naught. By 3 February elements from 15 German divisions, adding up to about five divisions in all, were in the Alban Hills and on the Anzio plain.[10] Most of these had been identified by VI Corps Intelligence. The situation looked serious indeed.

2. *VI Corps on the Defensive, 1–29 February*

From 2 February, when Captain Harry Sanders took it over, naval participation in the Anzio operation was continuous, in the form of escort, logistic supply and gunfire support of troops ashore.[11] It was imperative to protect the Naples–Anzio lifeline, but General Lucas wanted every available gunfire ship off the beachhead. Admiral Cunningham, despite his caution about the use of cruisers in the roadstead, generally managed to have one there every day, and it took only five or six hours to get one up from Naples in sudden need.[12] It gave the troops confidence, when

[8] General Clark ordered Lucas on 3 Feb.: "Your beachhead should now be consolidated and dispositions should be made suitable for meeting an attack. . . . Previous orders to . . . take Cisterna are canceled." Lucas Diary; *Calculated Risk* p. 298.

[9] Kesselring *Soldat bis zum Letzten Tag* p. 272 (*Memoirs* p. 195).

[10] Sacmed *Report* p. 22; "The German Operation at Anzio" p. 15. None of these divisions were full strength. Germans had remarkable proficiency in combining units from widely scattered divisions into effective combat teams.

[11] With the withdrawal of Rear Adm. Lowry, the main action reports of this operation come to an end; neither Admiral Morse nor Admiral Mansfield seems to have made one.

[12] On 2 Feb. H.M.S. *Phoebe* was at the roadstead with U.S.S. *Trippe,* which

they raised their heads from the scarred plain where they were dug in, to see cruisers' and destroyers' guns trained on the enemy and at instant call.

Hitler now ordered Kesselring to cut out the "abscess," as he is said to have called Anzio beachhead. While his Tenth Army held the American Fifth and British Eighth on the Gustav Line, the Fourteenth Army (General Eberhard von Mackensen) made every effort to perform the desired surgical operation. On the night of 3 February British troops who had driven a salient into the German defense line east of Campoleone were attacked. The British, especially the Guards Brigade, fought doggedly; but on the 5th were forced back three miles to a line north of Aprilia, after losing more than 1400 killed, wounded and missing.[13]

General Lucas, remembering the sensational German counterattack at Salerno which had very nearly split the beachhead, braced himself for something similar, and he had not long to wait.

On the evening of 5 February the enemy put an intense concentration of gunfire on the 3rd Division facing Cisterna, and forced them to give up a crossroad about a mile and a half southwest of the town. The Germans now had 95 tanks and 372 artillery pieces (154 of calibers over 105-mm) concentrated around this area, and were able to fire into any part of the roadstead or beachhead.[14] Their aim was not very good, but the beachhead was so congested that almost any shot had lethal results. The Luftwaffe was equally active, and more deadly than the artillery.

Ludlow on 8 February, the third day of heavy fighting ashore, was steaming slowly between the Peter and X-ray sectors. Her tall, lean skipper, Commander Liles Creighton, was relaxing in his chair

---

was relieved by *Edison* that day. On 3 Feb. Rear Adm. Mansfield put *Brooklyn* and *Dido* on half-hour notice, and *Orion* and *Penelope* on 4-hour notice. *Brooklyn* relieved *Phoebe* 4 Feb. and *Ludlow* relieved *Edison. Brooklyn* expended 201 rounds on enemy concentrations and motor transport on 5 Feb. That afternoon, Capt. Cary recommended that his cruiser stay away from Anzio until there was more evidence of the expected German counterattack, and she returned to Naples. When the attack broke on 8 Feb., *Brooklyn, Orion, Phoebe* and *Mauritius* were sent right up to Anzio.

[13] *Anzio Beachhead* p. 46.

[14] "German Operation at Anzio" p. 53.

on the bridge, one foot on a port and the other on the navigator's desk. A 170-mm shell dropped at a 60-degree angle right between his legs, burning them severely, and spent itself in a crazy course of destruction. It tossed 20-mm ammunition into the captain's cabin, destroyed confidential publications in the wardroom passageway, and finally came to rest, unexploded, three feet from the ship's skin. There it was gingerly picked up by J. D. Johnson, chief gunner's mate, carried to the main deck and dropped overboard.[15] "Lucky Lud's" luck still held.

Naval gunfire ships continued their unflagging support on the 9th. *Brooklyn*, in her final shoot on the Anzio beachhead, fired 580 rounds of 6-inch shell and then retired to Tunis to become Rear Admiral Davidson's flagship, releasing *Philadelphia* (Captain Walter Ansel) for cruiser support off Anzio. Three British cruisers were already there. The Germans had been throwing in everything to wrest Aprilia and Carroceto, two contiguous towns four miles south of Campoleone, from the hard-pressed British 1st Division. Cruiser gunfire did its best to help the exhausted Micks, Jocks and Tommies; but the 1st Division was down to half its effective strength, and it was unable to hold the two towns.

General Lucas on 10 February committed two regiments of the 45th Infantry Division (Major General W. W. Eagles USA) from his corps reserve, to help the British. After two days' frantic fighting, the 45th had not attained its objective. Combat came to a halt on the 12th; the 56th British Division was brought up to relieve the battered 1st. VI Corps steeled itself for the next counterattack.

A sense of desperation now prevailed on the beachhead and on board the ships in the roadstead. Several news correspondents at the beachhead "took off, wishing to avoid another Dunkirk," and spread alarm at Naples.[16] Field Marshal Smuts, watching events from afar, telegraphed to the Prime Minister that he supposed Anzio beachhead was intended to "link up with the Cassino front";

[15] *Ludlow* Action Report 11 Feb. 1944.
[16] Lucas Dairy.

but "an isolated pocket has now been created, which is unconnected with enemy's main southern front, and which is itself besieged instead of giving relief." [17] That was the bald truth. As days passed and nothing important happened on land, the situation began to look brighter to those who were not sweating it out on the spot. Mr. Churchill declared on 12 February that both General Wilson and General Alexander had assured him that the battle for Rome would be won. "All battles are anxious as they approach the climax, but there is no justification for pessimism, according to the latest reports from responsible authorities." [18]

The campaign was indeed mounting a climax, but there was much more than natural anxiety to justify pessimism. Against about four Allied divisions the Germans had nearly 92,000 troops in the battle area, and more were coming up.[19] Nor were signs on the Fifth Army front any more favorable. Monte Cassino was the key to that region. Almost continuous attacks on it by the United States II Corps during the first twelve days of February were thrown back with heavy loss. General Clark reluctantly decided to destroy the monastery on the summit of the mountain, since many people believed (mistakenly it has since been proved) that the enemy was using it for observation and gun emplacements. Very heavy air bombings, beginning 15 February, completely razed that ancient home of the Benedictine Order. The Germans promptly moved into the rubble and counterattacked.

While this battle for Monte Cassino teetered and tottered, General Mackensen renewed his attack on Anzio beachhead on February 16, with six divisions in the initial assault. The previous evening, the Luftwaffe deprived VI Corps of part of its ammunition to meet the assault, by a successful radio-directed bombing attack on Liberty ship *Elihu Yale*, which was discharging artillery shells into *LCT–35* about half a mile off the beach. A bomb that exploded in

[17] *Closing the Ring* p. 492.
[18] *O.N.I. Weekly* III No. 7 (16 Feb. 1944) pp. 481–82.
[19] "German Operation at Anzio" p. 46; *Anzio Beachhead* p. 67 states there were at least 120,000 troops in Fourteenth Army on 12 Feb. 1944. Allied battle order in Truscott p. 318.

an empty hold gutted the ship and set off the ammunition in the LCT. Both were a total loss.[20]

The Germans attacked in two waves. The first, whose mission was to break the VI Corps lines, consisted of two motorized infantry divisions, the 3rd Panzer Grenadiers and a pet Nazi outfit, the Lehr. The second wave – 29th Panzer Grenadier Division, 26th Panzer Division and two additional battalions – was to drive down both sides of the main road to Anzio and Nettuno. And three other divisions – the 1st Parachute, 65th Infantry and the Hermann Goerings – delivered harassing attacks on VI Corps flanks.[21]

The first German wave, attacking on a four-mile front, drove a salient four miles deep into the center of the VI Corps line and reached a point seven miles from the beach. There the Allied defensive positions held; the second wave and the flank attackers never got going. The United States Army now took the offensive. On 19–20 February, counterattacks led by General Harmon of the 1st Armored Division and General Eagles of the 45th forced the enemy to fall back and brought the greatest German effort on this front to a halt. British cruisers, and destroyers of both navies, piled shells on the storming enemy during the counteroffensive. The German naval chronicler alluded gloomily to the tenacity of Allied troops, and to naval gunfire which "hindered the battle's progress"; he admitted the "casualties from hits by ships' batteries (cruisers and destroyers)" were "not insignificant." [22]

The Germans also gave credit for stopping this drive to Allied fighter bombers. Allied aircraft based on southern Italian fields gave close and continuous support to the troops and went after supply dumps and vehicle parks in the enemy's rear. Some 800 planes of Tactical dropped 972 tons of bombs during this action, while Stra-

20 Moran "Anzio-Nettuno Landings" p. 62; Summary of Survivors' Statements.

21 "Feldzug in Italien" chap. xii; "The German Operation at Anzio" pp. 39–41.

22 War Diary German Naval Staff 18 and 20 Feb. 1944. The extent of the gunfire supplied by naval forces cannot now be ascertained. The R.N. was in charge of the port of Anzio, gunfire support and all naval operations off the beachhead, and we shall have to await the official British history of this campaign to know the details.

tegic Air Force flew missions against Grottaferrata, Albano, Genzano and Velletri.

On 22 February, only two days after his VI Corps had won this outstanding defensive battle against the overwhelming enemy forces, General Lucas's "head fell in a basket," as he had predicted. General Clark, who only two days before had congratulated him on defeating the German drive, said "that he could no longer resist the pressure . . . from both Alexander and Devers." [23] It seems that all the "higher-ups" were chagrined because SHINGLE had turned out the way it did; and the "lower-downs" had lost confidence in Lucas.[24]

Major General Truscott, who had been Lucas's deputy for the past week, now relieved him as Commanding General VI Corps. On 29 February the enemy made his final effort against the American sector south of Cisterna. Three divisions with 90 tanks, and smaller groups on the flanks, smashed at the battered 3rd Division, 1st Armored, and part of the 45th. After two more days of bloody give-and-take, mostly under heavy rain, the Germans gave up trying. Fourteenth Army was too exhausted to continue an offensive, and Marshal Kesselring had committed all his reserves. Over one thousand German prisoners were taken on the last day of February.

Since the Axis still held the ports of Leghorn, Genoa, Cannes, Toulon and Marseille, it is surprising that there were neither submarine nor torpedo boat attacks on ships off Anzio for almost four weeks. Prince Borghese, whose villa General Clark was using as headquarters, raided the roadstead on the night of 18 February with a few of the motor torpedo boats which he had brought into the

[23] Lucas Diary 22 Feb. 1944. Lt. Gen. J. L. Devers USA was "Jumbo" Wilson's Deputy Sacmed.

[24] Gen. Truscott writes (*Command Missions* p. 320) that Lucas "lacked some of the qualities of positive leadership that engenders confidence, and that he leaned heavily upon his staff and trusted subordinates in difficult decisions." On pp. 328–31 Truscott discusses faults in the Corps organization and gives reasons why the German offensive was not stopped earlier. He says nothing about naval gunfire support, probably regarding it as of secondary importance to the Army's own artillery. Fitzgerald *History of the Irish Guards* pp. 209–10 confirms the poor staff work of VI Corps.

service of Mussolini's puppet government. U.S.S. *PC–545* sank one of them in a sharp ten-minute encounter; *PC–627* got another on the night of 22 February.

Air attacks came every night. On the 25th H.M.S. *Inglefield* was hit by guided bombs. U.S.S. *LCI–12*, equipped as salvage vessel, closed the sinking destroyer in a strong sirocco and heavy sea, and managed to rescue 23 of her crew under extremely hazardous conditions. But *Inglefield* and most of her men were lost.[25]

Now the convoy route for the Naples–Anzio run was becoming dangerous. On 18 February H.M.S. *Penelope* was torpedoed and sunk by *U–410* between Ponza and Cape Circe. On the 20th, *LST–348* met the same fate. One torpedo blew off her bow, a second broke her in two, and she went down with 24 members of her crew. Escorts were strengthened, but the inner channel to Anzio was not abandoned. Ships continued to pass under the eyes of German gunners on Cape Circe, whose summit rises 1775 feet above the sea. The former resort of the enchantress had become as inimical to us as to Ulysses' crew.

3. *Stagnation, March–April*

At 1840 March 1 Marshal Kesselring ordered General Mackensen to halt; and that evening Fourteenth Army began to dig in.[26] As if to implement his decision, the weather cleared on 2 March, permitting Allied Air Forces to put on the biggest show of the campaign. Two hundred and forty-one Liberators and 100 Flying Fortresses, with 113 P–38s and 63 P–47s providing fighter cover, dropped thousands of fragmentation bombs around Cisterna, Velletri and Carroceto. An almost equally large force of medium, light and fighter-bombers concentrated on enemy tanks, gun positions and assembly areas, particularly along the Cisterna–Campoleone railway.

The third of March, almost six weeks after D-day, began a

[25] *Philadelphia* War Diary Feb. 1944, Enclosure A; Moran p. 64.

[26] *Soldat bis zum Letzten Tag* p. 275. He sent the 114th Division to his Tenth Army and the hard-worked Hermann Goering to Leghorn, fearing another end run near that city. "Feldzug in Italien" chap. xii; "The German Operation at Anzio" p. 78.

long period of stagnation on Anzio beachhead. The enemy could not spare enough troops to make another bid at cutting out the "abscess," nor were the Allies strong enough to pierce his lines, cut his communications or take the Alban Hills. The only military value of the Anzio undertaking for them during the next three months was to pin down several first-line German divisions which might otherwise have been used against the Fifth and Eighth Armies, or deployed to meet the invasion of Normandy.

The problem of supplying the now bloated VI Corps with available shipping was met by the average daily dispatch of six LSTs carrying 50 loaded trucks or dukws each, a shuttle of 15 LCTs per week, and 4 Liberty ships every ten days.

"There could be no hope now of a break-out from the Anzio beachhead," wrote Mr. Churchill, "and no prospect of an early link-up between our two separated forces until the Cassino front was broken." [27] There never had been, for that matter. Still interested in his "baby," despite disappointment over its progress, the Prime Minister on 12 March inquired into the ration and vehicle strength at Anzio beachhead. He was told that 90,200 U. S. and 35,500 British troops were present, and that "nearly 25,000 vehicles" had been landed.[28]

Deadlock on the beachhead was a severe trial to VI Corps, and to sailors in the ships standing by. Cold, drenching rains and gusty winds made any movement ashore difficult, and life itself a burden; beaching craft in the roads rolled and tossed in the steep Mediterranean winter seas, almost worse than those of the North Atlantic. Evening brought no rest to the weary sailor who, like as not, had been at general quarters since dawn. Crepuscular air attacks were the rule rather than the exception, because Allied fighter planes had to retire to their fields near Naples at twilight. The Germans had an air observation post high in the Alban Hills, from which they could identify and follow any ship in the roadstead, and dispatch a

[27] *Closing the Ring* p. 501.

[28] *Closing the Ring* pp. 487–8, 501. Mr. Churchill became steamed up over a mental picture of 25,000 soldiers driving that many vehicles; actually the figure 25,000 represented repeated appearances of the same trucks, operating by the preloaded shuttle system devised by Gen. Lucas's staff.

guided missile attack from the Roman airfields at a few minutes' notice. The strain on the American and British sailors of endless alerts, frequent firing, constant dodging of guided missiles and enemy shellfire, created a number of noncombatant casualties greatly exceeding those that stemmed from direct action with the enemy – a most unusual state of affairs for either navy. Fortunately, by alternating gunfire support ships and by a quick turnaround of the LST shuttles, it was possible to give the sailors a little rest in Naples.

"Never had I seen a war zone so crowded," wrote Ernie Pyle. "If a plane went down in no man's land, more than half the troops on the beachhead could see it fall. New units in the fighting, or old units wishing to change positions, had great difficulty in finding a place. The space problem was almost as bad as in Washington." [29]

Visiting Anzio beachhead shortly after hostilities there had ceased, I found over half the buildings in Anzio and Nettuno to be wholly or partially destroyed. The plain, for a space of seven to ten miles inland, was pockmarked with shell and bomb craters; not one isolated farmhouse was intact; Aprilia was a heap of rubble. The plain looked more like no man's land on the Western Front during World War I than did even the most plowed-up and beaten-down atoll in the Pacific.

Fortunately for the civilians who lived on this beachhead, the Allied Military Government organization (AMGOT) began evacuating them to southern Italy in good time, and in all took out about 20,000 Italian men, women and children by sea. Evacuation of the sick and wounded from the exposed field hospitals was also done by sea to Naples, for the minute airstrip at Nettuno was too vulnerable. Since hospital ship *St. David* had been sunk, LSTs, specially fitted and provided with hospital corpsmen, Army medicos, supplies and utilities, became the principal carriers. At most it was an 18-hour passage for a wounded man from the beach to the base hospital at Naples.[30]

[29] *Brave Men* p. 162, by permission of Henry Holt & Co.

[30] "Fifth Army Medical Service, History 1944" p. 29; 2nd Lt. Glenn Clift USA "Field Operations of Medical Dept. in Mediterranean Theater" 10 Nov. 1945.

In March, VI Corps consisted of the 3rd, 45th and 1st Armored Divisions United States Army, and 1st and 56th Divisions British Army, together with a number of attached units. Replacements, brought in almost daily, did not make up for the attrition.

Kesselring withdrew two German divisions, the 26th Panzer and 29th Panzer Grenadier, from the Anzio front shortly after 4 March, and added only two battalions of the Italian infantry that had stuck by Mussolini. By the end of March, the enemy had five divisions and three regiments on Anzio beachhead, a total of over 135,000 troops, and still outnumbered the Allies at that point. After 4 March there was no heavy fighting, but a constant exchange of armed patrolling, night raids, air attacks and artillery fire kept the beachhead lively.[31]

Both the Army and naval authorities at the beachhead occasionally had trouble with Liberty ships manned by merchant mariners. In part this was caused (as Admiral Lowry observed) by lack of proper communications with shore control, want of clear knowledge by shipmasters of their places in the organization, and inadequate instructions on convoy and routing. On the other hand, merchant mariners frequently refused to handle the lines of LCTs coming alongside "after working hours." The Navy-manned craft, under orders to work around the clock, came alongside at all hours, only to be left waiting for want of line handlers on the merchant vessels. The 450 dukws employed at the beachhead "proved an invaluable asset in unloading Liberty ships moored at a distance off shore," recorded General Wilson; and the British naval officers praised the Negroes who drove the American dukws "for their cheerfulness, cleanliness and courage. Shelling or no shelling . . . those American Negroes and their white comrades kept the unending chain of 'ducks' running to and from the anchorage." [32]

[31] *Fifth Army History* Part IV 159–66.

[32] Rear Adm. Lowry Supplementary Action Report 17 May 1944 pp. 16–17; Sacmed *Report* p. 20; Lt. Cdr. Trevor Blore RNVR *Commissioned Bargees, the Story of the Landing Craft* (London 1952) pp. 49–50. The "white comrades" were the British Army drivers of dukws attached to R.N. units.

During the month of March masters of merchant vessels became so nervous about anchoring close inshore, within range of German guns, that Admiral Lowry had to issue arguments to back up his orders. He pointed out that, by moving out to sea to avoid enemy shelling, the ships not only lost the protection of inshore smoke screen, antiaircraft umbrella and naval patrols, but delayed their unloading and increased the length of their stay in the roadstead. "The chances of being hit by a shell from a shore battery," he observed, "are negligible. . . . If shells are falling near you, there is no objection to your moving a few hundred yards, but remember that you are just as likely to move into as you are out of the path of the next shell." [83] The Admiral even took the unusual course of assuming responsibility for any damage that the merchant vessels might sustain as a result of obeying his orders.

On 12 March the United States Navy lent a hand on the main Fifth Army front by delivering counter-battery fire at and around the town of Fórmia, on the Gulf of Gaëta between Naples and Anzio. The green U.S. 88th Infantry Division had recently relieved the British on this flank, and it was thought that naval gunfire support would have a good effect on its morale. *Philadelphia*, *Hilary P. Jones* and *Lansdale* entered the Gulf of Gaëta through a swept channel on the morning of the 12th, but rain closed in so rapidly that the projected shoot had to be postponed. The problem was resumed next day under a cloudless sky. Allied air spot searched in vain for the enemy guns, which fired with uncanny accuracy on all three ships. Brisk evasive maneuvers were executed as shells bracketed *Philadelphia* and threw splinters on board *Jones*, then belching forth smoke in the hope of concealing the group. *Philadelphia* fired at extreme range, and so was unable to comply when the Spitfire that was spotting signalled "up 300." Finally, as enemy shellfire continued to churn the waters where this fire-support unit was maneuvering, its objective changed from one of bolstering infantry morale to that of preserving three valuable ships. When

[83] "Guide to Merchant Vessels Unloading at Anzio" 17 Mar. 1944, a mimeographed sheet; U.S. Naval Inst. *Proceedings* LXXX 29.

Captain Ansel, O.T.C. in *Philadelphia*, reported this state of affairs to Rear Admiral Mansfield, he was advised to retire to Naples.

Well to the south, 60 miles northeast of Palermo, there took place a unique destroyer–submarine battle in which both antagonists were sunk. H.M. destroyer *Laforey* reported a contact on the morning of 29 March. In the attack that developed, the destroyer was torpedoed. She sent out a call for assistance which was promptly answered by U.S.S. *Kearny* and *Ericsson*, two PCs, and several British vessels. One of them sank the submarine, *U–223*, but not before it had got another torpedo into *Laforey*, which sank her.[34]

April brought sunlight, moderate breezes and some measure of physical comfort to the weary troops dug in on the Anzio plain. Flowers bloomed in the cratered fields for Easter week; the untended gardens of abandoned villas were a riot of cyclamen and freesia. But there was still rage in this heaven. A German 280-mm railroad gun, called "Leopold" by its German masters and "Anzio Annie" by the Americans, began on 24 March to lob shells into both towns and the roadstead.[35] It destroyed a number of buildings in Anzio and Nettuno. The Luftwaffe continued to raid throughout the month of April, but its guided bombs were now effectively dealt with by the standby destroyer escort.

Other unwelcome spring flowers were German midget submarines. At 0230 April 21, *PC–591*, patrolling six miles south of Anzio lighthouse, made a radar contact and set course to intercept. The target, never seen, turned inside the PC's turning circle, and at 0307 an underwater explosion was heard dead astern.[36] In view of what happened a few hours later, this was undoubtedly a midget. For *PC–558* at 0715 picked up a small wake on her starboard bow. She closed range and presently observed a glass dome about 24 inches in diameter extending less than a foot above the surface. The mechanism proved to be a one-man submarine. *PC–558* roared in to drop depth charges, and her crew picked up an *Oberleutnant*

[34] *Brooklyn* War Diary 29–30 Mar. 1944; *PC–626* War Diary.
[35] *Anzio Beachhead* p. 113.
[36] Moran "Anzio-Nettuno Landings"; *PC–691* Action Report.

of the German Navy floundering in the water, his submarine gone. Within a few minutes *PC–558* sighted another small boat, attacked it with the aid of *PC–626*, and made a second kill. A third was made by *SC–651*. The vulnerability of these tiny submarines was now apparent. Vigilant lookouts could easily pick them up; depth charges with shallow settings demolished them in short order.[37]

In Chapter XIV we described the early operations of American and British motor torpedo boats based on Bastia, Corsica. Their efforts to break up German coastal traffic north of Rome continued through Operation SHINGLE.

Lieutenant Commander Barnes, with three PTs, was patrolling the Italian coast opposite Corsica on the night of 18–19 February 1944 when he made contact with a group of F-lighters escorted by E-boats. The PTs, which had been equipped with rocket launchers, fired a rocket salvo which did not find its target, and the German escorts opened up with heavy gunfire. In the confusion which followed, Barnes's boat had all three engines fail, the second lost all electric power, and the third had a jammed rudder. But the Germans, firing indiscriminately in the darkness and smoke, slowly drew away, leaving three unhurt but much relieved PTs in their wake. Rocket launchers were now discarded.

Some means had to be found to cope with German coastal traffic. A combined striking group was built around the American PTs, the only radar-equipped small craft; the British LCGs, which were LCTs armed with 4.7-inch and 40-mm guns; and the British MTBs, which had more reliable torpedoes than ours. The leader of this group, Commander R. A. Allan RNVR, used one of the American boats for his "flagship" and organized his "fleet" as if for a classic naval battle, in a "scouting group" of two American PTs under Lieutenant E. A. DuBose USNR, and a "battle group" of three LCGs as "capital ships" with a screen of PTs and MTBs. His first success came on the night of 27–28 March north of Elba. At 2145 DuBose's

[37] *PC–558* "Report of Action against One-Man Submarines" 23 Apr. 1944; *PC–626* War Diary Apr. 1944.

radar picked up a convoy of six F-lighters headed south. Allan maneuvered his "battle group" into position to intercept. In the meantime the "scouting group" picked up two torpedo boats closing rapidly from the direction of Spezia, attacked them with torpedoes from a range of 400 yards, and retired under smoke cover while being straddled by 4-inch shells. An explosion was heard in one of the torpedo boats, and both retired up the coast. As soon as they were at a safe distance, Allan illuminated the German convoy with star shell which the F-lighter gunners mistook for aircraft flares and began firing skyward. Allan's gunners, who now had a perfect setup, sank all six lighters.

This excellent piece of teamwork pointed the way for more of the same kind, and a similar attack in the night of 24–25 April was equally successful. Each of the two groups picked up an F-lighter convoy, one southbound and the other northbound. Allan took on the one, and DuBose the other; and in three fights, lasting an hour and a half, five F-lighters, four flak lighters and a tug were sunk, and twelve prisoners were taken.

German corvettes, though not nearly as fast as torpedo boats, were also used by the enemy as escorts. Two of them on the night of 23–24 May were picked up by a PT-scouting unit commanded by Lieutenant DuBose, who promptly fired a torpedo spread. The leading corvette, *UJ–2223*, took two hits and sank; the other was so badly damaged that the Germans had to abandon her, but not before she had driven the PTs off with heavy gunfire.

Out-gunned by their enemy, and armed with torpedoes ill suited for shoal-draft targets, the PTs nevertheless made a gallant record. Operating where large vessels could not venture because of mines, they proved that properly designed and armed small naval craft have an important and useful function in modern warfare.[38]

[38] MTBron 15 Action Reports No. 31 and 37; Bulkley ms. PT History pp. 399–406; Lt. Cdr. Barnes War Diary and conversations with him, 1953.

CHAPTER XVIII

Breakout

11 May–4 June 1944

1. *Gustav Line Broken, 11–25 May*

BY THE FIRST of May the naval part of the Anzio campaign had become routine. All the troops and supplies that the beachhead could hold were already there; calls for gunfire support were few and far between. But in May the Army was called upon to perform the deeds which had been planned for January.

Since March, General Alexander had been rearranging forces on both fronts. Troops were rested and trained; fresh divisions were brought up. The resulting distribution was as follows: –

At Anzio the VI Corps, General Truscott, comprised seven infantry divisions (five United States and two British) by the second week in May.[1] It still belonged to General Mark Clark's Fifth Army, the rest of which [2] was deployed in front of the German Gustav Line from the Gulf of Gaëta to the confluence of the Liri and Garigliano Rivers. From that point the British Eighth Army (Lieutenant General Sir Oliver Leese) carried the line to the Adriatic.

Total Allied forces on this main front amounted to about 20 divisions, in addition to the seven on the Anzio beachhead. Against these Marshal Kesselring could deploy about 26 divisions – 12 on the Gustav Line, six to contain Anzio beachhead, and eight in reserve.

An all-out attack on the Gustav Line was scheduled for 11 May.

[1] The U.S. 1st, 3rd, 34th, 36th, and 45th; British 1st and 5th Infantry Divisions.

[2] II Corps U.S. Army, commanded by Maj. Gen. Geoffrey Keyes, and a French Army Corps commanded by General Juin.

Eighth Army's mission was to break enemy defenses along the Rapido and advance into the Liri Valley, while the U.S. II Corps and the French Corps broke out of the Garigliano bridgehead. The mission of VI Corps was to advance from Anzio beachhead and get astride enemy communications to Rome. In the hope that the southern attack would suck all the German reserves out of the Alban Hills, VI Corps would jump off several days later, at a time to be set by General Alexander. After securing Highway No. 6, the Via Casilina, it would press on into Rome.[3]

General Juin's French Expeditionary Corps established the first bridgehead across the Garigliano and II Corps fought its way to positions two and a half miles northeast of Fórmia, by noon of the 16th. British XIII Corps and a Polish division, after a seesawing struggle, invested the entire Monte Cassino position. The Poles stormed up the mountain and, after suffering terrible casualties, captured the ruins of the monastery on the morning of 19 May. For the Allied armies in Italy, particularly the pent-up forces at Anzio, there could have been no brighter omen. The Germans now fell back to a new line of defense, the so-called Adolf Hitler Line which stretched from Terracina near Cape Circe to Monte Cairo northwest of Cassino.

During this advance both Navies were called upon to support II Corps by pounding enemy guns lying beyond Army artillery range. The bombardment force, commanded by Rear Admiral Lyal A. Davidson, comprised *Philadelphia*, *Brooklyn*, H.M.S. *Dido* and several U.S. destroyers, all based at Naples.

The first targets were in and near Gaëta and Fórmia, and Itri a few miles inland. H.M.S. *Dido* opened on the afternoon of May 12, shooting 242 rounds at a battery of 88-mm guns south of Itri, and 200 rounds at a road junction near Terracina.[4] *Brooklyn*, next in turn, found a more responsive enemy on 13 May. Captain F. R. Dodge remarked that his ship had not "heretofore been fired at as frequently as during this operation. Fortunately the enemy was

[3] General Alexander to Mr. Churchill 17 May 1944, *Closing the Ring* p. 603.
[4] Moran "Anzio-Nettuno Landings," section on Gaëta operations.

never good enough to make a hit, although he came uncomfortably close at times." *Brooklyn* found enemy gunfire so well registered on the only practicable firing area that she was forced to retire prematurely.[5]

May 14 began early for the Navy. The Luftwaffe called on Naples at 0340 and dropped circling torpedoes, which fortunately found no targets, and the early hours off Anzio were enlivened by a visit from the enemy's mosquito fleet. *PC–627* had a spirited brush with an Italian MAS-boat and sank it by gunfire. By sunup, *Philadelphia* and destroyers *Boyle* and *Kendrick* were off the Gaëta shore, ready to shoot. The coast remained invisible most of the day, but planes spotted for the cruiser as she fired on enemy batteries and on the command post of the German 94th Division at Itri.

Cruiser bombardment continued to support II Corps' coastwise progress, on a rotating schedule. Terracina, for instance, was well pounded from the sea before Corps artillery actually took over. The 85th and 88th Infantry Divisions of II Corps, which were doing their first fighting in this war, wanted all the naval gunfire they could get. Gaëta and Itri were in their possession by the 19th, but the Germans made a determined stand at Terracina, southern hinge of the Hitler Line. On the morning of 25 May, II Corps began swarming — and swimming — along roads ramifying through the Pontine Marshes, which the retiring Germans had flooded.

Now came an event which the Allies had been awaiting for four months. At 0731 May 25, on a small bridge near the village of Borgo Grappa in the Pontine Marshes, Lieutenant Francis X. Buckley USA, leading a II Corps reconnaissance mission west of Terracina, bumped into Captain Benjamin H. Sousa, leading a platoon of VI Corps engineers southeast from Anzio. "Where in hell do you think you're going?" shouted Sousa. "Anzio!" replied Buckley. "Boy, you've made it!" was the response.[6]

[5] *Brooklyn* Action Reports 12–19 May and 23 May–4 June 1944.
[6] Army Combat Film THC–4, "Cassino to Rome."

2. *On to Rome, 22 May–4 June*

These movements on the southern front dictated the timetable at Anzio beachhead. By 22 May, when the French captured Pontecorvo and the Americans had reached the mountains north of Terracina, it was clear that the Hitler Line had been turned, and the bell tolled for VI Corps to break its bonds at Anzio beachhead. The hour before dawn on 23 May was chosen.

Orders for supporting naval gunfire were passed to Rear Admiral Davidson. The fire of two cruisers was wanted, to guard against counterattack on the north flank facing the Alban Hills, and to support troops on the south flank in the Pontine Marshes. Thus, VI Corps would be enabled to concentrate its entire energies on the capture of Cisterna and Velletri, after which it would press through the valley between the Alban and Lepini Hills to Valmontone. This was a mighty mission for VI Corps, because Valmontone lay in the center of the Sacco River Valley on the Via Casilina, the only line of retreat for Germans from the main battlefront, now that the Via Appia was in Allied hands.

Philadelphia, screened by *Kendrick* and *Laub*, steamed up to Anzio's troubled waters late on 22 May. *Brooklyn*, *Kearny* and *Ericsson* had no sooner returned to Ponza to await orders than they got the word: "Proceed to Anzio at once. Assume duties of bombardment cruiser. *Philadelphia* in collision with *Laub*." That untimely event sent *Philadelphia* to Malta for extensive repairs to a bashed-in bow, and *Laub*, too, was *hors de combat.*

Brooklyn hastened to the beachhead, and that afternoon fired on enemy batteries and concentrations. Her shoot was well delivered, and the German fire in reply was light and inaccurate. With her destroyer screen she retired that evening to take on board Admiral Davidson and staff from crippled *Philadelphia.*

On the morning of 24 May *Brooklyn* and two destroyers returned to Anzio, where a well-trained aviator in a Piper Cub spotted the cruiser's fire on guns and troops. Her guns enfiladed ravines and gullies which the artillery could not penetrate because they crossed the Army's line of advance.

Cisterna, which the Germans had turned into a miniature Monte Cassino, was captured on the afternoon of 25 May after two days' bitter fighting. *Brooklyn* fired her last shot in this campaign on the 26th, evoking complimentary comments from her spotters. French cruiser *Émile Bertin*, relieving *Philadelphia*, acquitted herself with equal skill. With destroyers *Ordronaux* and *MacKenzie* screening, she silenced three enemy gun emplacements on the 27th while *MacKenzie*, operating at short range, evaded 18 "heavy and accurate" enemy salvos. For the next two days these ships supported the Allied left flank at extreme ranges.

No more cruiser fire was wanted. United States destroyers took up fire support as the Germans withdrew. From 31 May to 3 June *Kendrick*, *Parker*, *MacKenzie*, *Champlin* and *Kearny* took turns pouring hundreds of rounds upon guns, vehicles and troops around Ardea and Practica di Mare, villages halfway between Anzio and the mouth of the Tiber. U.S.S. *Kearny* was the last to fire in these concluding hours of the Anzio operation; H.M.S. *Dido* and French *Émile Bertin* came up on 4 June just in time to hear that it was all over.

These were glorious days for VI Corps, but costly; it suffered 4000 combat casualties in less than a week. Shortly after Cisterna had been captured on the 25th, General Clark altered the plan, greatly to General Truscott's dismay, and threw the weight of VI Corps across and south of the Alban Hills.[7] Here the Germans were still holding strongly, and it took the Corps four days to overrun the site of Campoleone. On the last day of May the 36th Division broke through in the center and seized high ground in the Alban Hills. The Germans withdrew, after two ancient imperial galleys which the Italians had salvaged from the bottom of Lake Nemi had burst into flames.

[7] Truscott pp. 375–78. He believes that this shift of plan prevented the cutting off and destruction of the German Tenth Army; that it was a mistake similar to that of Gen. Montgomery before Catania. Compare Linklater *Campaign in Italy* chap. v.

During the night of 2–3 June, the Germans broke off all along the front and rapidly withdrew northward, leaving only rear-guard detachments to harass the advance of the victorious Fifth Army. On the evening of 3 June, General Clark communicated to his troops his "most urgent desire" that they "protect both public and private property in the City of Rome." [8]

Kesselring spared Rome from the destruction and ignominy to which he had subjected Naples. By 4 June, most of his forces were retiring towards a new defense line that was being prepared in the northern Apennines.

On that fateful day, flying columns of eager Allied troops converged on the city along all main roads. A patrol of the 88th Division passed a ROMA sign on the Via Casilina at 0800 June 4, and entered the city by the Porta Maggiore. Throughout the day other American and British units thrust in to secure bridges and other key points.

As the Germans marched out of the city every street was deserted and the shutters closed; not one Roman wished them Godspeed. But no sooner had their rear guards departed than windows opened, Allied and Italian colors were displayed, and the streets filled with joyful crowds so dense that only with difficulty could the troops drive their flower-decked tanks and vehicles through. By midnight 4 June, Fifth Army was deployed along the Tiber from its mouth to well north of the city. Thus the Anzio operation and the advance on Rome were concluded simultaneously, exactly nineteen weeks after Admiral Lowry had landed VI Corps on Anzio beachhead.

For one brief day the liberation of Rome held the attention of the Allied nations. Then, on 6 June, came the news that the Allies had landed on the coast of Normandy. And with that the Italian campaign became a secondary front.

[8] *Fifth Army History* V p. 156.

3. *Conclusion*

CASUALTIES IN OPERATION SHINGLE

	Killed and Missing	*Wounded in Action*	*Non-Combat Casualties*
U. S. Navy [9]	160	166	?
Royal Navy [10]	366	63	?
	Killed Only		
U. S. Army [11]	2,800	11,000	26,000
British Army [11]	1,600	7,000	11,000

Of the two Navies engaged, the British sustained the heavier loss in ships: two cruisers, three destroyers, three LSTs one LCI and a hospital ship. The United States Navy lost one minesweeper, one small minecraft, one LST, two LCIs, three LCTs and two Liberty ships.

Operation SHINGLE was doomed by its very nature to drag along for months. Originally conceived as an end run coördinated with the drive up central Italy, it was nevertheless carried out after that drive had stalled. Consequently it could only be a diversion; and like other operations of that kind, it depleted the assailant by as much as or more than it diverted the defense. General Eisenhower describes it as "a draining sore in the side of the attacker"; but "in the final outcome," he writes, "the Anzio operation paid off handsomely. . . . The move undoubtedly convinced Hitler that we in-

[9] These figures obtained by adding up casualties of all U.S. ships known to have been hit or sunk.

[10] Figures communicated by Rear Adm. Roger Bellairs RN, 13 Jan. 1954.

[11] Approximate figures only, from *Anzio Beachhead* p. 116, which says, "British combat losses were relatively heavier than American, in terms of the number of troops engaged"; the British units of VI Corps lost 27 per cent of their strength; the American, 17 per cent, during the first 30 days. The enemy reported capture of 6800 P.O.W., "including about 2400 American troops." Naval non-combat casualties, of which apparently no record was kept, were, by Admiral Lowry's statement, much greater than the combat casualties. It should be understood by the reader that non-combat casualties include disabilities from fatigue, neuroses, etc., that stem from the fighting, as distinct from actual wounds inflicted by shellfire, air bombs, mines and other lethal weapons, and reflect no discredit on the men or units that suffer them.

tended to push the Italian campaign as a major operation, and he reinforced his armies there with eight divisions." [12]

Mr. Churchill, too, put a good face on it, and in a message to Stalin on 5 June 1944 wrote: "Although the amphibious landing at Anzio and Nettuno did not immediately fructify as I had hoped when it was planned, it was a correct strategic move, and brought its reward in the end." Said reward, he asserted, was the pulling in of ten, not eight, German divisions from various theaters; a "defensive battle" in which the Germans, he believed, lost 30,000 men to our 25,000; and the probable "entrapping" of more German divisions south of Rome.[13]

Those divisions avoided the trap; and although no exact statistics of German losses are available, Marshal Kesselring in 1947 said that his total casualties were 40,000, of which 5000 were killed.[14] However, the main object of the Anzio landings was not to kill Germans but to liberate Rome quickly, which was not done. Surprise was obtained in the faultless landings, for which Admirals Lowry and Troubridge deserve high praise. But there were not enough Allied forces available to exploit that surprise, and the Germans turned an amphibious assault into a siege.

"A correct strategic move" Anzio certainly was not. By splitting the Fifth Army and landing a part of it outside mutually supporting distance, the smaller part was exposed to destruction in detail; and that is probably just what would have happened, but for General Lucas's much criticized caution. If a "left hook" was wanted to employ Allied amphibious forces, a short one to Gaëta or Terracina would have been wiser than the long one to Anzio. Unfortunately both were too far from Rome and the Alban Hills to interest Mr. Churchill.

Yet, if we conclude that Operation SHINGLE was wrong, does it not follow that the entire Campaign of Italy was mistaken; that its

[12] *Crusade in Europe* pp. 264, 213.

[13] *Closing the Ring* p. 611.

[14] Interview in Jan. 1947, quoted by Vice Adm. Lowry in U. S. Naval Inst. *Proceedings* LXXX 31. He also confirmed that 10 of his 30 divisions were committed at Anzio. The Allies captured about 4500 Germans.

possible prizes were altogether incommensurate with the necessary expenditure, let alone the sufferings of Italian civilians and the damage to their unfortunate country? One of the avowed objects of that invasion – knocking Italy out of the war – was achieved before a single Allied soldier had set foot on the mainland. And, in a sense, that knockout was undone when the invasion began; for invasion made Italy a major battlefield. And, once we were in Italy, there could be no turning back.

Was President Roosevelt right when he predicted at the TRIDENT Conference in May 1943 that committing large armies to Italy "might result in attrition for the United Nations and play into Germany's hands"? Was Admiral King wrong in predicting that the invasion of Italy would "create a vacuum into which Allied forces would be sucked"? Before that campaign was over – and it was not finished until eleven months after the liberation of Rome – an army contributed by ten Allied nations [15] faced Vietinghoff's Southwestern Army Group; and the Germans were still on Italian soil when that group surrendered on 2 May 1945.

Yet there is much to be said in defense of the Italian campaign, in the light of its other object as stated in the original directive to General Eisenhower: – "To contain the maximum number of German forces." Granted that the Allies had to fight Germans somewhere during the ten months that would elapse between the conquest of Sicily and D-day in Normandy, where else could they have fought them with any prospect of success? What was the alternative to Italy? Search the coasts of Europe and the Near East as you will, there was none, other than invading islands of slight strategic value, which the Germans would probably have evacuated in any case; or taking the long and tortuous Balkans route which every military commander regarded as impracticable. We instinctively resent campaigns in which there is great suffering with little result, as the American public in 1864 resented Grant's Wilderness campaign. But let us admit that the Italian campaign, like Grant's, was fought *because it had to be fought.*

[15] The U.S., U.K., Canada, Australia, New Zealand, India, France, Brazil, Poland, Italy.

There were tactical mistakes, of course. Putting a cork in the bottleneck of the Strait of Messina would have eliminated three German divisions. The planned air drop on Rome on 9 September, if carried out, should have forced the Germans back to northern Italy nine months earlier. Employing VI Corps on the southern front might have been more efficacious than throwing it into Anzio. But every military planner and commander makes mistakes, and the side wins that makes the least number. The Germans, although they made war their principal business, made more mistakes than we did. They should have quit early in 1943. They should have withdrawn to the Po late in 1943, as Rommel advised. But, with a master like Hitler, they could not quit short of total defeat; and they could not retire unless forced to do so.

"I can say this," said Marshal Kesselring on the third anniversary of the Anzio landings: "if you had never pitted your divisions in the Mediterranean, as at Anzio–Nettuno, you would not have won the victory in the West." [16]

There should no longer be any doubt that the campaigns covered by this volume contributed very materially to the defeat of Germany. HUSKY and AVALANCHE were certainly worth their cost. In both campaigns the Navy not only put the Army ashore in good order, with a minimum of casualties, but stood by for days and weeks to augment with its own gunfire the work of the Army artillery, and the sporadic efforts of the Army Air Forces, Possession of Sicily made the Mediterranean almost an Allied lake, and the Salerno beachhead led straight to Naples, the first major European port lost by the Axis.

In comparison with Sicily and Salerno, the Anzio operation may suffer in popular esteem from the belief that it was fruitless; but Anzio beachhead should endure in our memories as a symbol of heroic tenacity. It was primarily an Army operation, in which the United States and British Navies performed an almost faultless landing, and then played the part of ferry and feeder. Naval gunfire,

[16] U.S. Naval Inst. *Proceedings* LXXX 31. In his later published *Memoirs*, however, Kesselring concludes that his Italian campaign paid off, because it engaged so many Allied divisions and saved southern Germany from invasion.

like air support, was important in defeating the enemy, but not vital as it had been at Gela and on the Salerno plain. The dogged valor of the American and British infantrymen and gunners, and the good tactics of their commanders, were responsible for VI Corps' repelling formidable counterattacks and eventually breaking out to Rome. This was their battle, this their victory; of which the United States Navy is proud to say, "We helped you; and we too suffered, at Anzio beachhead."

APPENDIX I

United States Naval Forces Engaged in the Assault on Sicily[1]

10 July–17 August 1943

WESTERN NAVAL TASK FORCE

Vice Admiral H. Kent Hewitt

TG 80.1 FORCE FLAGSHIP GROUP

Embarking Commanding General Seventh Army, Lt. Gen. George S. Patton jr. USA and staff.

MONROVIA Cdr. T. B. Brittain; DD MCLANAHAN Lt. Cdr. H. R. Hummer.

TG 80.2 ESCORT GROUP, Capt. Charles Wellborn (Comdesron 8)

WAINWRIGHT Cdr. R. H. Gibbs; MAYRANT Cdr. E. K. Walker; TRIPPE Lt. Cdr. R. C. Williams; RHIND Lt. Cdr. O. W. Spahr; ROWAN Lt. Cdr. R. S. Ford; PLUNKETT (Cdr. G. L. Menocal, Comdesron 7, on board) Lt. Cdr. E. J. Burke; NIBLACK Lt. Cdr. R. R. Conner; BENSON Lt. Cdr. R. J. Woodaman; GLEAVES Lt. Cdr. B. L. Gurnette.

TG 80.3 SCREENING GROUP, Lt. Cdr. Robert Brodie

DD ORDRONAUX Lt. Cdr. Brodie; MTBron 15 Lt. Cdr. S. M. Barnes: 17 PTs.

TG 80.4 DEMONSTRATION GROUP, Cdr. H. R. Robinson USNR

8 air-sea rescue craft and *PT–213*.

TG 80.5 MINELAYING GROUP, Cdr. G. F. Mentz

KEOKUK Cdr. Leo Brennan USNR; WEEHAWKEN Lt. Cdr. R. E. Mills USNR; SALEM Cdr. H. G. Williams.

[1] Many of these ships and craft were attached to and detached from the different task units during the operation, but are listed only once.

TG 80.6 RESERVE GROUP (KOOL), Capt. K. S. Reed

Embarking 18th RCT 1st Infantry Division, HQ and 2 Combat Commands 2nd Armored Division, 8000 officers and men. Maj. Gen. H. J. Gaffey USA.

Transports ORIZABA Cdr. L. E. Kelley; CHATEAU THIERRY Cdr. B. W. Cloud; 6 LSTs; 11 LCIs of divs. 5 and 6; 16 British LCIs of Flotilla 9; 5 LCTs; Cargo vessels JOSEPH PULITZER, *ROBERT ROWAN, LAUGHTON B. EVANS, EZRA MEEKER, FRANCIS PARKMAN, NICHOLAS GILLMAN, TABITHA BROWN.

TF 86 LICATA ATTACK FORCE (JOSS)
Rear Admiral Richard L. Conolly

Embarking 3rd Infantry Div., reinforced; 3rd Ranger Bn.; Combat Command A of 2nd Armored Division; 20th and 36th Engineers; 27,650 officers and men. Maj. Gen. L. K. Truscott jr. USA

Flagship BISCAYNE Cdr. R. C. Young; DD BRISTOL Cdr. J. A. Glick.

TG 86.1 SUPPORT GROUP, Rear Admiral L. T. DuBose (Comcrudiv 13)

BROOKLYN Capt. H. W. Ziroli; BIRMINGHAM Capt. John Wilkes.

Screen, Cdr. E. R. Durgin (Comdesron 13): BUCK Lt. Cdr. M. J. Klein; LUDLOW Lt. Cdr. L. W. Creighton.

Beach Identification Group: H.M. submarine SAFARI Lt. R. B. Lakin RN; BRISTOL; *PC–546*.

TG. 86.2 GAFFI ATTACK GROUP, Capt. L. S. Sabin in *LCI–10*

Gunfire Support: SWANSON Lt. Cdr. E. L. Robertson; ROE Lt. Cdr. R. L. Nolan; 3 British LCG(L) and 2 British LCF(L); Minesweeper SEER Cdr. A. F. Block.

Landing and Control Craft

LST Group 2, Lt. Cdr. S. H. Pattie: 7 LSTs.

LCI(L) Flot. 2, Capt. Sabin: 1st Wave, Lt. Cdr. E. W. Wilson: 6 LCI(L)s.

2nd Wave, Lt. Cdr. R. G. Newbegin USNR: 9 LCI(L)s.

LCT Group, Lt. Gordon Raymond USNR: 21 LCTs, 2 PCs, 5 SCs.

TG 86.3 MOLLA ATTACK GROUP, Cdr. R. M. Morris in *LST–6*

Gunfire Support: DD EDISON Lt. Cdr. H. A. Pearce; 1 British LCG(L), 1 British LCF(L); minesweeper *SENTINEL Lt. Cdr. G. L. Phillips USNR.

* Lost in this operation.

Landing and Control Craft

British LSI(S)s PRINCESS JOSEPHINE CHARLOTTE Capt. A. I. Robertson RNR; PRINCESS ASTRID Lt. Cdr. C. E. Hall RNR; 6 LSTs, 3 LCTs; *LCI–32;* 2 PCs; 5 SCs.

TG 86.4 SALSO ATTACK GROUP, Cdr. W. O. Floyd in *LCI–95*

Gunfire Support: DD WOOLSEY Lt. Cdr. H. R. Wier; 3 British LCG(L)s, 2 British LCF(L)s.

Landing and Control Craft

12 LSTs, including **158* and *386* (carrying 4 Cub planes); *LCI–96.*
25 LCTs, Lt. Cdr. J. B. Freese; 2 PCs; 5 SCs.

TG 86.5 FALCONARA ATTACK GROUP, Cdr. R. E. Nelson in *LCI–86*

Gunfire Support: DD WILKES Lt. Cdr. Frederick Wolsieffer (Cdr. Vernon Huber, Comdesdiv 26, on board); NICHOLSON Cdr. L. M. Markham; 2 British LCG(L)s; 2 British LCF(L)s.

Landing and Control Craft

10 LSTs.
1st Wave, Lt. Cdr. A. C. Unger USCG: 8 LCI(L)s.
2nd Wave, Lt. Cdr. J. A. Bresnan USCG: 8 LCI(L)s, 9 LCTs, 4 SCs, *PC–562.*

TG 86.7 SALVAGE [2]

Tugs MORENO Lt. V. H. Kyllberg; INTENT.

TG 86.8 RESERVE, Cdr. M. H. Imlay USCGR

2 LSTs; 15 LCIs; 8 LCTs; 12 British LCTs; 6 SCs; 6 YMSs.

TF 81 GELA ATTACK FORCE (DIME)

Rear Admiral J. L. Hall in *Samuel Chase*

Embarking 1st Infantry Division reinforced (less 18th RCT), 1st and 4th Ranger Bns.; Chemical Warfare Bns.; 19,250 officers and men. Maj. Gen. T. de la M. Allen USA.

Beach Identification Group: Destroyer COLE Lt. Cdr. Briscoe Chipman; H.M. submarine SHAKESPEARE Lt. Cdr. M. F. R. Ainslie RN.

* Lost in this operation.

[2] The rest of TF 84, U. S. Naval Salvage Force Northwest African Waters, to which TG 86.7, TG 81.9 and the tugs in TG 85.1 belonged, remained in Africa; but its C.O., Capt. William A. Sullivan, was embarked in *Monrovia.*

TG 81.2 TRANSPORT GROUP, Capt. C. D. Edgar in *Barnett*

Section 1, Capt. C. W. Harwood USCG: JOSEPH T. DICKMAN Capt. Harwood; British LSIs PRINCE CHARLES Cdr. S. H. Dennis RN; PRINCE LEOPOLD Lt. Cdr. J. A. Lowe RNR.

Section 2, Capt. Edgar: BARNETT Cdr. G. E. Maynard; MONROVIA; LYON Cdr. T. C. Sorenson; OBERON Cdr. Ion Pursell. LCI Div. 3, Lt. T. Gore USNR: 9 LCIs. Control Group 2: *PC-621;* 3 SCs.

Section 3, Capt. R. A. Dierdorff: ELIZABETH C. STANTON Capt. Dierdorff; THURSTON Capt. J. E. Hurff; SAMUEL CHASE Cdr. R. C. Heimer USCG; BETELGEUSE Cdr. J. F. Grube. LCI Div. 4, Lt. Cdr. H. B. Taliaferro USNR: 8 LCIs; Control Group 3: *PC-627*, *PC-625*, *SC-694*.

TG 81.3 LST GROUP, Cdr. W. D. Wright, 14 LSTs including **LST-313*

TG 81.4 LCI GROUP, Capt. J. H. Leppert, 16 LCIs

TG 81.5 FIRE SUPPORT GROUPS, Capt. L. Hewlett Thébaud

Light cruisers BOISE Capt. Thébaud; SAVANNAH Capt. R. W. Cary; DDs SHUBRICK Lt. Cdr. L. A. Bryan; JEFFERS Lt. Cdr. W. T. McGarry.

TG 81.6 SCREEN, Capt. D. L. Madeira (Comdesron 17)

NELSON Lt. Cdr. M. M. Riker; MCLANAHAN Lt. Cdr. H. R. Hummer; MURPHY Lt. Cdr. L. W. Bailey (Comdesdiv 33); GLENNON Cdr. F. C. Camp; *MADDOX *Lt. Cdr. E. S. Sarsfield; DALLAS Cdr. A. C. Roessler (Comdesdiv 60); GHERARDI Lt. Cdr. J. W. Schmidt (Comdesdiv 34, Cdr. J. B. Rooney on board); BUTLER Lt. Cdr. M. D. Matthews; HERNDON Lt. Cdr. G. A. Moore; BERNADOU Lt. Cdr. B. L. E. Talman.

TG 81.7 CONTROL GROUP, Lt. Cdr. R. D. Lowther USNR, 4 PCs, 5 SCs

TG 81.8 SWEEPER GROUP, Lt. Cdr. M. H. Harris USNR

SUSTAIN Lt. Cdr. Harris; STEADY Lt. Cdr. F. W. Maennle USNR; 6 YMSs.

TG 81.9 SALVAGE GROUP, Lt. O. W. Huff

Tug HOPI Lt. Huff; salvage vessel BRANT Lt. H. M. Andersen; 4 harbor tugs.

TF 85 SCOGLITTI ATTACK FORCE (CENT)

Rear Admiral A. G. Kirk

Embarking Lt. Gen. Omar N. Bradley USA and staff of II Corps and 45th Infantry Div. reinforced; 25,800 officers and men. Maj. Gen. T. H. Middleton USA.

* Lost or killed in this operation.

TG 85.1 ATTACK GROUP ONE ("Wood's Hole"), Rear Admiral Kirk

Amphibious force flagship ANCON Capt. P. L. Mather; DD EARLE Cdr. H. W. Howe.

Beach Identification Group: H.M. submarine SERAPH Lt. N. L. A. Jewell RN: DD COWIE Cdr. C. J. Whiting.

Transdiv 1, Capt. W. B. Phillips: LEONARD WOOD Capt. Merlin O'Neill USCG; JAMES O'HARA Capt. Charles Allen; HARRY LEE Cdr. J. G. Pomeroy; DOROTHEA L. DIX Capt. L. B. Schulten; FLORENCE NIGHTINGALE Capt. J. W. McColl; ANDROMEDA Cdr. W. A. Fly; ALCYONE Capt. D. M. McGurl.

Transdiv 7, Capt. D. W. Loomis: CALVERT Capt. L. A. Thackrey; NEVILLE Cdr. O. R. Swigart; FREDERICK FUNSTON Cdr. J. E. Murphy; ANNE ARUNDEL Capt. L. Y. Mason; BELLATRIX Cdr. O. H. Ritchie USNR: 8 LSTs; 6 LCIs; 6 LCTs; tugs NARRAGANSETT Lt. C. J. Wichmann; NAUSET Lt. Joseph Orleck.

Screen, Capt. T. L. Wattles (Comdesron 16)

PARKER Lt. Cdr. J. W. Bays; LAUB Cdr. J. F. Gallaher; MACKENZIE Lt. Cdr. D. B. Miller; KENDRICK Cdr. C. T. Caufield; DORAN Lt. Cdr. H. W. Gordon; 4 PCs, 2 SCs.

Minecraft, Cdr. W. L. Messmer: STRIVE Cdr. Messmer; STAFF Cdr. R. T. McDaniel USNR; SKILL Lt. Cdr. E. J. Kevern; SPEED Lt. R. C. Dryer; 5 YMSs.

TG 85.2 ATTACK GROUP TWO ("Bailey's Beach"), Rear Admiral L. A. Davidson in *Philadelphia*

Transdiv 5, Capt. W. O. Bailey: CHARLES CARROLL Cdr. Harold Biesemeier; THOMAS JEFFERSON Capt. P. P. Welch; WILLIAM P. BIDDLE Capt. P. R. Glutting; SUSAN B. ANTHONY Capt. Henry Hartley; ARCTURUS Cdr. J. R. McKinney; PROCYON Cdr. B. A. Hartt; 5 LSTs.

Screen, Cdr. B. R. Harrison (Comdesdiv 32)

BOYLE Lt. Cdr. B. P. Field; CHAMPLIN Lt. Cdr. C. L. Melson; NIELDS Lt. Cdr. A. R. Heckey; DAVISON Lt. Cdr. W. C. Winn; 2 PCs; 2 SCs.

Minecraft, Lt. L. F. Danz: 5 YMSs.

TG 85.3 FIRE SUPPORT GROUPS, Rear Admiral Davidson

PHILADELPHIA Capt. Paul Hendren; H.M.S. ABERCROMBIE Capt. G. V. B. Faulkner RN; DDs MERVINE Lt. Cdr. D. R. Frakes; DORAN Lt. Cdr. H. W. Gordon: QUICK Lt. Cdr. P. W. Cann; TILLMAN Cdr. F. D. McCorkle; KNIGHT Lt. Cdr. J. C. Ford; COWIE; BEATTY Cdr. F. C. Stelter.

TF 87 TRAIN, Capt. R. B. Tuggle

Repair ships VULCAN Capt. Tuggle; DELTA Capt. C. D. Headlee; ammo. ship MOUNT BAKER Cdr. F. D. Hamblin; storeship TARAZED Cdr. R. W. Chambers USNR; oilers WINOOSKI Cdr. J. P. B. Barrett; MATTAPONI Cdr. M. C. Barrett; CHICOPEE Capt. G. Bannerman; SALAMONIE Cdr. L. J. Johns; CHEMUNG Capt. J. J. Twomey; NIOBRARA Capt. T. G. Haff; RAPIDAN Cdr. M. D. Mullen USNR; salvage ship W. R. CHAMBERLIN, JR.

Follow-Up Convoys of Liberty Ships

To arrive Gela 14 July: S.S. WALTER FORWARD, WILLIAM BRADFORD, EDWARD P. COSTIGAN, FILIPPE DE NEVE, HUGH WILLIAMSON, SAMUEL ADAMS, JAMES IREDELL, WALTER RANGER, WILLIAM FEW, MARION MCKINLEY BOVARD. Escorted by TG 80.5.

To arrive Scoglitti, 14 July: S.S. THOMAS W. BICKETT, WINFIELD SCOTT, ALEXANDER MARTIN, JOHN H. PAYNE, GEORGE MATTHEWS, DAVID CALDWELL, JAMES WOODROW.

To arrive Gela 18 July: S.S. CHARLES PIEZ, BUSHROD WASHINGTON, WILLIAM DEAN HOWELLS, ALEXANDER GRAHAM BELL, DANIEL WEBSTER, OLIVER HAZARD PERRY, LEWIS MORRIS; fuel barge ANTICLINE.

APPENDIX II

Naval Forces Engaged in the Salerno Operation[1]

9 September–13 October 1943

TF 80 WESTERN NAVAL TASK FORCE

Vice Admiral H. Kent Hewitt

Force flagship ANCON, embarking Commanding General Fifth Army, Lt. Gen. Mark W. Clark USA, and Staff.

H.M.S. ULSTER QUEEN and PALOMARES, embarking Fighter-Director teams.

Beacon submarine H.M.S. SHAKESPEARE.

TF 81 SOUTHERN ATTACK FORCE, Rear Admiral John L. Hall in *Samuel Chase*

Embarking VI Corps U. S. Army, Maj. Gen. E. J. Dawley USA (36th and 45th Infantry Divisions), Maj. Gen. Fred Walker USA and Maj. Gen. Troy Middleton USA.

TG 81.5 FIRE SUPPORT GROUP, Rear Admiral L. A. Davidson

PHILADELPHIA, SAVANNAH, BOISE, BROOKLYN; H.M.S. ABERCROMBIE.

Desron 13, Cdr. E. R. Durgin: WOOLSEY, LUDLOW, *BRISTOL, EDISON.

TG 81.6 SCREEN, Capt. Charles Wellborn

Desron 8, Capt. Wellborn: WAINWRIGHT Cdr. W. W. Strohbehn; TRIPPE, RHIND Cdr. H. T. Read; *ROWAN.

Desron 7, Cdr. G. L. Menocal: PLUNKETT Cdr. W. H. Standley; NIBLACK, BENSON Lt. Cdr. C. A. Fines; GLEAVES, MAYO Lt. Cdr. F. S. Habecker.

Desdiv 60, Cdr. A. C. Roessler: DALLAS, BERNADOU, COLE.

* Lost in this operation.

[1] Compiled from Vice Adm. H. K. Hewitt's Op. Plan 7-43 and Admiralty records. Commanding Officers are not repeated if same as in Appendix I. All ships are U.S.S. unless otherwise stated. The transport groups here are those of the assault convoy only; most of them also participated in follow-up convoys.

TG 81.2 TRANSPORT GROUP, Capt. C. D. Edgar

Section 2, Capt. Edgar, carrying 142nd RCT: BARNETT, JOSEPH T. DICKMAN, LYON, OBERON, British MARNIX VAN ST. ALDEGONDE, DERWENTDALE.

Section 3, Capt. W. O. Bailey, carrying 141st RCT: CHARLES CARROLL, JAMES O'HARA, THOMAS JEFFERSON, ARCTURUS, British ORONTES, EMPIRE CHARMAIN.

Section 1, Capt. R. A. Dierdorff, carrying 143rd RCT: SAMUEL CHASE, ELIZABETH C. STANTON, FREDERICK FUNSTON, ANDROMEDA, PROCYON; British DUCHESS OF BEDFORD.

Section 4, Cdr. G. B. Herbert-Jones RNR: "Killer" class LSTs, H.M.S. BOXER, BRUISER, THRUSTER.

SUPPORT BOAT GROUP, Lt. R. K. Margetts

4 Scout Boats (for names of skippers, see text); 2 in reserve

TG 81.3 LANDING CRAFT GROUP, Capt. F. M. Adams

13 LSTs assigned to 36th Division; 3 LSTs, 20 LCI(L)s assigned to 82nd Airborne Division; 9 British LSTs and 6 British LCI(L)s embarking part of the 45th Division; 2 LSTs assigned to Northwest African Air Force; 6 LCI(L)s assigned to Rangers; 6 LCTs carrying vehicles of 36th Division.

TG 81.7 CONTROL GROUP, Cdr. R. D. Lowther USNR

8 PCs, 4 LCSs.

TG 81.8 MINESWEEPER GROUP, Cdr. A. H. Richards

Unit 1, Cdr. Richards: SEER, PILOT, SUSTAIN, SPEED, PREVAIL, STEADY, *SKILL, SYMBOL.

Unit 2, Cdr. W. L. Messmer: STRIVE and 12 YMSs.

TG 81.9 SALVAGE GROUP, Lt. V. H. Kyllberg: tugs MORENO, HOPI

TG 80.2 PICKET GROUP, Lt. Cdr. S. M. Barnes: 16 PTs

TG 80.4 DIVERSION GROUP, Capt. C. L. Andrews

KNIGHT Lt. Cdr. J. C. Ford; 1 PT; 6 British MTBs; 4 SCs; 6 Motor Launches; gunboat H.N.M.S. FLORES; 10 U.S. air-sea rescue craft.

TF 85 NORTHERN ATTACK FORCE, Commodore G. N. Oliver RN

Carrying X Corps, Lt. Gen. Sir R. McCreery, comprising 46th and 56th Infantry Divisions, 7th Armored Division, 3 U. S. Ranger Battalions and 2 Commando forces.

* Lost in this operation.

Flagship H.M.S. HILARY; U.S.S. BISCAYNE with Rear Adm. Richard L. Conolly USN embarked.

Cruisers, Rear Admiral C. H. J. Harcourt RN: H.M.S. MAURITIUS, UGANDA, ORION, DELHI; monitor ROBERTS.

Desron 19, Capt. R. M. J. Hutton RN: H.M.S. LAFOREY, LOOKOUT, LOYAL, NUBIAN, TARTAR.

Desron 21, Capt. C. R. L. Parry RN: H.M.S. MENDIP, DULVERTON, TETCOTT, BELVOIR, BROCKLESBY, QUANTOCK, BLACKMORE, BRECON, BEAUFORT, EXMOOR, PINDOS (Greek), LEDBURY, BLANKNEY.

Minesweepers, Capt. J. W. Boutwood RN: H.M.S. FLY, ALBACORE, MUTINE, CIRCE, CADMUS, ACUTE, ROTHESAY.

U.S. tugs NARRAGANSETT Lt. C. J. Wichmann; *NAUSET Lt. Joseph Orleck, RESOLUTE, INTENT.

Transports and LSIs: GLENGYLE, SOBIESKI (Polish), DEVONSHIRE, ROYAL ULSTERMAN, ROYAL SCOTSMAN, PRINCESS BEATRIX, ULSTER MONARCH, PRINCESS ASTRID.

LSIs for Rangers and Commandos: PRINCE ALBERT, PRINCE CHARLES, PRINCE LEOPOLD, PRINCESS JOSEPHINE CHARLOTTE.

Beaching Craft Groups

Of R.N.: 45 LSTs, 60 LCTs (including **154*, **391*, **572*, **601*, **624*), 48 LCI(L)s, 13 Trawlers, 32 Motor Launches, 27 Minecraft.

Of U.S.N.: 23 SCs, 45 LSTs, 24 LCTs, 48 LCI(L).

TF 88 SUPPORT CARRIER FORCE, Rear Admiral Sir P. L. Vian RN

Cruisers H.M.S. EURYALUS, SCYLLA, CHARYBDIS; light carrier H.M.S. UNICORN; escort carriers H.M.S. BATTLER, ATTACKER, HUNTER, STALKER.

Destroyers, Cdr. R. Tyminski (Polish Navy): SLAZAK, KRAKOWIAK (Polish); H.M.S. CLEVELAND, HOLCOMBE, ATHERSTONE, LIDDESDALE, FARNDALE, CALPE, HAYDON.

COVERING FORCES

FORCE "H," Vice Admiral Sir A. U. Willis RN

Battleships H.M.S. NELSON, RODNEY (Rear Admiral J. W. Rivett-Carnac RN embarked); WARSPITE (Rear Admiral A. W. la T. Bisset RN embarked); VALIANT.

CARRIERS, Rear Admiral C. Moody RN

H.M.S. ILLUSTRIOUS (12 Barracuda, 28 Martlet, 10 Seafire), FORMIDABLE (28 Martlet, 5 Seafire, 12 Albacore), Rear Admiral A. G. Talbot RN.

* Lost in this operation.

Desron 4, Capt. S. H. Carlill RN: H.M.S. QUILLIAM, QUEENBOROUGH, QUAIL, PETARD.

Desron 24, Capt C. L. Firth RN: H.M.S. TROUBRIDGE, TYRIAN, TUMULT, OFFA, PIORUN (Polish).

Desron 8, Capt. A. K. Scott-Moncrieff RN: H.M.S. FAULKNOR, INTREPID, ECLIPSE, INGLEFIELD, FURY, ILEX, RAIDER, ECHO, H.H.M.S. QUEEN OLGA; LE FANTASQUE and LE TERRIBLE (French).

British hospital ships *NEWFOUNDLAND, LEINSTER, SOMERSETSHIRE.

* Lost in this operation.

APPENDIX III

Naval Forces Engaged in the Assault on Anzio[1]

22 January 1944

TASK FORCE 81

Rear Admiral Frank J. Lowry in *Biscayne*

Embarking VI Corps U.S. Army (Maj. Gen. J. P. Lucas USA), comprising 3rd Infantry Division (Maj. Gen. L. K. Truscott, Jr.) and 1st Division British Army (Maj. Gen. W. R. C. Penney)

Force Flagship BISCAYNE Cdr. E. H. Eckelmeyer, screened by destroyer escort FREDERICK C. DAVIS Lt. Cdr. R. C. Robbins USNR.

TG 81.2 RANGER GROUP, Capt. E. C. L. Turner RN

All these British: LSI(*M*)s ROYAL ULSTERMAN, PRINCESS BEATRIX; transport WINCHESTER CASTLE; *LST–410;* 3 LCTs; 3 SCs; 1 LCI(H).

X-RAY FORCE, Rear Admiral Lowry

TG 81.3 RED BEACH GROUP, Cdr. William O. Floyd

12 LSTs, 31 LCIs, 22 LCTs; British: 1 LCG, 1 LCF, 1 LCT(R); 4 PCs, 6 SCs.

TG 81.4 GREEN BEACH GROUP, Cdr. O. F. Gregor[2]

Assault Flagship *LCI*(*L*)*–196*, British LSI(L)s CIRCASSIA, ASCANIA; 16 LCI(L)s, 11 LCTs, 1 LCG, 1 LCF, 1 LCT(R); 2 PCs, 2 SCs.

TG 81.5 FIRST FOLLOW-UP GROUP, Capt. J. P. Clay[3]

39 British LSTs, 20 LCI(L)s, 6 LCTs.

[1] Compiled from Commander Amphibious Task Force Op-plan 147–43, 12 Jan. 1944, and the action reports and war diaries of the forces and ships involved.

[2] *LST–348*, LCIs *–20*, *–32*, and LCTs *–35*, *–36*, *–220* in Red and Green Groups were sunk.

[3] H.M.S. *LST–305*, *–418*, *–422*, and *LCI–273* of this group were sunk.

TG 81.6 ESCORT GROUP, Capt. Clay

DDs PLUNKETT, GLEAVES, NIBLACK, H.M.S. CROOME, H.H.M.S. THEMISTOCLES; destroyer escorts HERBERT C. JONES Lt. Cdr. R. A. Soule USNR, FREDERICK C. DAVIS; minecraft STEADY, SUSTAIN.

TG 81.7 SWEEPER GROUP, Cdr. A. H. Richards

AMs PILOT, STRIVE, PIONEER, *PORTENT, SYMBOL, DEXTROUS, SWAY, PREVAIL; 14 YMSs (including **YMS–30*), *SC–770*.

TG 81.8 GUNFIRE SUPPORT GROUP, Capt. Robert W. Cary[4]

Light cruisers BROOKLYN Capt. Cary; H.M.S. *PENELOPE Capt. G. D. Belben RN.

Desron 13, Capt. Harry Sanders: WOOLSEY, Cdr. H. R. Wier; MAYO Cdr. A. D. Kaplan; TRIPPE Cdr. R. C. Williams; LUDLOW, EDISON.

MISCELLANEOUS

Beacon submarine H.M.S. UPROAR; destroyer H.H.M.S. CRETE; 3 PCs; 2 SCs; salvage ship RESTORER; British ocean tugs PROSPEROUS, WEAZEL; U.S. tug HOPI; LCI(L)s and LCTs equipped as salvage vessels.

PETER FORCE

Rear Admiral Thomas H. Troubridge RN
Embarking 1st Infantry Division British Army,
Maj. Gen. W. R. C. Penney

Transports: H.M.S. BULOLO,[5] GLENGYLE, DERBYSHIRE, SOBIESKI (Polish).

Antiaircraft and Fighter-Director ships: H.M.S. ULSTER QUEEN, PALOMARES.

Cruisers, Rear Adm. J. M. Mansfield RN: H.M.S. ORION, *SPARTAN.

Destroyers: H.M.S. *JANUS, JERVIS, *LAFOREY, URCHIN, TENACIOUS, KEMPENFELT, LOYAL, *INGLEFIELD.

Hunt class destroyers: H.M.S. BEAUFORT, BRECON, WILTON, TETCOTT.

Gunboats: H.N.M.S. FLORES, SOEMBA.

Minesweepers: H.M.S. BUDE, ROTHSAY, RINALDO, FLY, CADMUS, WATERWITCH.

Killer class LSTs: H.M.S. BOXER, BRUISER, THRUSTER.

Patrol craft: H.M. trawlers TWO STEP, SHEPPEY, HORNPIPE, ST. KILDA.

* Lost in this Operation.

[4] Relieved on D-day plus 3 by Rear Adm. J. M. Mansfield RN in H.M.S. *Orion*.

[5] *Bulolo* and *Palomares* each had a U.S.A.A.F. fighter-director team on board.

Beaching craft: 14 British LSTs, 5 U.S. LSTs; 2 LCG(L)s, 31 LCIs, 1 LCI(H), 1 LCT(R), 6 miscellaneous.

Oiler BRITISH CHANCELLOR; net tender BARNDALE.

U.S. tugs EVEA, EDENSHAW; 2 U.S. PCs.

British hospital ships: ST. JULIEN, ST. ANDREW, LEINSTER, *ST. DAVID.

Beacon submarine: H.M.S. ULTOR.

* Lost in this operation.

Index

Index

Names of ships, and code names of operations, task forces and conferences, in SMALL CAPITALS
Numbers of lettered combatant ships, such as LSTs and U-boats, in *Italics*

In the Appendices, only flag and general officers have been indexed.

A

B

C

H

I

J

K